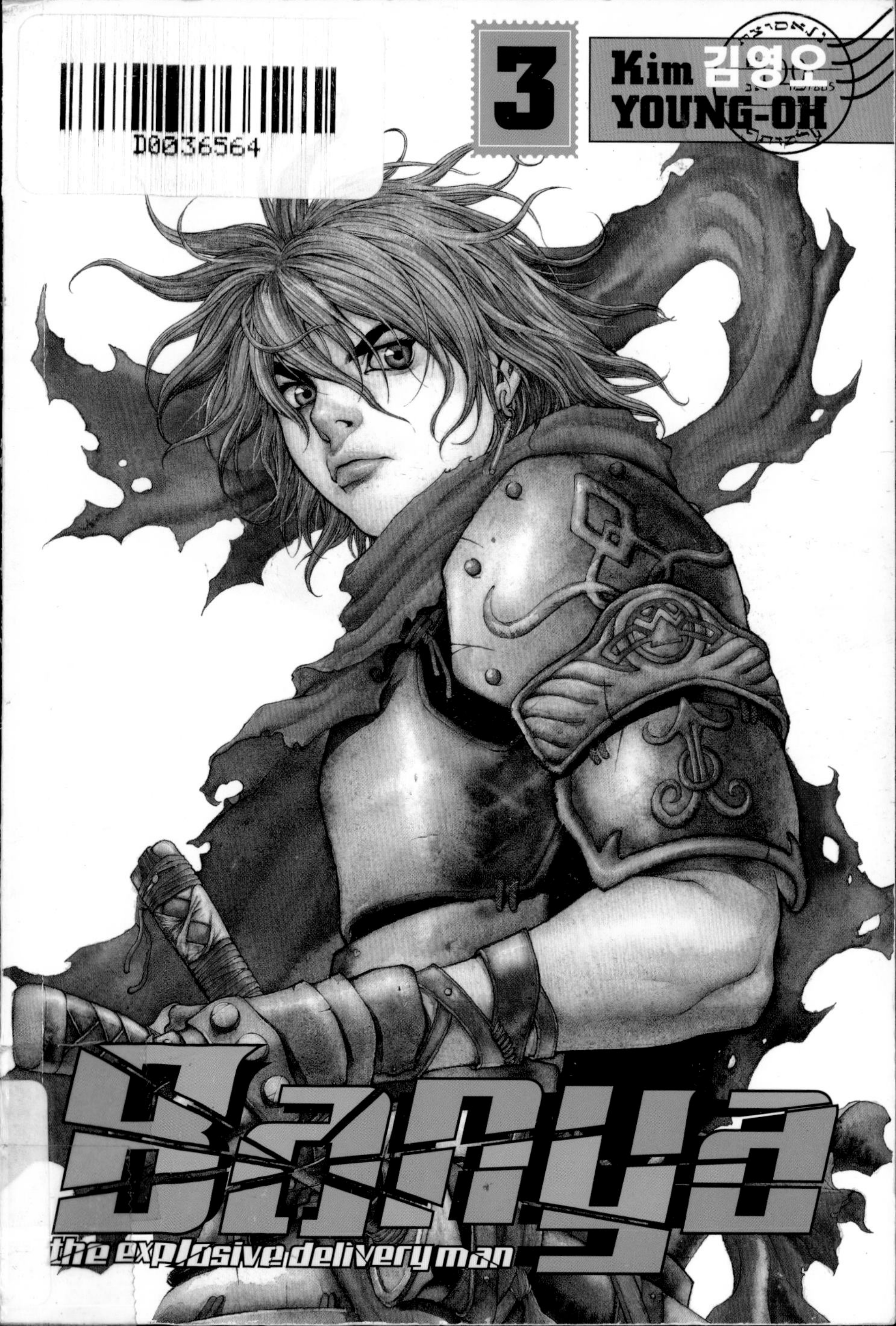
3
Kim 김영오
YOUNG-OH
Banya
the explosive delivery man

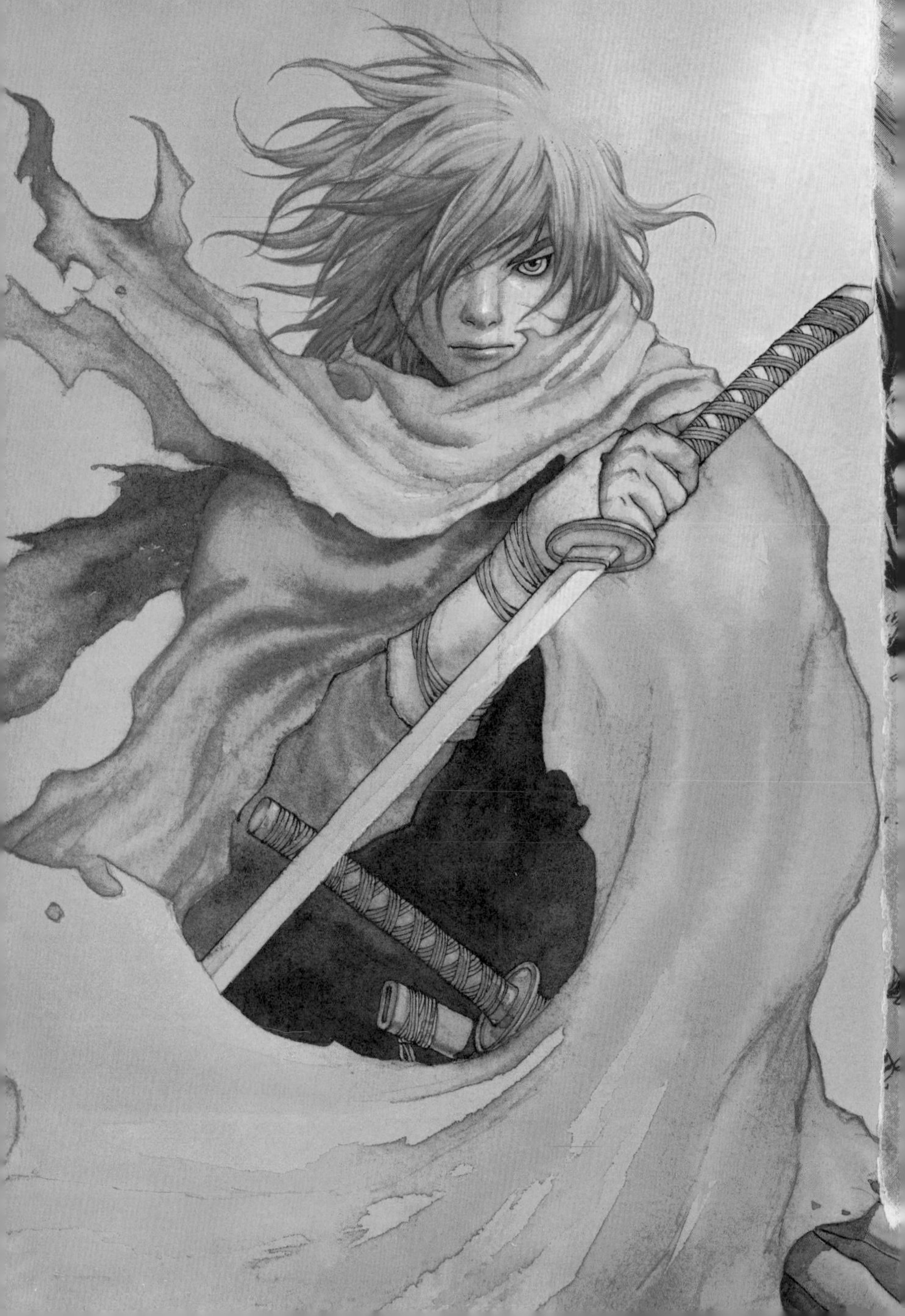

Banya
the explosive delivery man

IN THE HEART OF THE MOUNTAINS

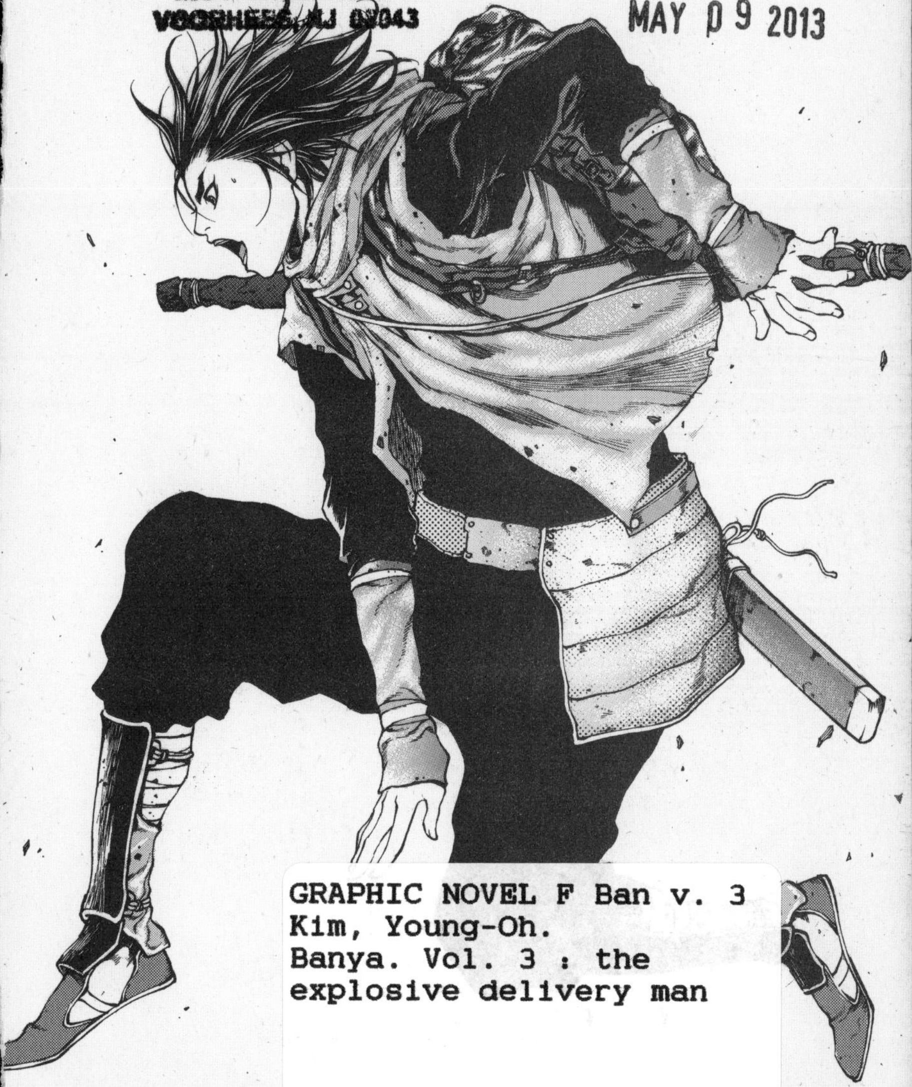

STORY AND ART BY KIM YOUNG-OH
TRANSLATION TAESOON KANG & DEREK KIRK KIM LETTERING STEVE DUTRO

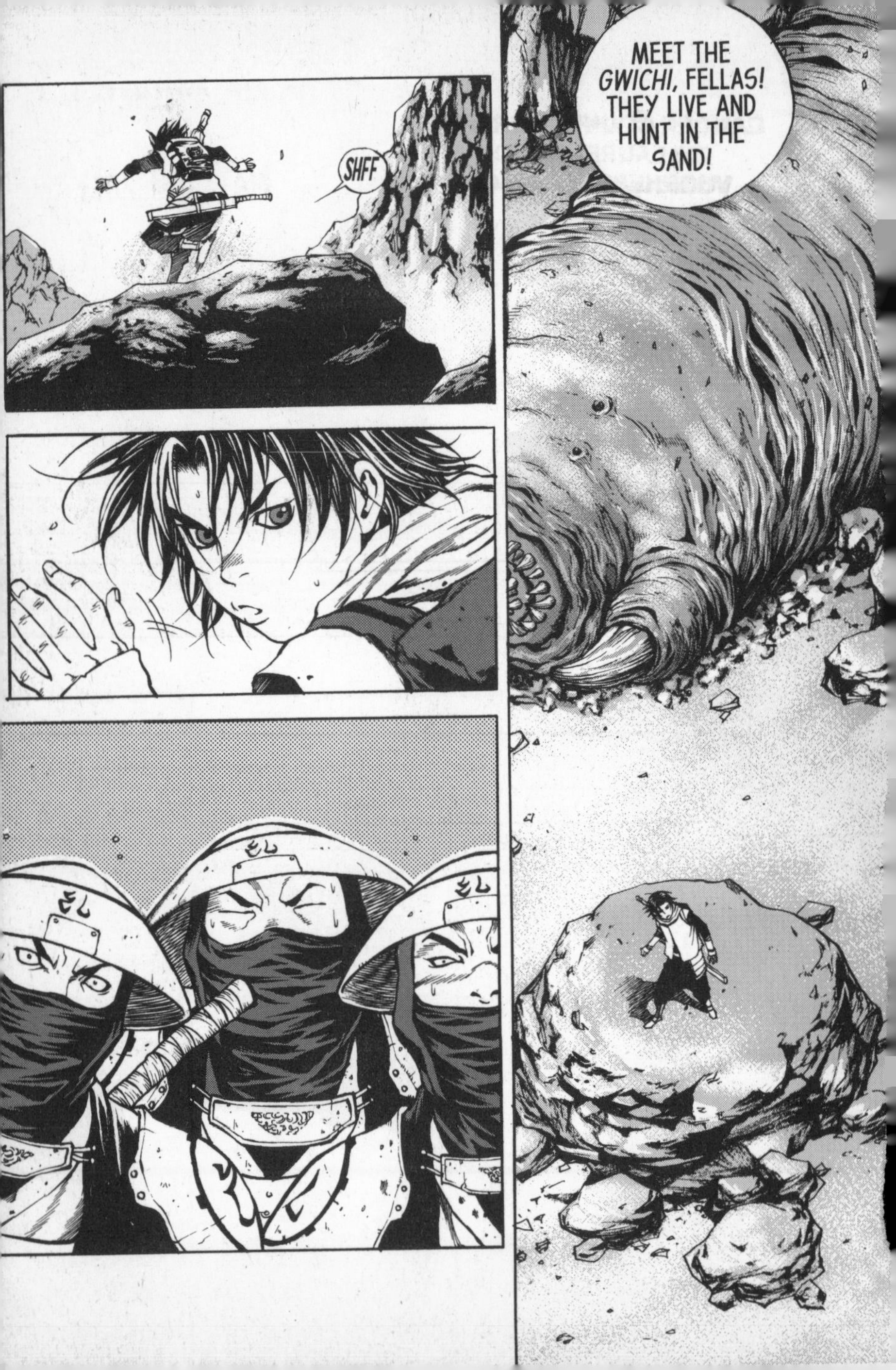
MEET THE *GWICHI*, FELLAS! THEY LIVE AND HUNT IN THE SAND!
SHFF

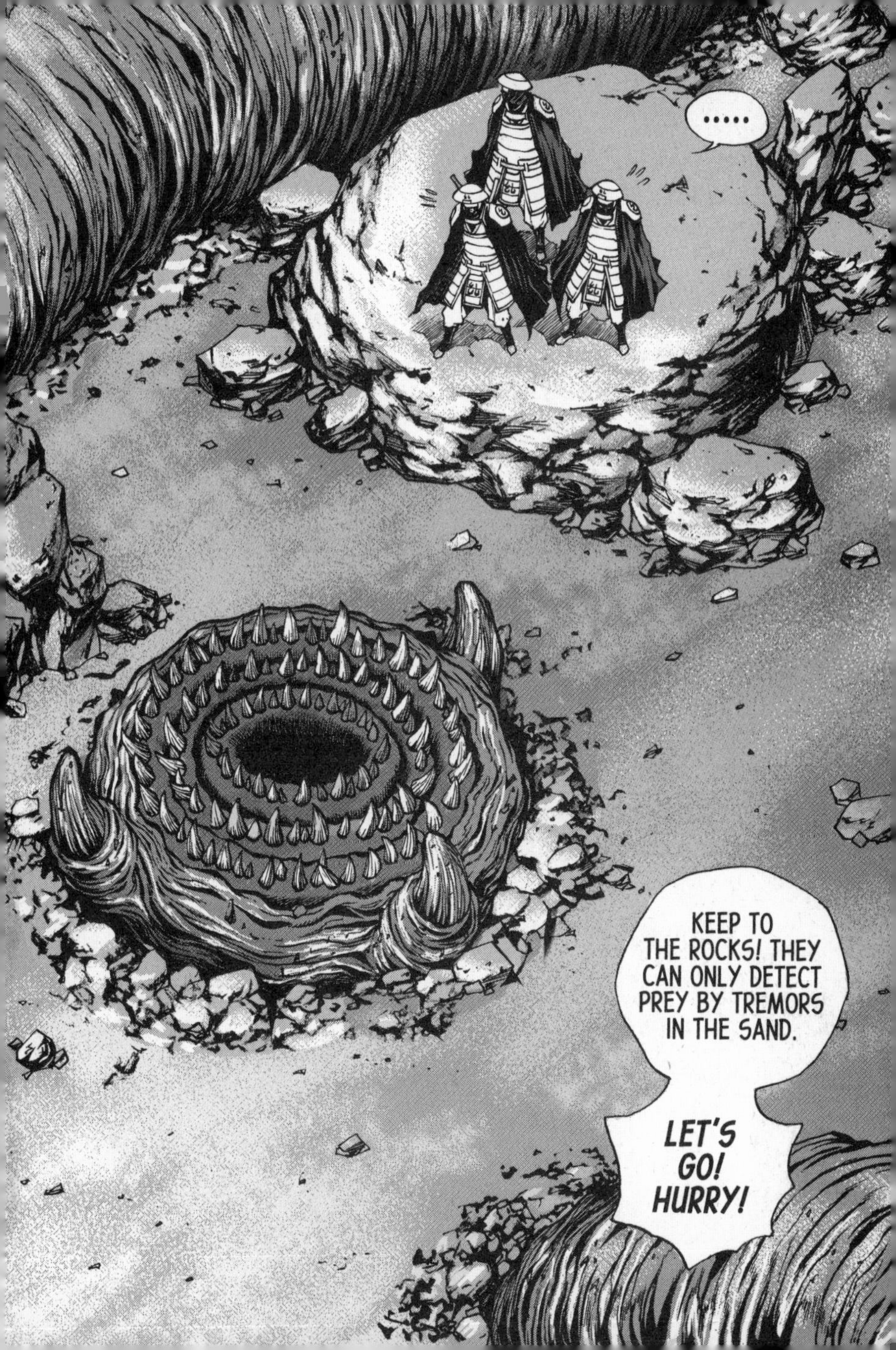
......
KEEP TO THE ROCKS! THEY CAN ONLY DETECT PREY BY TREMORS IN THE SAND.
LET'S GO! HURRY!

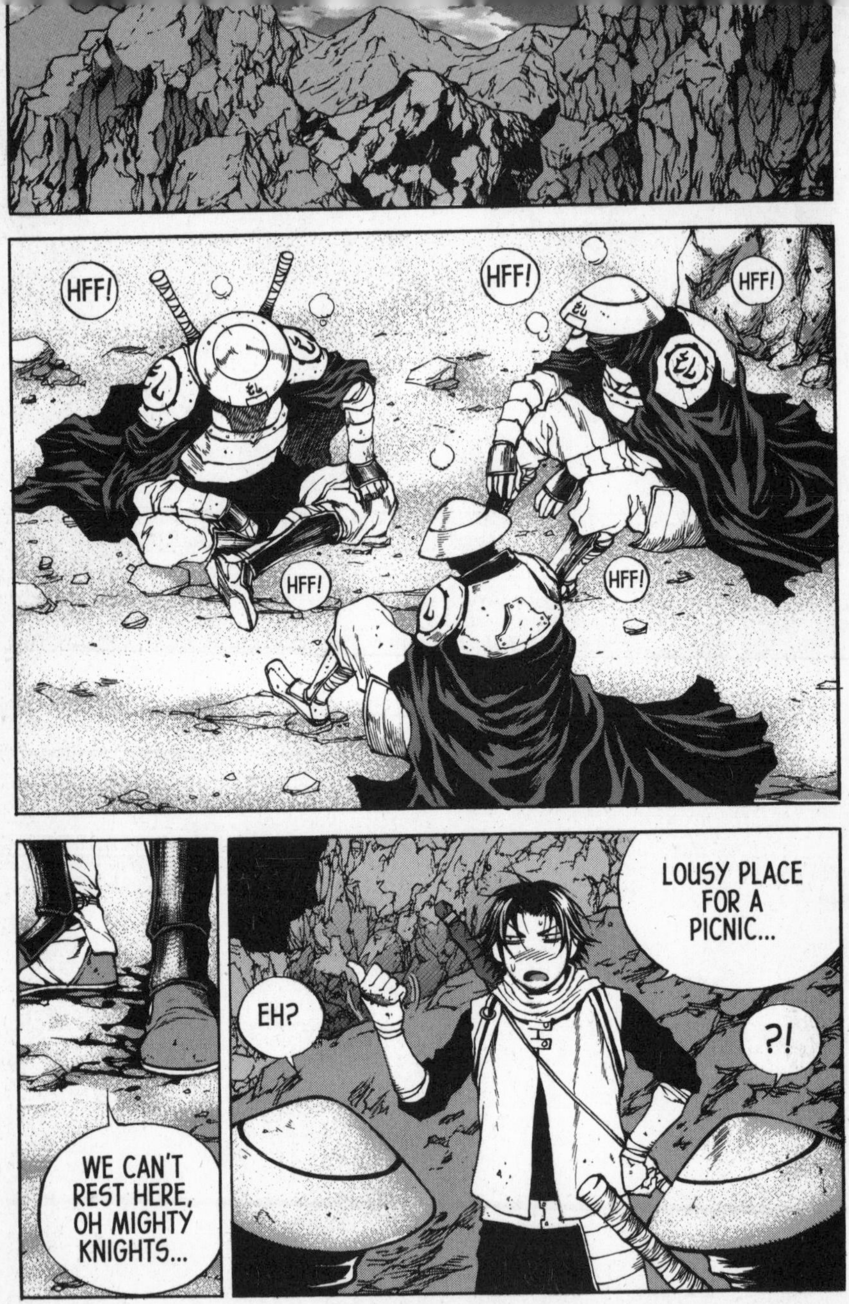
HFF!
HFF!
HFF!
HFF!
HFF!
LOUSY PLACE FOR A PICNIC...
EH?
?!
WE CAN'T REST HERE, OH MIGHTY KNIGHTS...

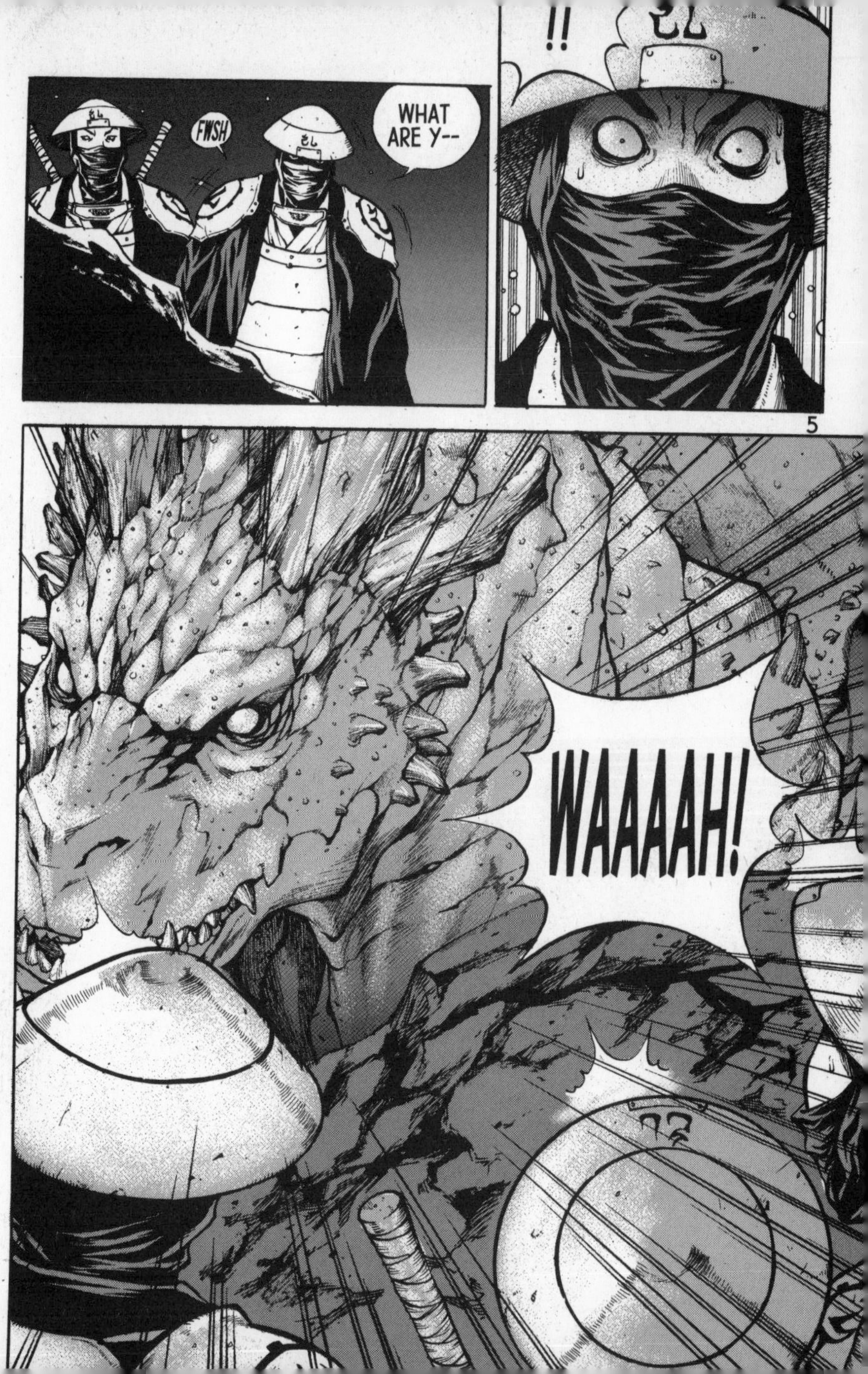
FWSH
WHAT ARE Y--
!!
WAAAAH!

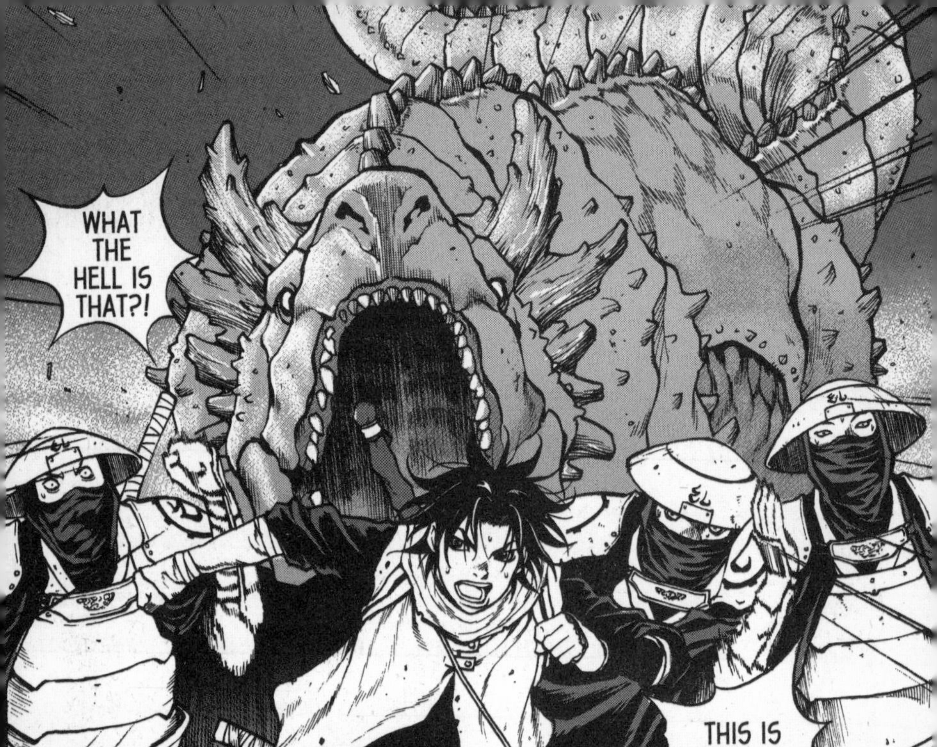
WHAT THE HELL IS THAT?!
THIS IS *GORIGON* TERRITORY...
...AND THEY'RE NOT VERY FOND OF TRESPASSERS!

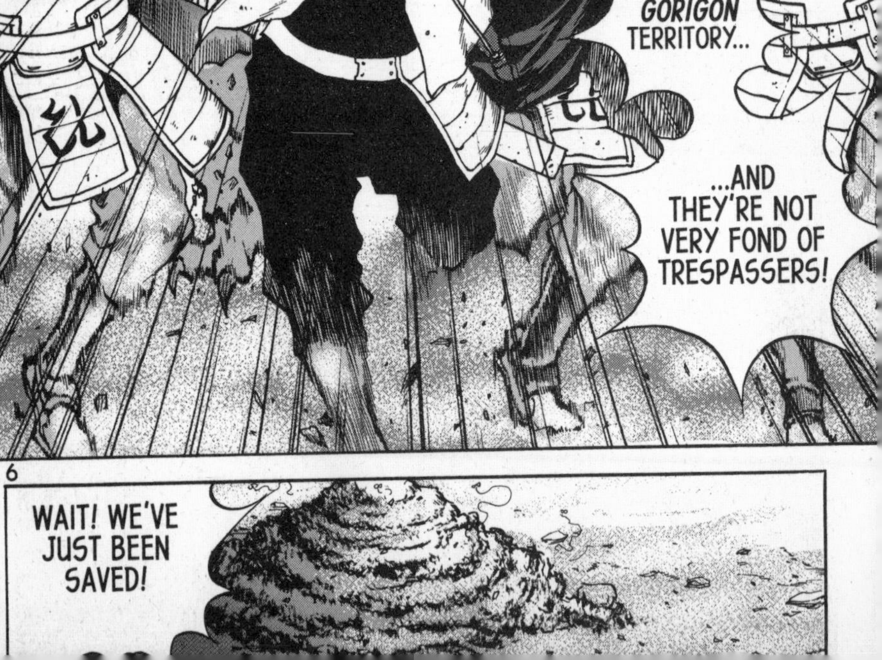
WAIT! WE'VE JUST BEEN SAVED!

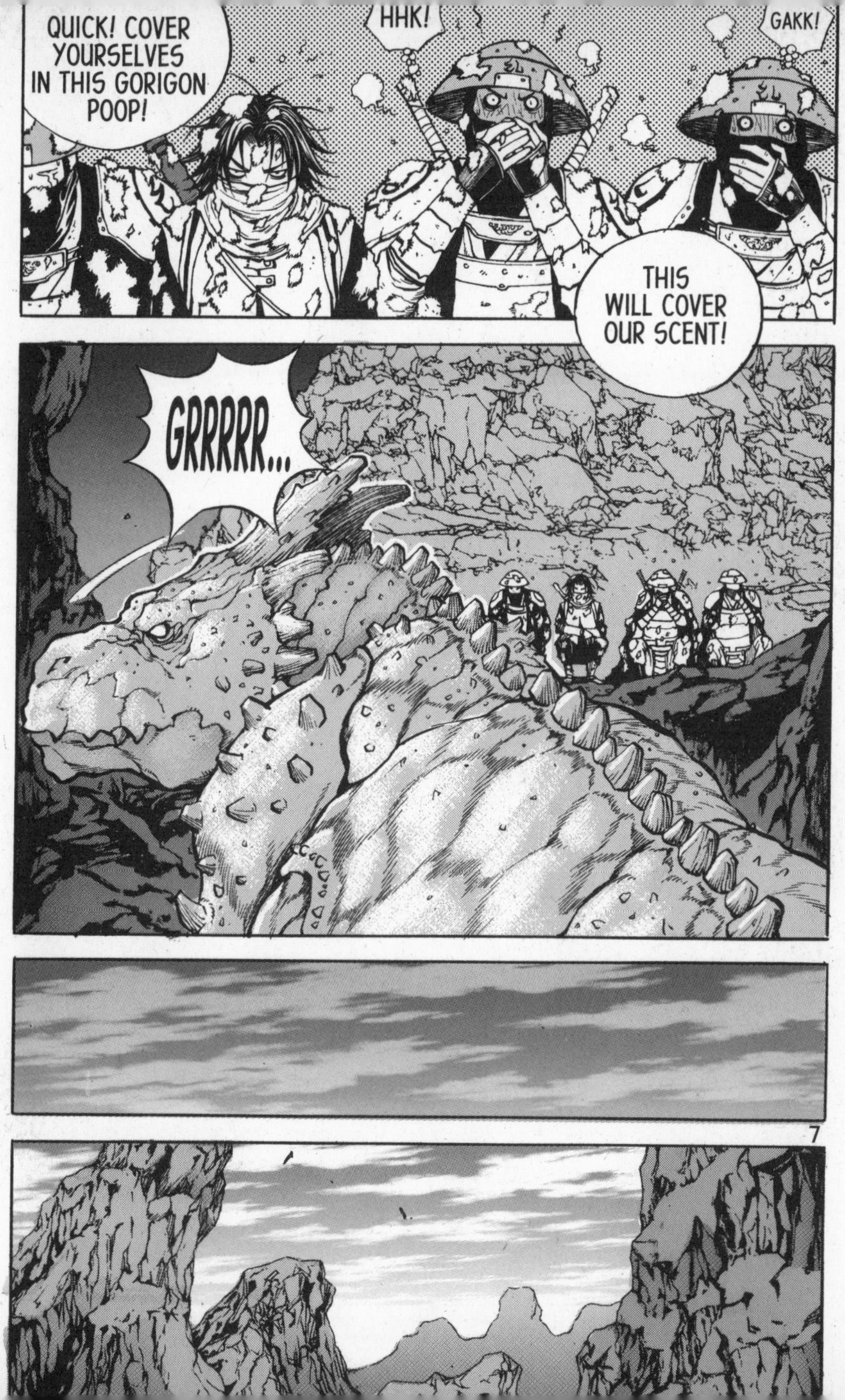
QUICK! COVER YOURSELVES IN THIS GORIGON POOP!
HHK!
GAKK!
THIS WILL COVER OUR SCENT!
GRRRRR...

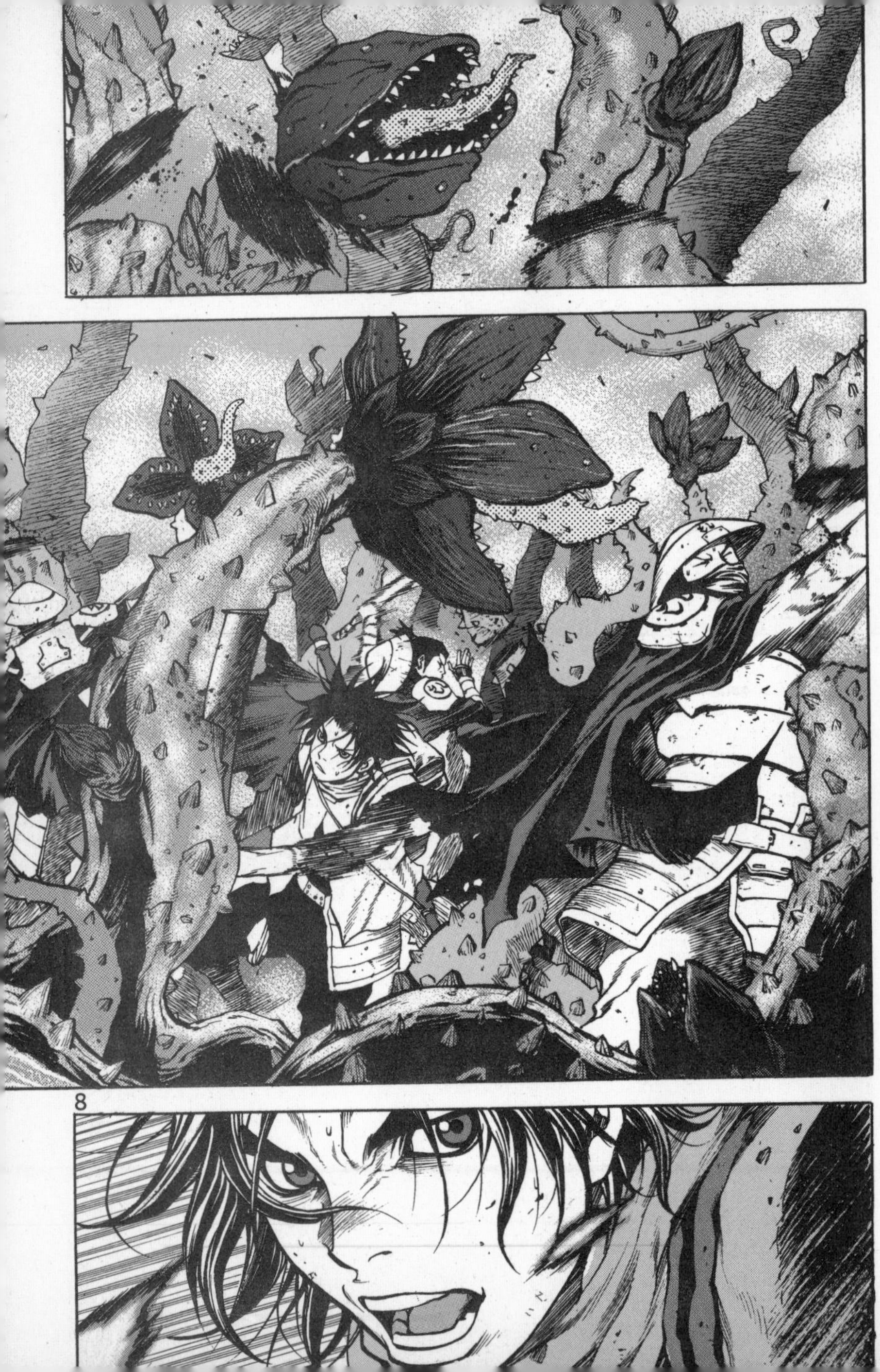

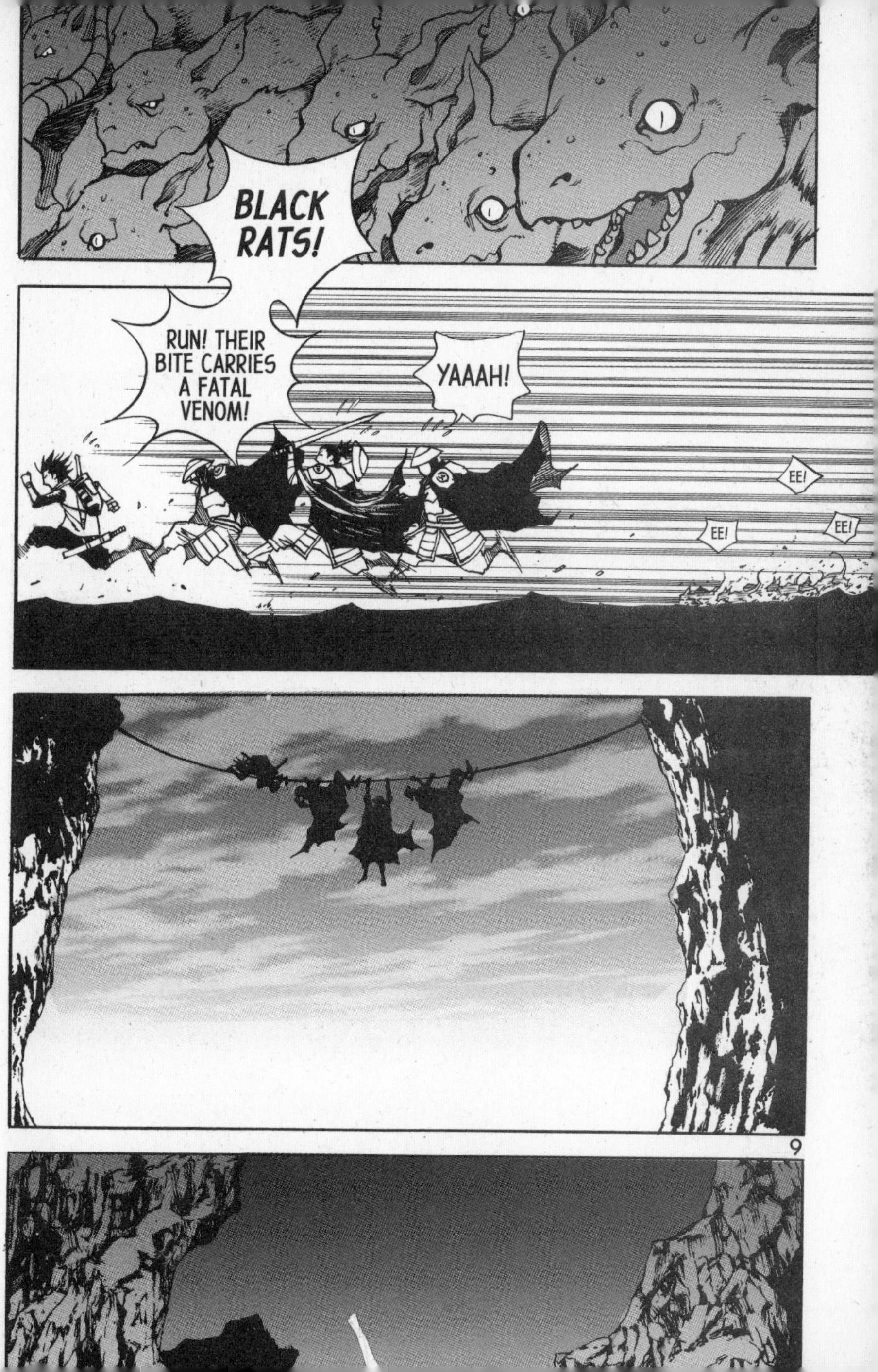

BLACK RATS!
RUN! THEIR BITE CARRIES A FATAL VENOM!
YAAAH!
EE!
EE!
EE!

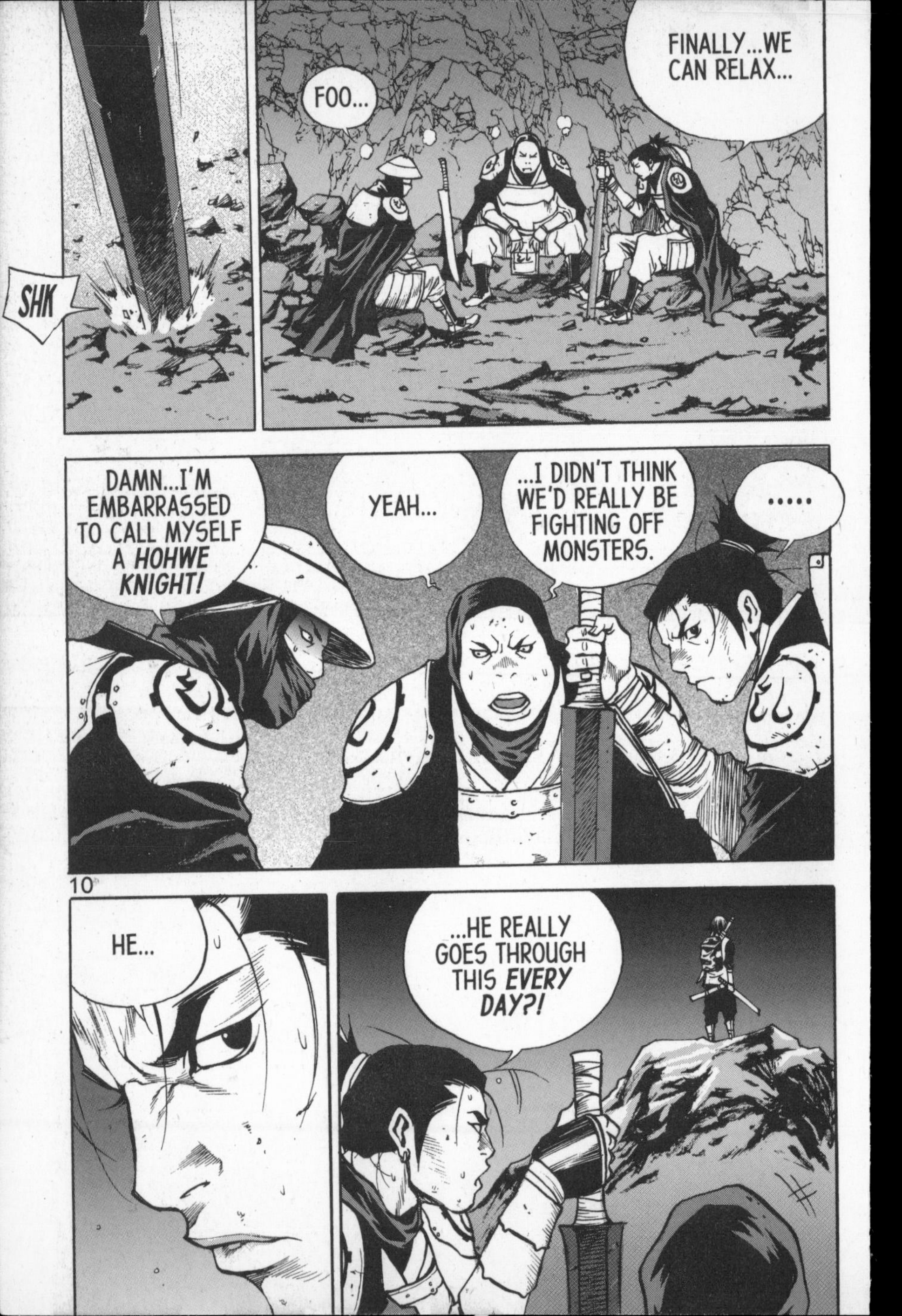
SHK
FOO...
FINALLY...WE CAN RELAX...
DAMN...I'M EMBARRASSED TO CALL MYSELF A *HOHWE KNIGHT!*
YEAH...
...I DIDN'T THINK WE'D REALLY BE FIGHTING OFF MONSTERS.
.....
HE...
...HE REALLY GOES THROUGH THIS *EVERY DAY?!*

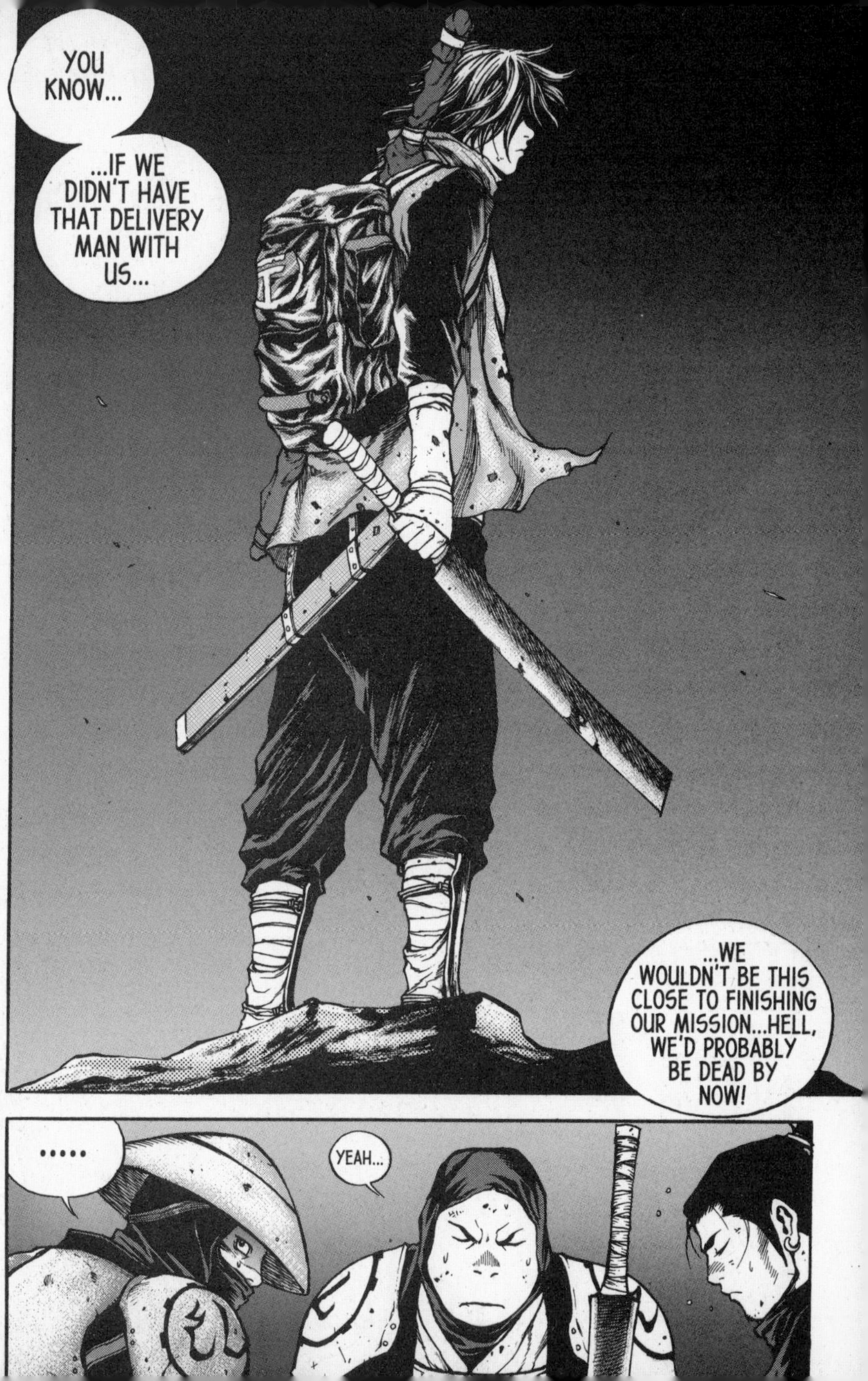
YOU KNOW...
...IF WE DIDN'T HAVE THAT DELIVERY MAN WITH US...
...WE WOULDN'T BE THIS CLOSE TO FINISHING OUR MISSION...HELL, WE'D PROBABLY BE DEAD BY NOW!
.....
YEAH...

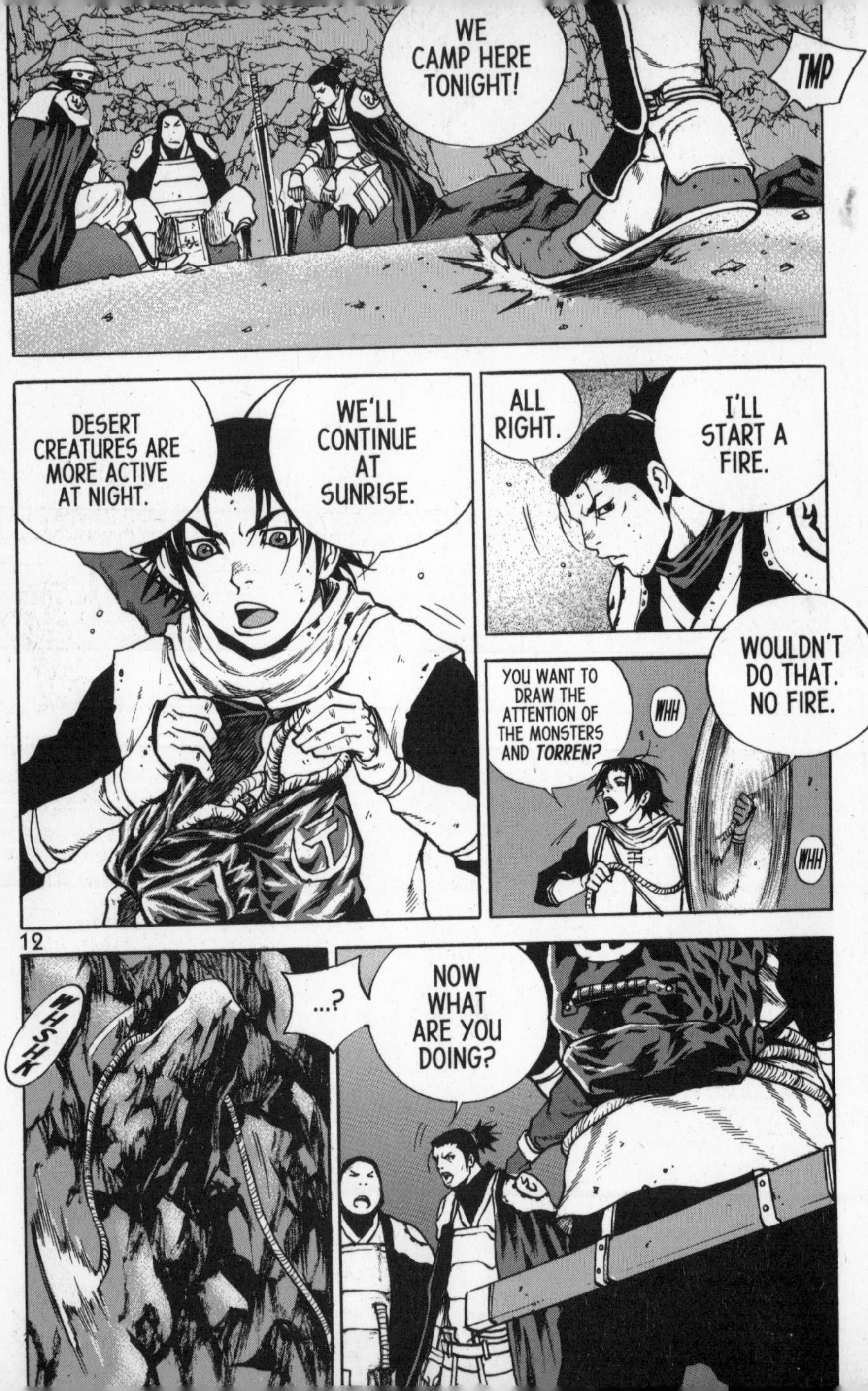
WE CAMP HERE TONIGHT!
TMP
DESERT CREATURES ARE MORE ACTIVE AT NIGHT.
WE'LL CONTINUE AT SUNRISE.
ALL RIGHT.
I'LL START A FIRE.
WOULDN'T DO THAT. NO FIRE.
YOU WANT TO DRAW THE ATTENTION OF THE MONSTERS AND *TORREN?*
WHH
WHH
WHSHK
...?
NOW WHAT ARE YOU DOING?

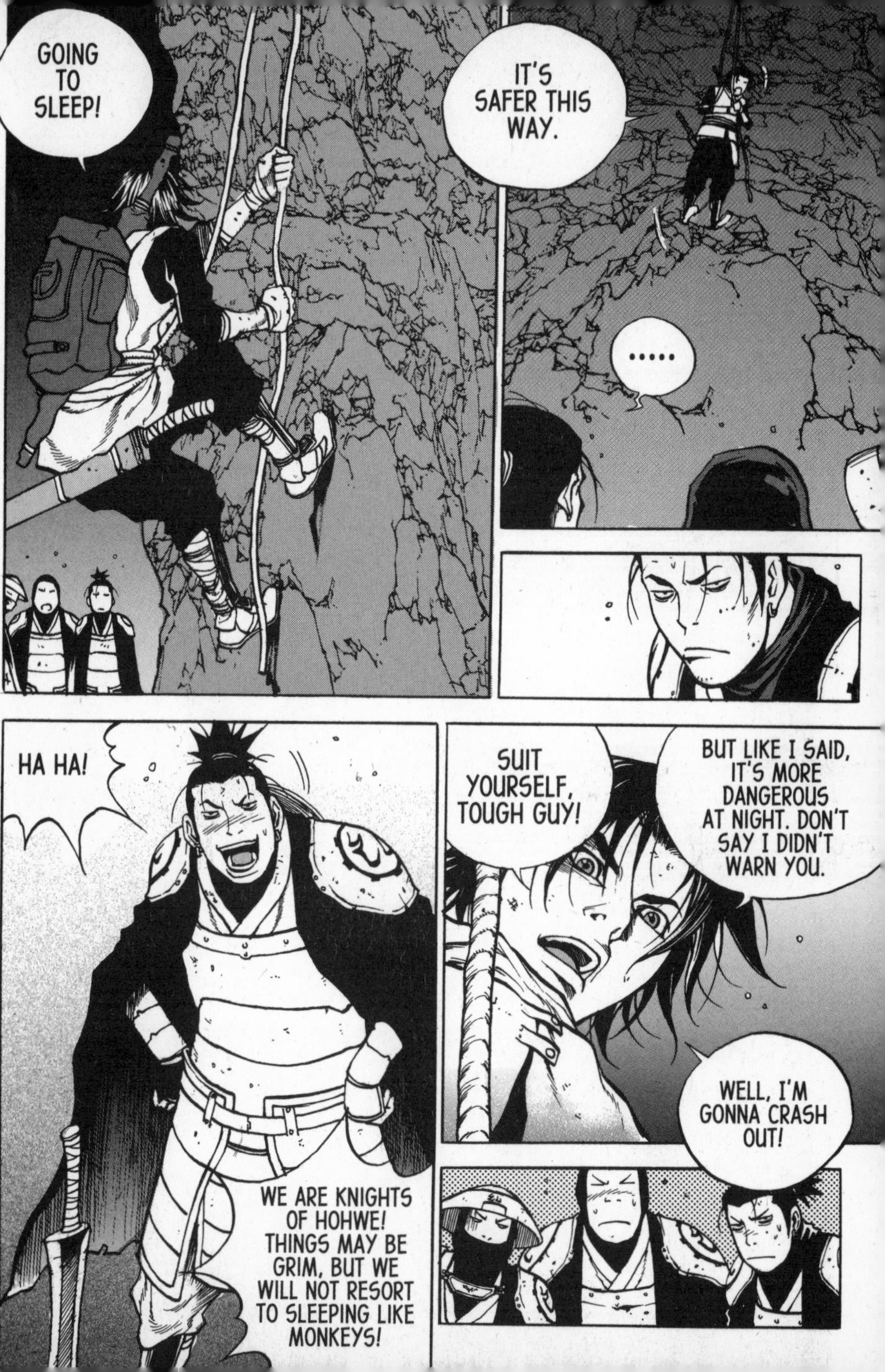
GOING TO SLEEP!
IT'S SAFER THIS WAY.
......
HA HA!
SUIT YOURSELF, TOUGH GUY!
BUT LIKE I SAID, IT'S MORE DANGEROUS AT NIGHT. DON'T SAY I DIDN'T WARN YOU.
WE ARE KNIGHTS OF HOHWE! THINGS MAY BE GRIM, BUT WE WILL NOT RESORT TO SLEEPING LIKE MONKEYS!
WELL, I'M GONNA CRASH OUT!

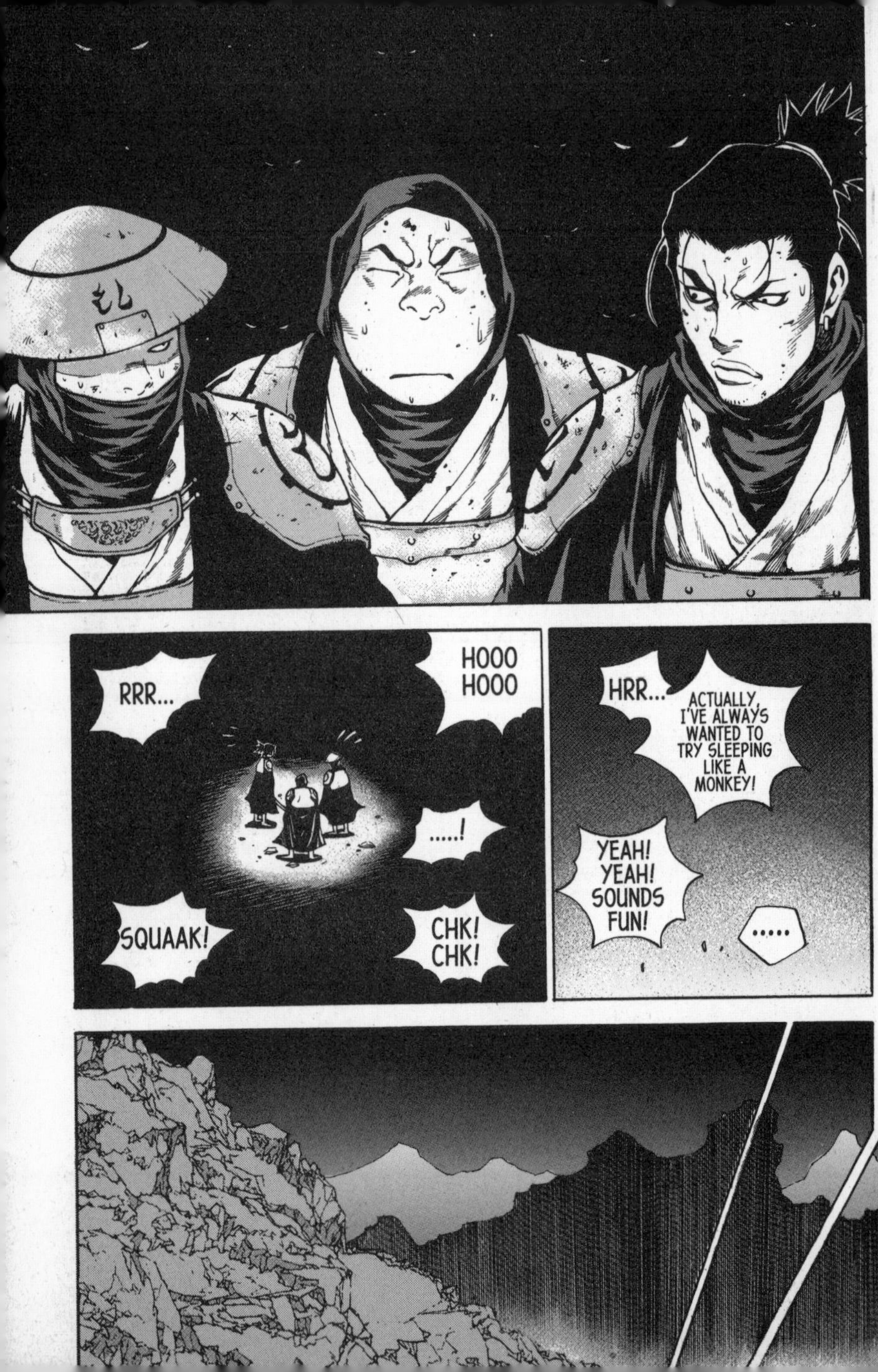
HOOO HOOO
RRR...
.....!
CHK! CHK!
SQUAAK!
HRR...
ACTUALLY, I'VE ALWAYS WANTED TO TRY SLEEPING LIKE A MONKEY!
YEAH! YEAH! SOUNDS FUN!
.....

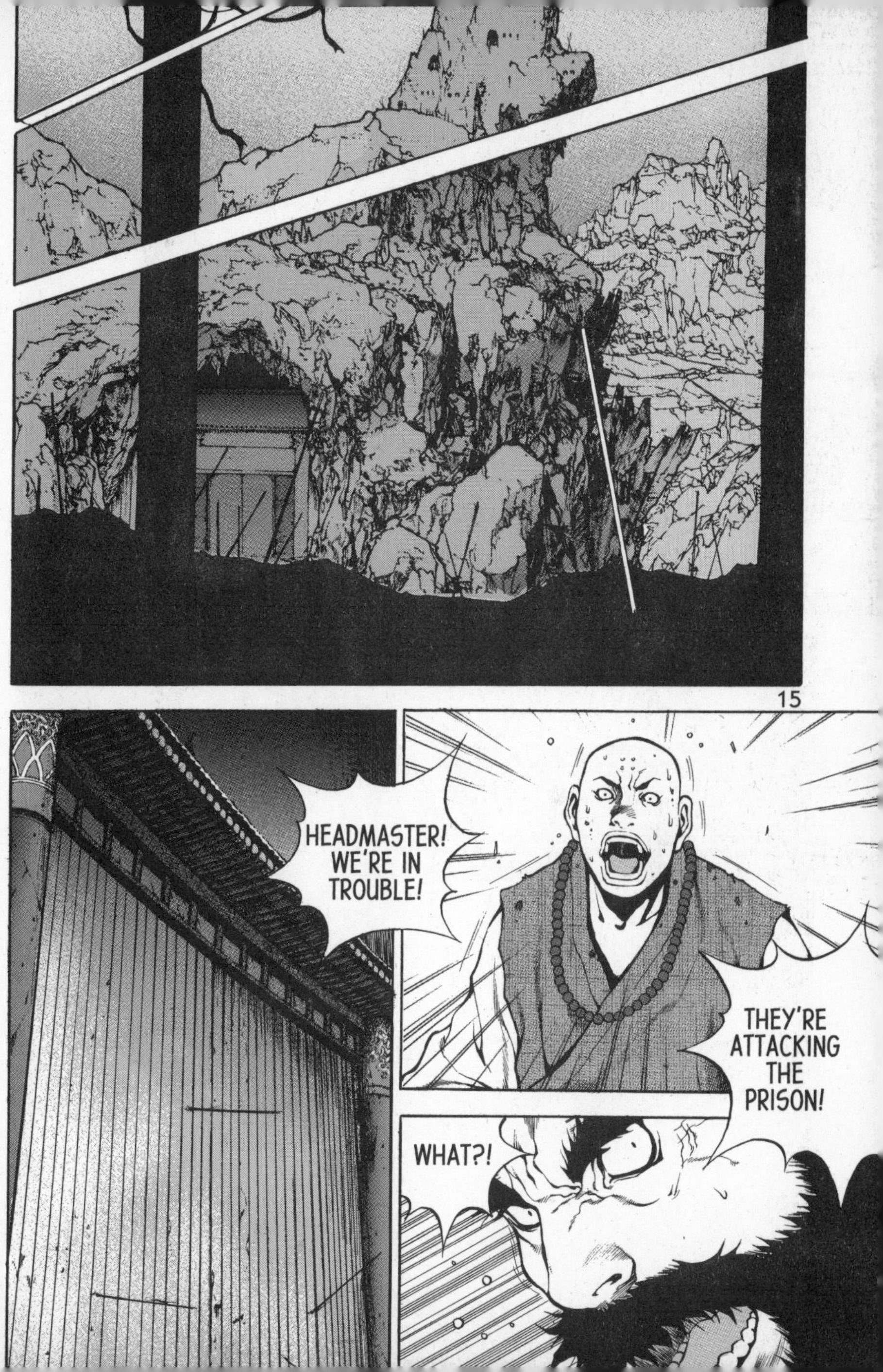
HEADMASTER! WE'RE IN TROUBLE!
THEY'RE ATTACKING THE PRISON!
WHAT?!

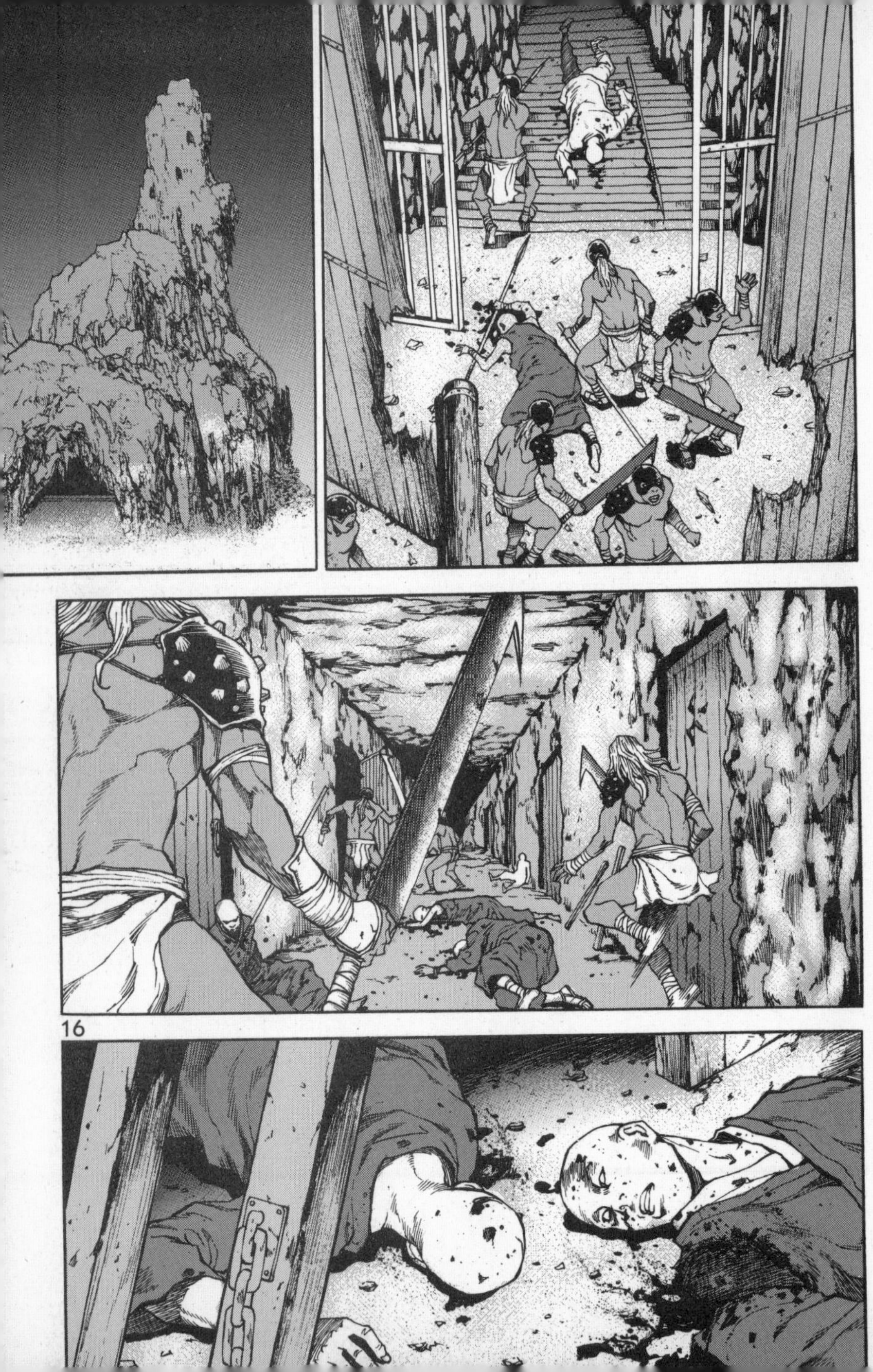

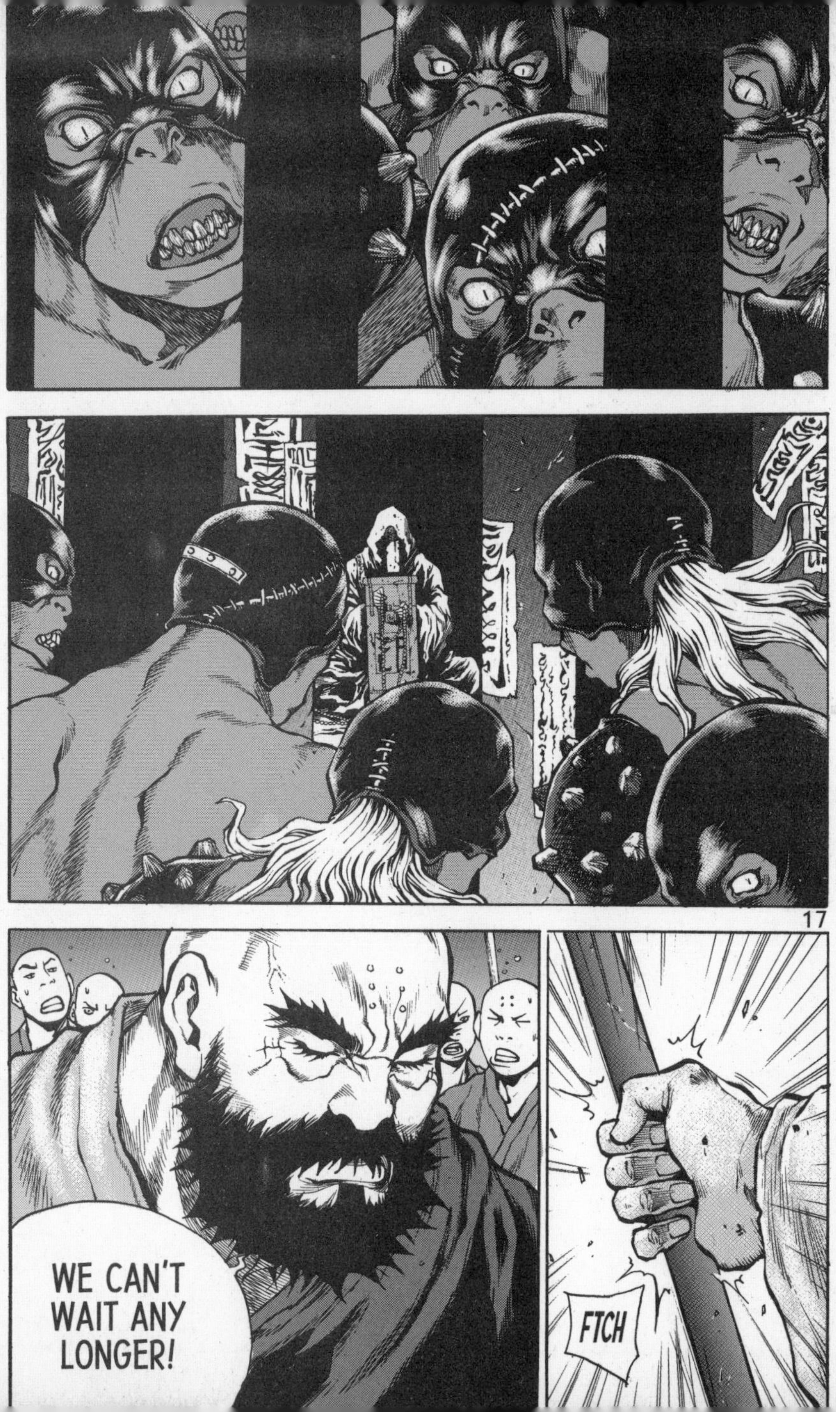
WE CAN'T WAIT ANY LONGER!
FTCH

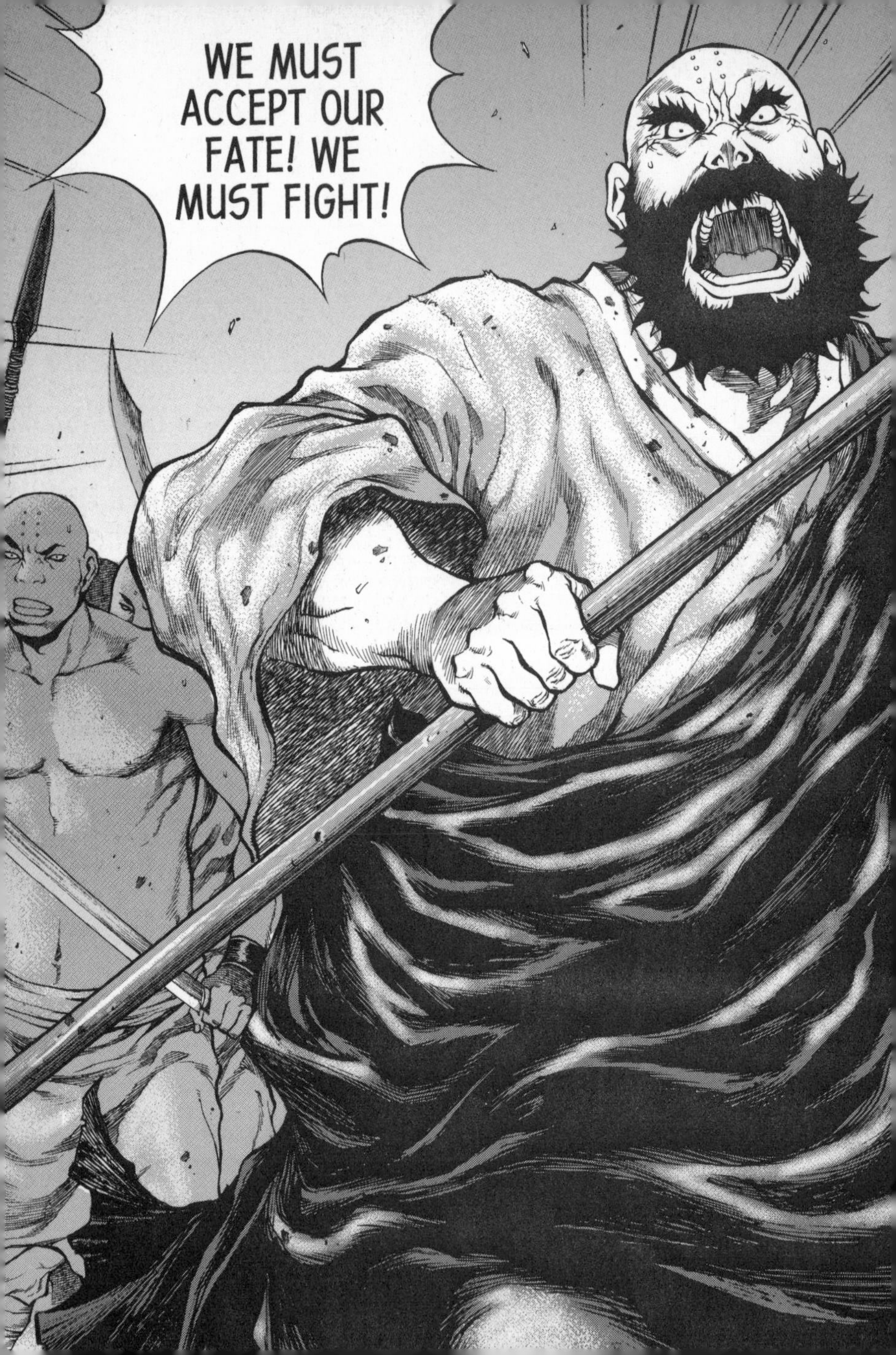
WE MUST ACCEPT OUR FATE! WE MUST FIGHT!

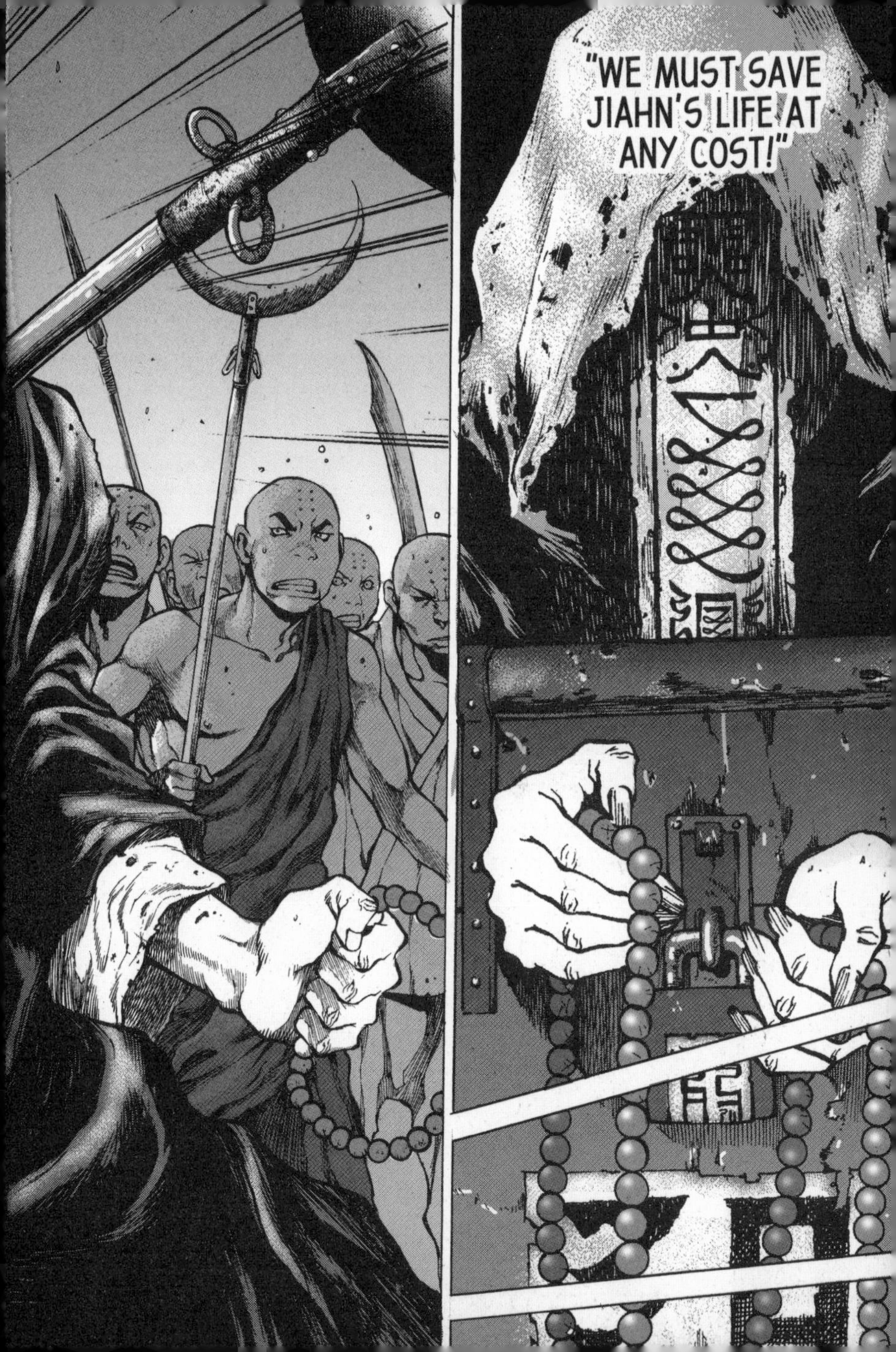
"WE MUST SAVE JIAHN'S LIFE AT ANY COST!"

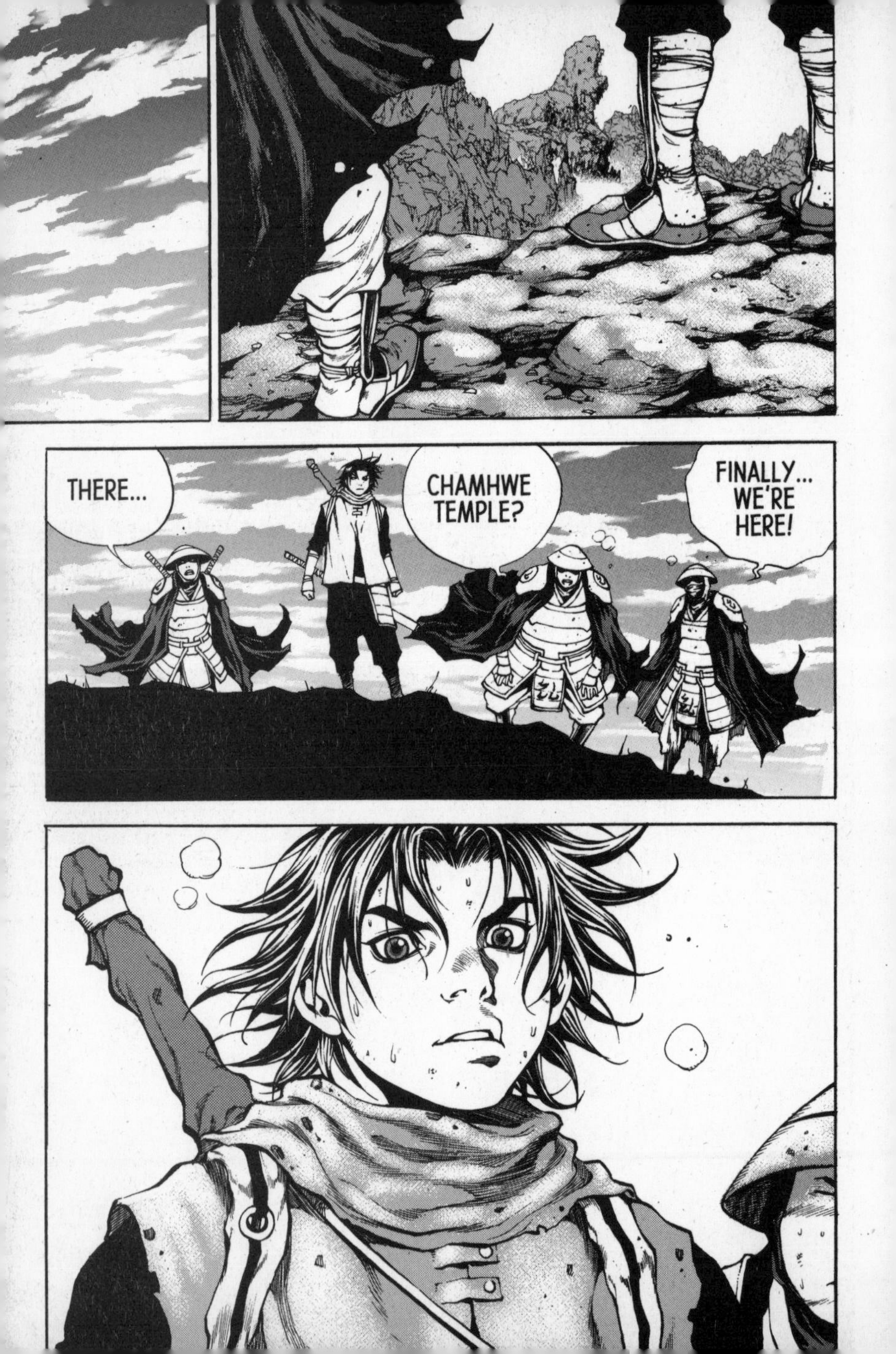
THERE...
CHAMHWE TEMPLE?
FINALLY... WE'RE HERE!

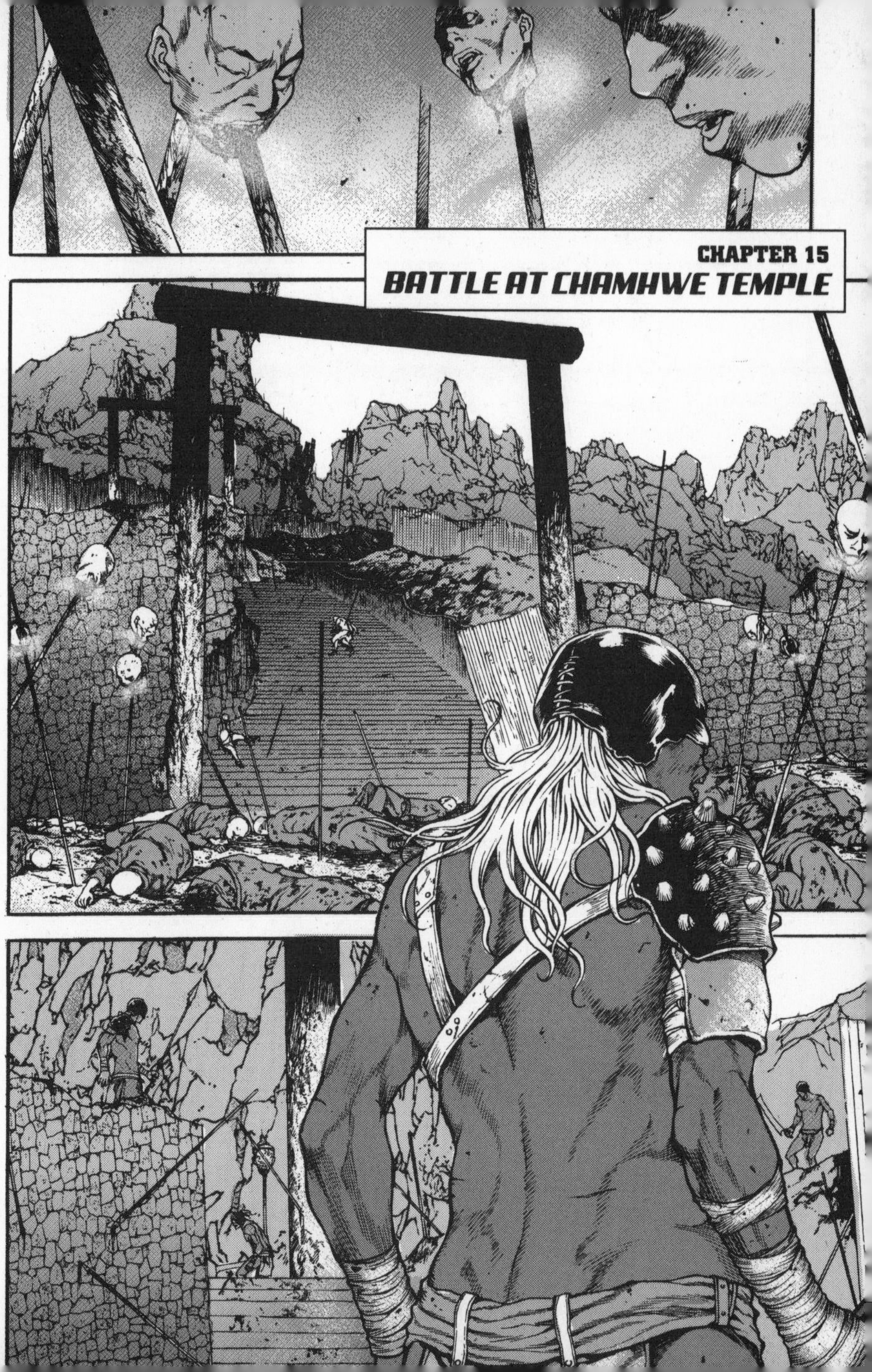
CHAPTER 15
BATTLE AT CHAMHWE TEMPLE

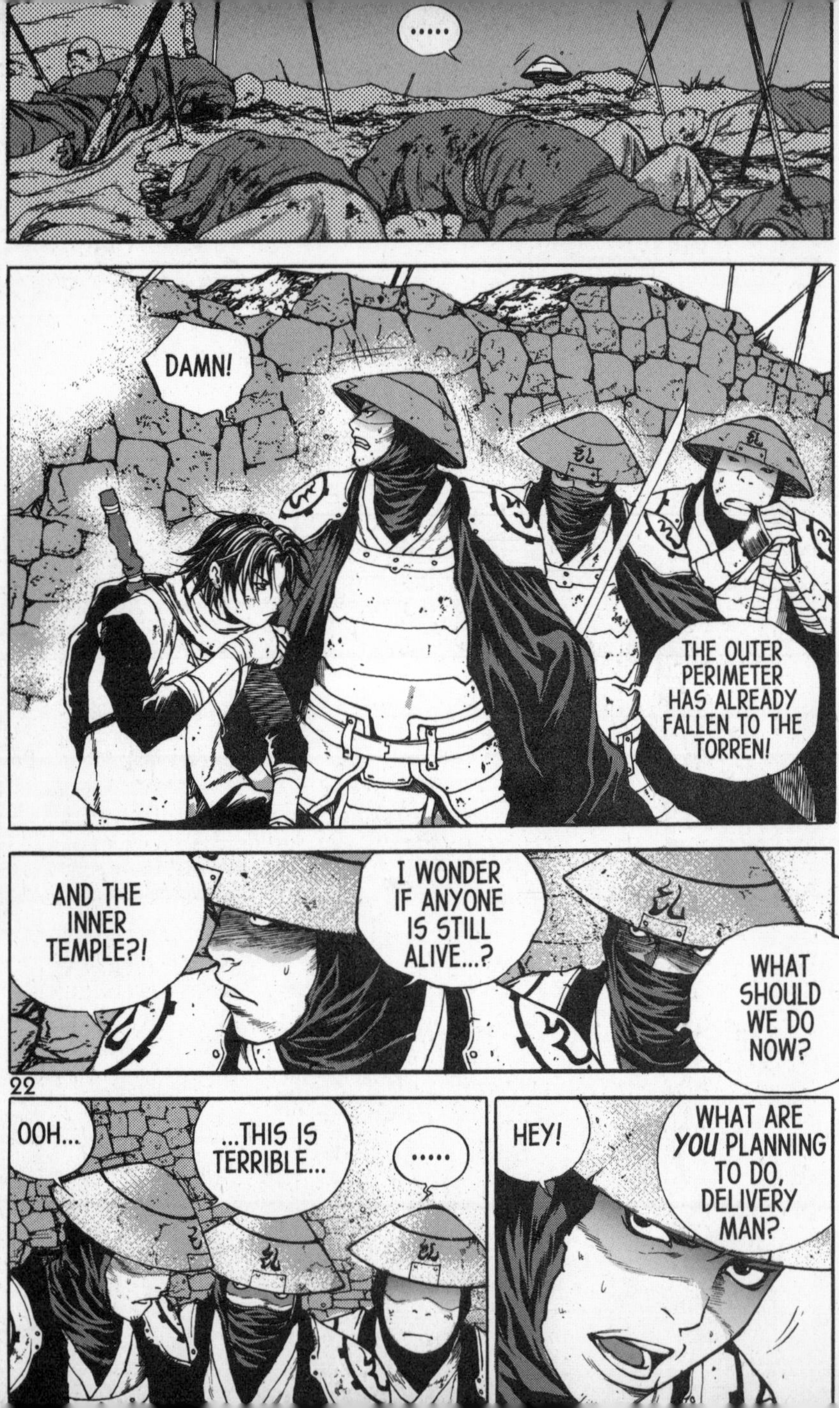
......
DAMN!
THE OUTER PERIMETER HAS ALREADY FALLEN TO THE TORREN!
AND THE INNER TEMPLE?!
I WONDER IF ANYONE IS STILL ALIVE...?
WHAT SHOULD WE DO NOW?
OOH...
...THIS IS TERRIBLE...
......
HEY!
WHAT ARE *YOU* PLANNING TO DO, DELIVERY MAN?

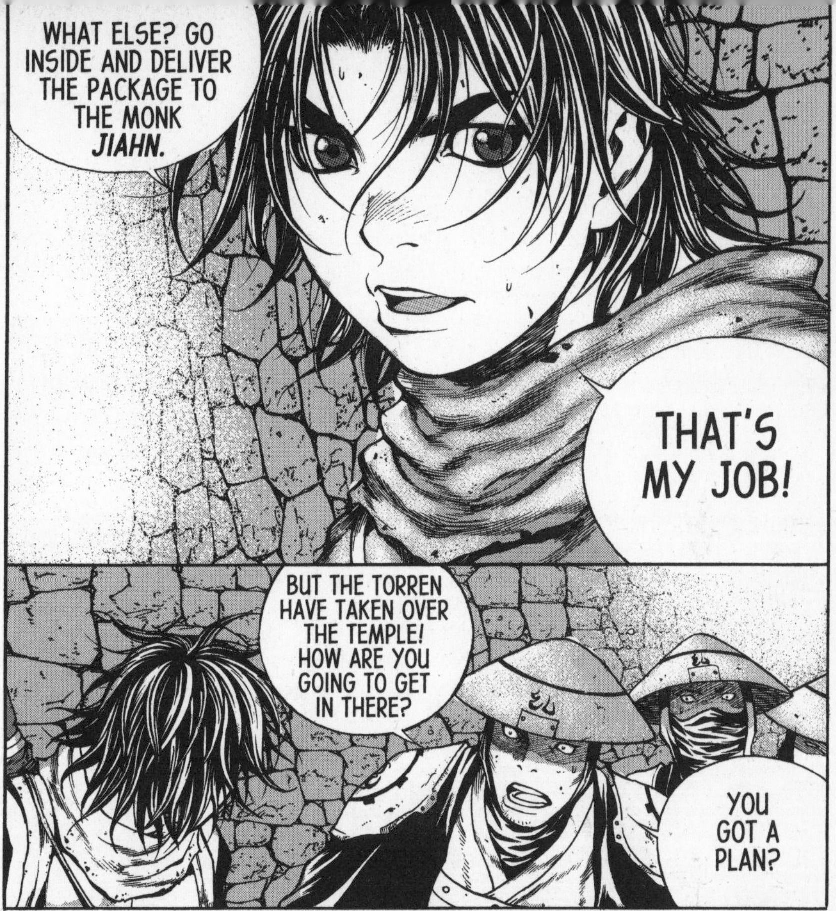
WHAT ELSE? GO INSIDE AND DELIVER THE PACKAGE TO THE MONK *JIAHN.*
THAT'S MY JOB!
BUT THE TORREN HAVE TAKEN OVER THE TEMPLE! HOW ARE YOU GOING TO GET IN THERE?
YOU GOT A PLAN?

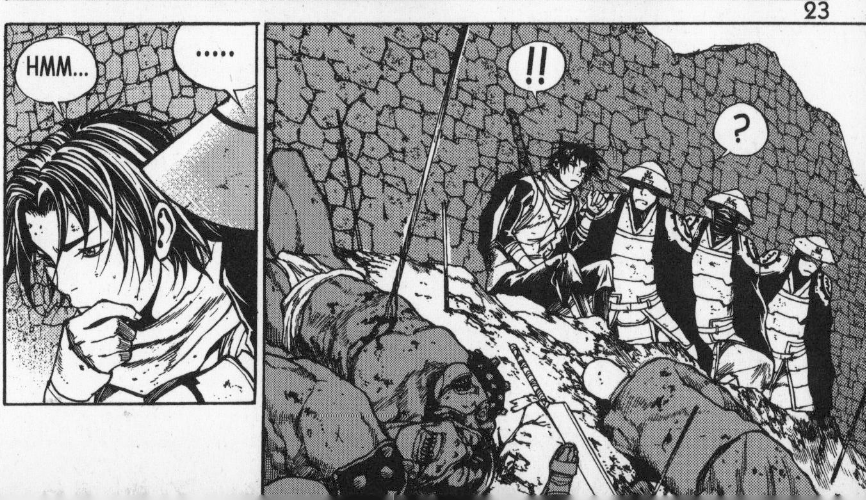
HMM...
.....
!!
?

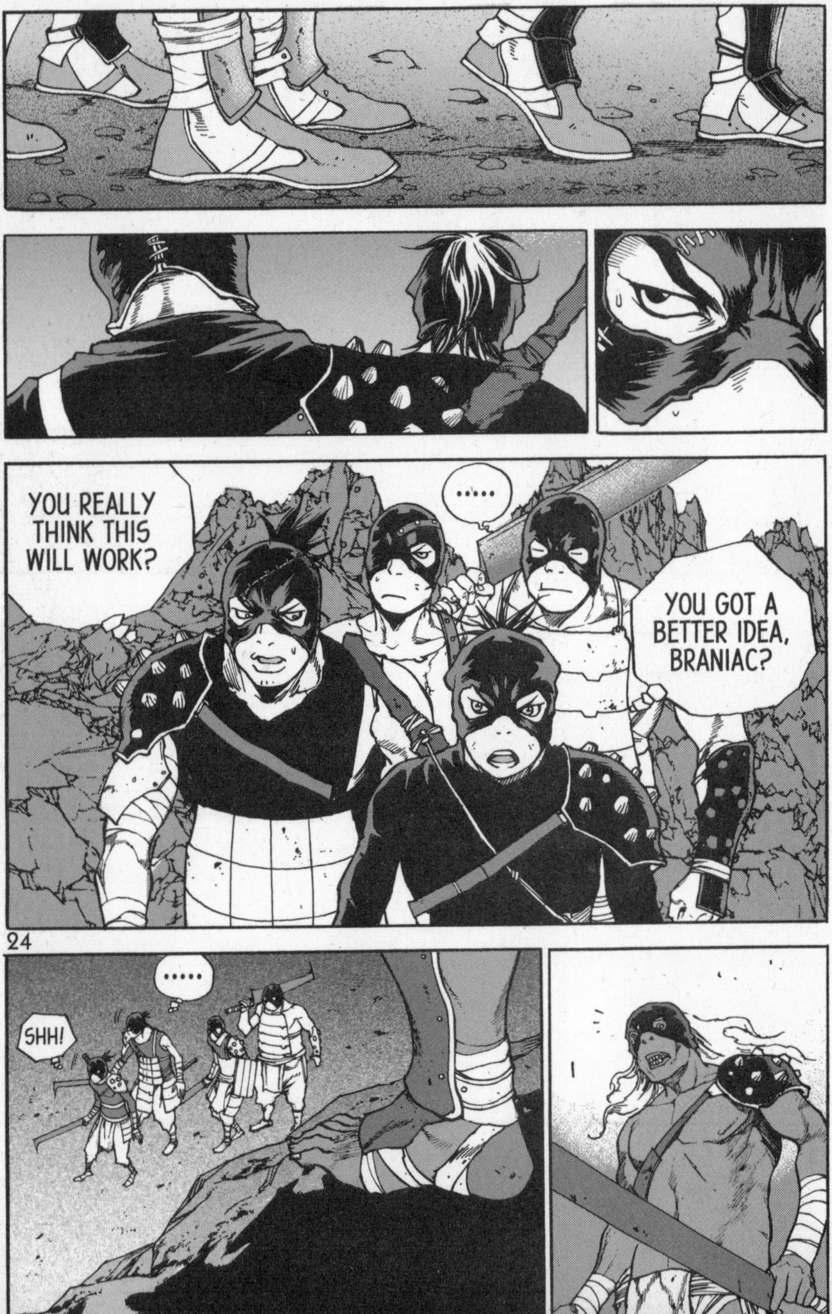
YOU REALLY THINK THIS WILL WORK?
......
YOU GOT A BETTER IDEA, BRANIAC?
......
SHH!

24

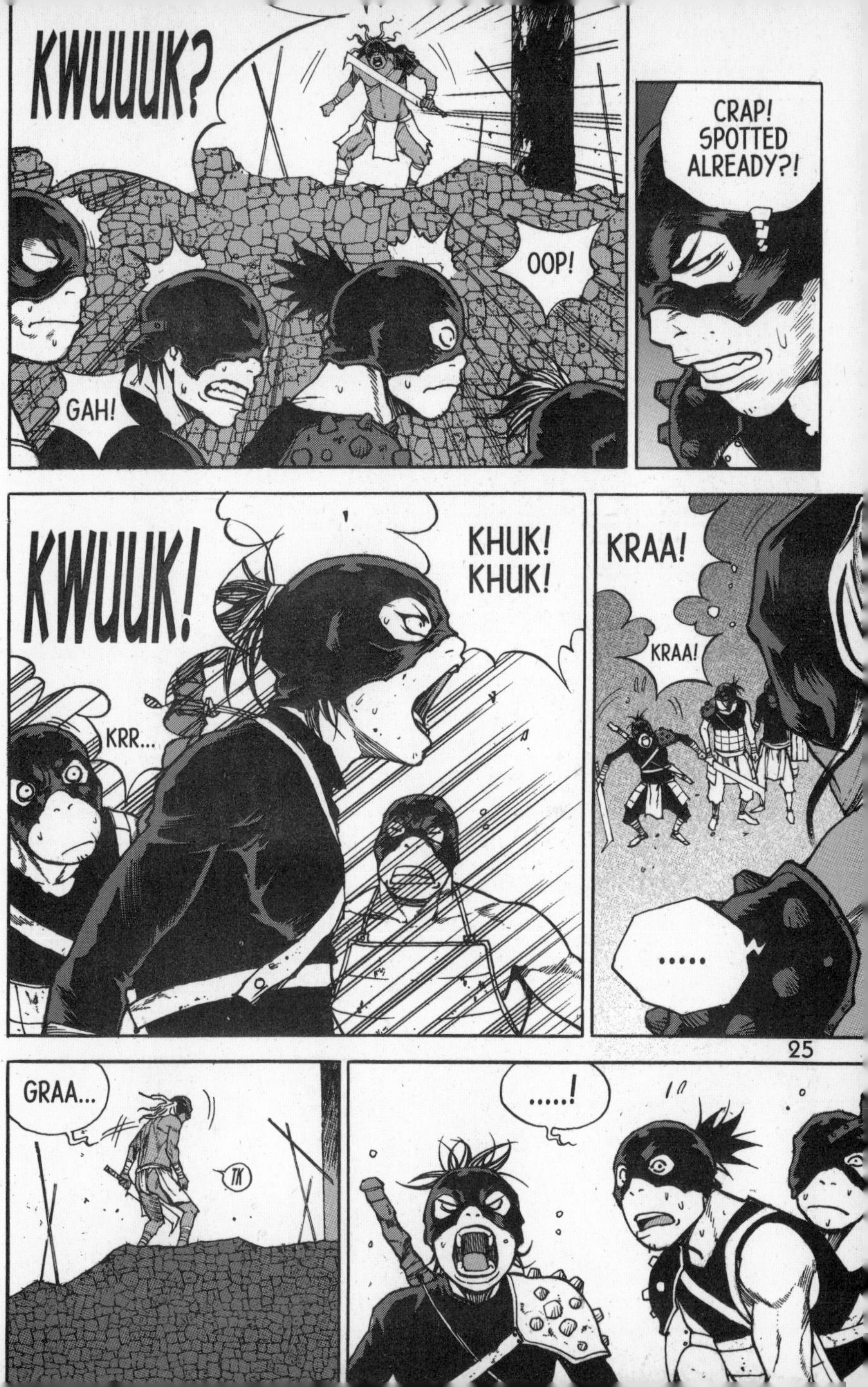
KWUUUK?
OOP!
GAH!
CRAP! SPOTTED ALREADY?!
KWUUK!
KHUK! KHUK!
KRR...
KRAA!
KRAA!
.....
GRAA...
TK
.....!

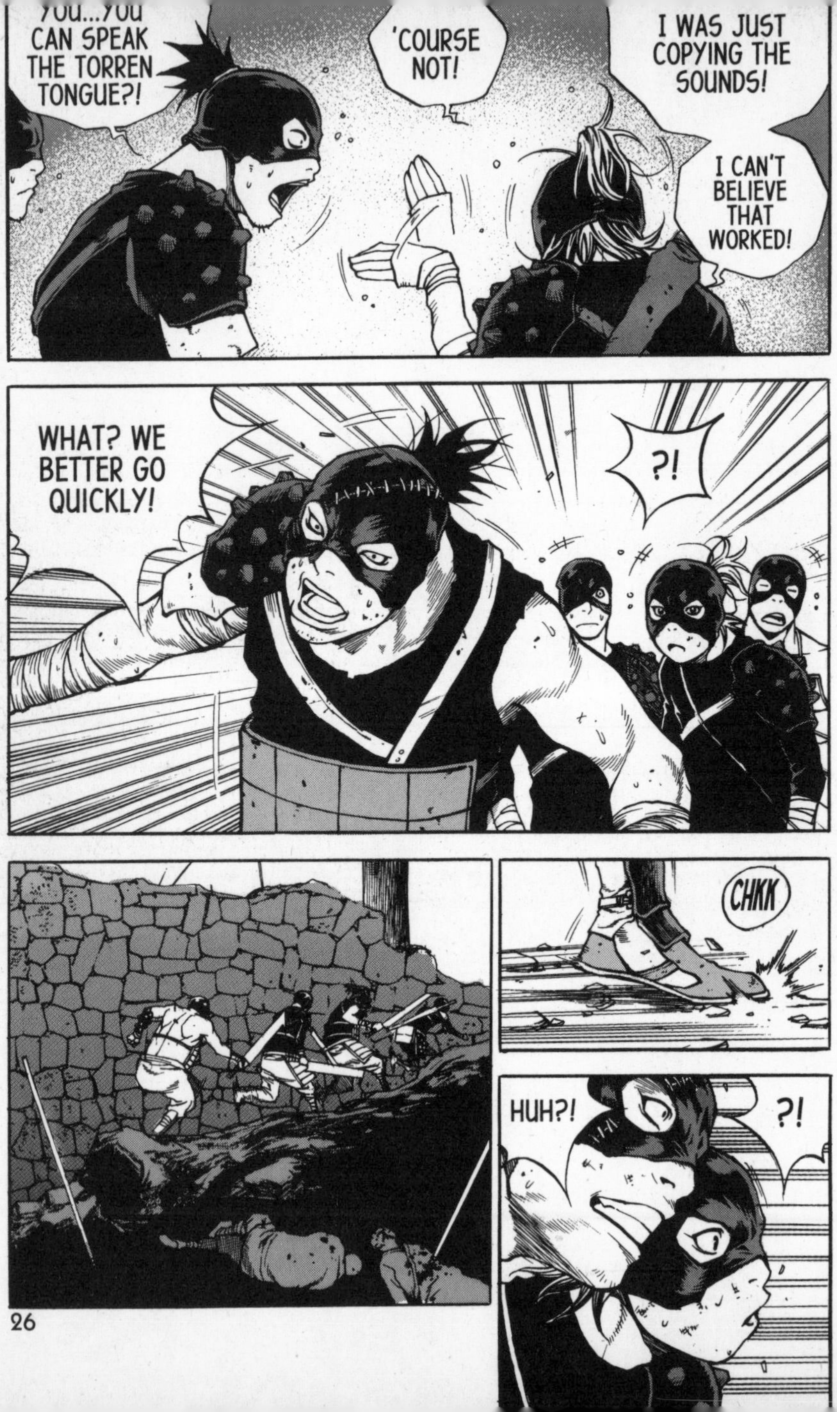
YOU...YOU CAN SPEAK THE TORREN TONGUE?!
'COURSE NOT!
I WAS JUST COPYING THE SOUNDS!
I CAN'T BELIEVE THAT WORKED!
WHAT? WE BETTER GO QUICKLY!
?!
CHKK
HUH?!
?!

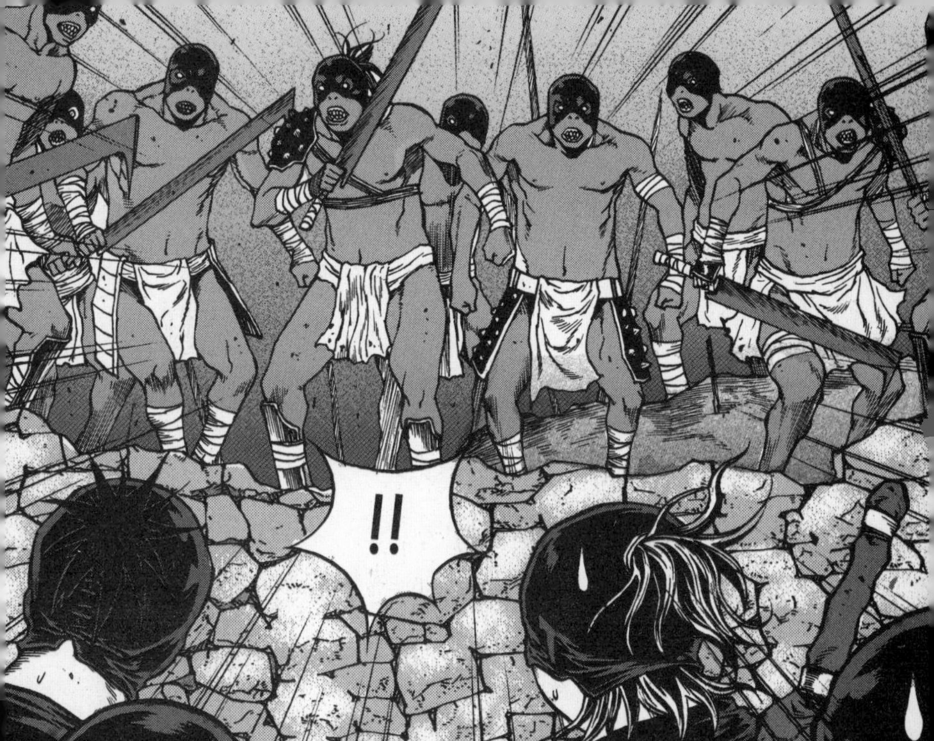
!!

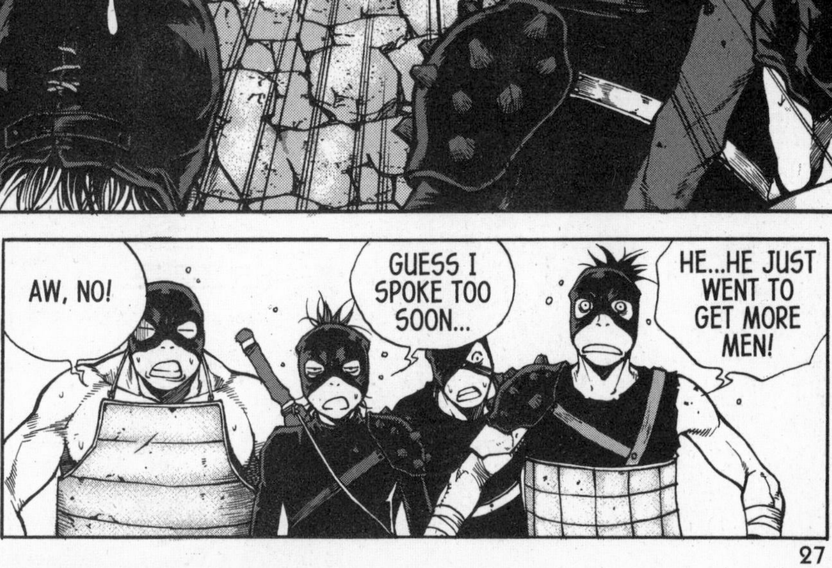
HE...HE JUST WENT TO GET MORE MEN!
GUESS I SPOKE TOO SOON...
AW, NO!

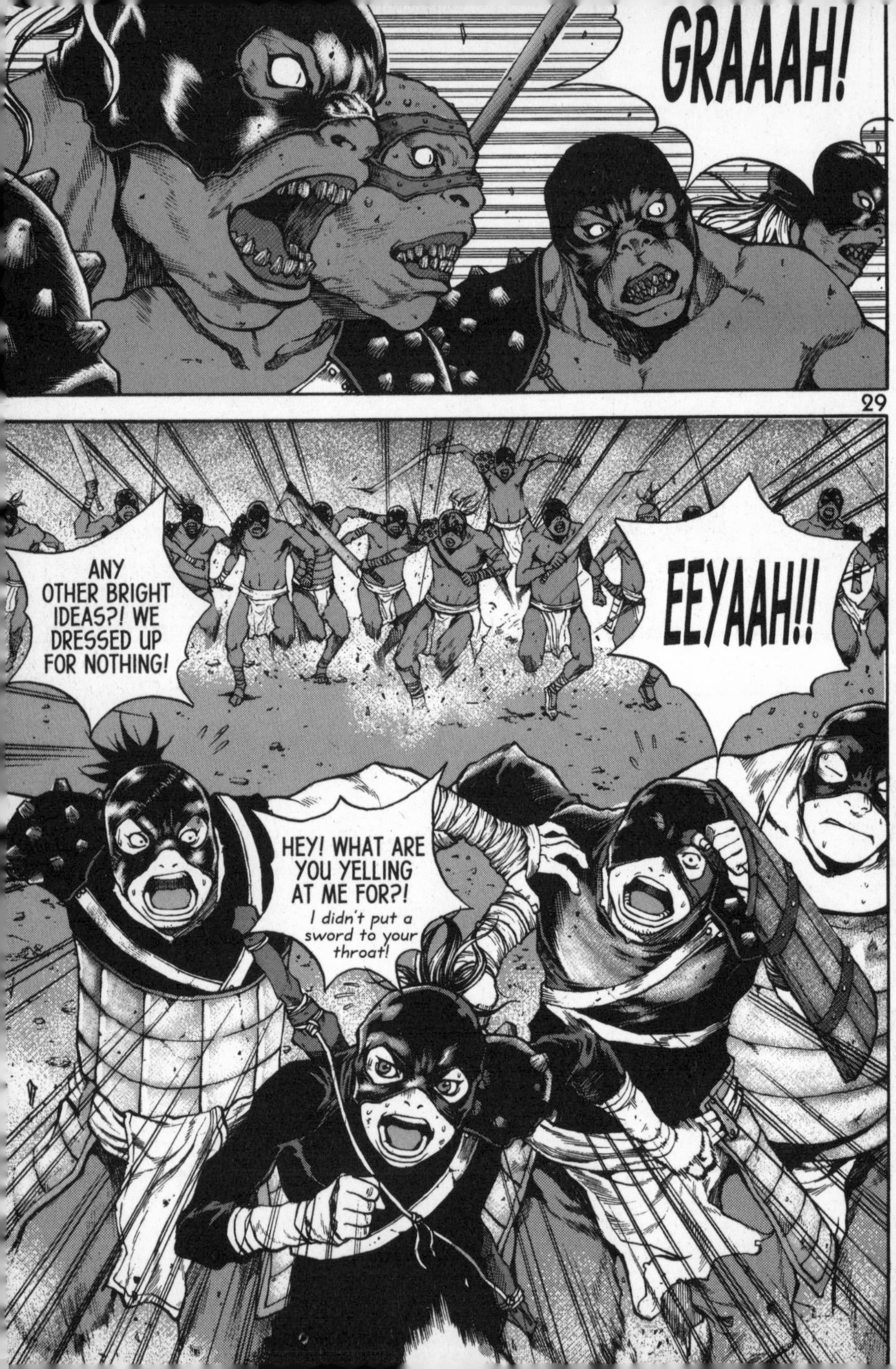
GRAAAH!
ANY OTHER BRIGHT IDEAS?! WE DRESSED UP FOR NOTHING!
EEYAAH!!
HEY! WHAT ARE YOU YELLING AT ME FOR?!
I didn't put a sword to your throat!

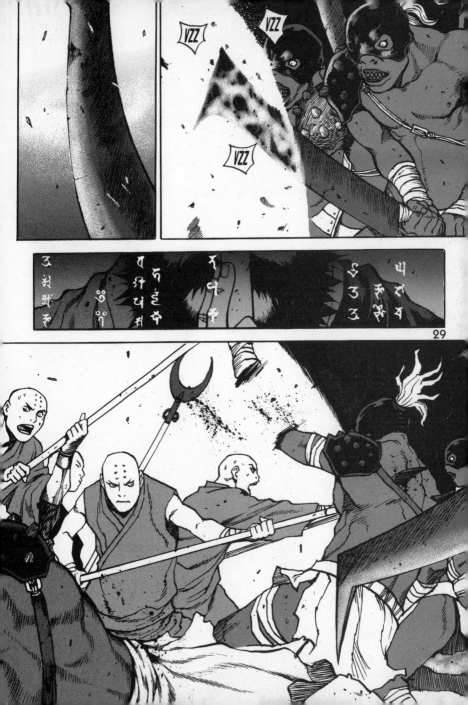

VZZ

VZZ

VZZ

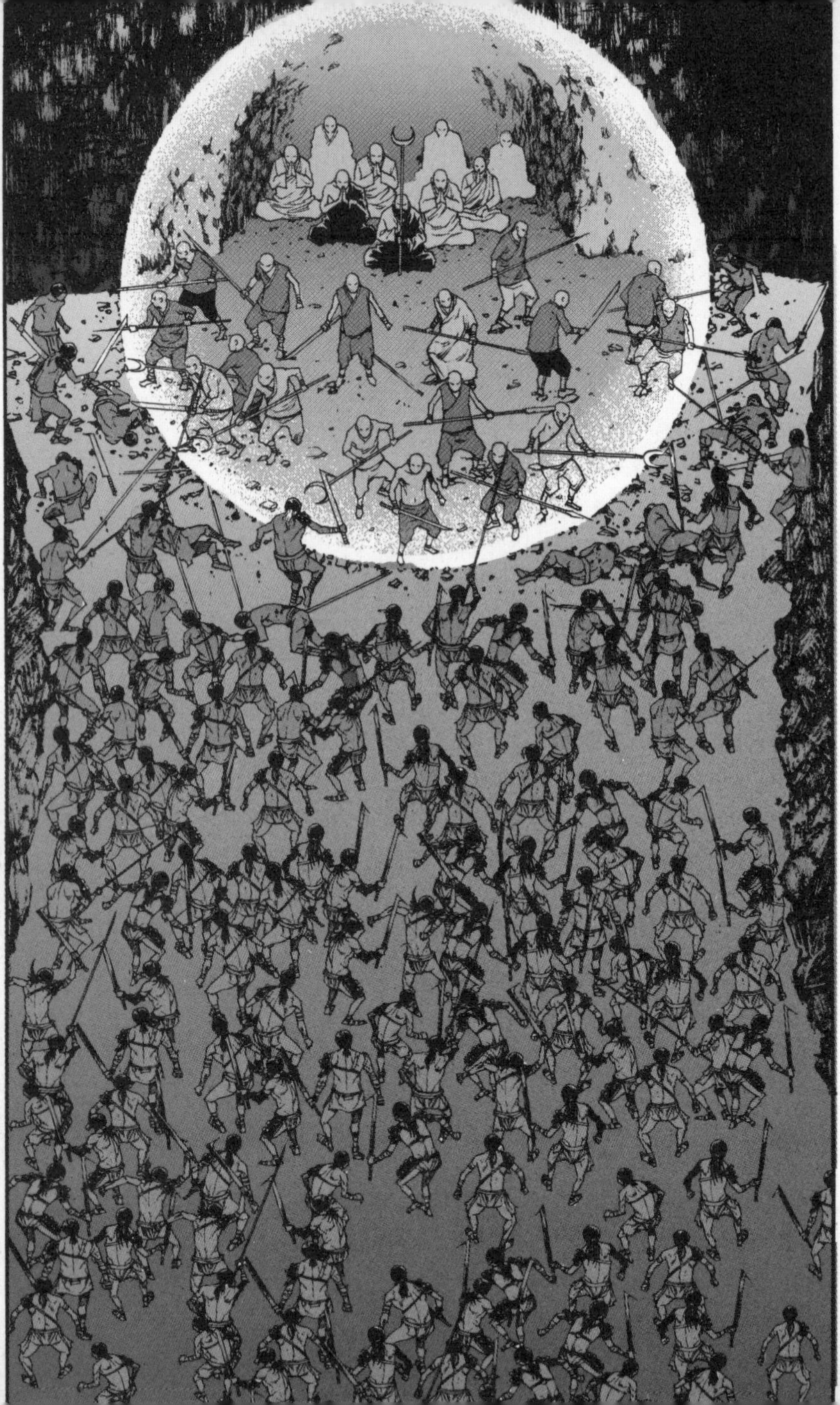

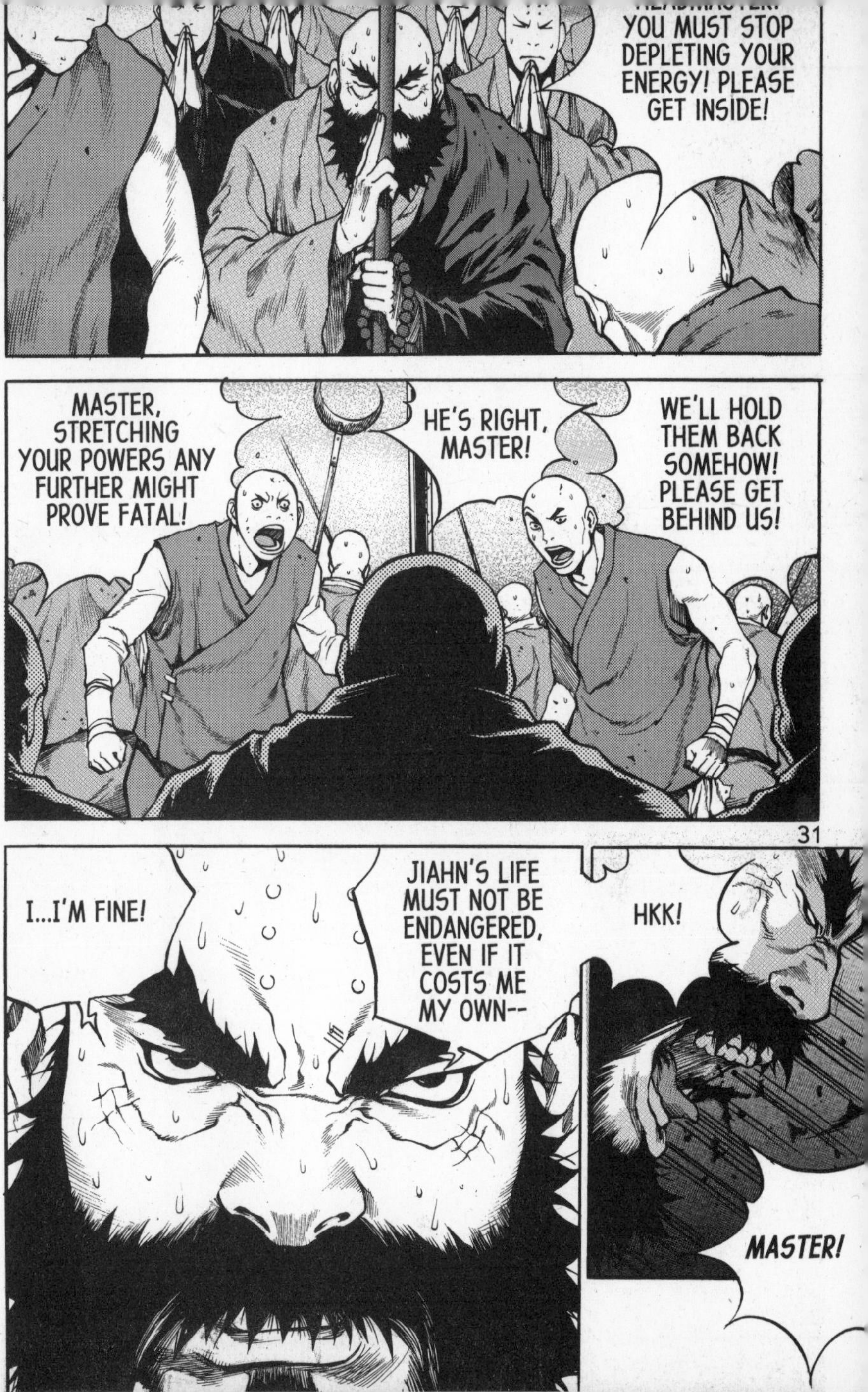
YOU MUST STOP DEPLETING YOUR ENERGY! PLEASE GET INSIDE!
MASTER, STRETCHING YOUR POWERS ANY FURTHER MIGHT PROVE FATAL!
HE'S RIGHT, MASTER!
WE'LL HOLD THEM BACK SOMEHOW! PLEASE GET BEHIND US!
I...I'M FINE!
JIAHN'S LIFE MUST NOT BE ENDANGERED, EVEN IF IT COSTS ME MY OWN--
HKK!
MASTER!

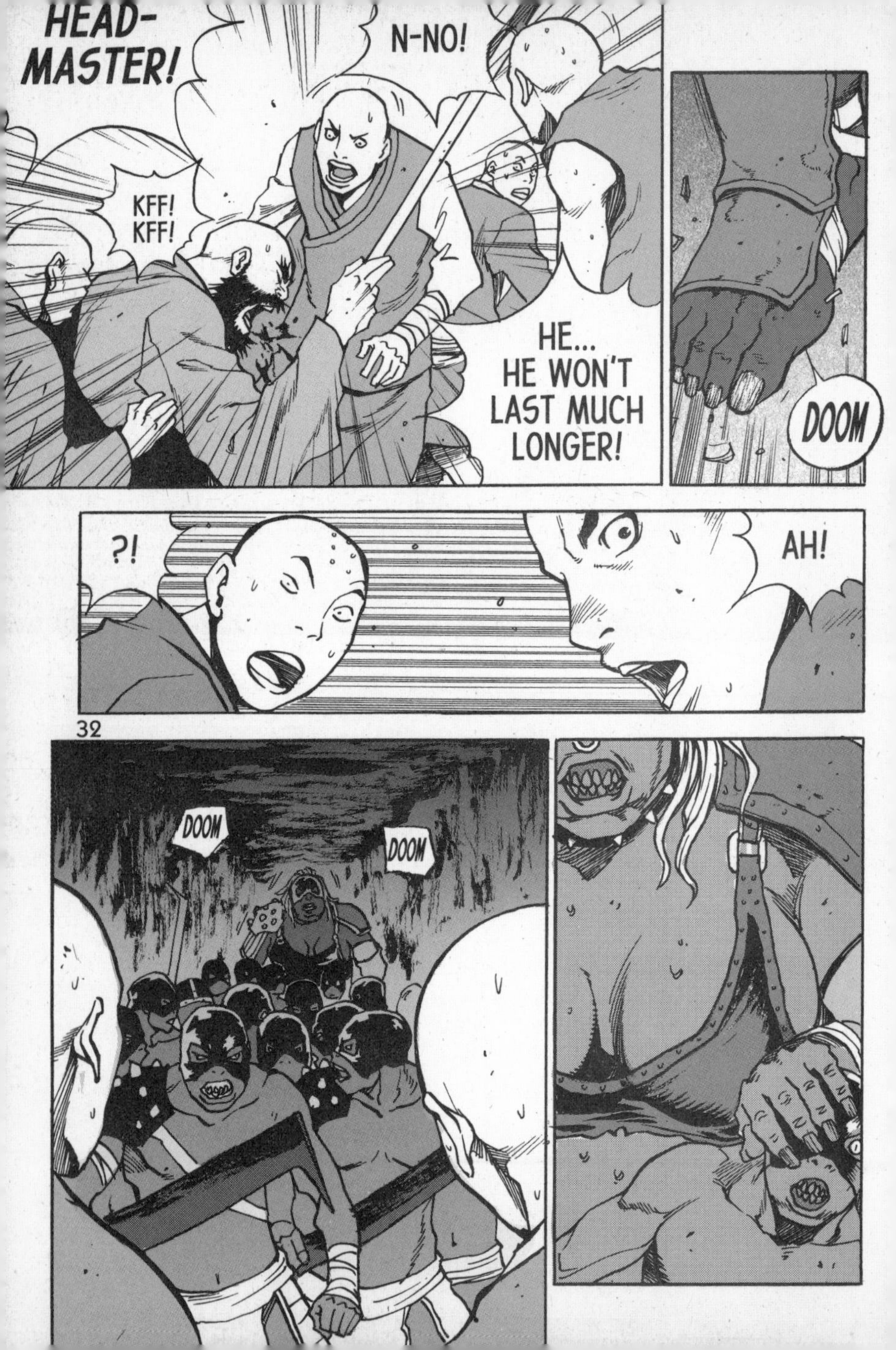
HEAD-MASTER!
N-NO!
KFF! KFF!
HE... HE WON'T LAST MUCH LONGER!
DOOM
?!
AH!
DOOM
DOOM
32

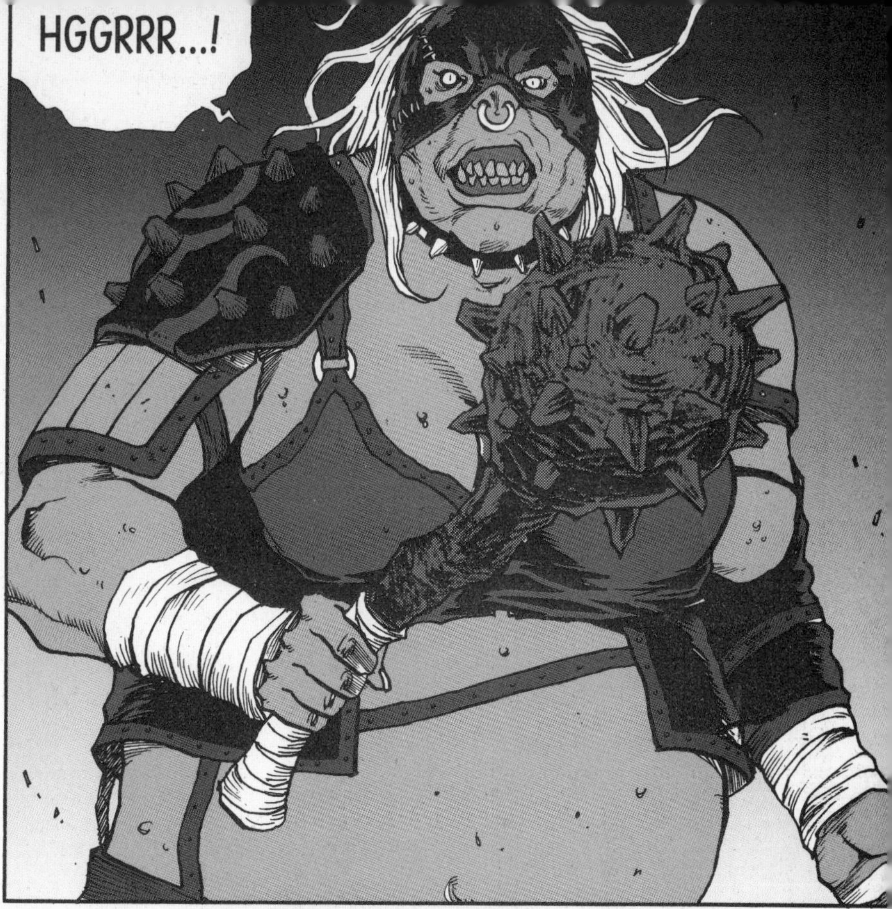
HGGRRR...!

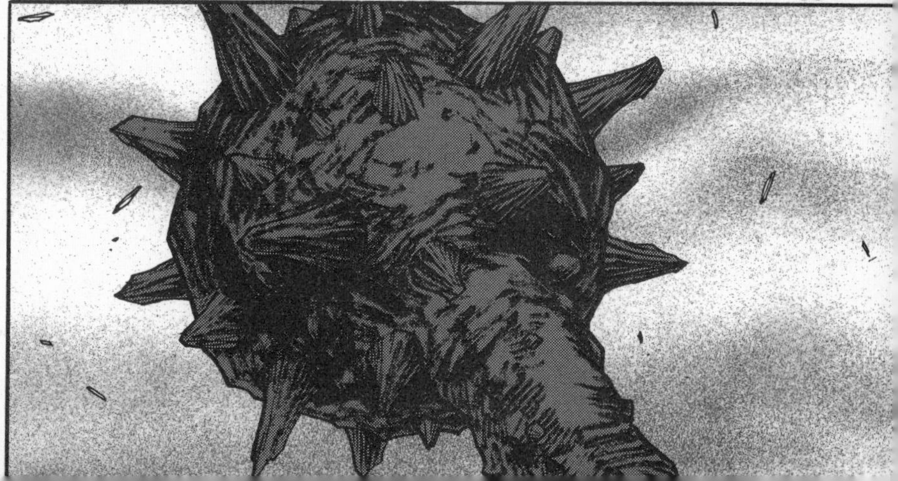

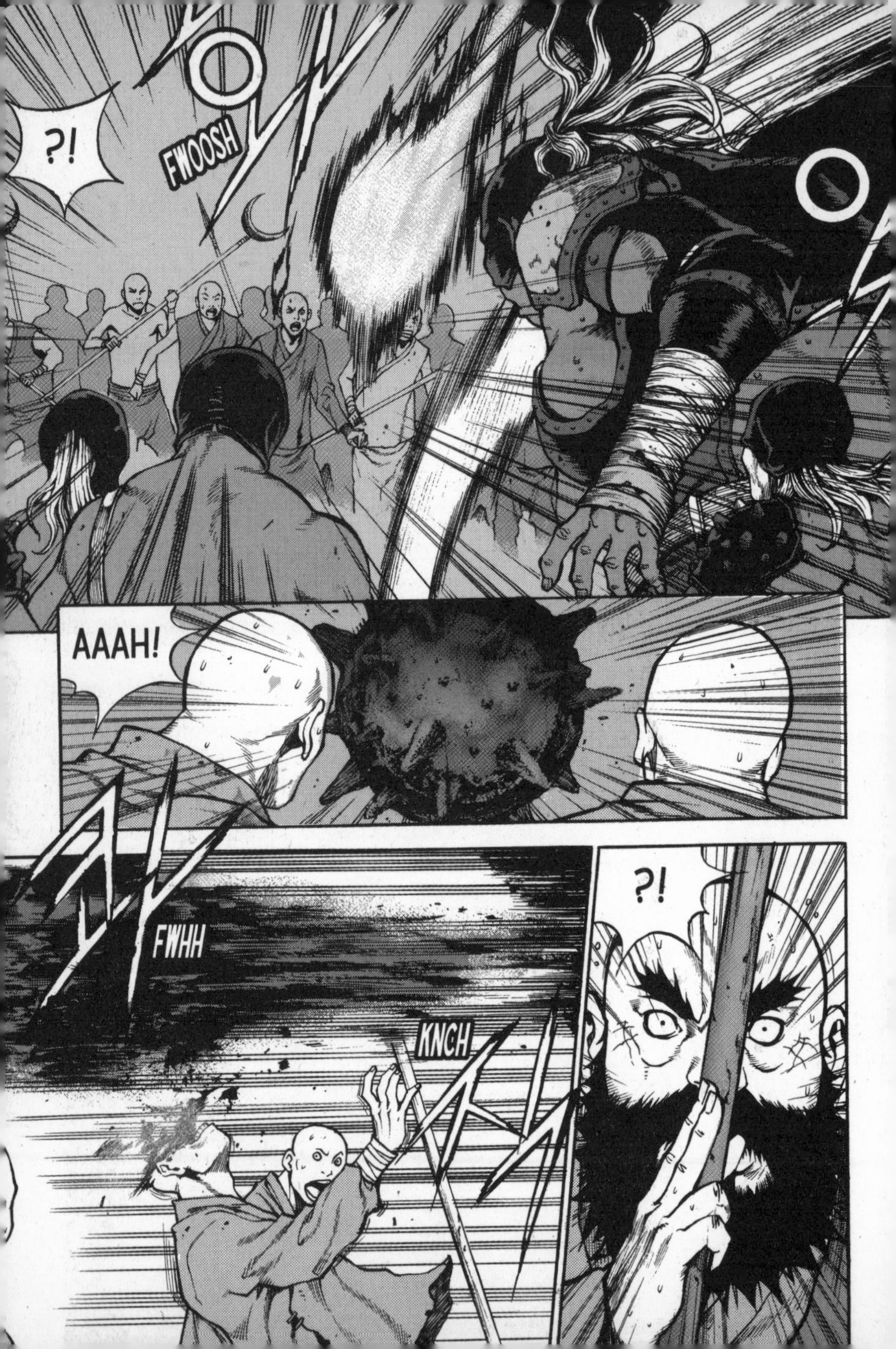
?!
FWOOSH
AAAH!
?!
FWHH
KNCH

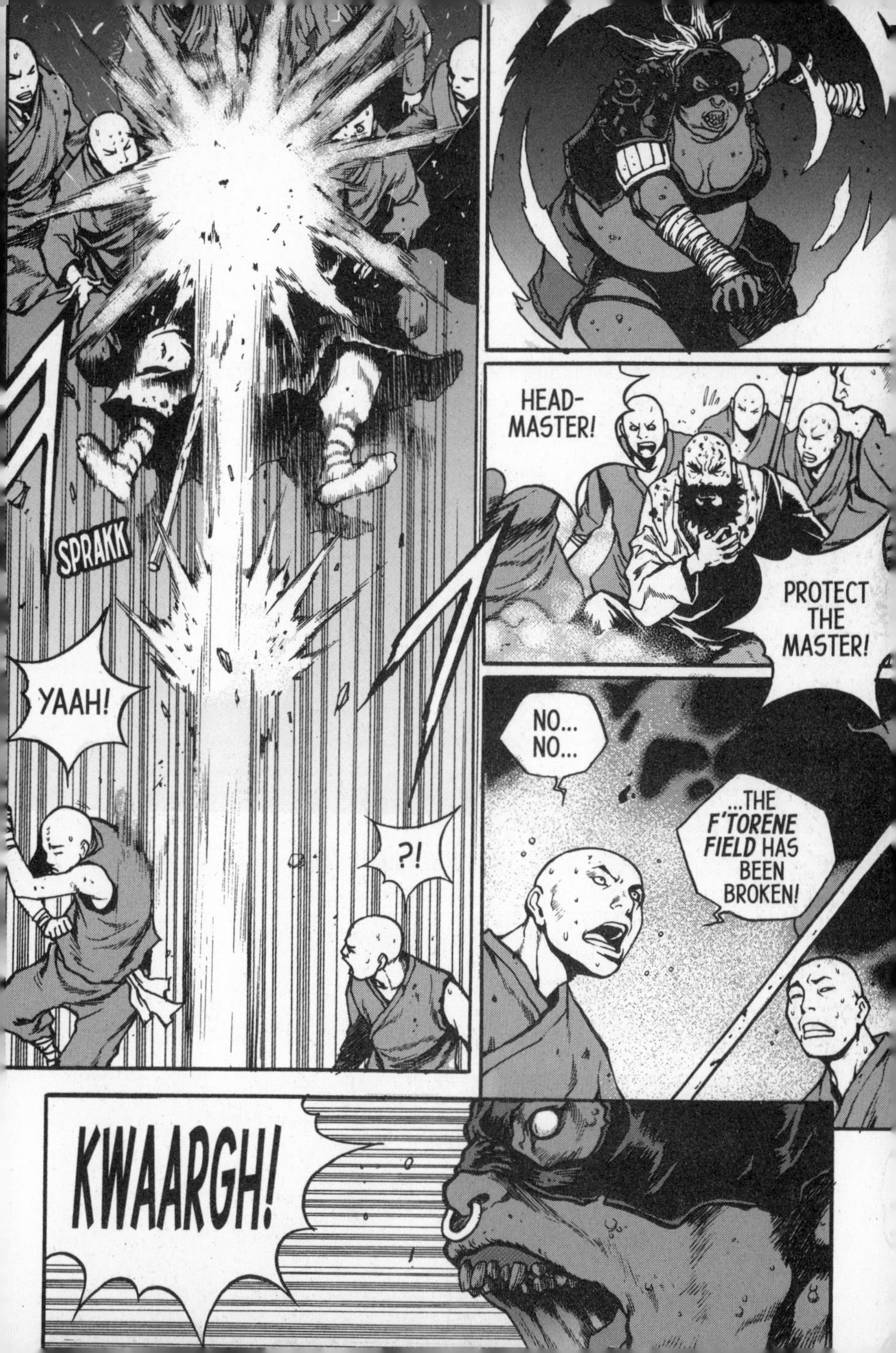
SPRAKK
YAAH!
?!
HEAD-MASTER!
PROTECT THE MASTER!
NO... NO...
...THE F'TORENE FIELD HAS BEEN BROKEN!
KWAARGH!

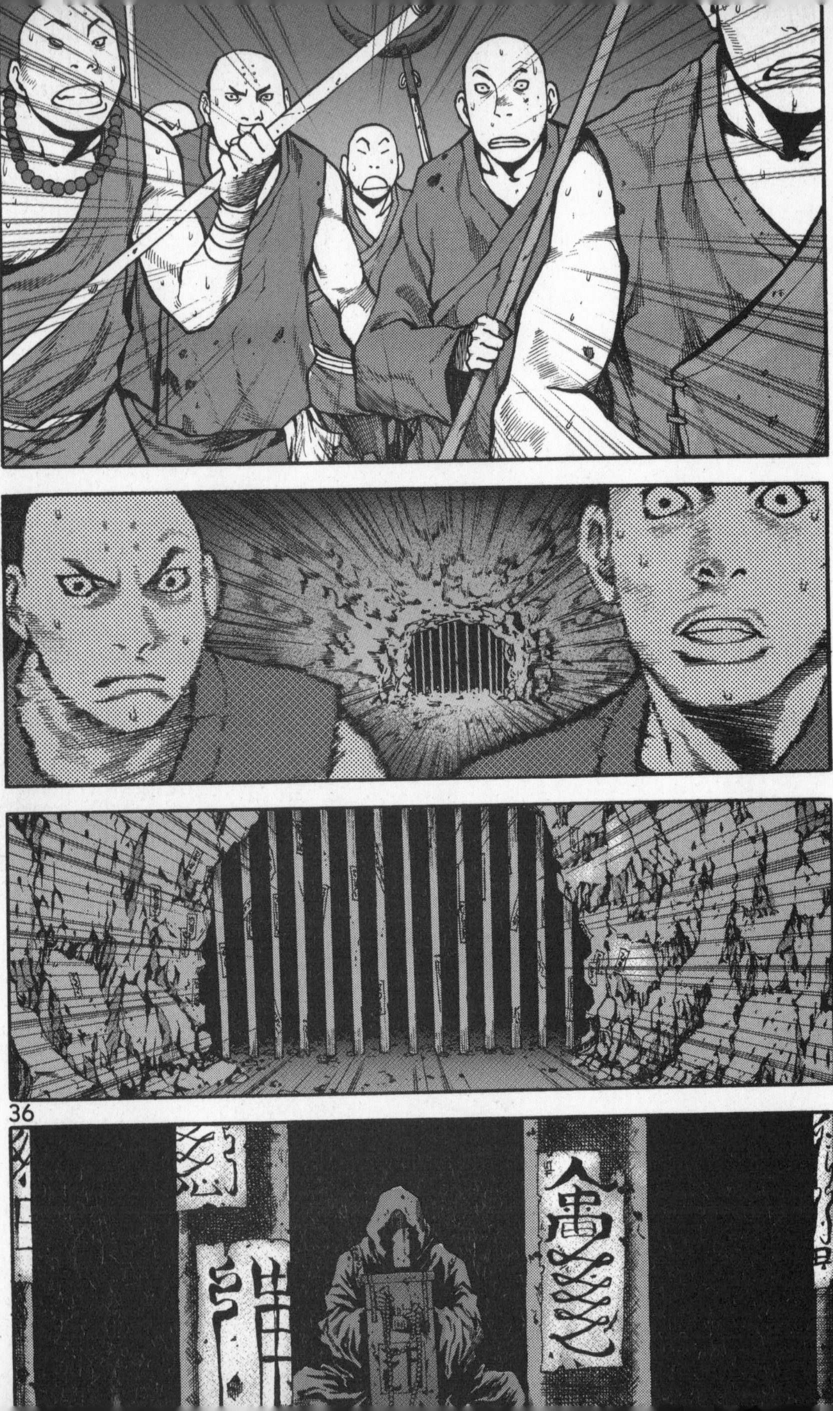

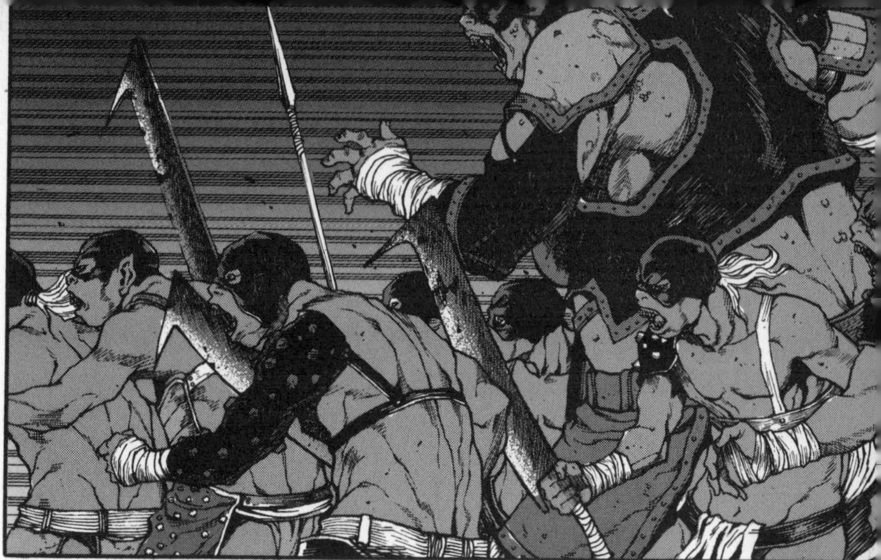

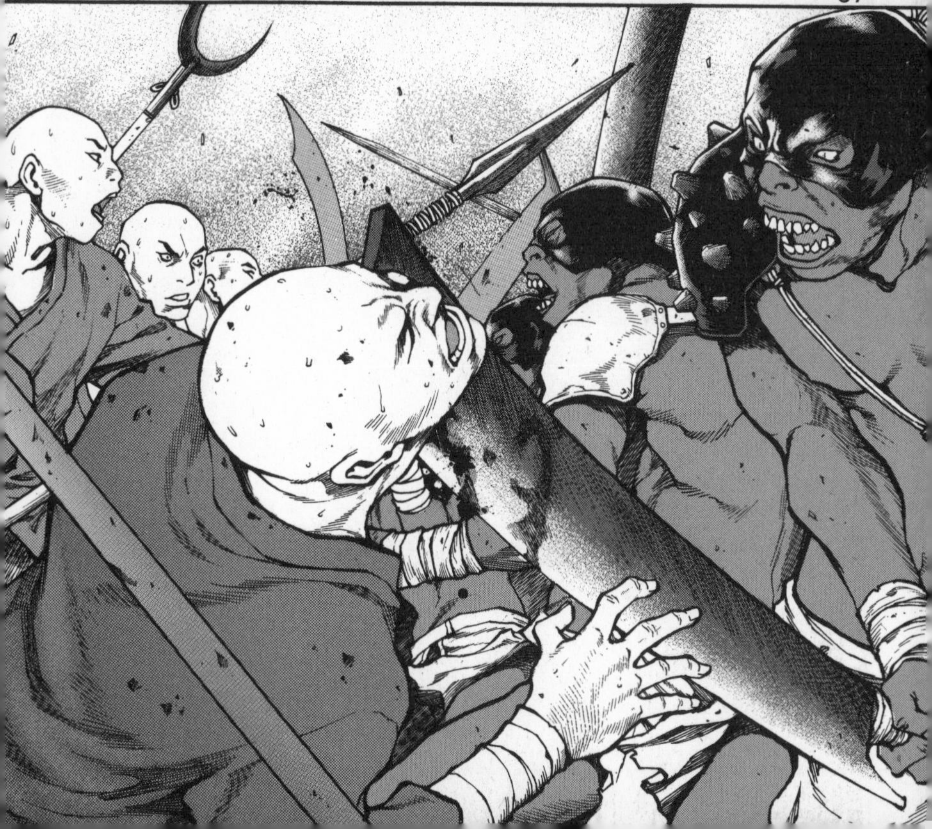

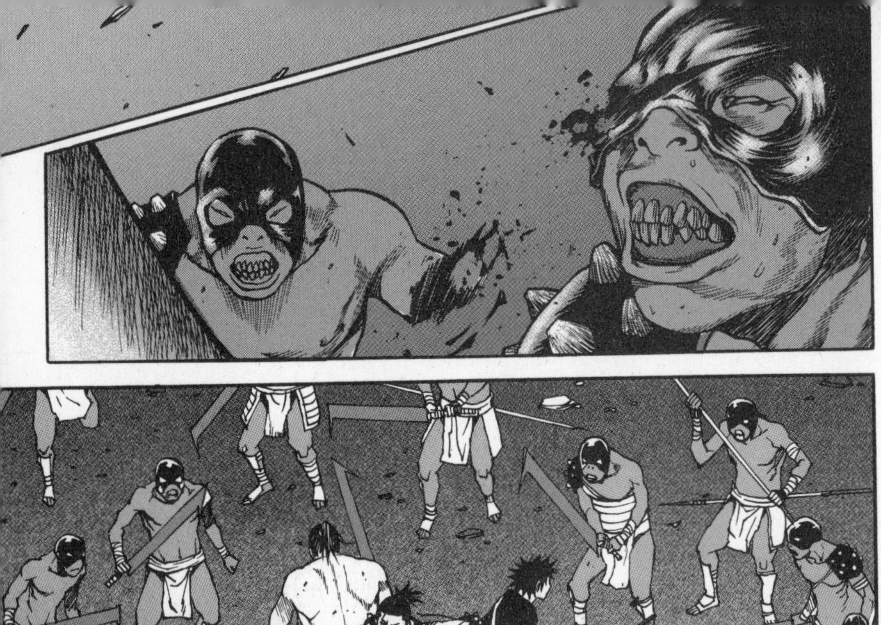

38

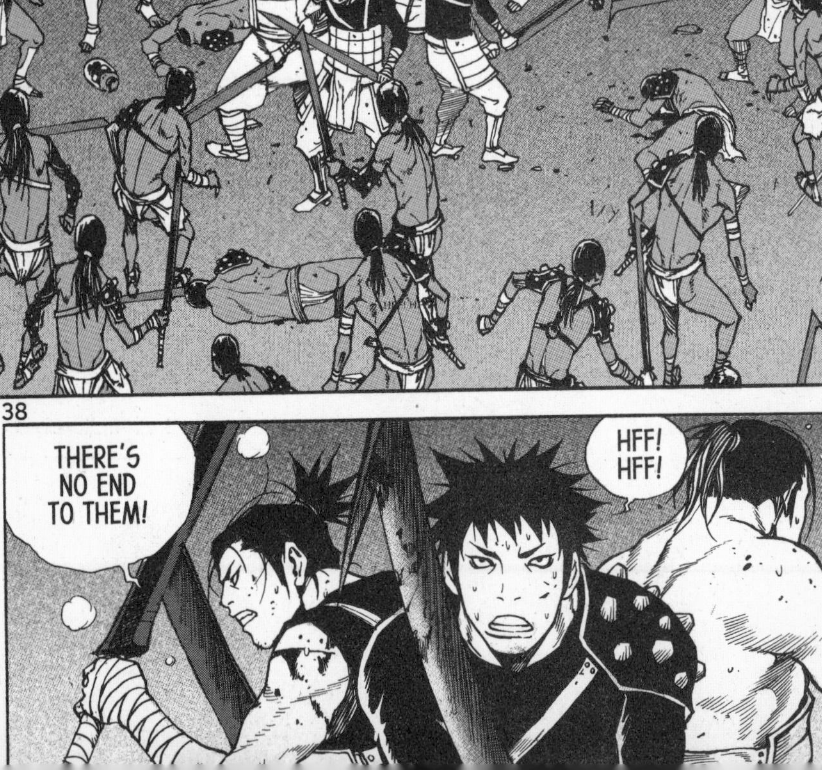
HFF! HFF!
THERE'S NO END TO THEM!

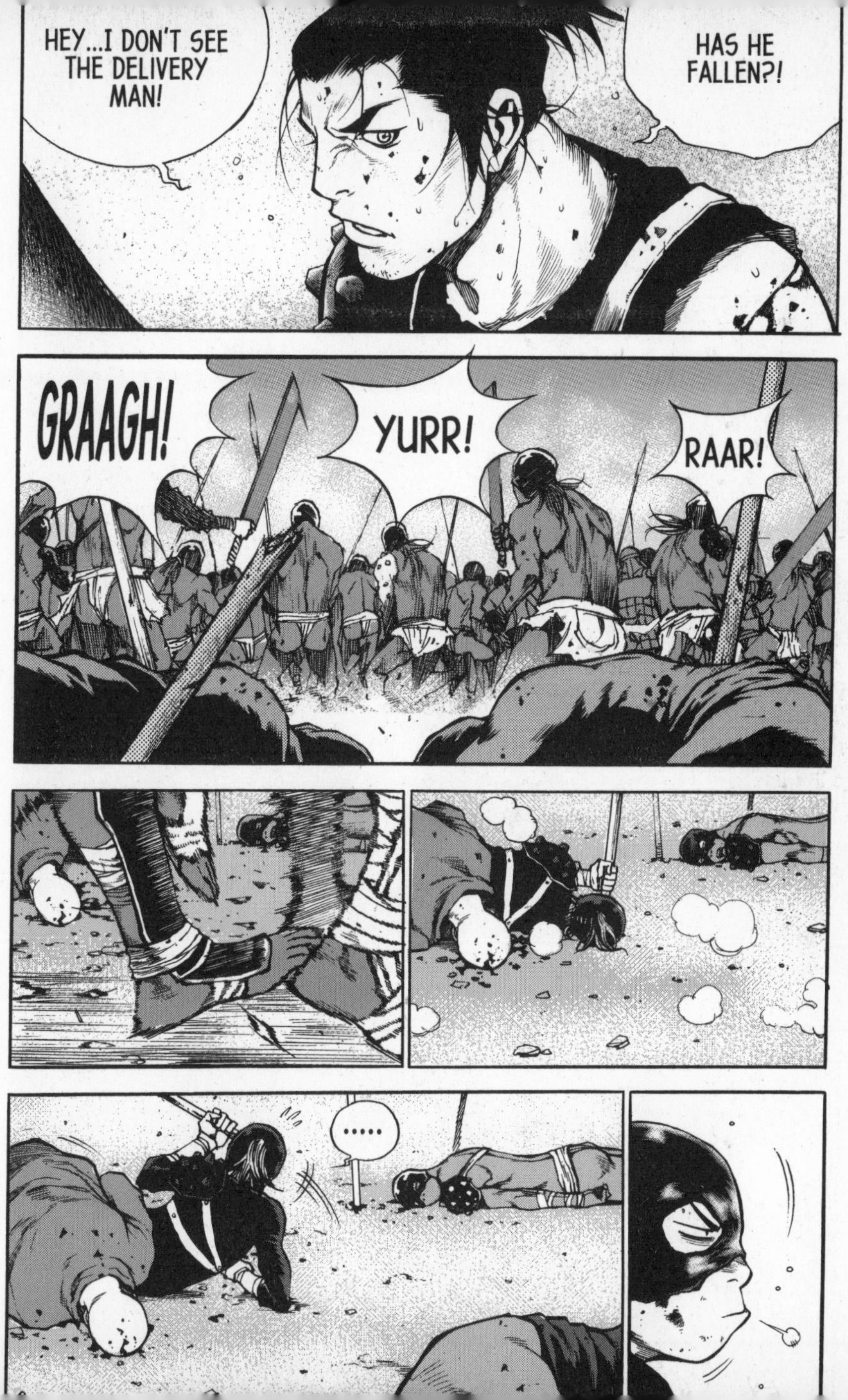
HAS HE FALLEN?!
HEY...I DON'T SEE THE DELIVERY MAN!
RAAR!
YURR!
GRAAGH!
......

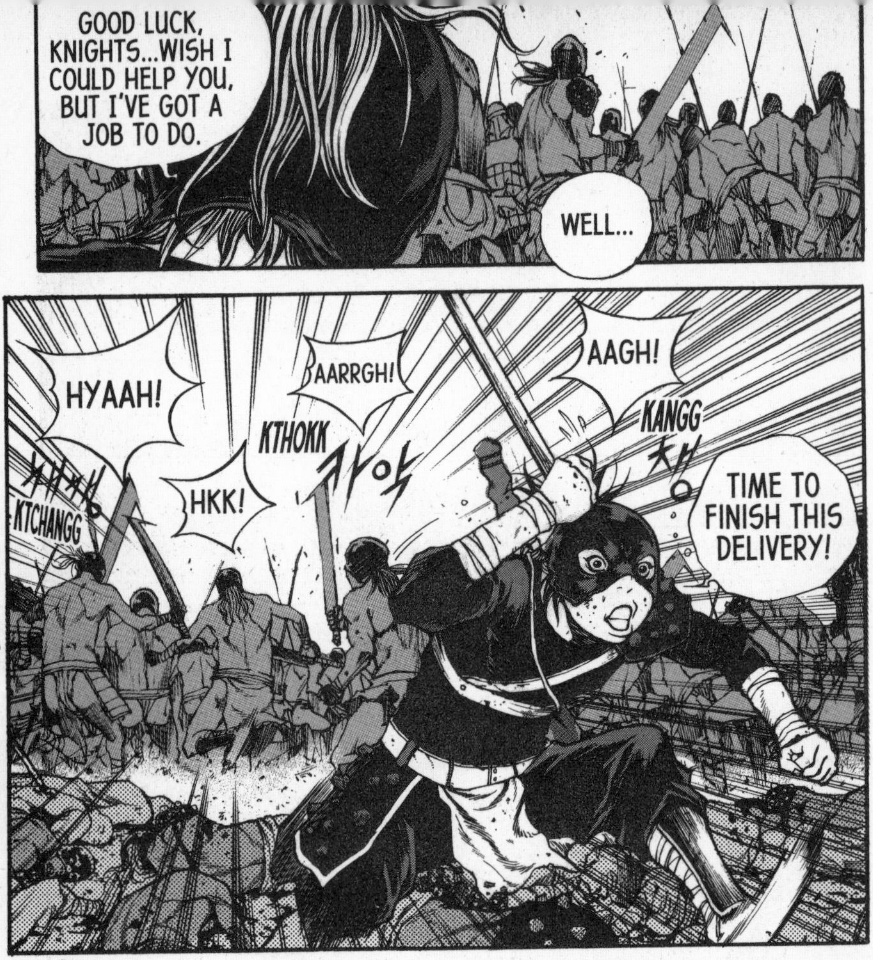
GOOD LUCK, KNIGHTS...WISH I COULD HELP YOU, BUT I'VE GOT A JOB TO DO.
WELL...
HYAAH!
KTCHANGG
HKK!
AARRGH!
KTHOKK
AAGH!
KANGG
TIME TO FINISH THIS DELIVERY!

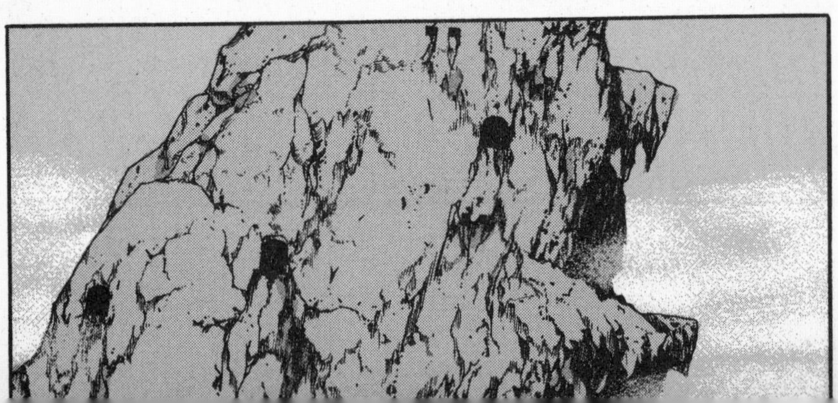

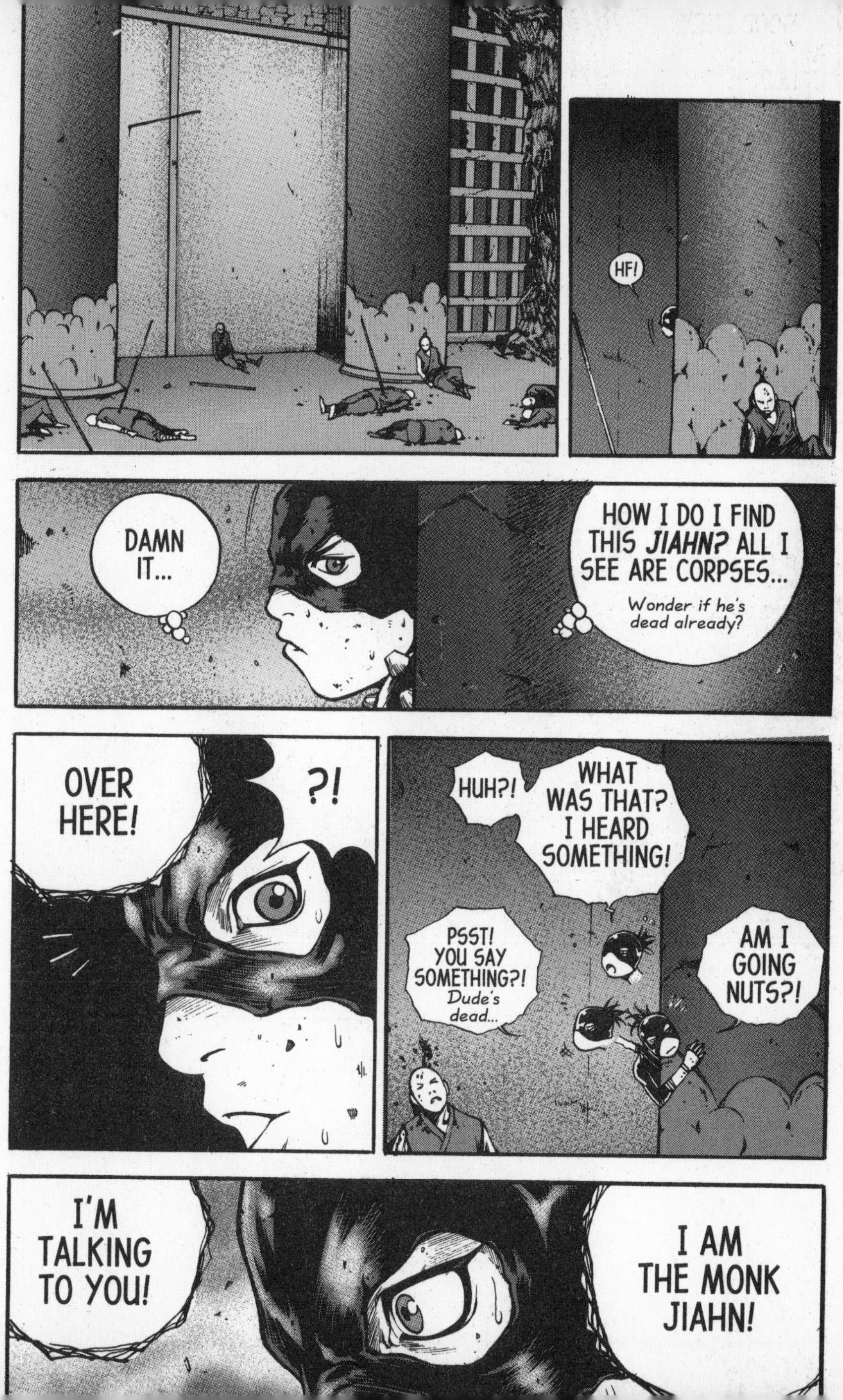
HF!
DAMN IT...
HOW I DO I FIND THIS JIAHN? ALL I SEE ARE CORPSES...
Wonder if he's dead already?
OVER HERE!
?!
HUH?!
WHAT WAS THAT? I HEARD SOMETHING!
PSSST! YOU SAY SOMETHING?! Dude's dead...
AM I GOING NUTS?!
I'M TALKING TO YOU!
I AM THE MONK JIAHN!

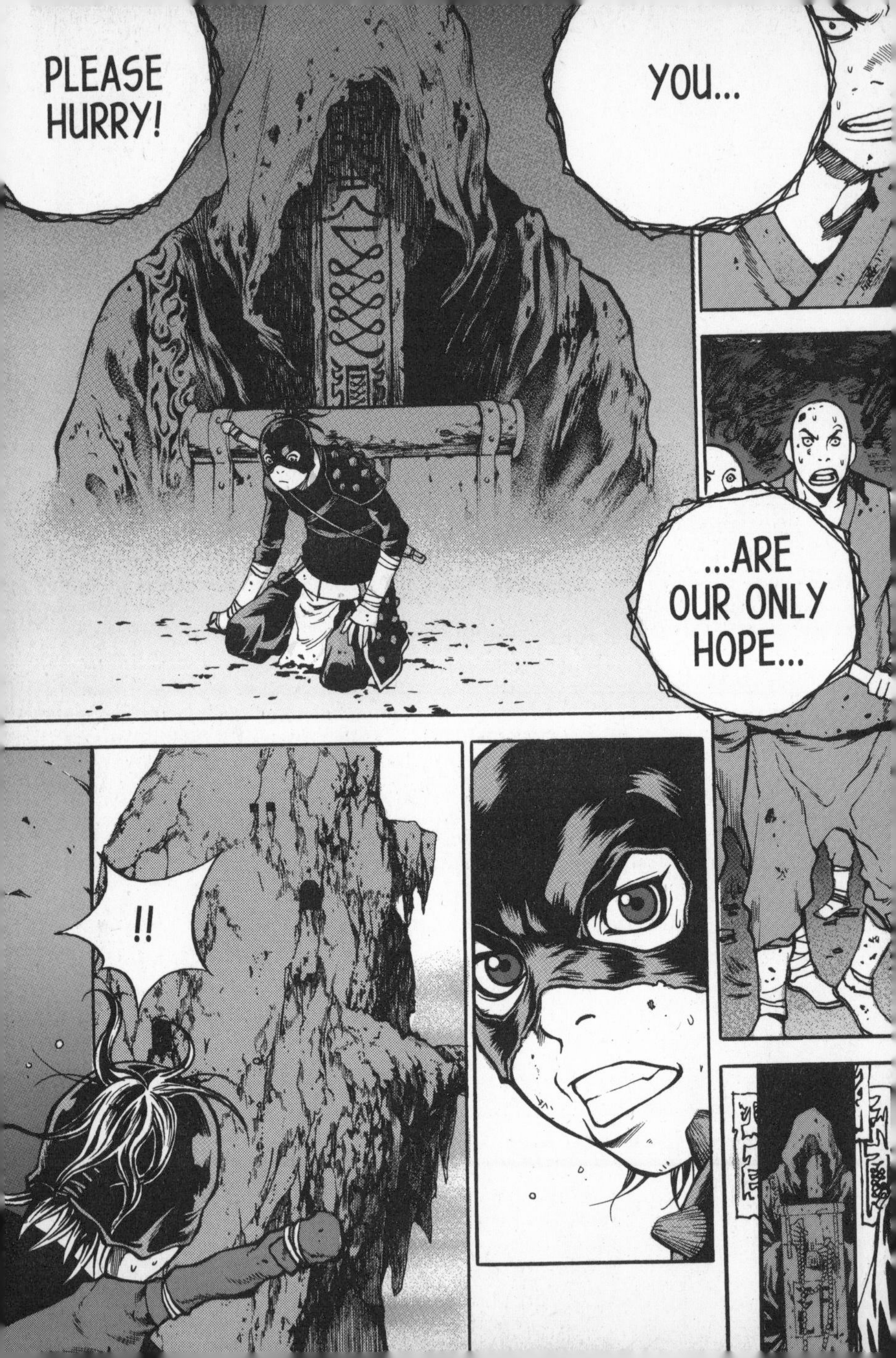
PLEASE HURRY!
YOU...
...ARE OUR ONLY HOPE...
!!

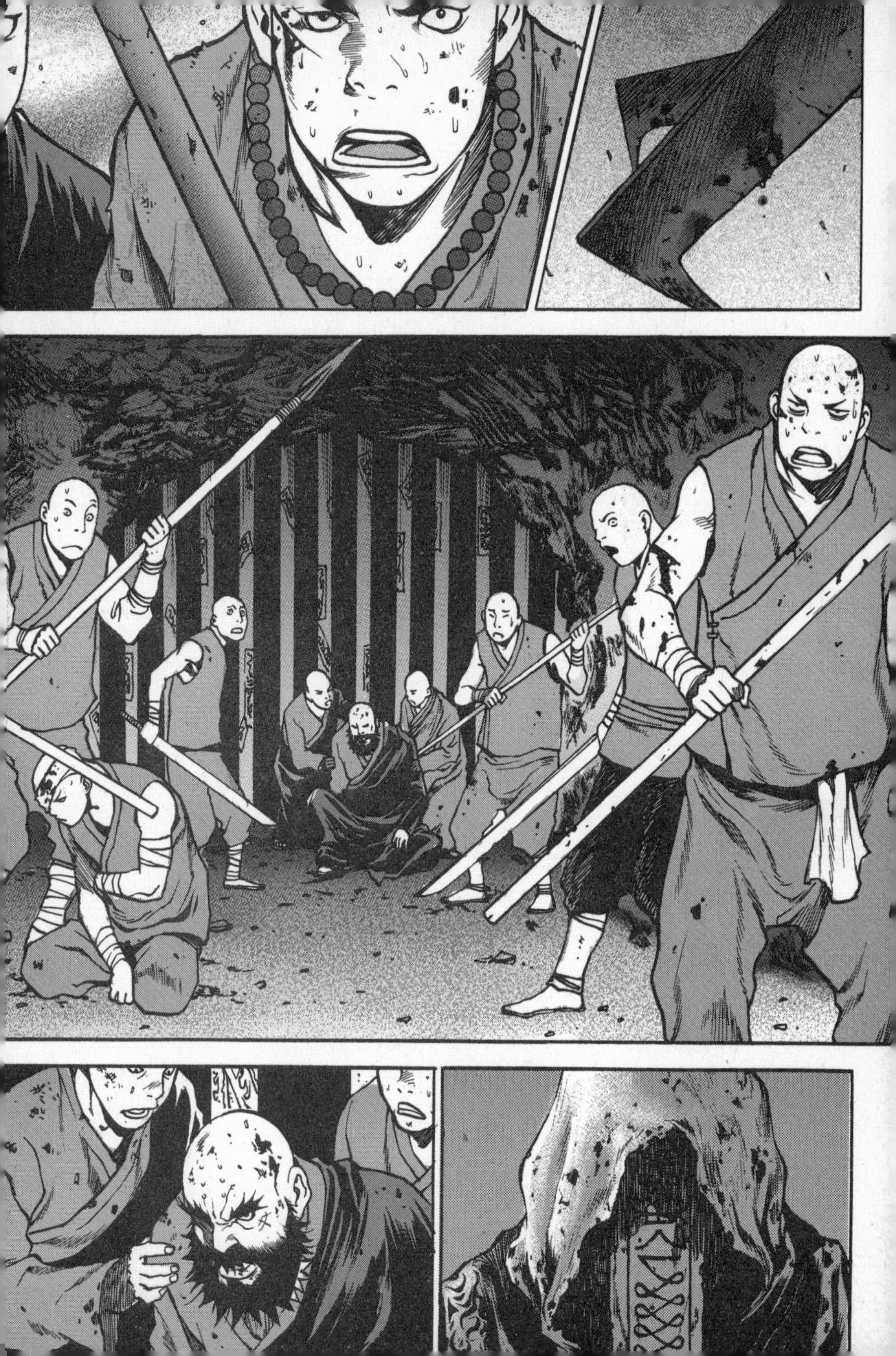

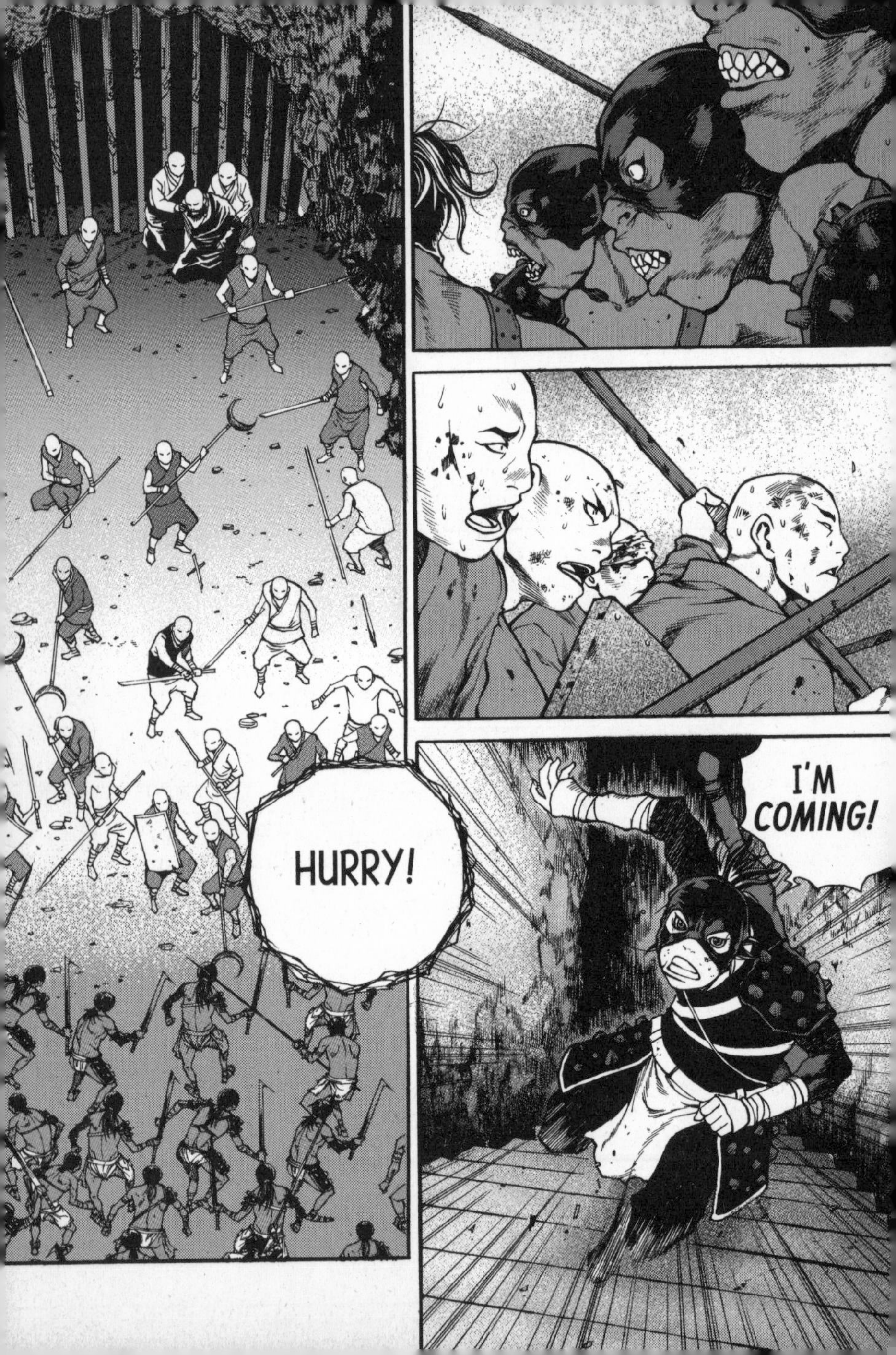
I'M COMING!
HURRY!

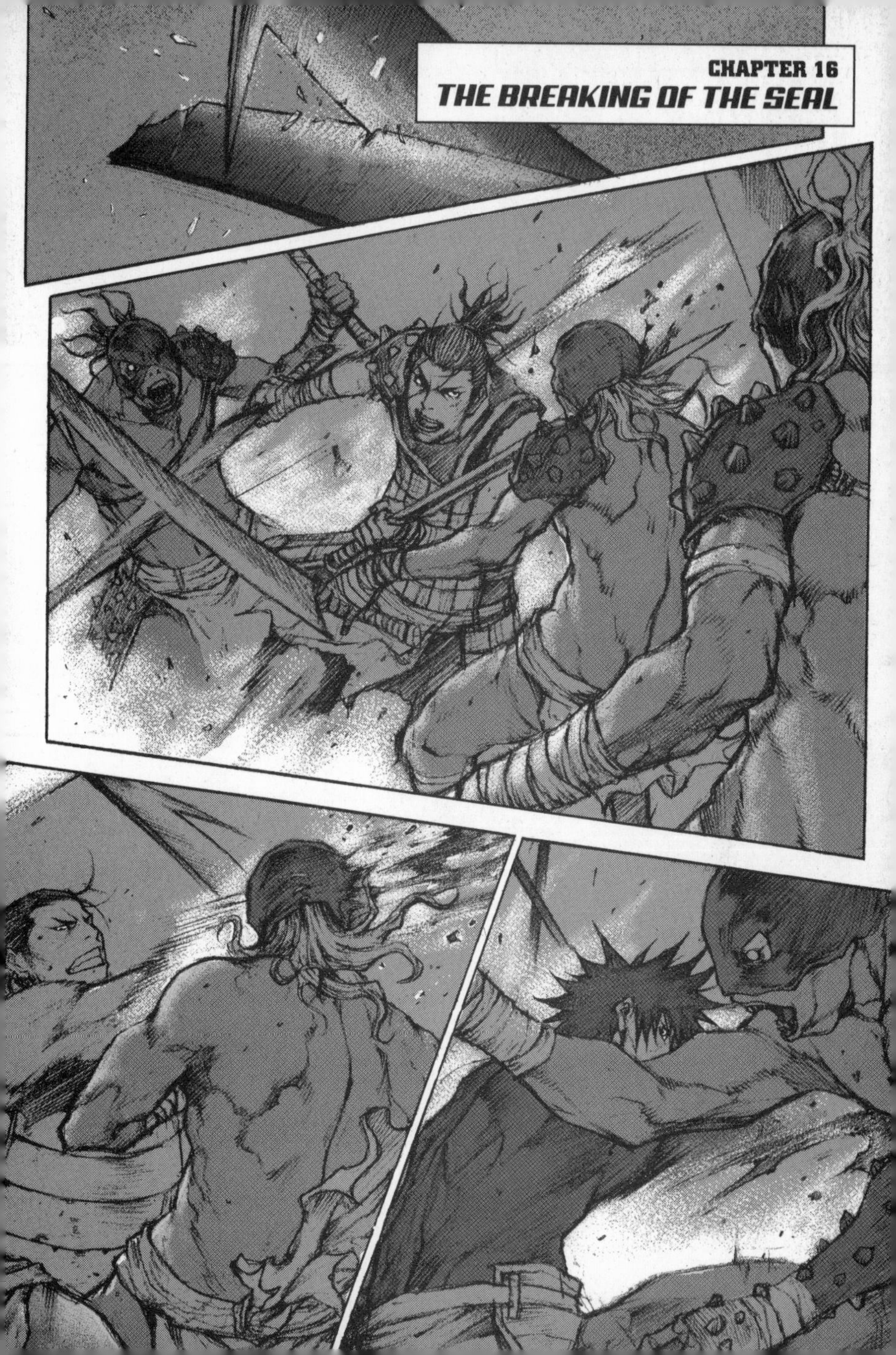
CHAPTER 16
THE BREAKING OF THE SEAL

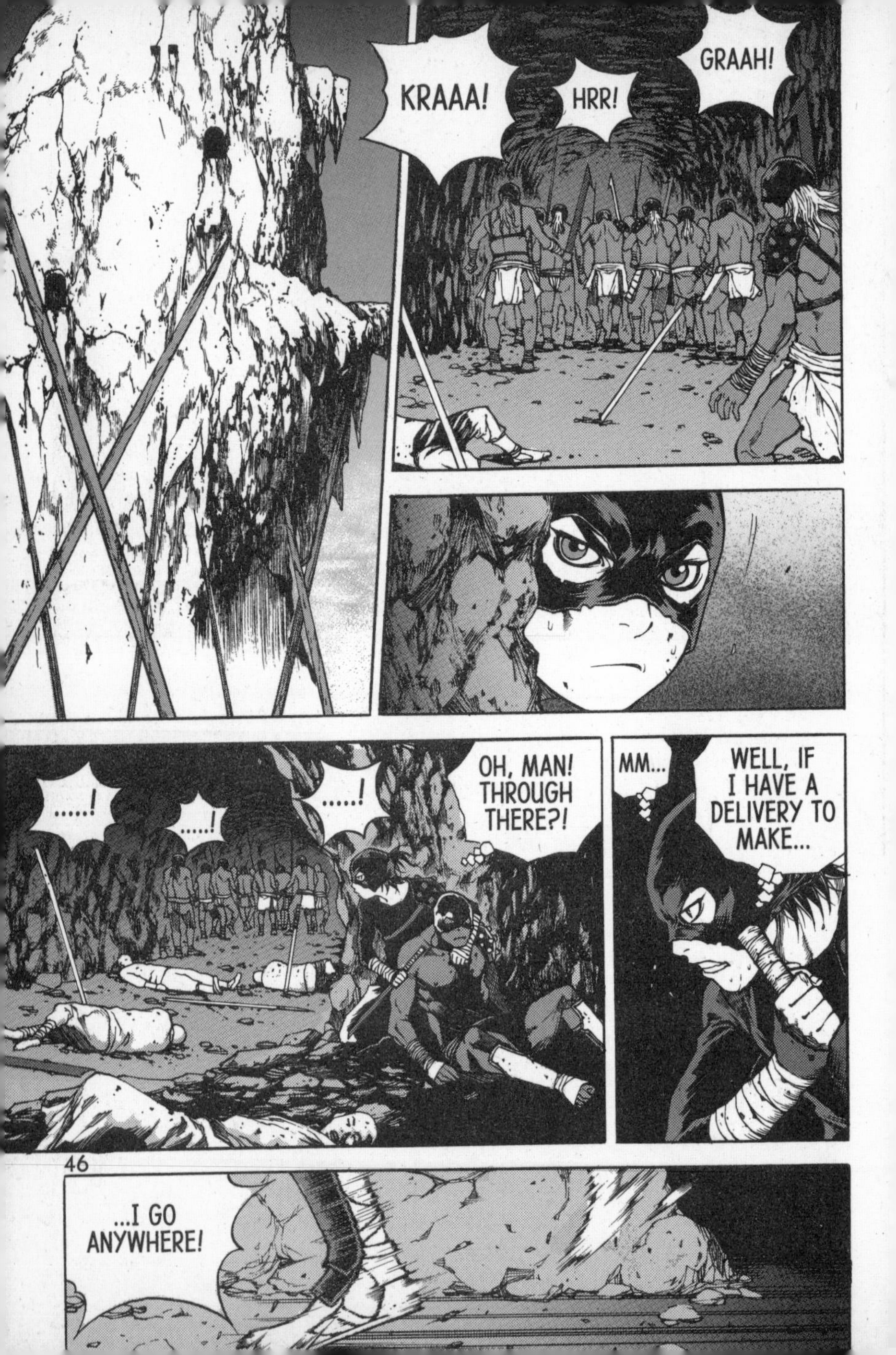
KRAAA!
HRR!
GRAAH!
.....!
.....!
.....!
OH, MAN! THROUGH THERE?!
MM...
WELL, IF I HAVE A DELIVERY TO MAKE...
...I GO ANYWHERE!

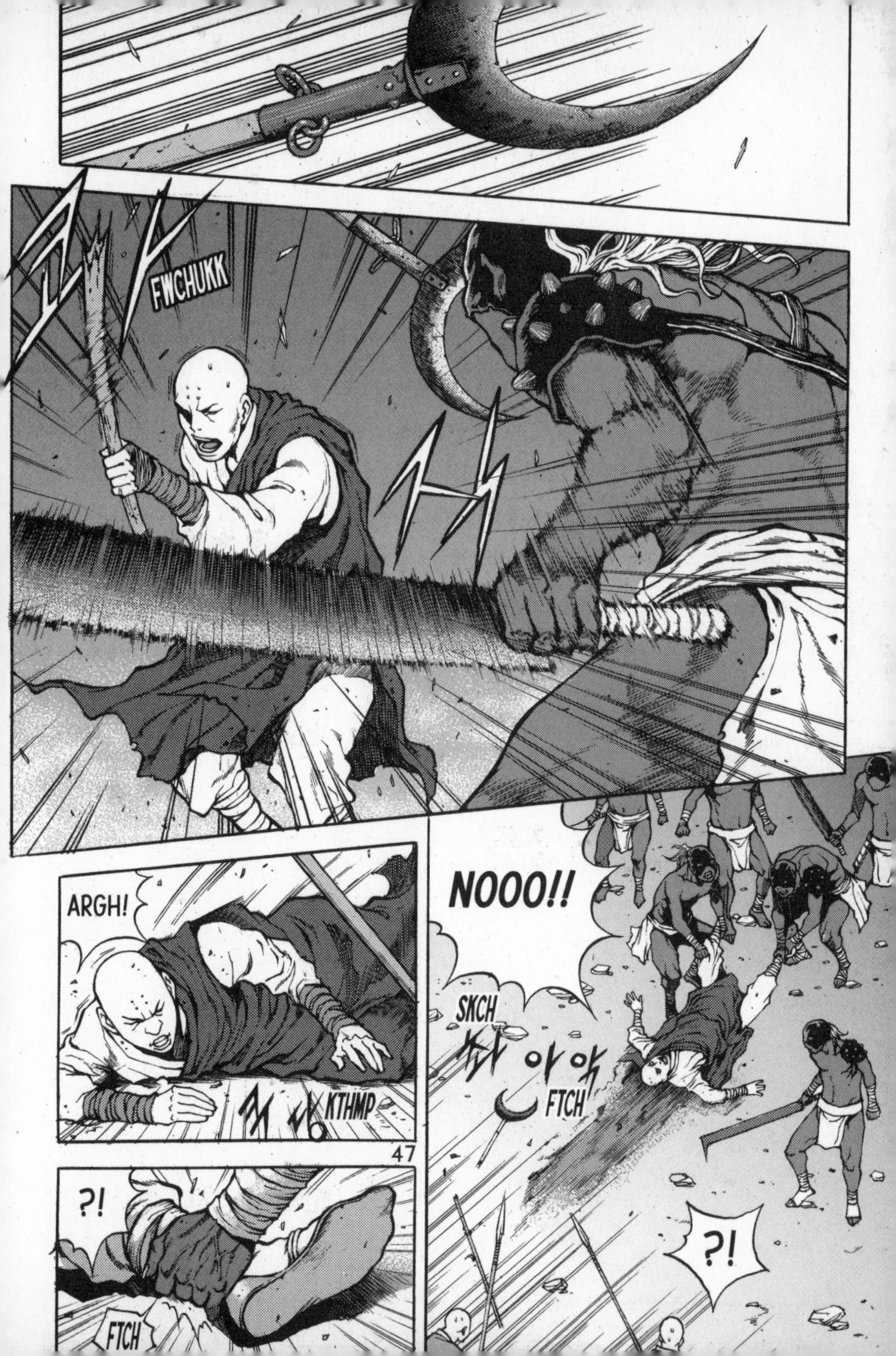

FWCHUKK
ARGH!
KTHMP
?!
FTCH
NOOO!!
SKCH
FTCH
?!

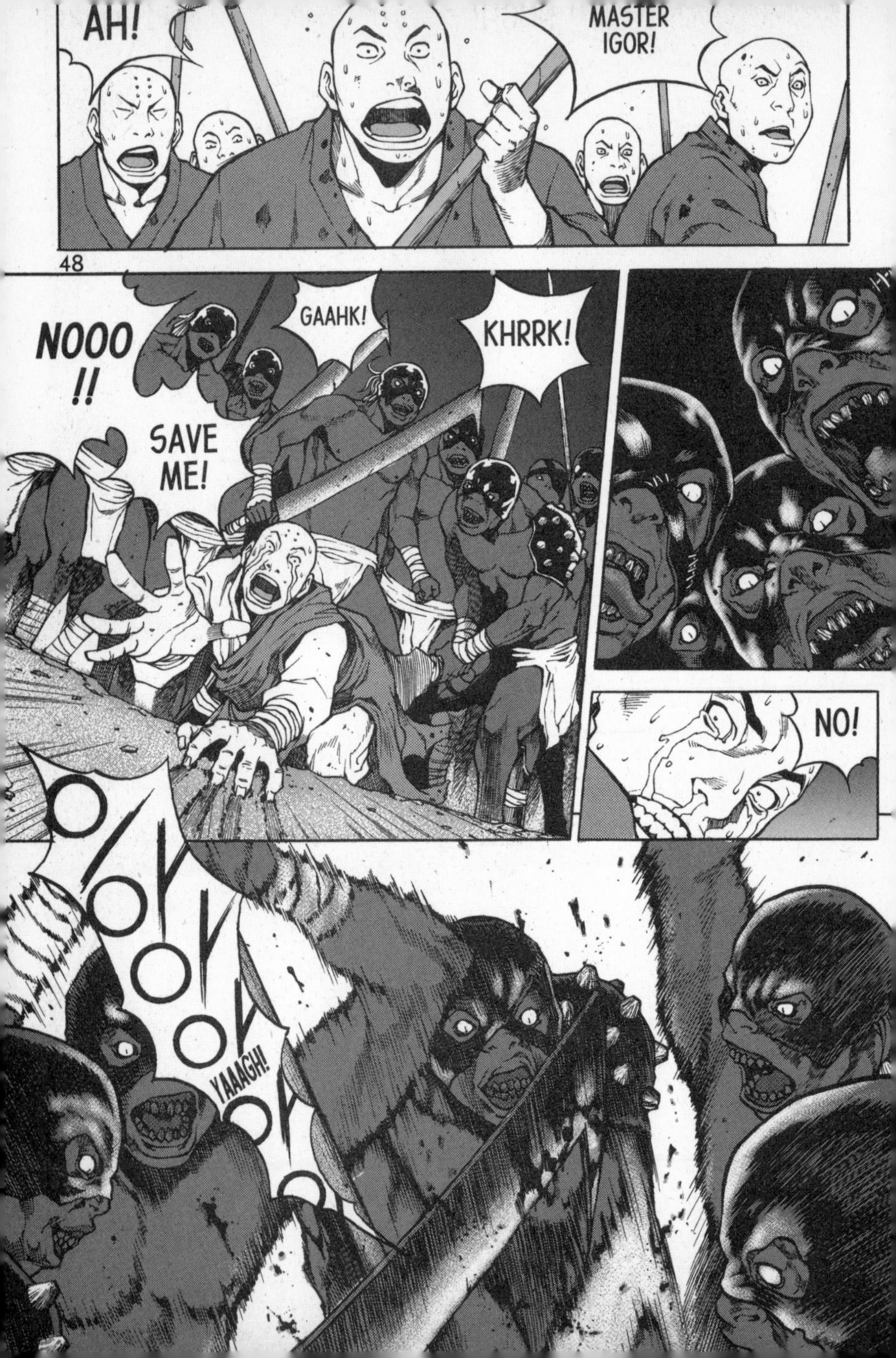
AH!
MASTER IGOR!
NOOO !!
GAAHK!
KHRRK!
SAVE ME!
NO!
YAAAGH!

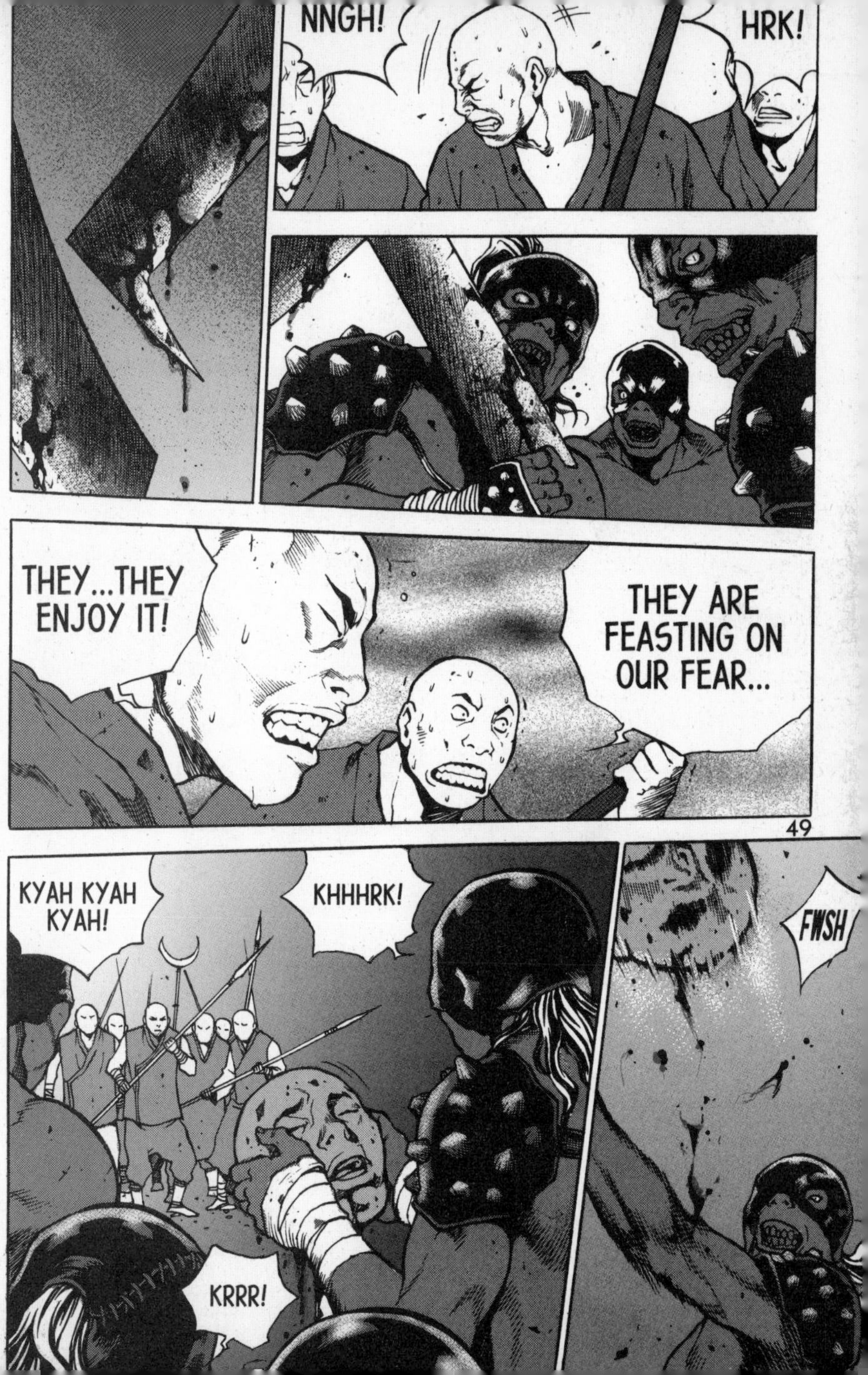
NNGH!
HRK!
THEY...THEY ENJOY IT!
THEY ARE FEASTING ON OUR FEAR...
FWSH
KHHHRK!
KYAH KYAH KYAH!
KRRR!

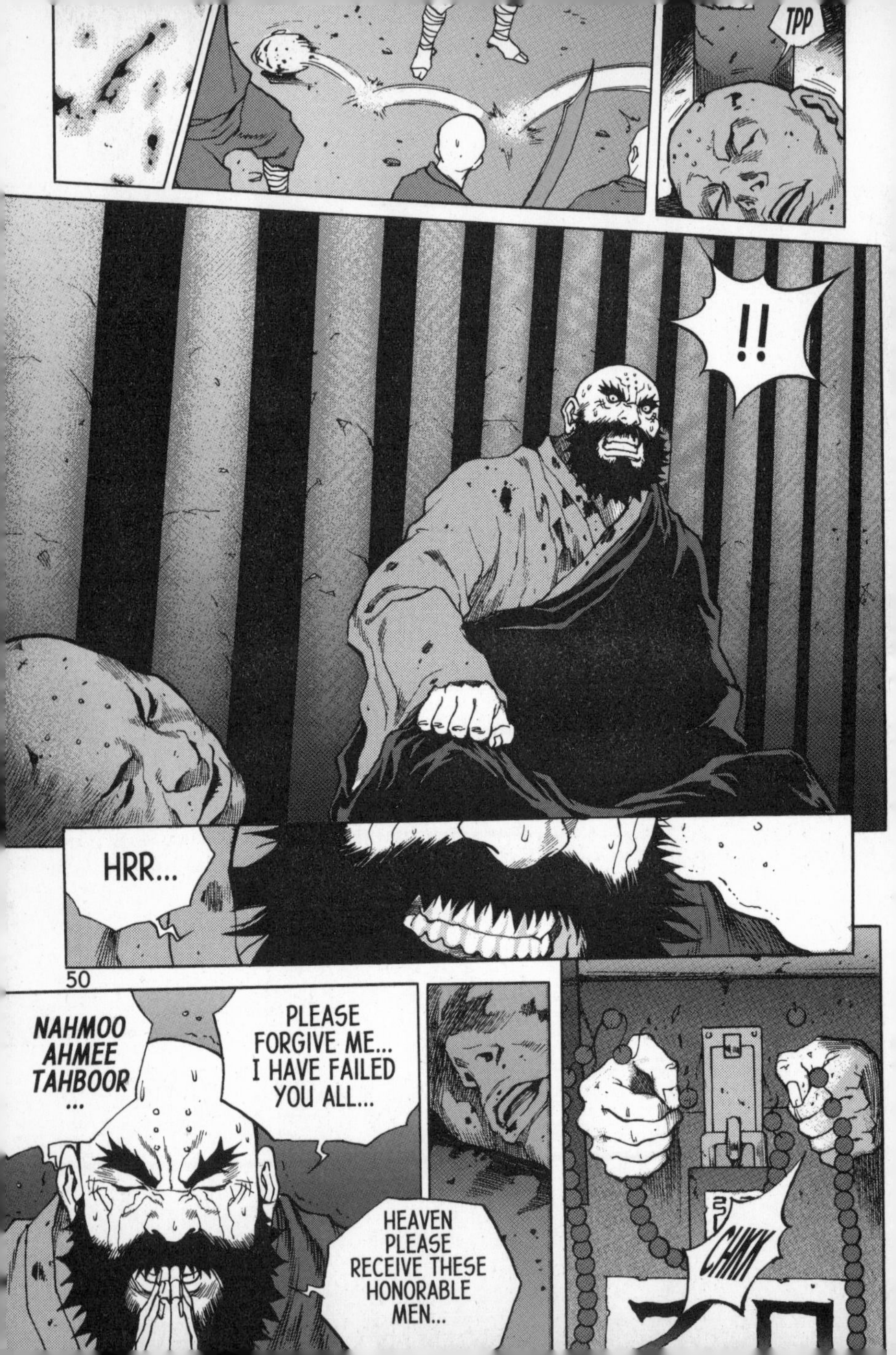
TPP
!!
HRR...
PLEASE FORGIVE ME... I HAVE FAILED YOU ALL...
NAHMOO AHMEE TAHBOOR ...
HEAVEN PLEASE RECEIVE THESE HONORABLE MEN...
CHAK

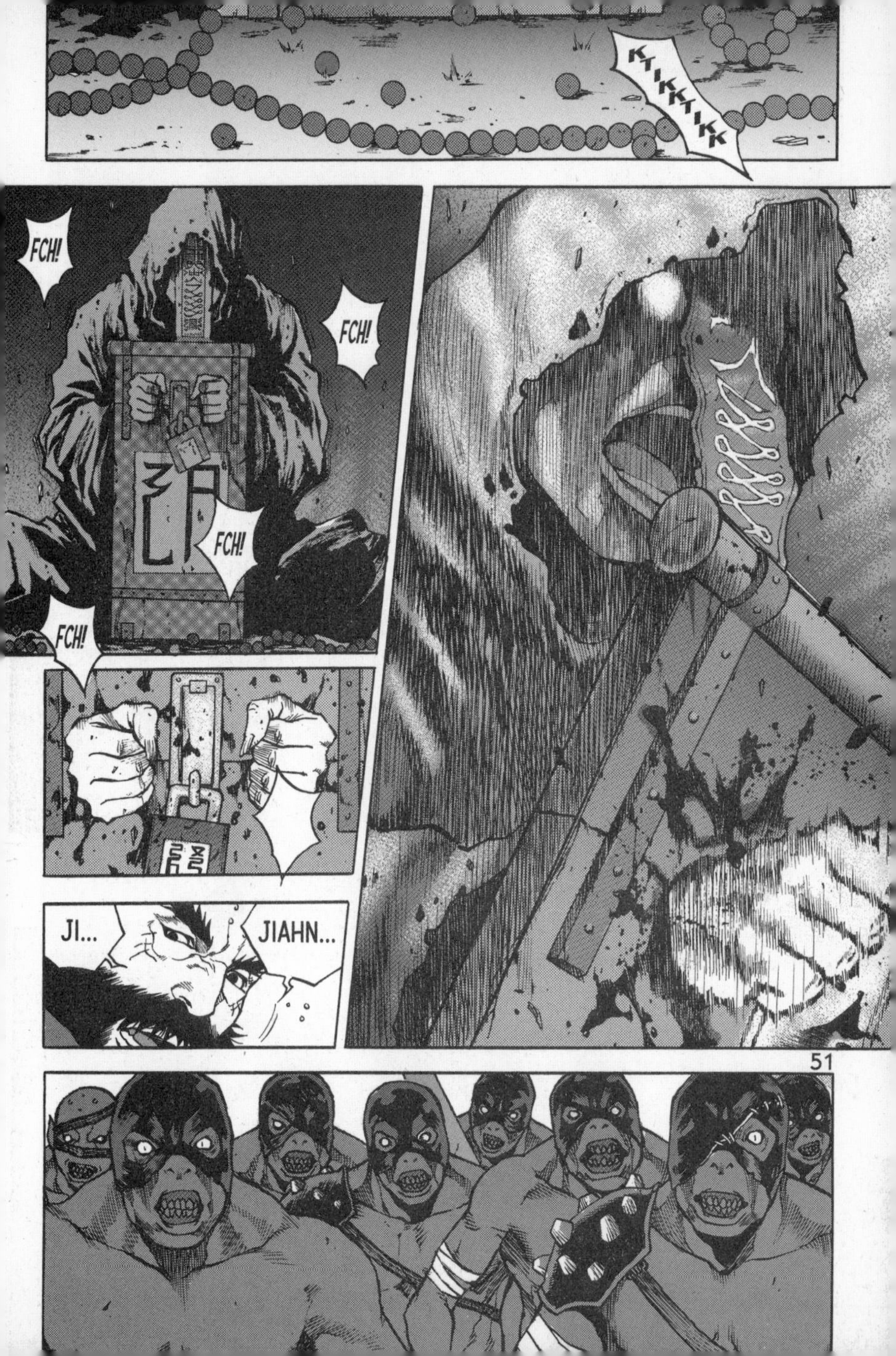
KTIKKTIKK
FCH!
FCH!
FCH!
FCH!
JI...
JIAHN...

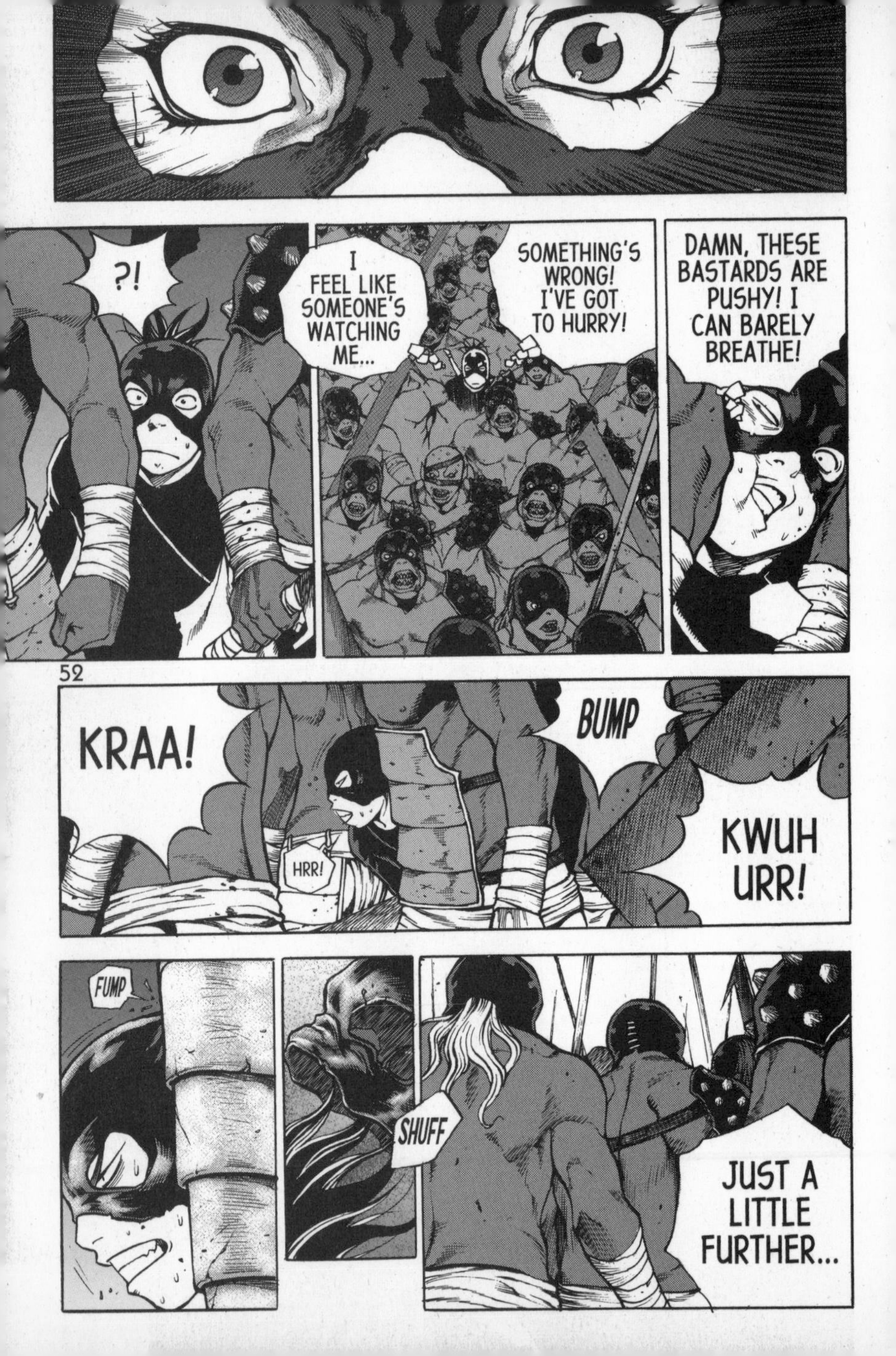
?!
I FEEL LIKE SOMEONE'S WATCHING ME...
SOMETHING'S WRONG! I'VE GOT TO HURRY!
DAMN, THESE BASTARDS ARE PUSHY! I CAN BARELY BREATHE!
KRAA!
BUMP
HRR!
KWUH URR!
FUMP
SHUFF
JUST A LITTLE FURTHER...

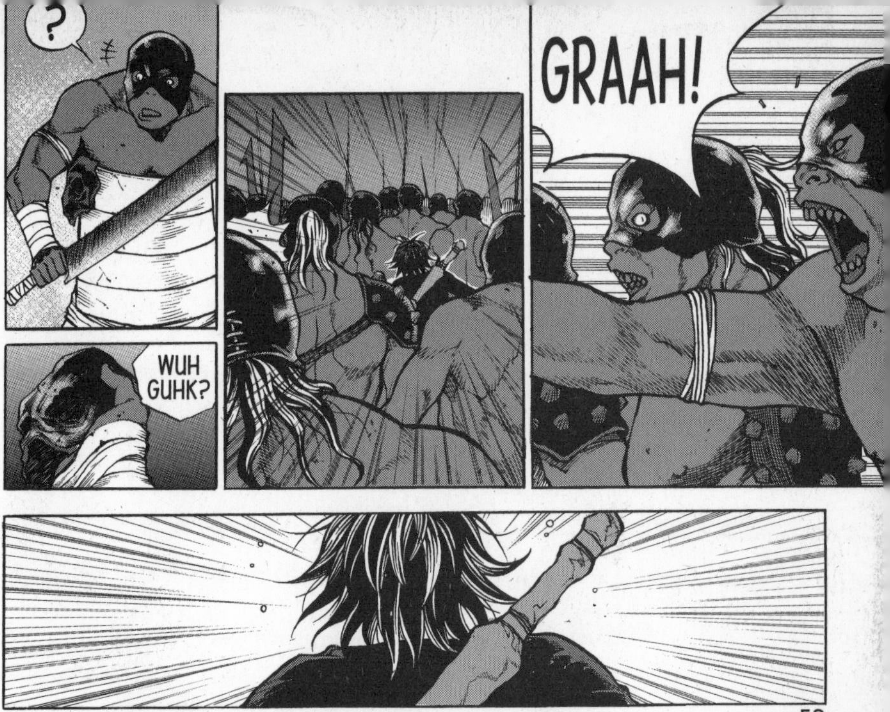
GRAAH!
?
WUH GUHK?

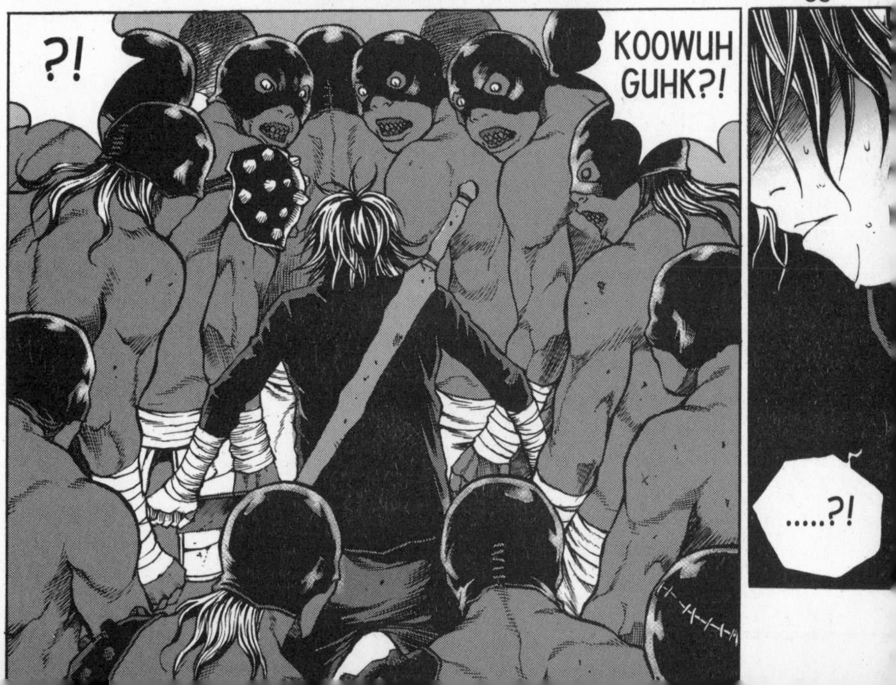
.....?!
KOOWUH GUHK?!
?!

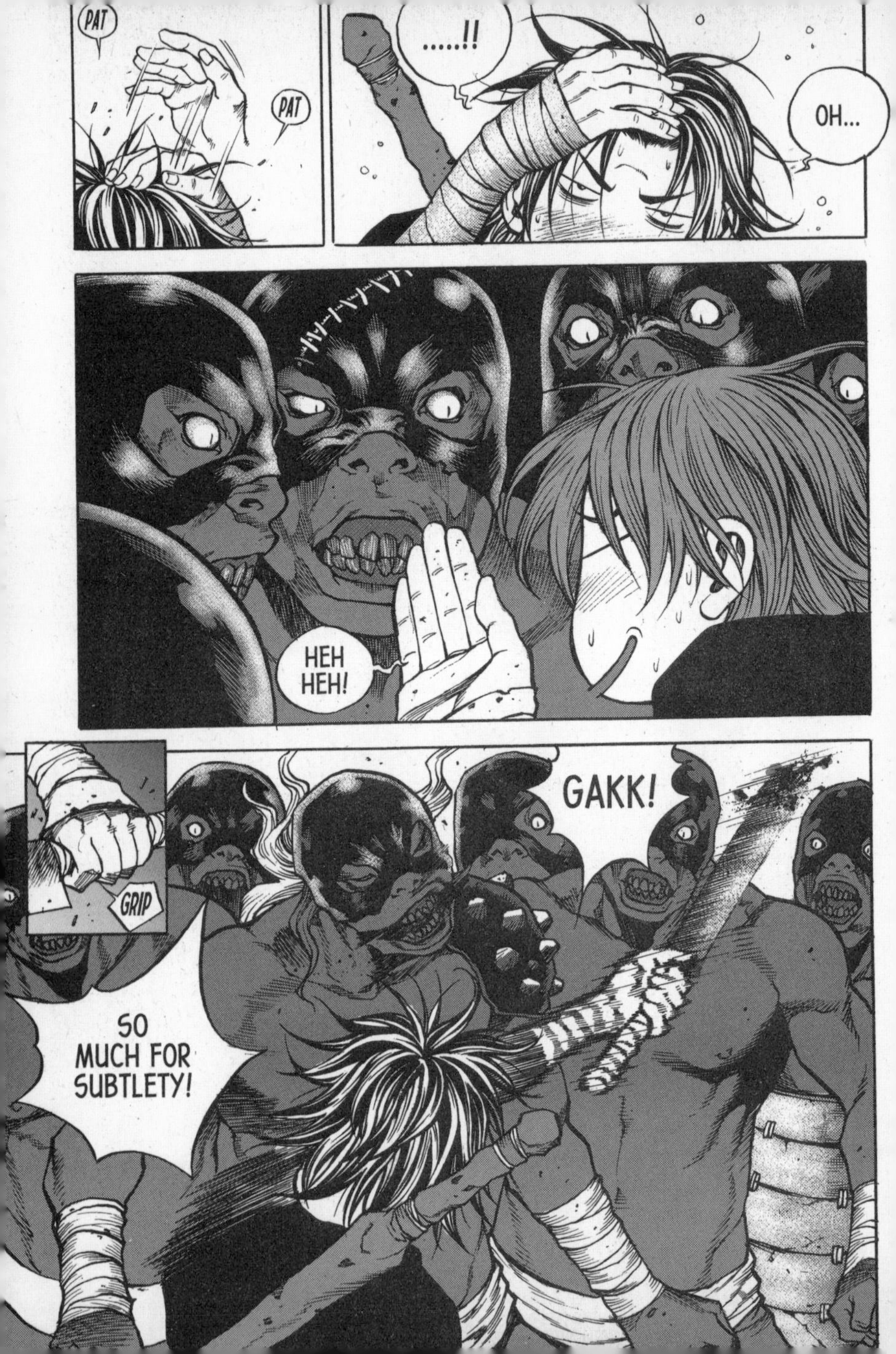
PAT
PAT
......!!
OH...
HEH HEH!
GRIP
GAKK!
SO MUCH FOR SUBTLETY!

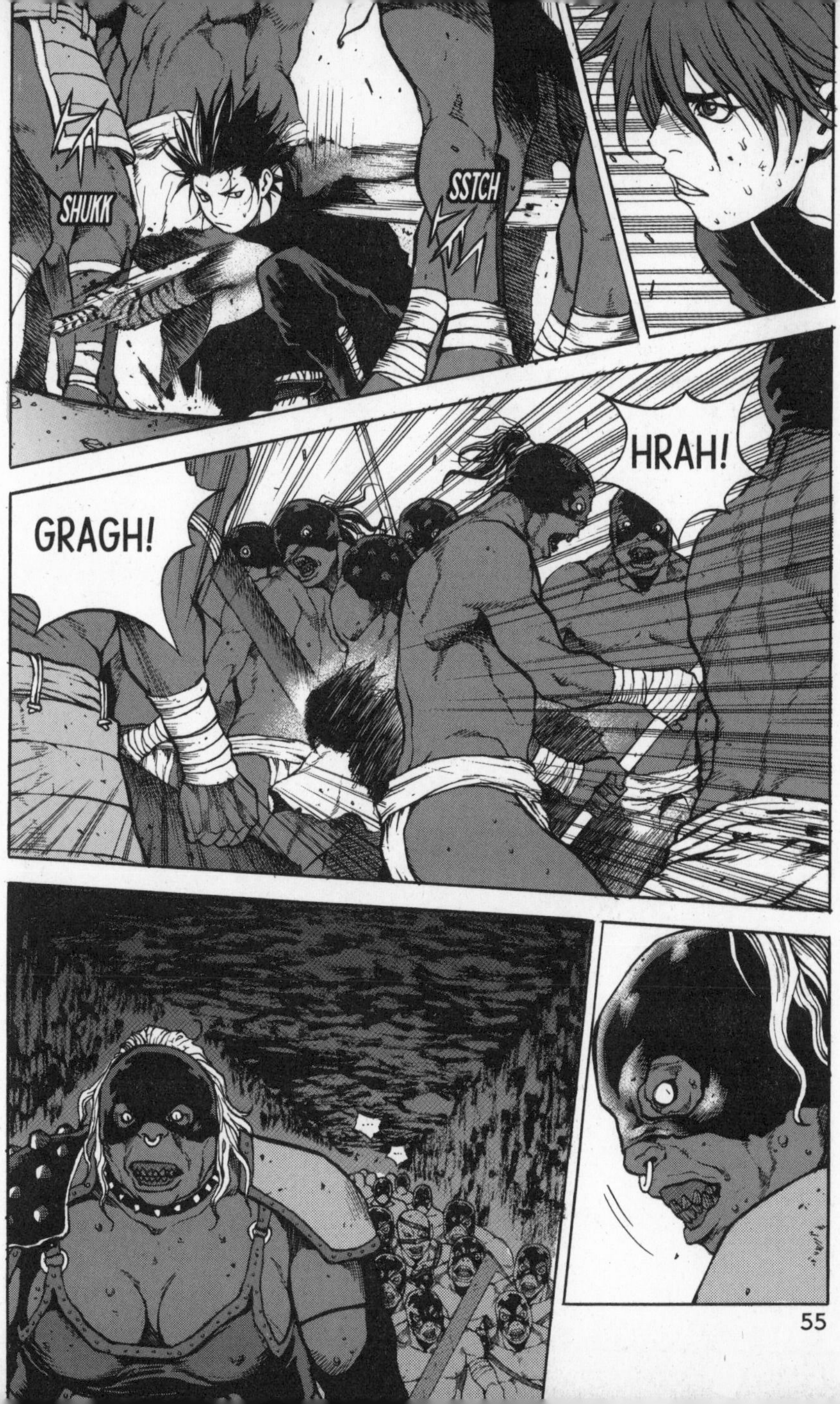
SSTCH
SHUKK
HRAH!
GRAGH!
...
...

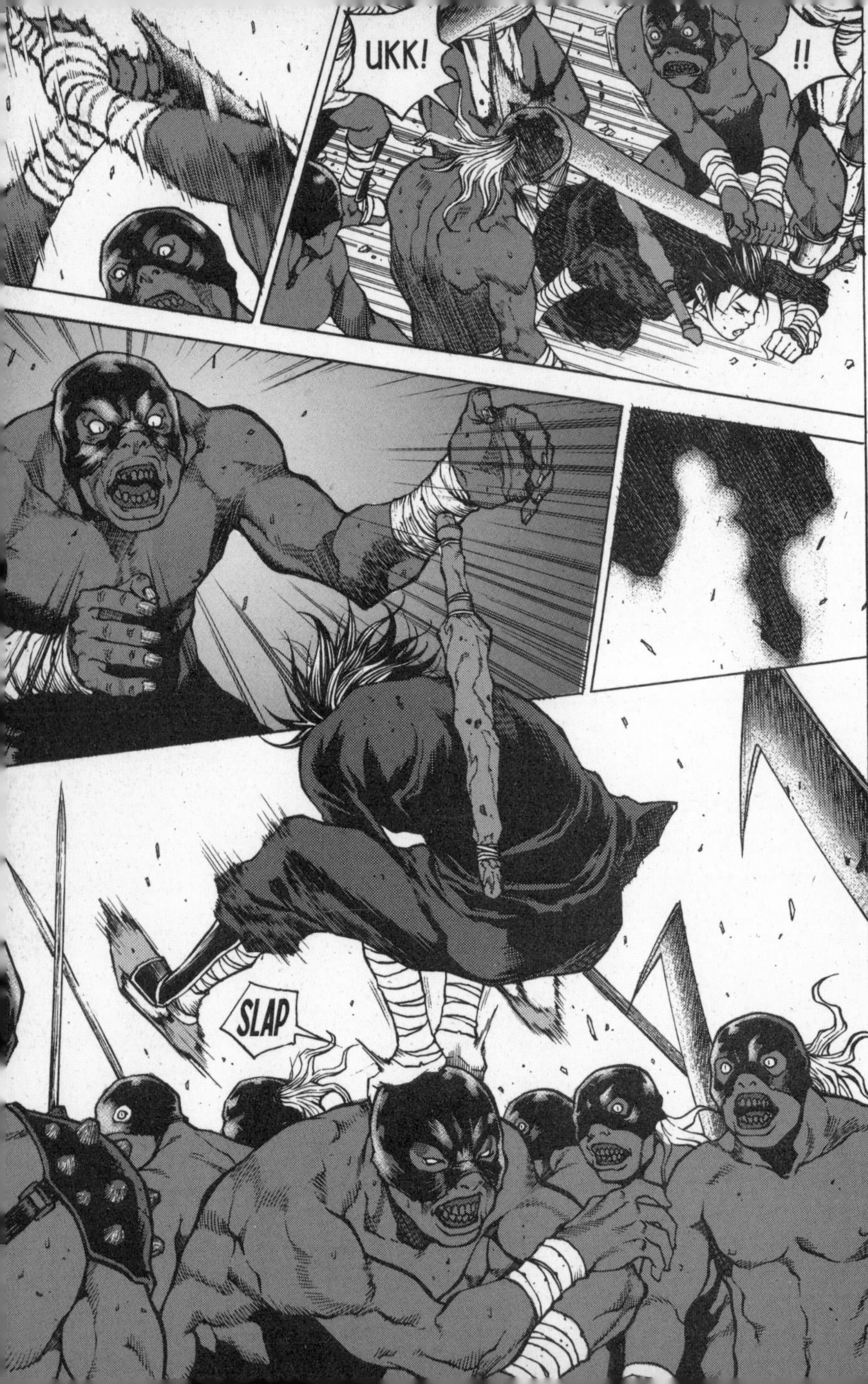
UKK!
!!
SLAP

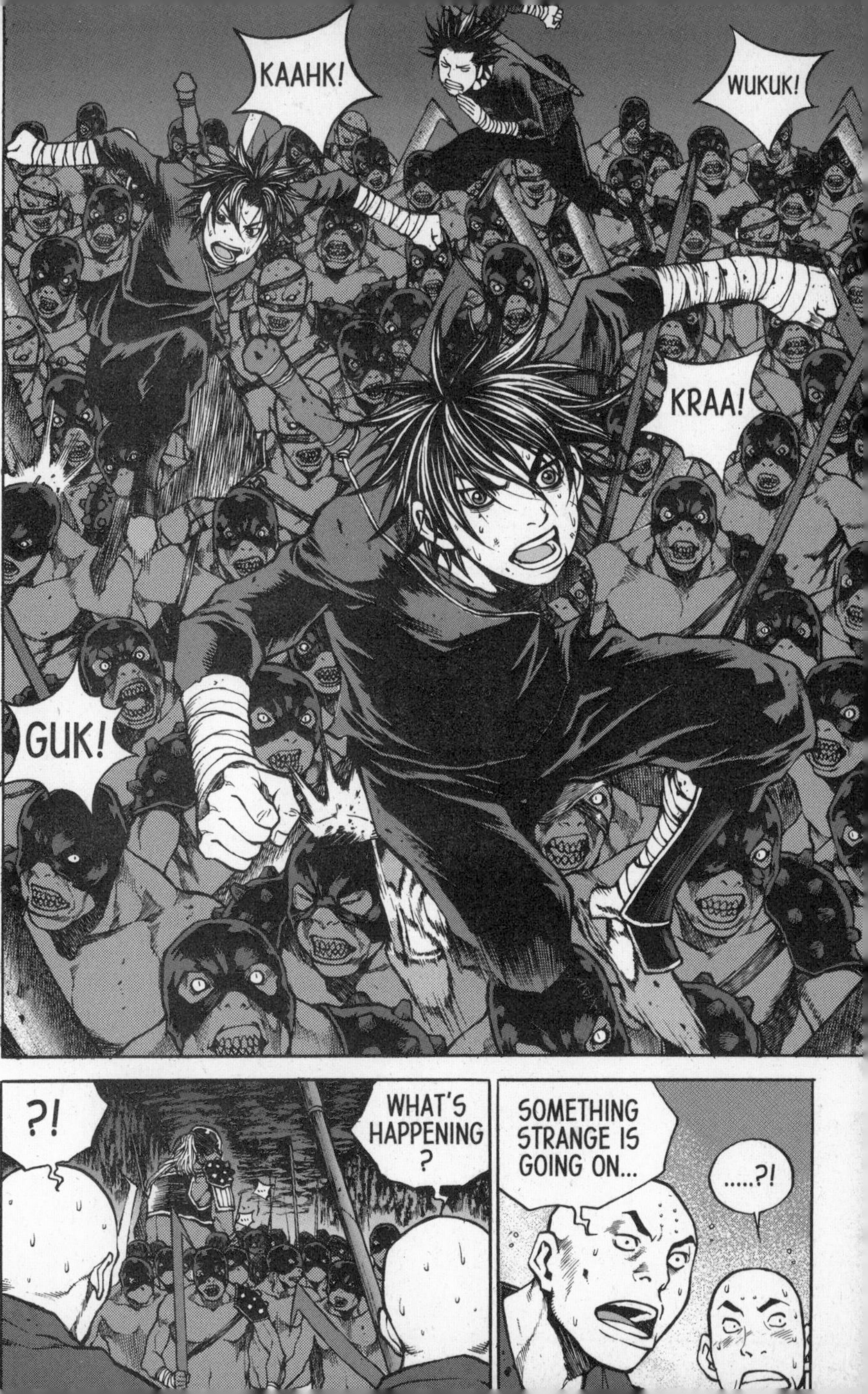

WUKUK!
KAAHK!
KRAA!
GUK!
SOMETHING STRANGE IS GOING ON...
.....?!
WHAT'S HAPPENING ?
?!

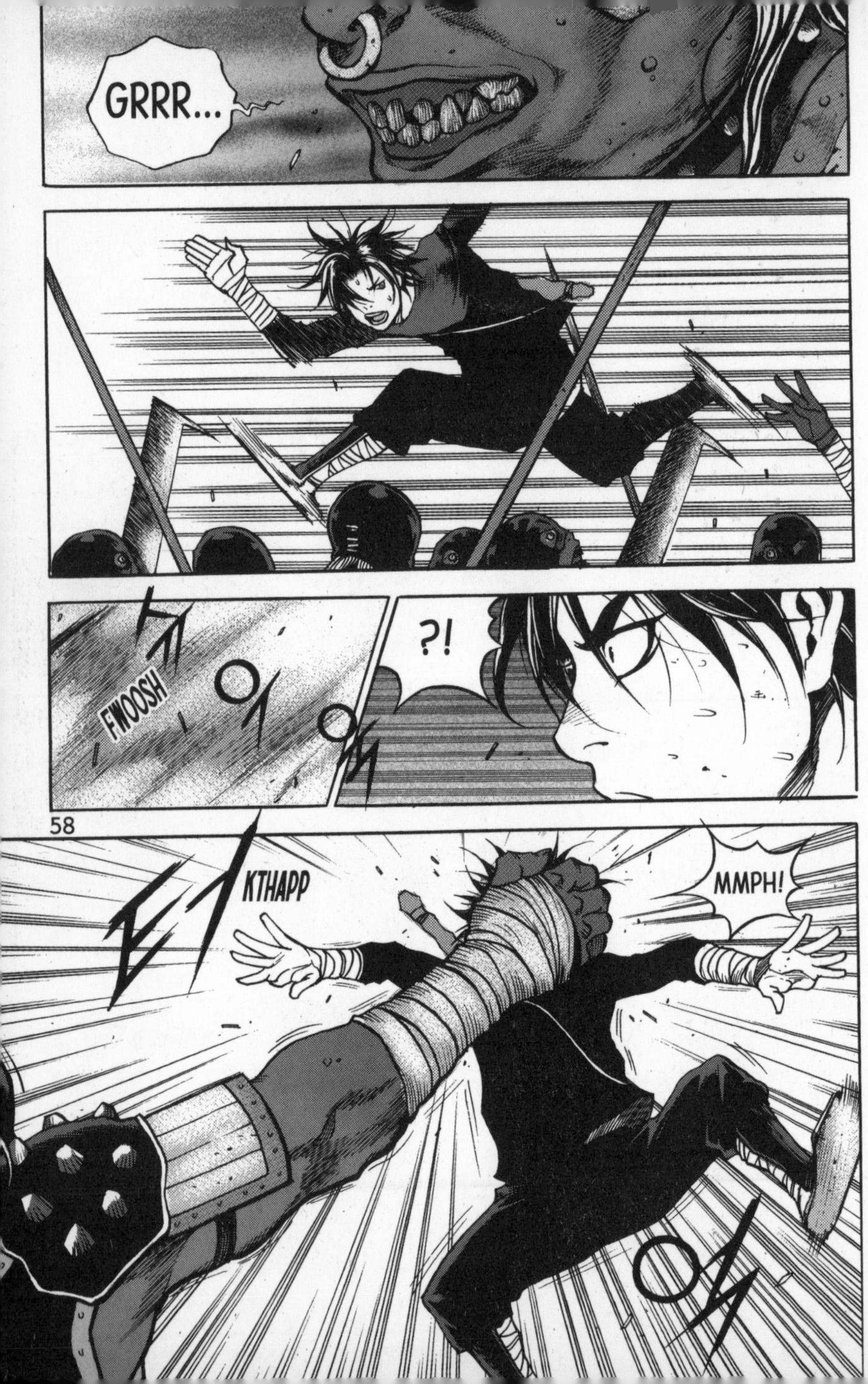
GRRR...
FWOOSH
?!
KTHAPP
MMPH!

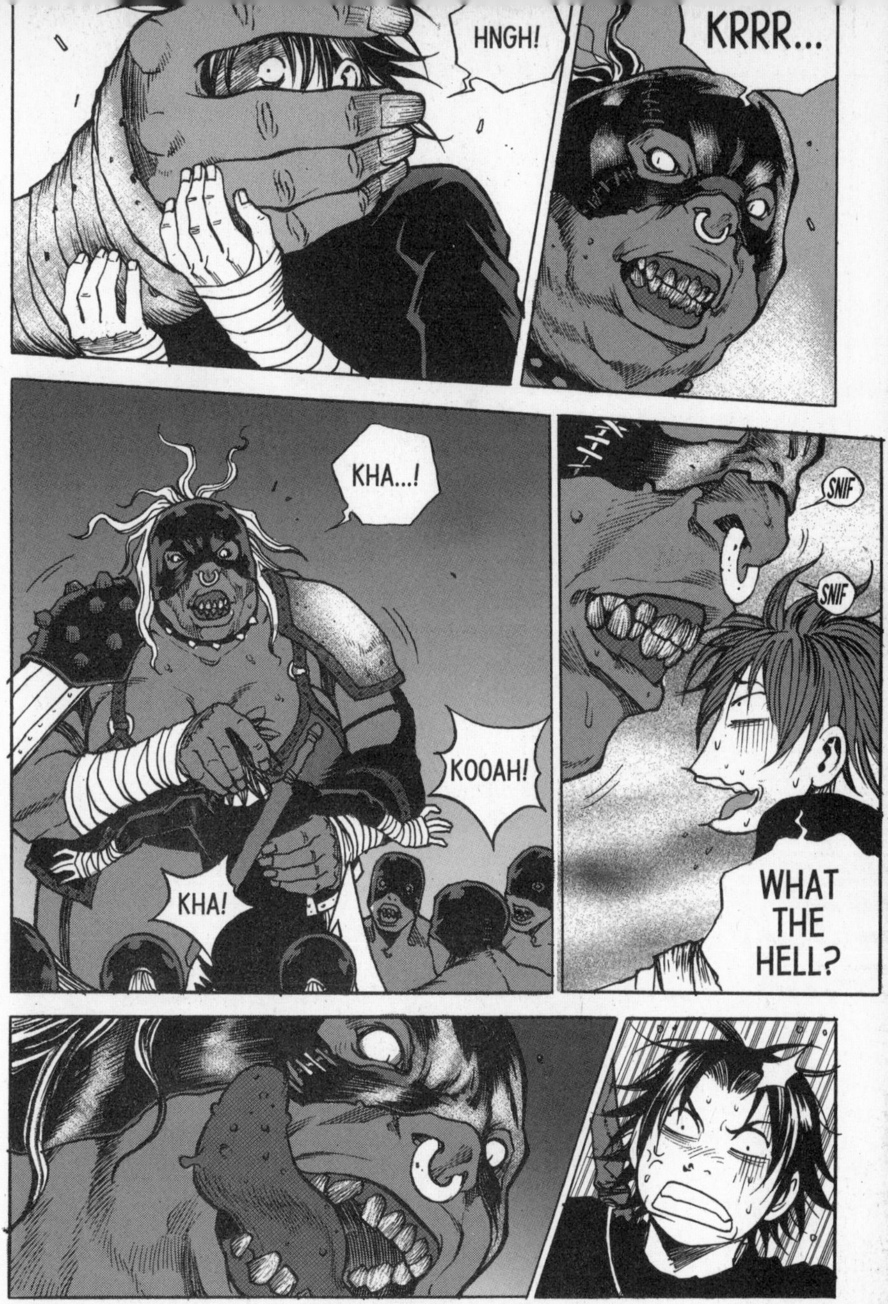

HNGH!
KRRR...
KHA...!
KOOAH!
KHA!
SNIF
SNIF
WHAT THE HELL?

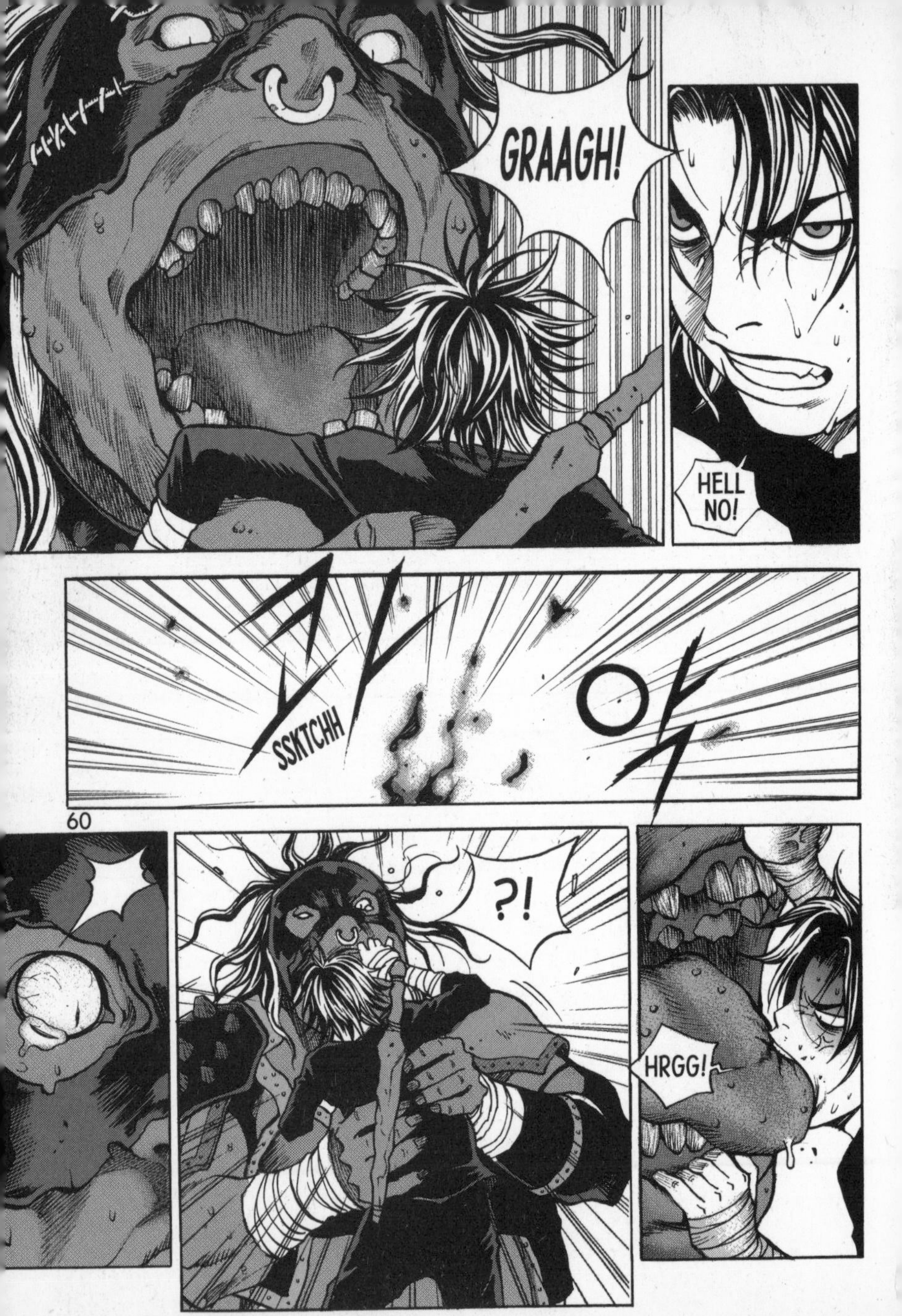
GRAAGH!
HELL NO!
SSKTCHH
?!
HRGG!

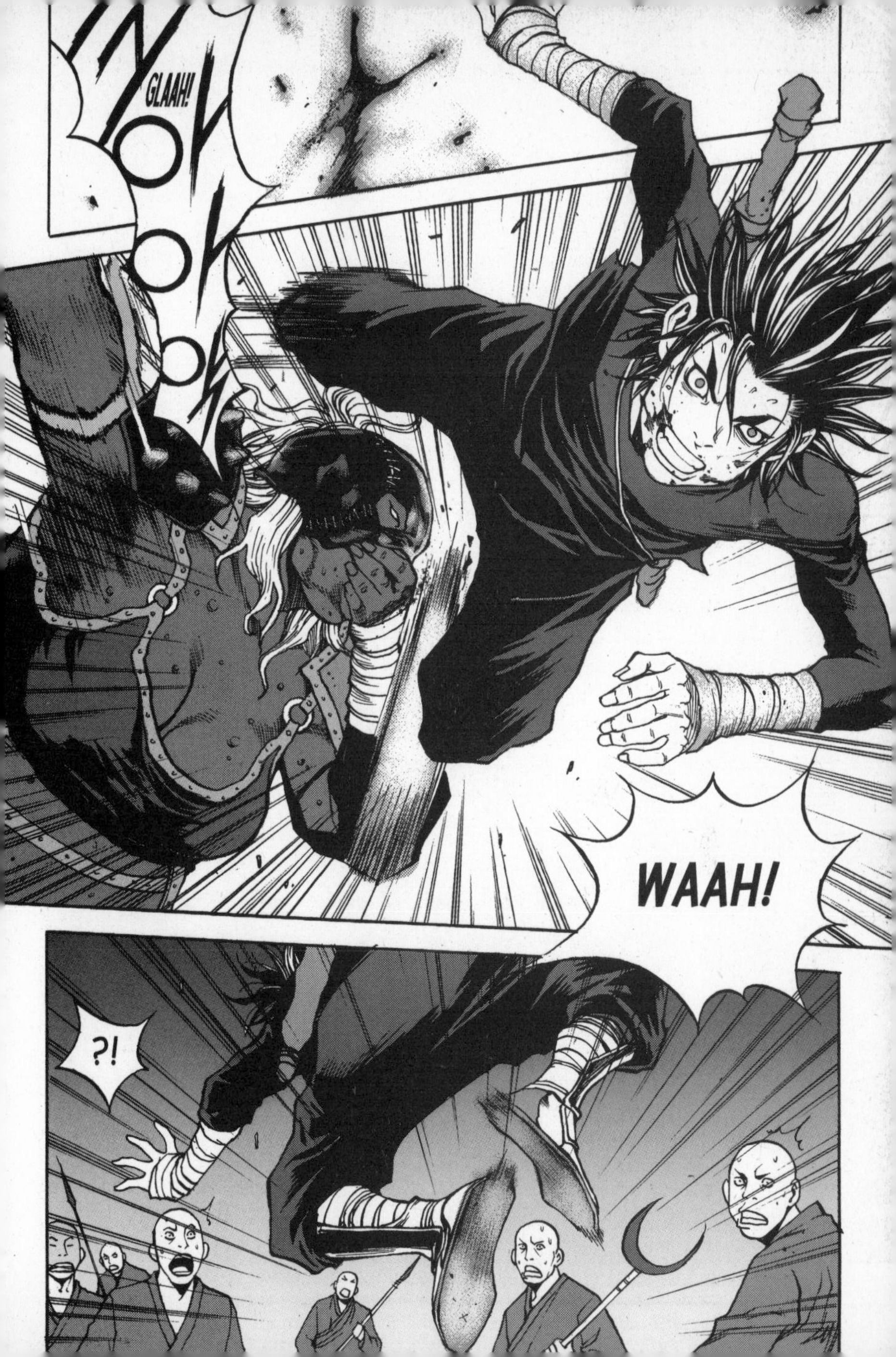
GLAAH!
WAAH!
?!

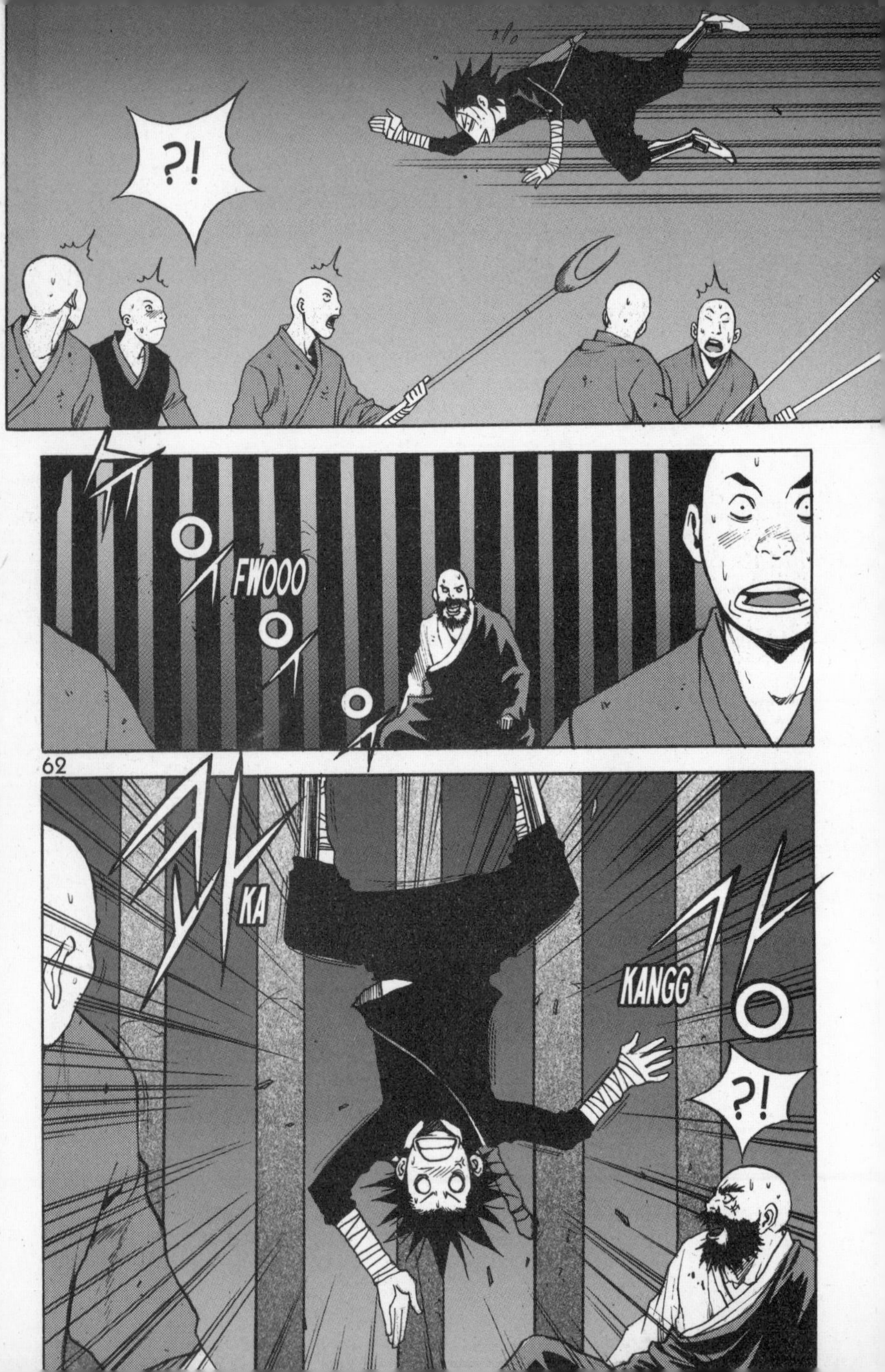
?!
FWOOO
KA
KANGG
?!

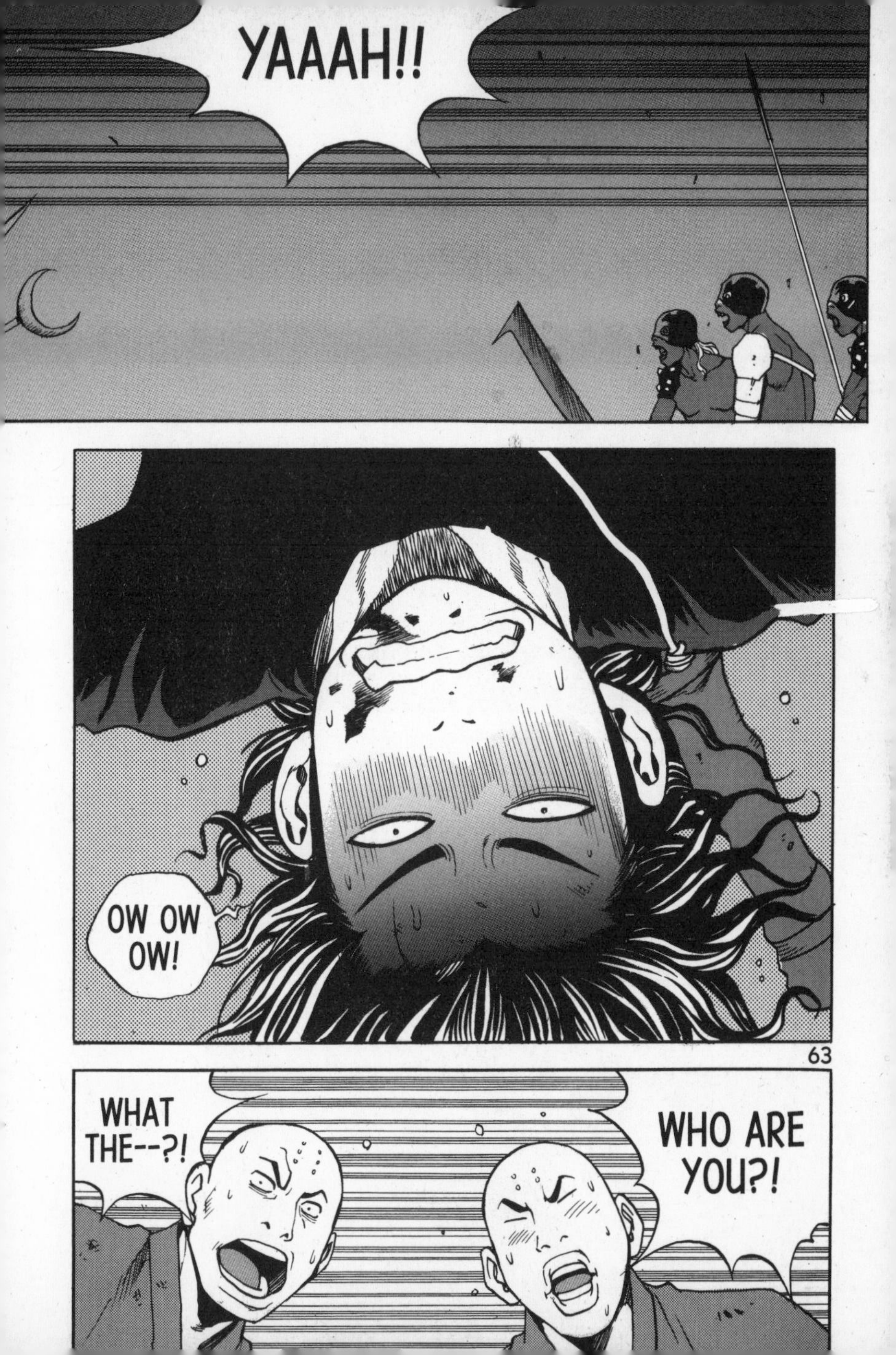
YAAAH!!
OW OW OW!
WHO ARE YOU?!
WHAT THE--?!

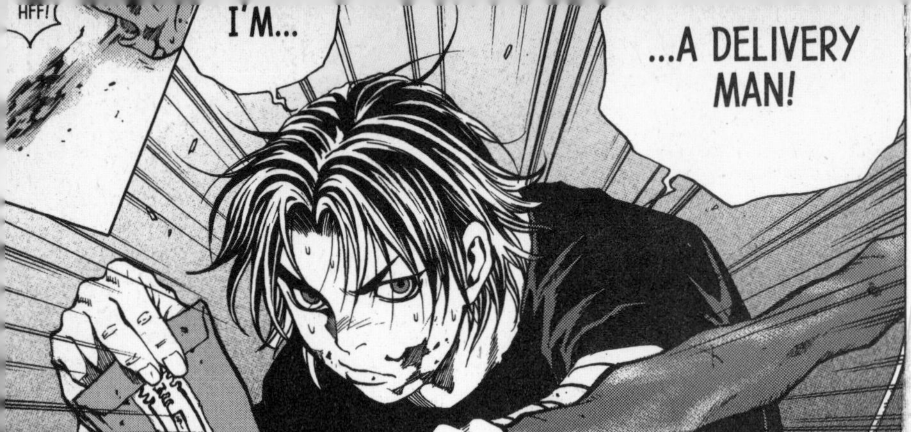
HFF!
I'M...
...A DELIVERY MAN!
I'VE GOT A DELIVERY FOR THE MONK JIAHN FROM THE HEAD TEMPLE!

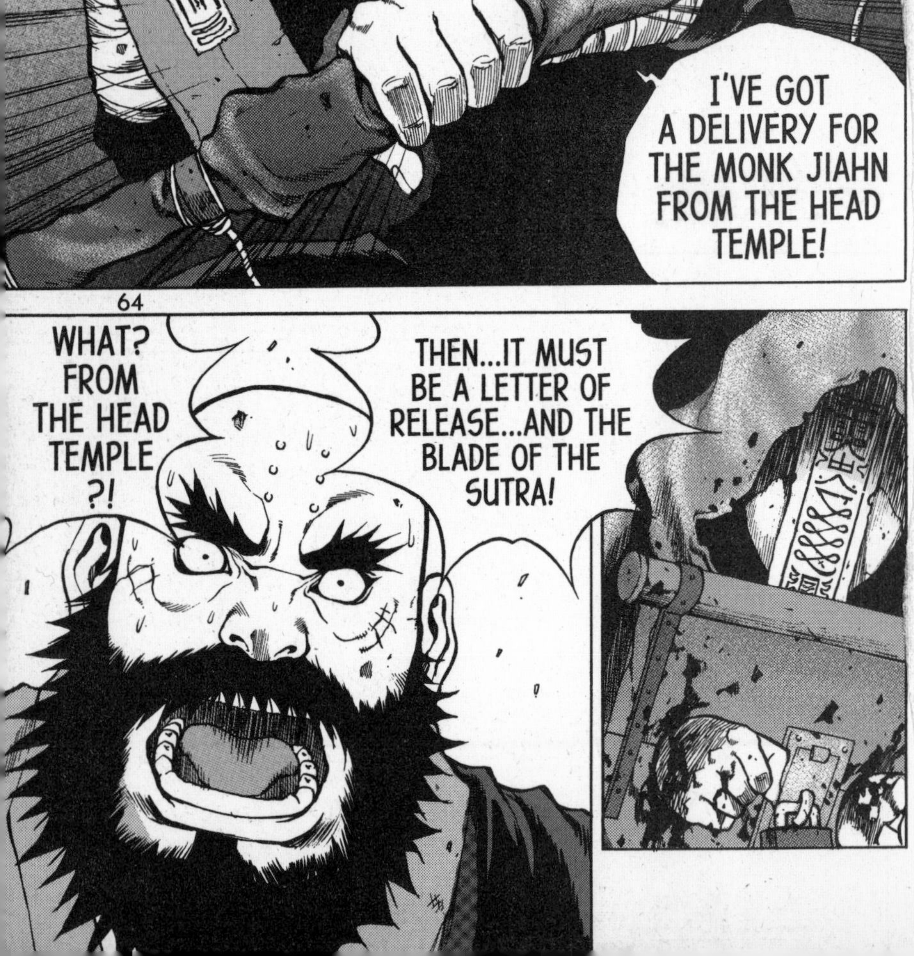
WHAT? FROM THE HEAD TEMPLE ?!
THEN...IT MUST BE A LETTER OF RELEASE...AND THE BLADE OF THE SUTRA!

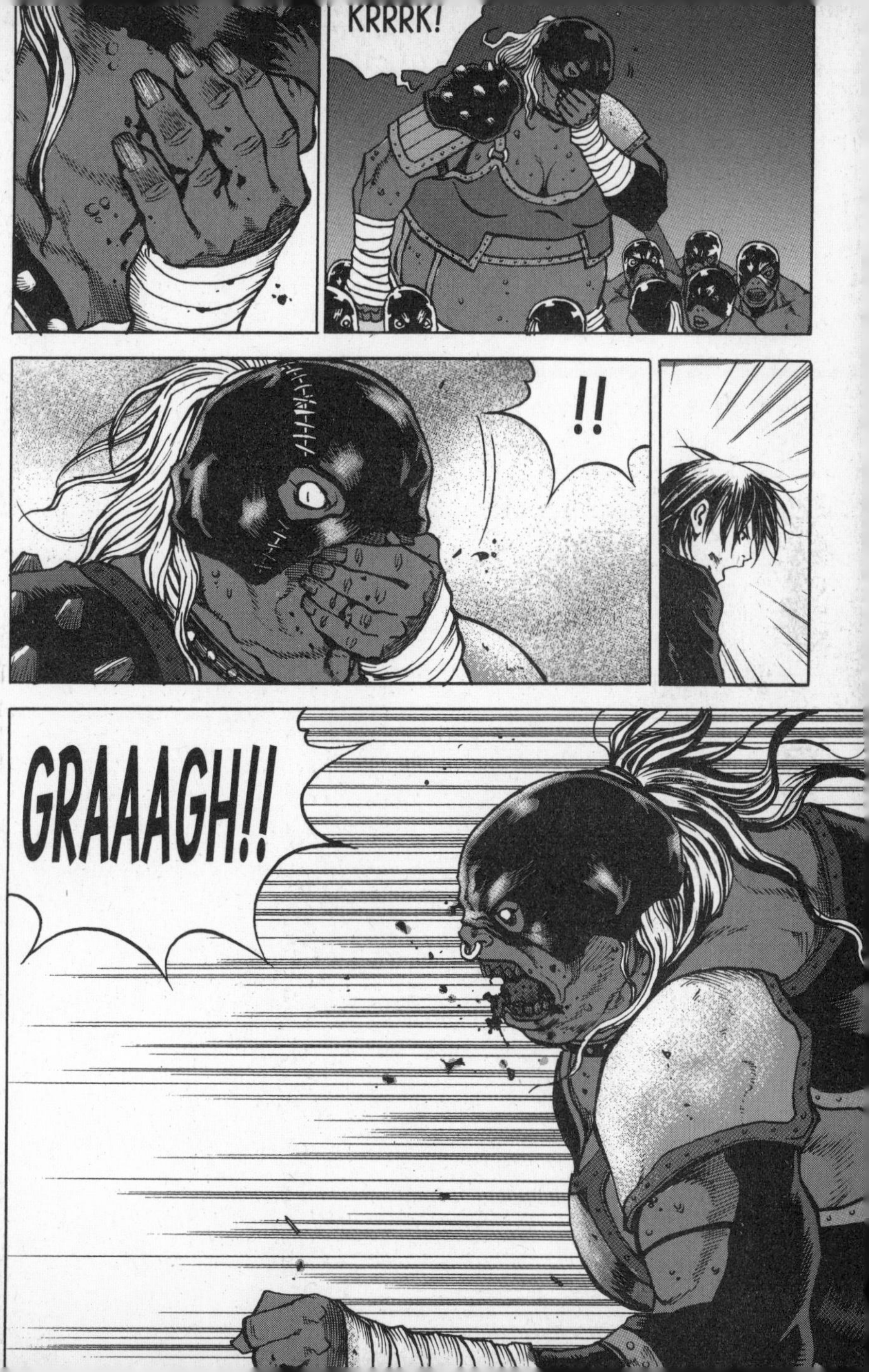
KRRRK!
!!
GRAAAGH!!

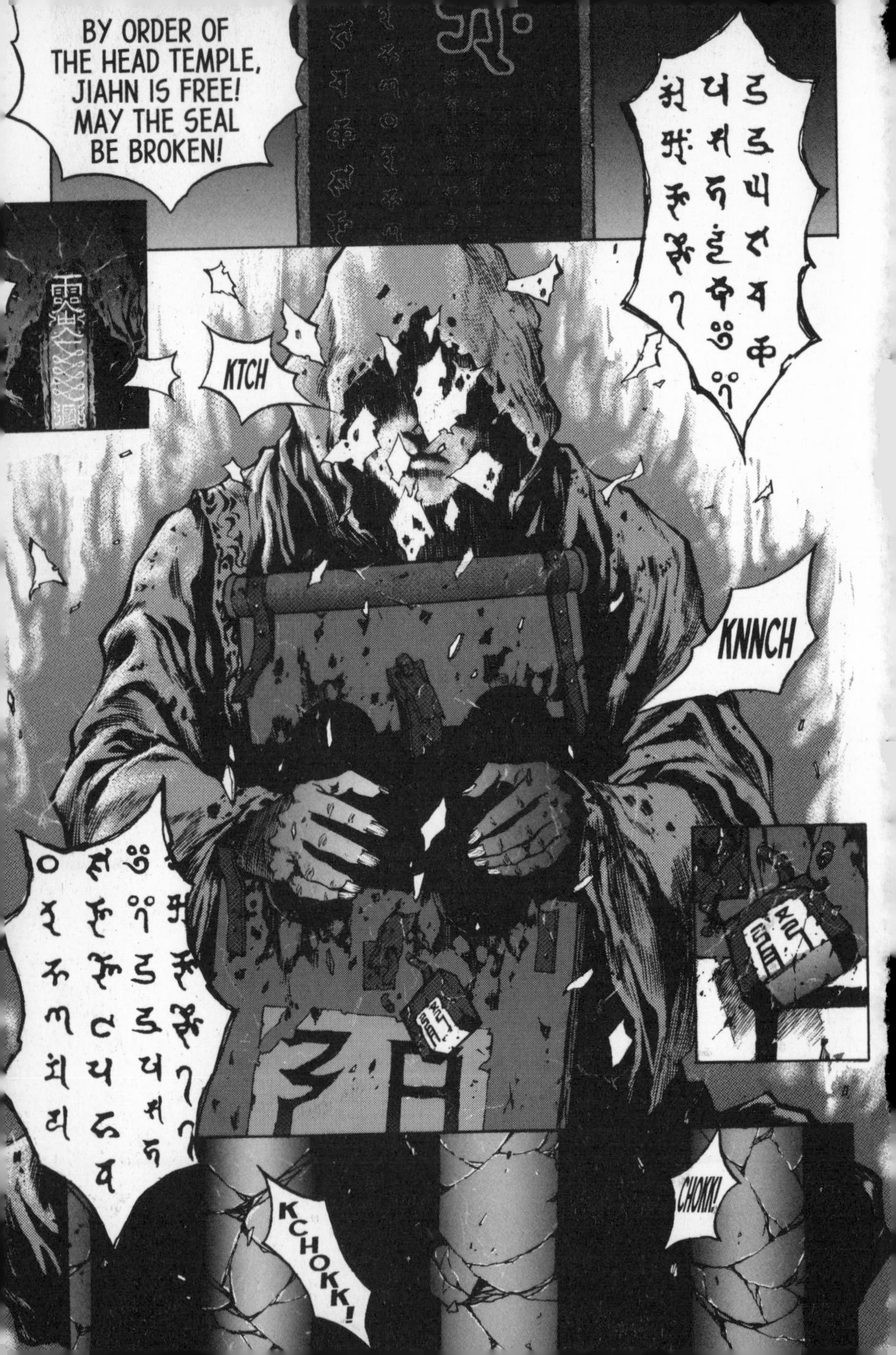
BY ORDER OF THE HEAD TEMPLE, JIAHN IS FREE! MAY THE SEAL BE BROKEN!
KTCH
KNNCH
KCHOKK!
CHOKK!

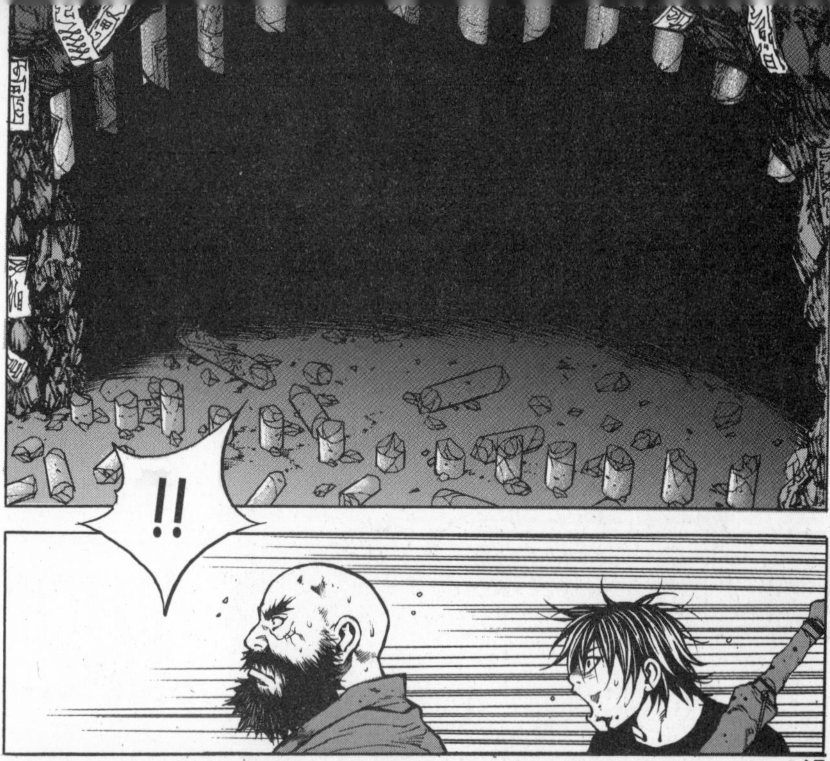
!!

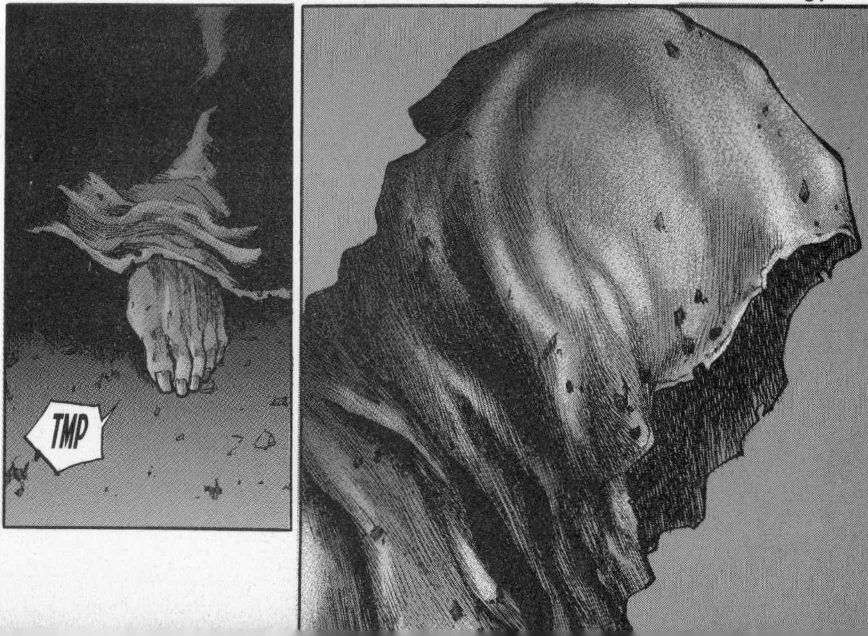
TMP

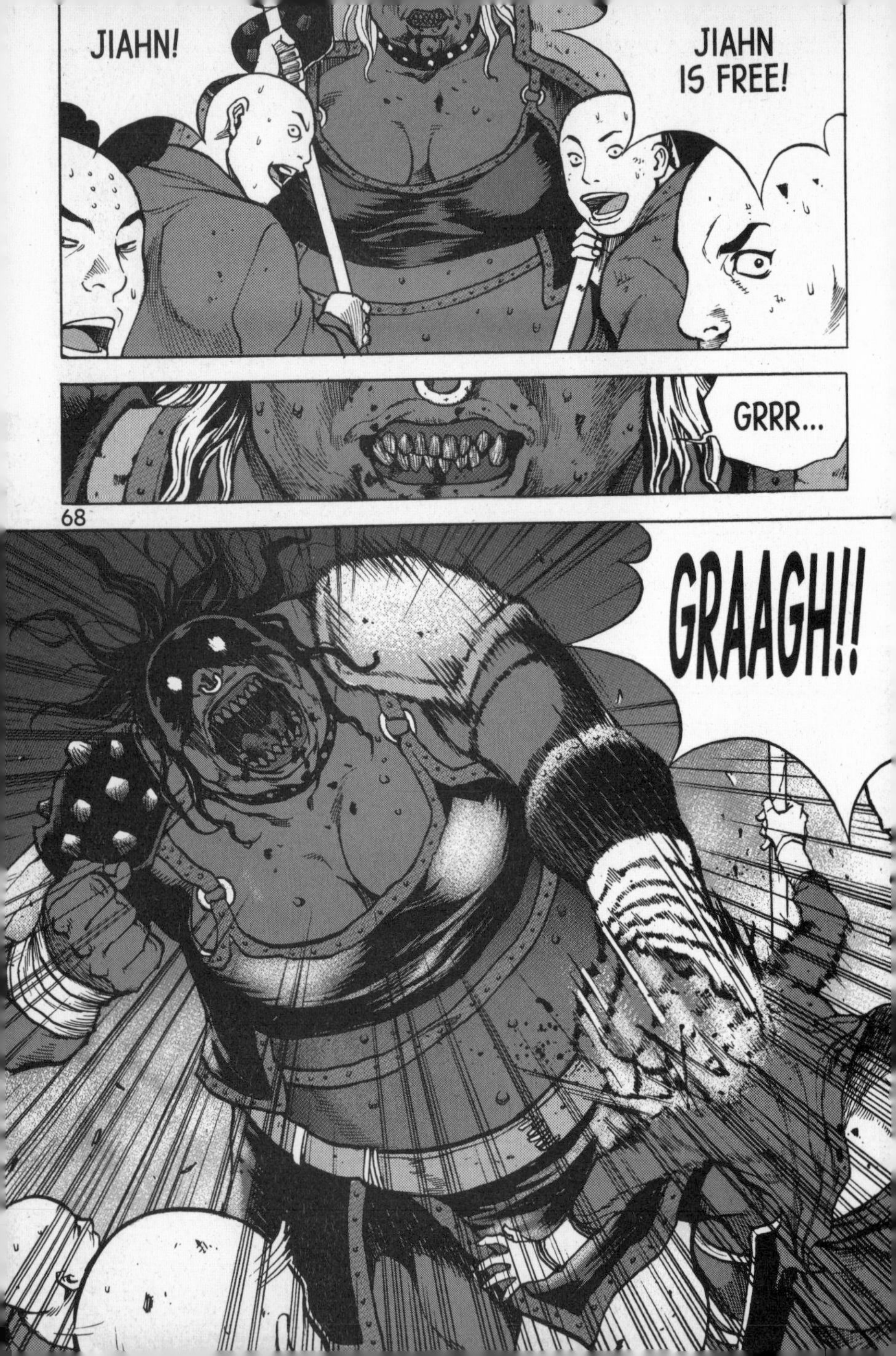
JIAHN
IS FREE!
JIAHN!
GRRR...
GRAAGH!!

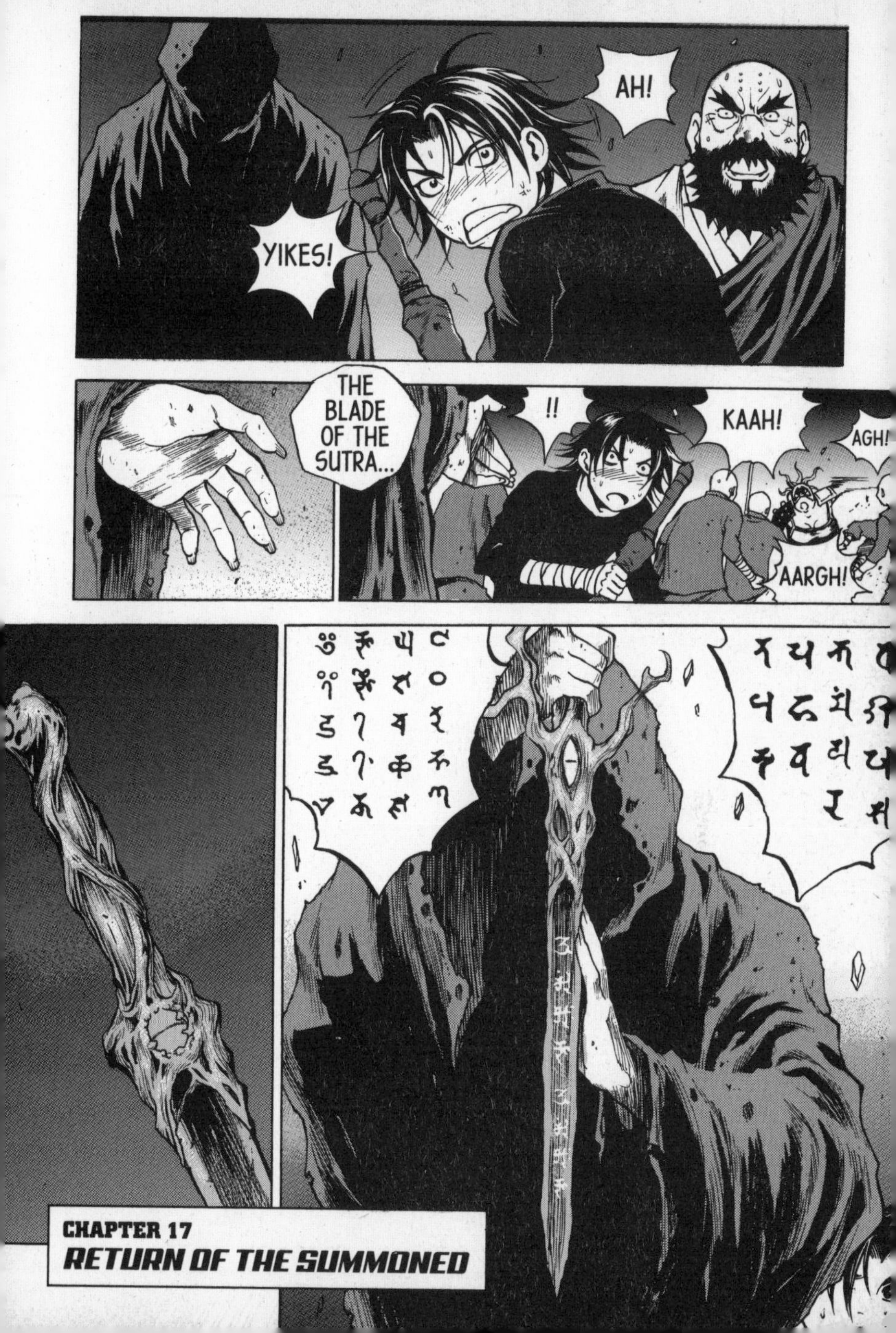
AH!
YIKES!
AGH!
KAAH!
!!
AARGH!
THE BLADE OF THE SUTRA...
CHAPTER 17
RETURN OF THE SUMMONED

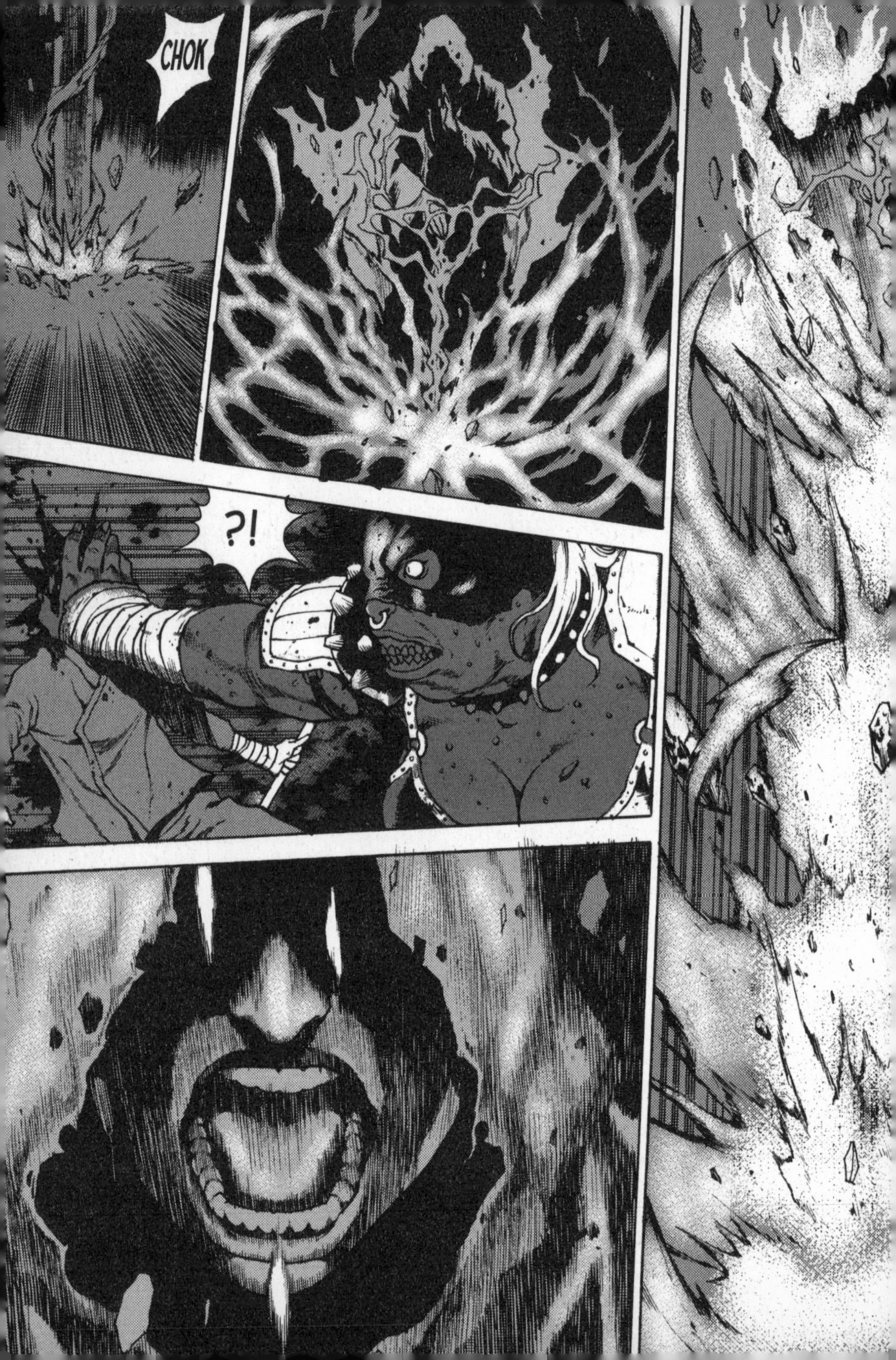
CHOK
?!

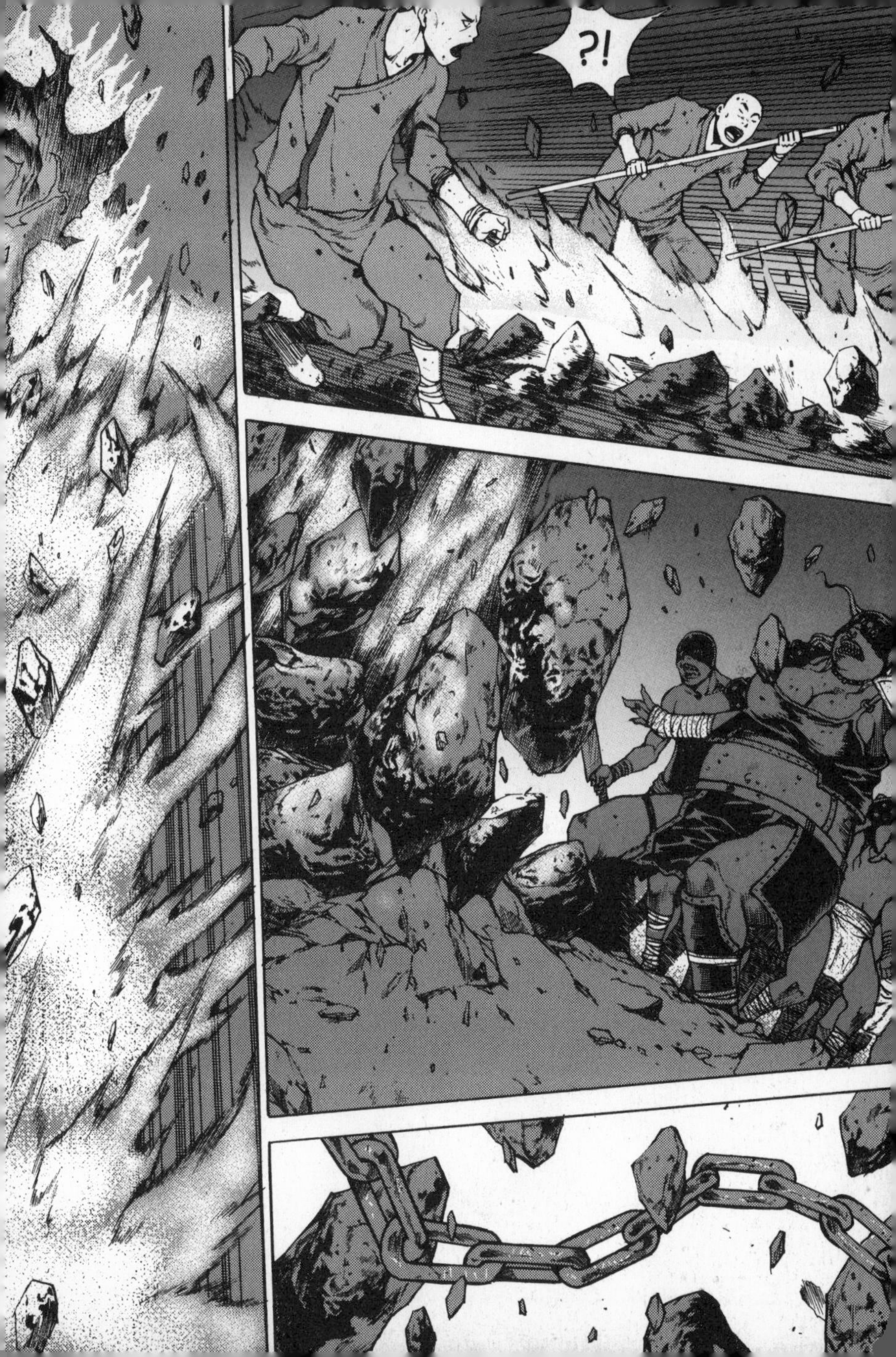
?!

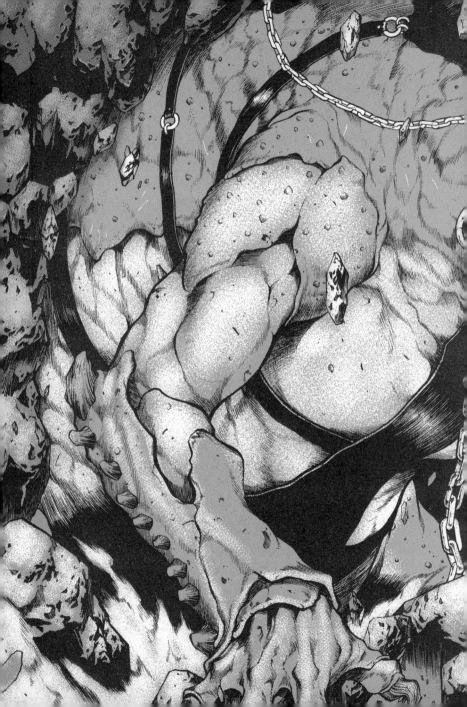

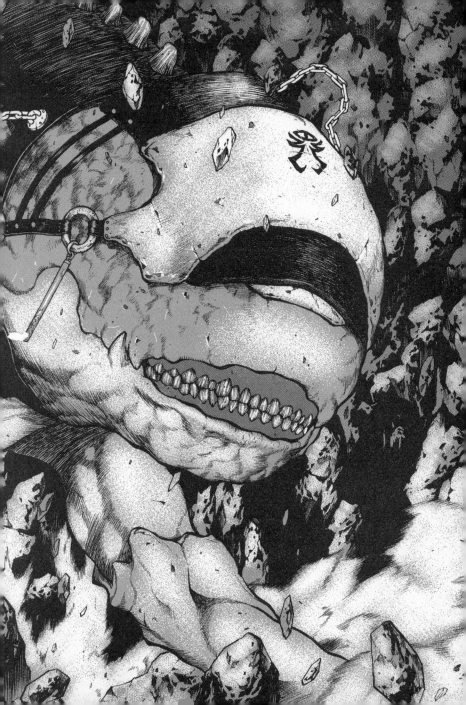

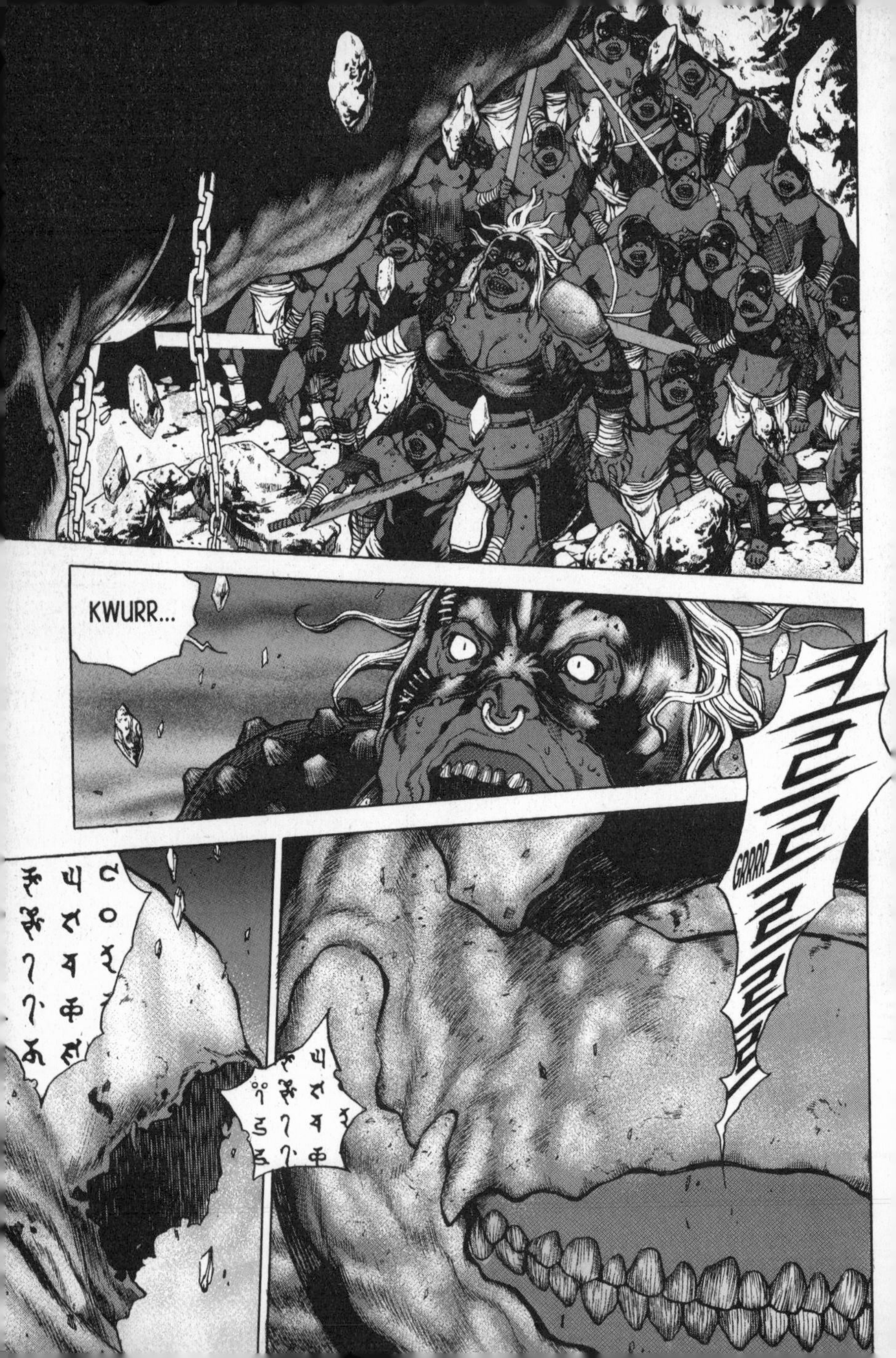
KWURR...
GRRRR

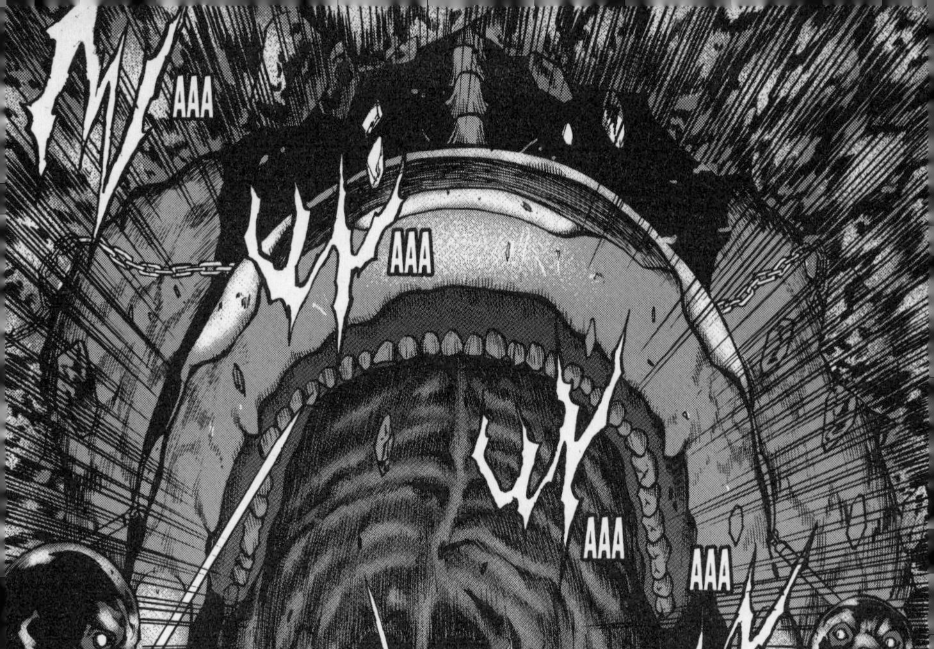
WAAA
WAAA
WAAA
AAA
WAAA

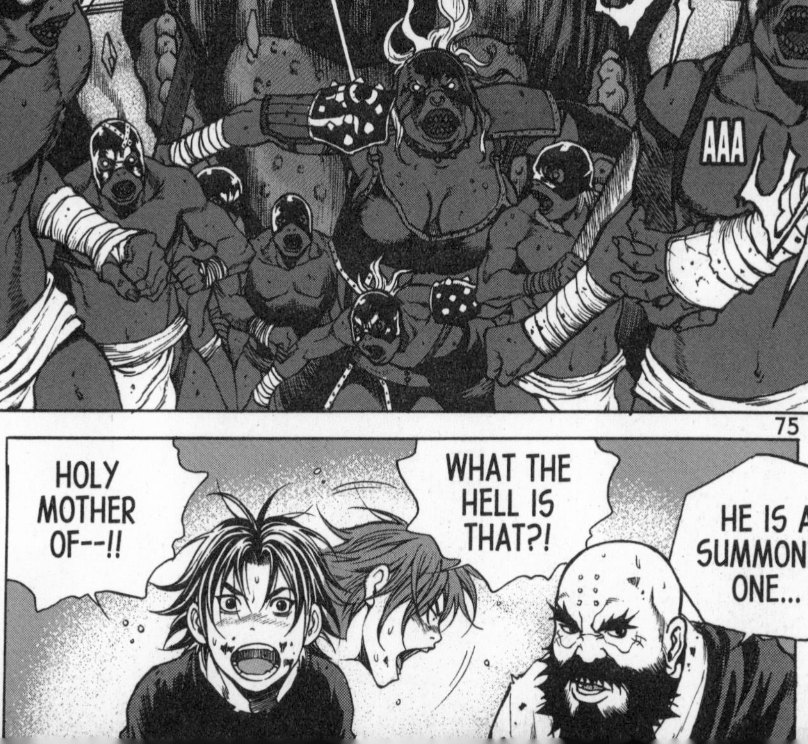
HOLY MOTHER OF--!!
WHAT THE HELL IS THAT?!
HE IS A SUMMONED ONE...

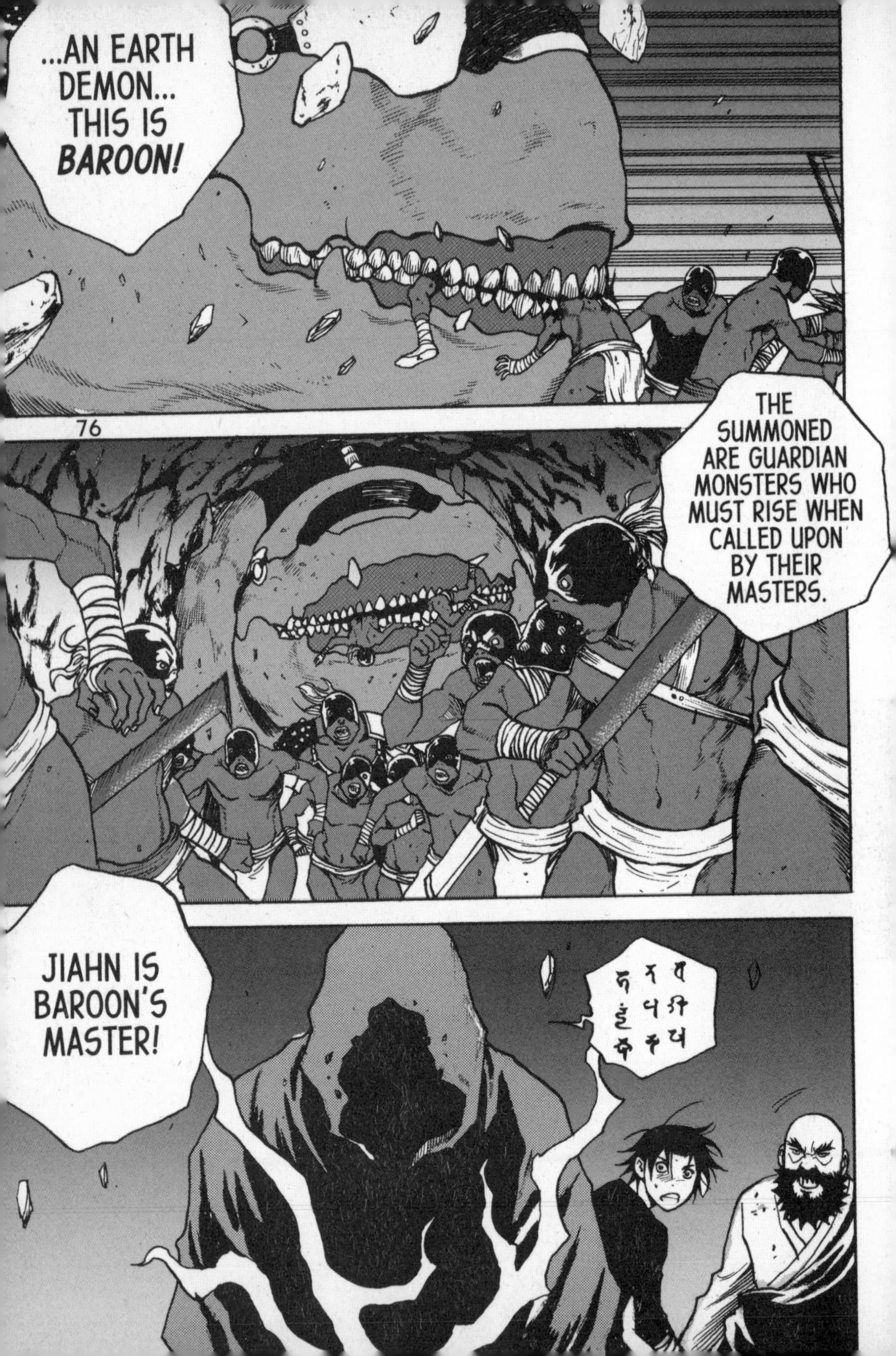
...AN EARTH DEMON... THIS IS BAROON!
THE SUMMONED ARE GUARDIAN MONSTERS WHO MUST RISE WHEN CALLED UPON BY THEIR MASTERS.
JIAHN IS BAROON'S MASTER!

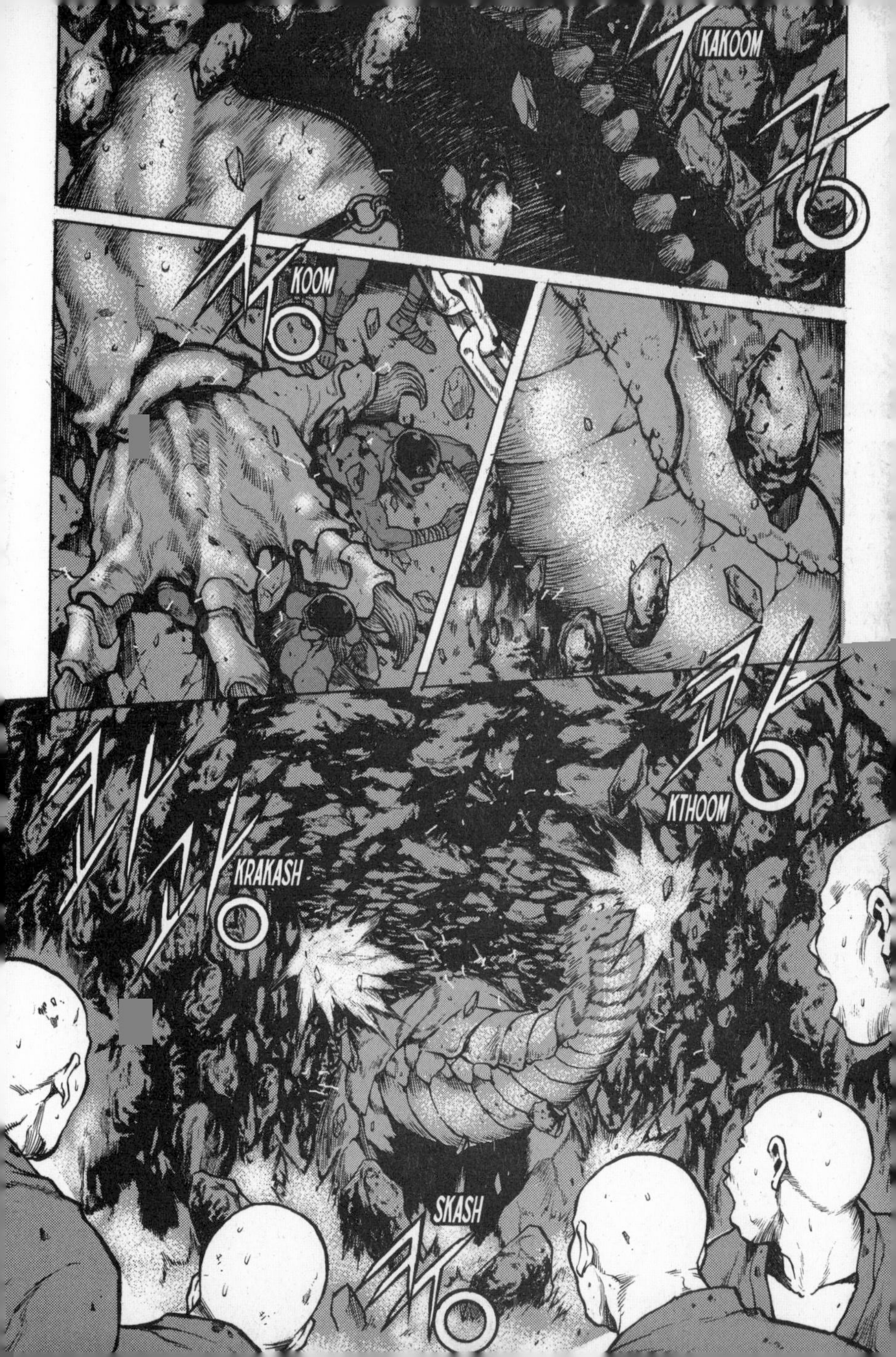
KAKOOM
KOOM
KTHOOM
KRAKASH
SKASH

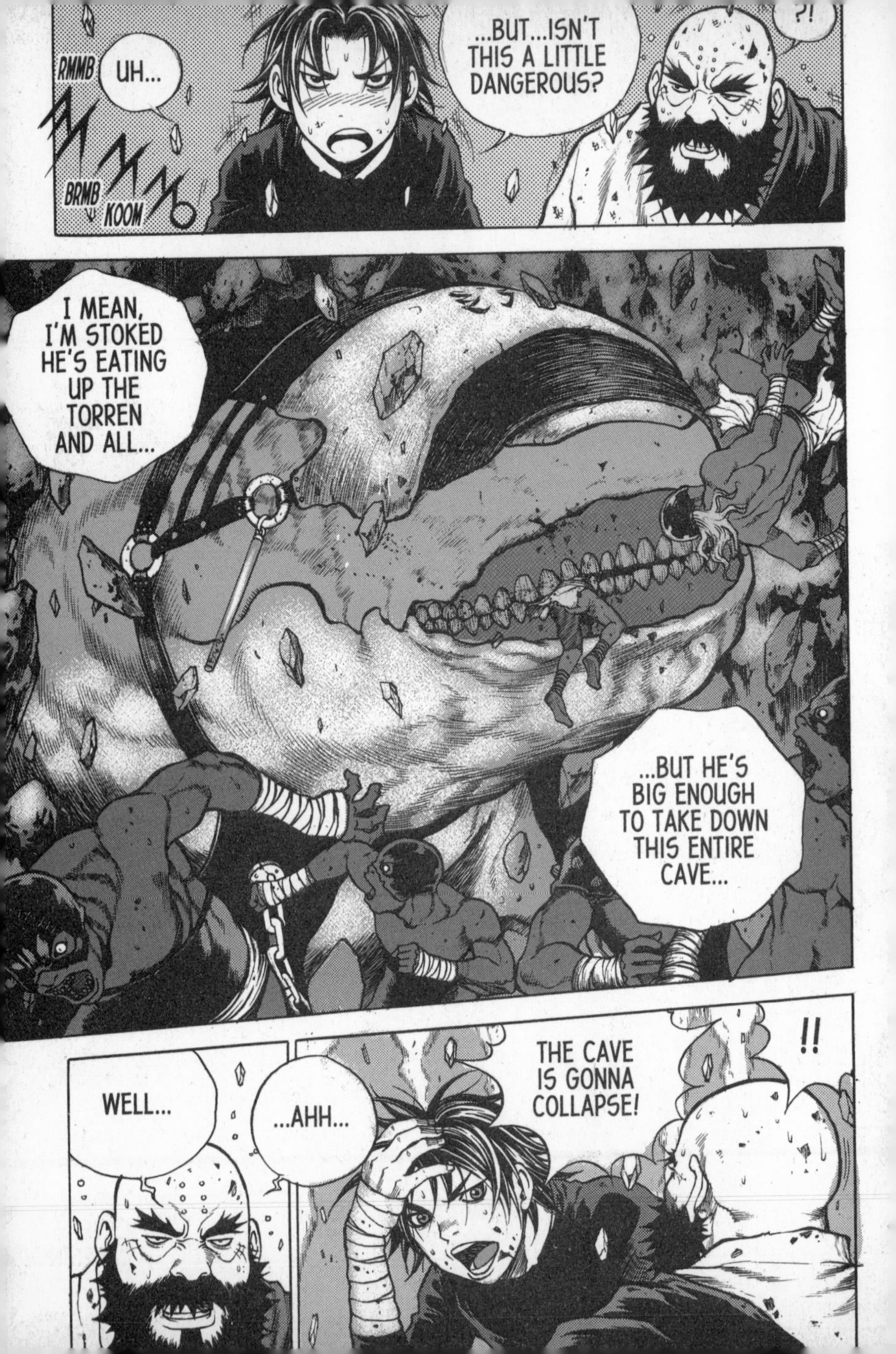
RMMB
UH...
...BUT...ISN'T THIS A LITTLE DANGEROUS?
?!
BRMB
KOOM
I MEAN, I'M STOKED HE'S EATING UP THE TORREN AND ALL...
...BUT HE'S BIG ENOUGH TO TAKE DOWN THIS ENTIRE CAVE...
WELL...
...AHH...
THE CAVE IS GONNA COLLAPSE!
!!

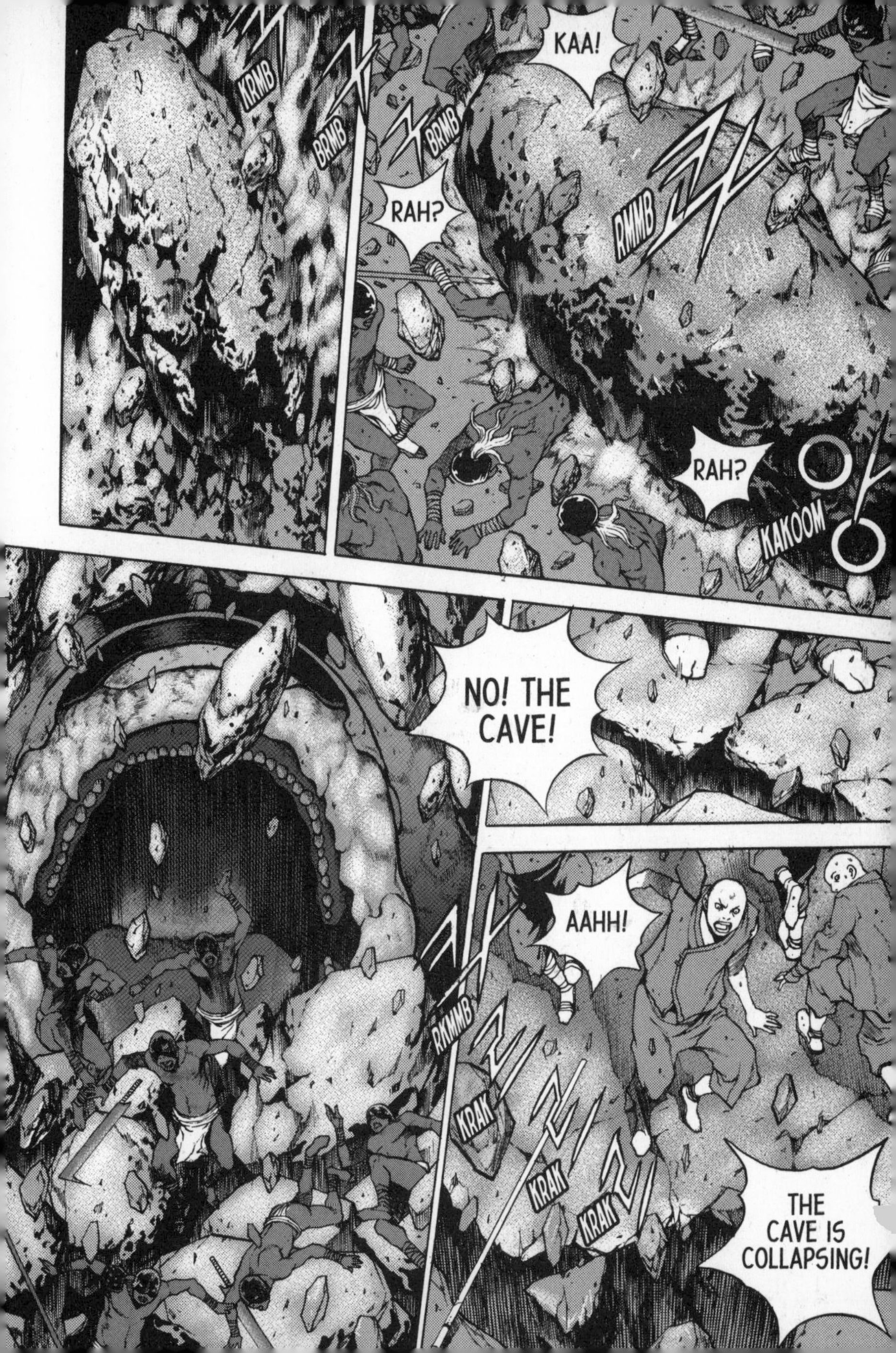
KRMB
BRMB
BRMB
KAA!
RAH?
RMMB
RAH?
KAKOOM
NO! THE CAVE!
AAHH!
RKMMB
KRAK
KRAK
KRAK
THE CAVE IS COLLAPSING!

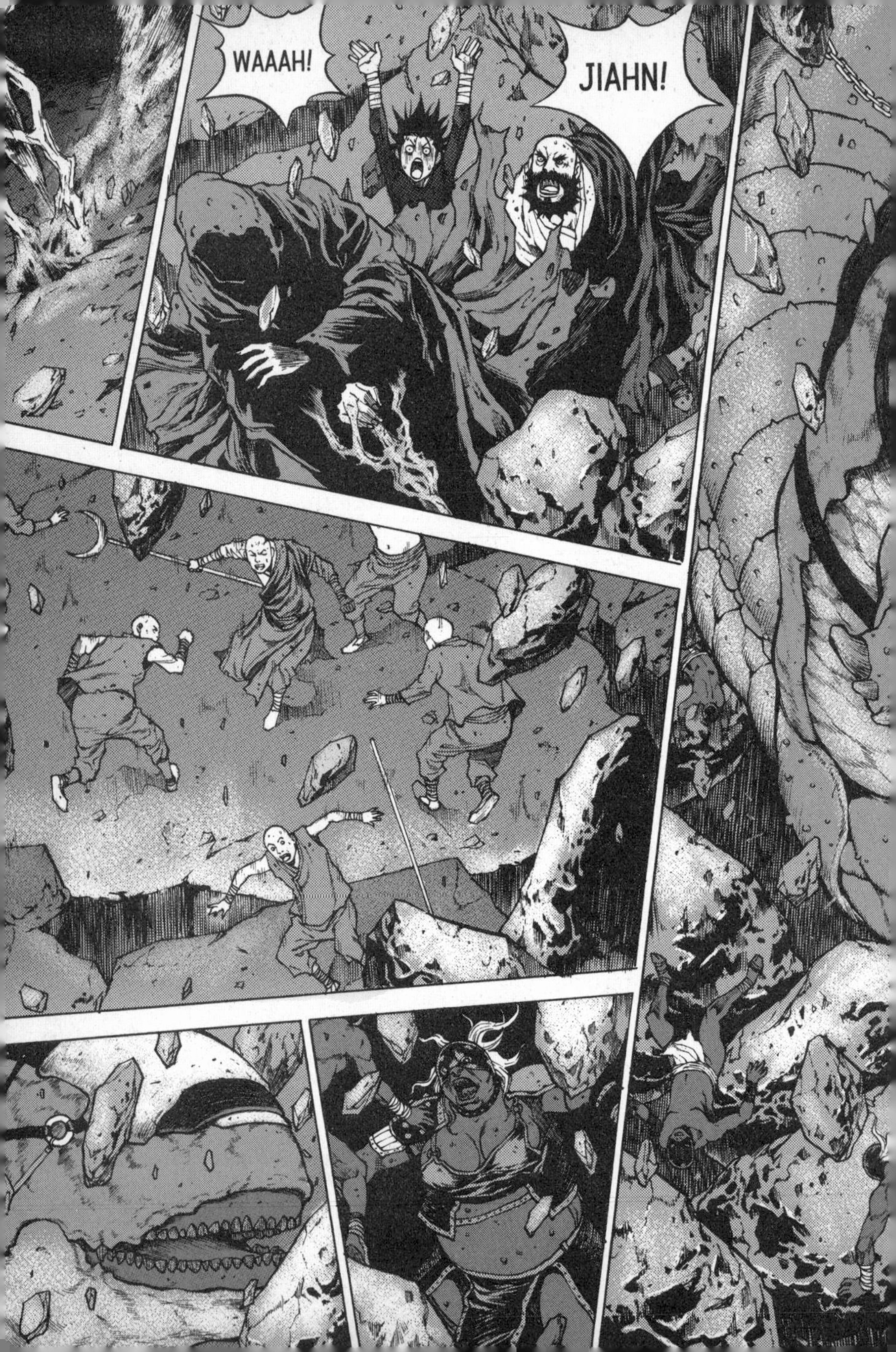
JIAHN!
WAAAH!

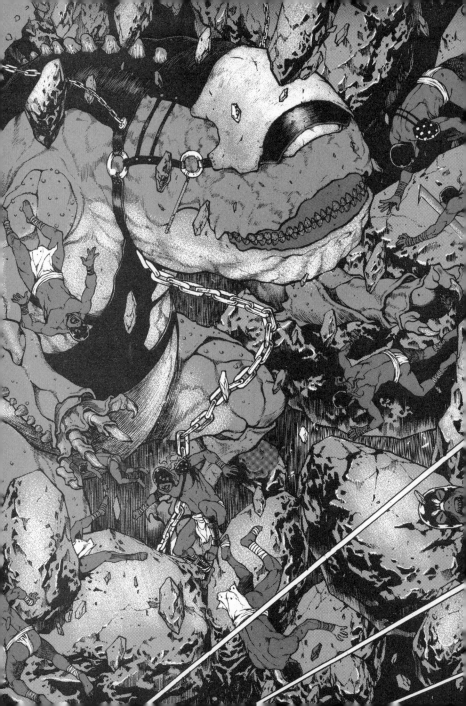

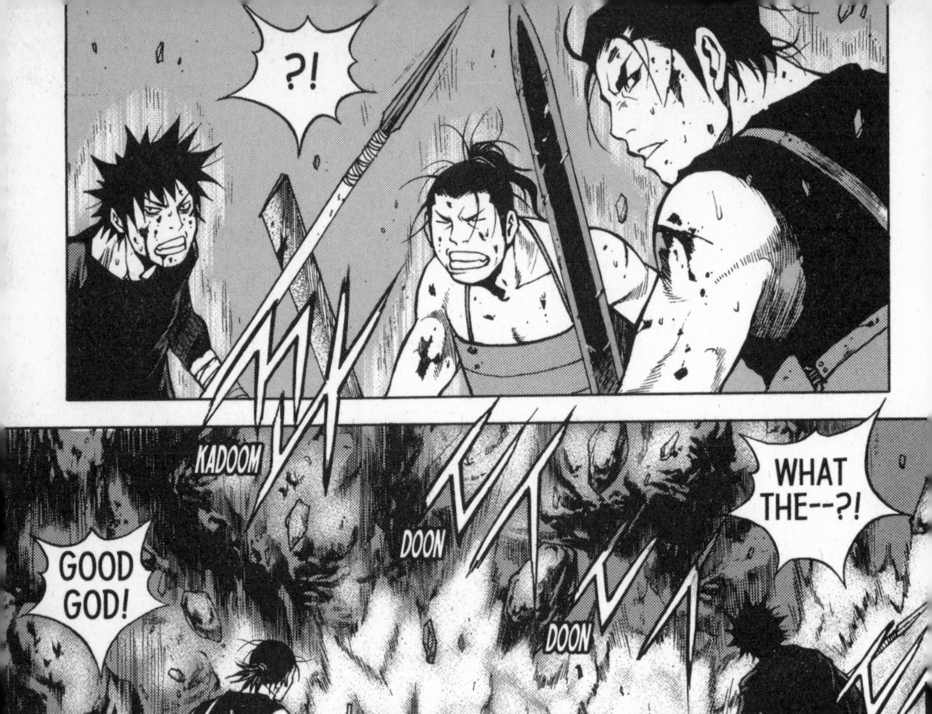
?!
WHAT THE--?!
DOON
DOON
DOON
KADOOM
GOOD GOD!

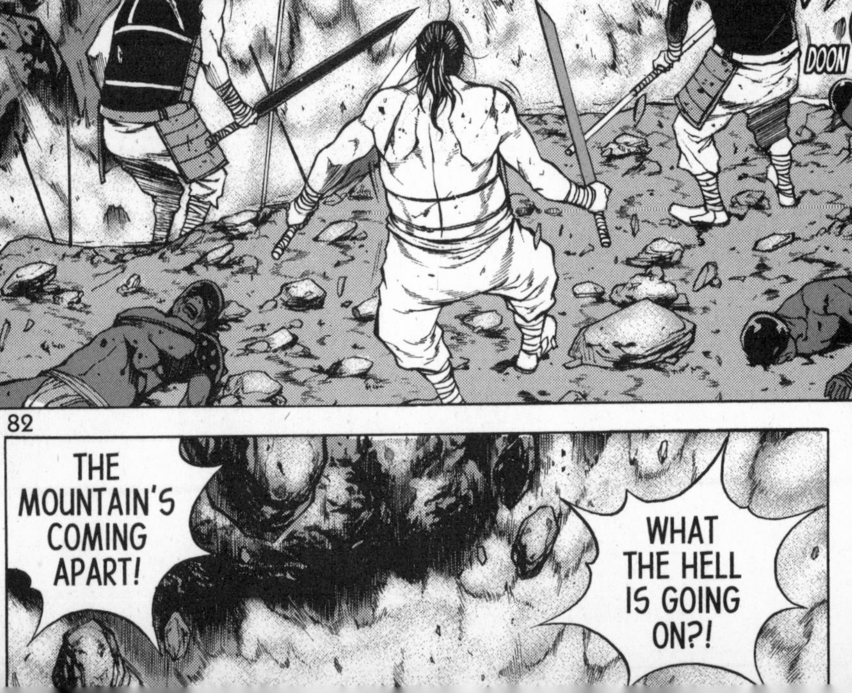
WHAT THE HELL IS GOING ON?!
THE MOUNTAIN'S COMING APART!

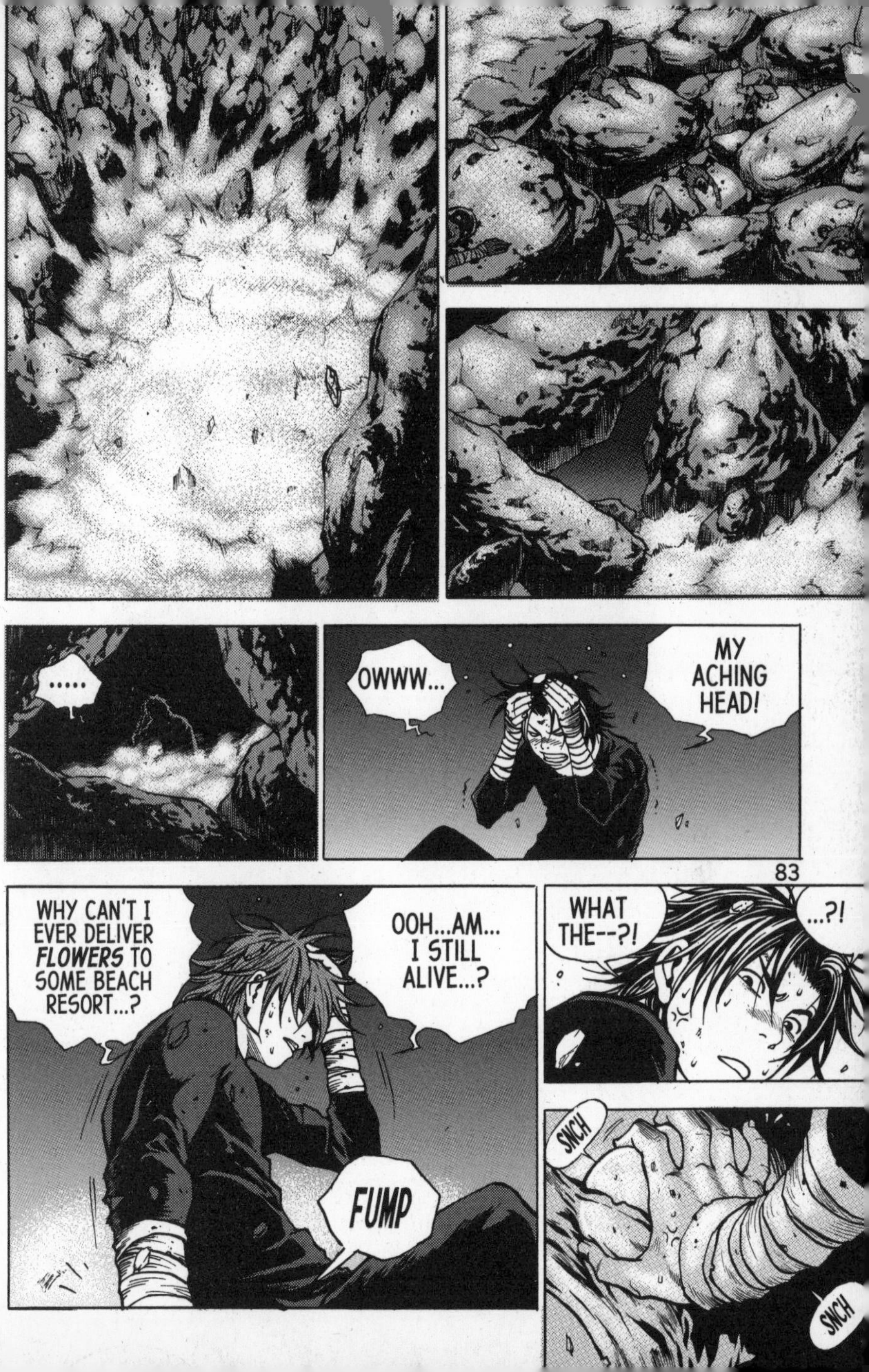
.....
OWWW...
MY ACHING HEAD!
WHY CAN'T I EVER DELIVER *FLOWERS* TO SOME BEACH RESORT...?
OOH...AM... I STILL ALIVE...?
FUMP
WHAT THE--?!
...?!
SNCH
SNCH

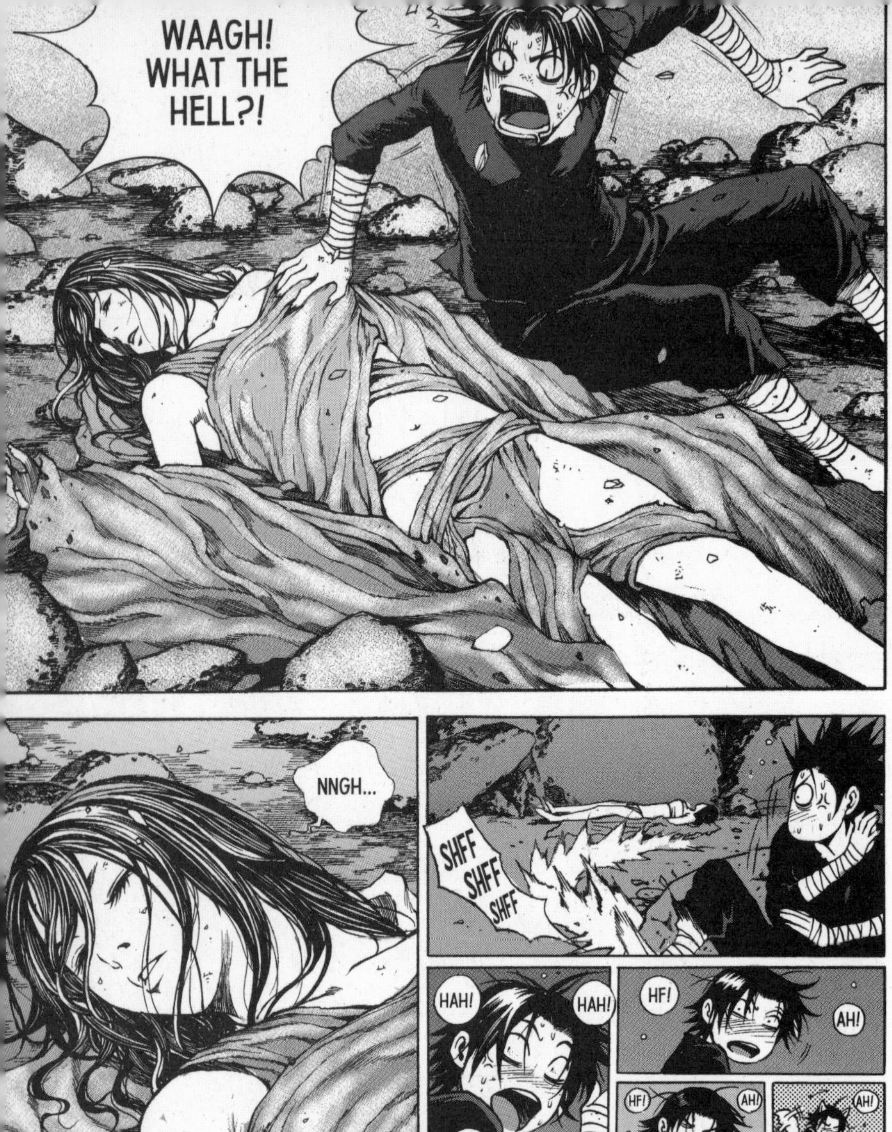
WAAGH! WHAT THE HELL?!
NNGH...
SHFF SHFF SHFF
HAH!
HAH!
HAH!
HF!
AH!
HF!
AH!
AH!

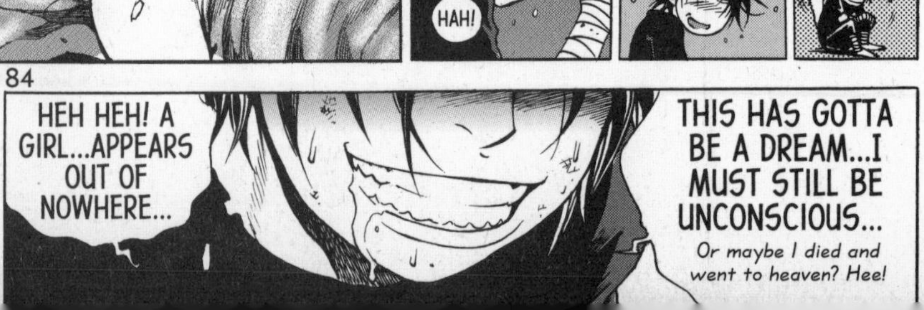
HEH HEH! A GIRL...APPEARS OUT OF NOWHERE...
THIS HAS GOTTA BE A DREAM...I MUST STILL BE UNCONSCIOUS...
Or maybe I died and went to heaven? Hee!

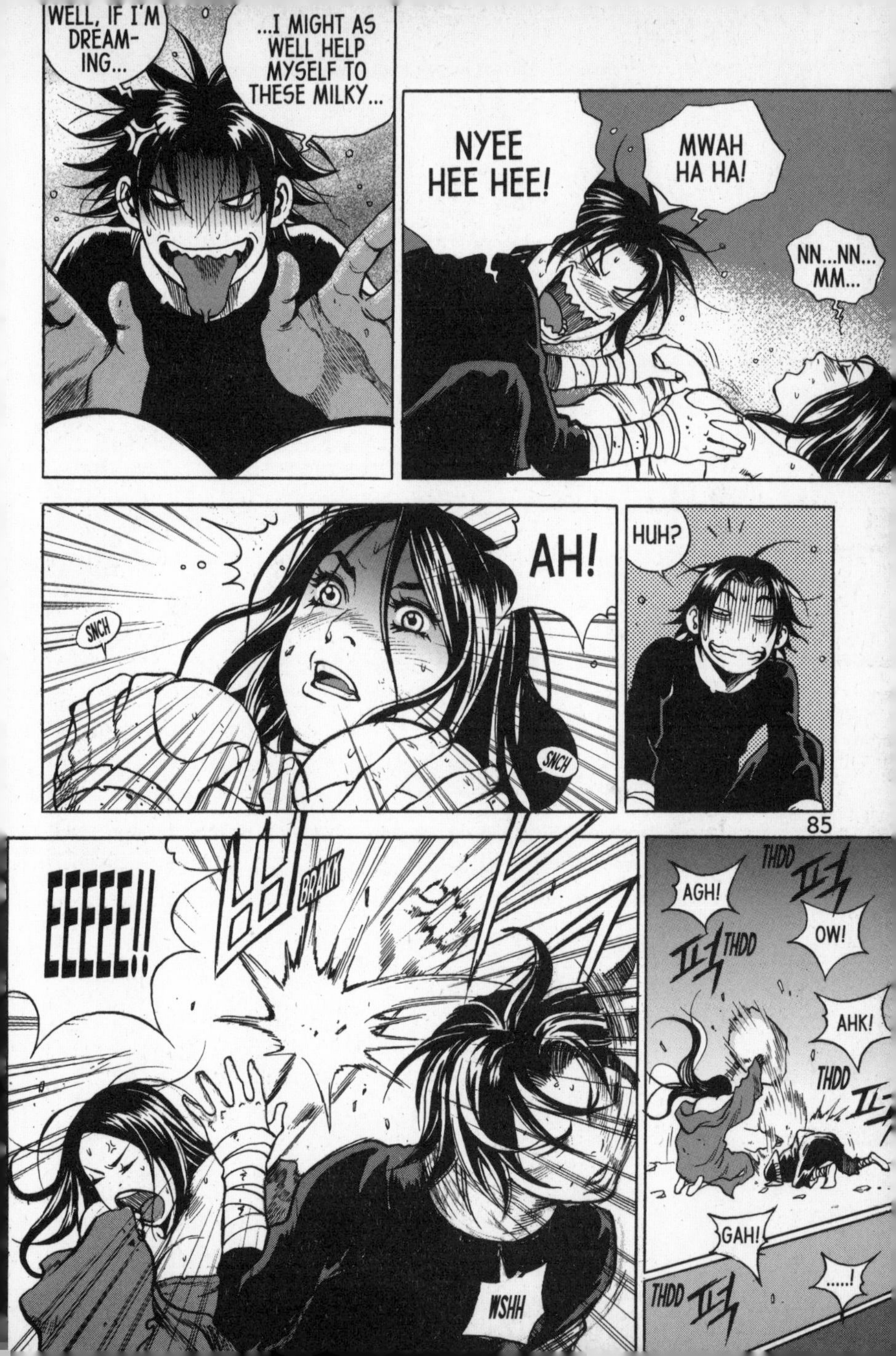

WELL, IF I'M DREAMING...
...I MIGHT AS WELL HELP MYSELF TO THESE MILKY...
NYEE HEE HEE!
MWAH HA HA!
NN...NN... MM...
SNCH
AH!
SNCH
HUH?
EEEEE!!
BRAKK
WSHH
THDD
AGH!
OW!
THDD
AHK!
THDD
GAH!
THDD
.....!

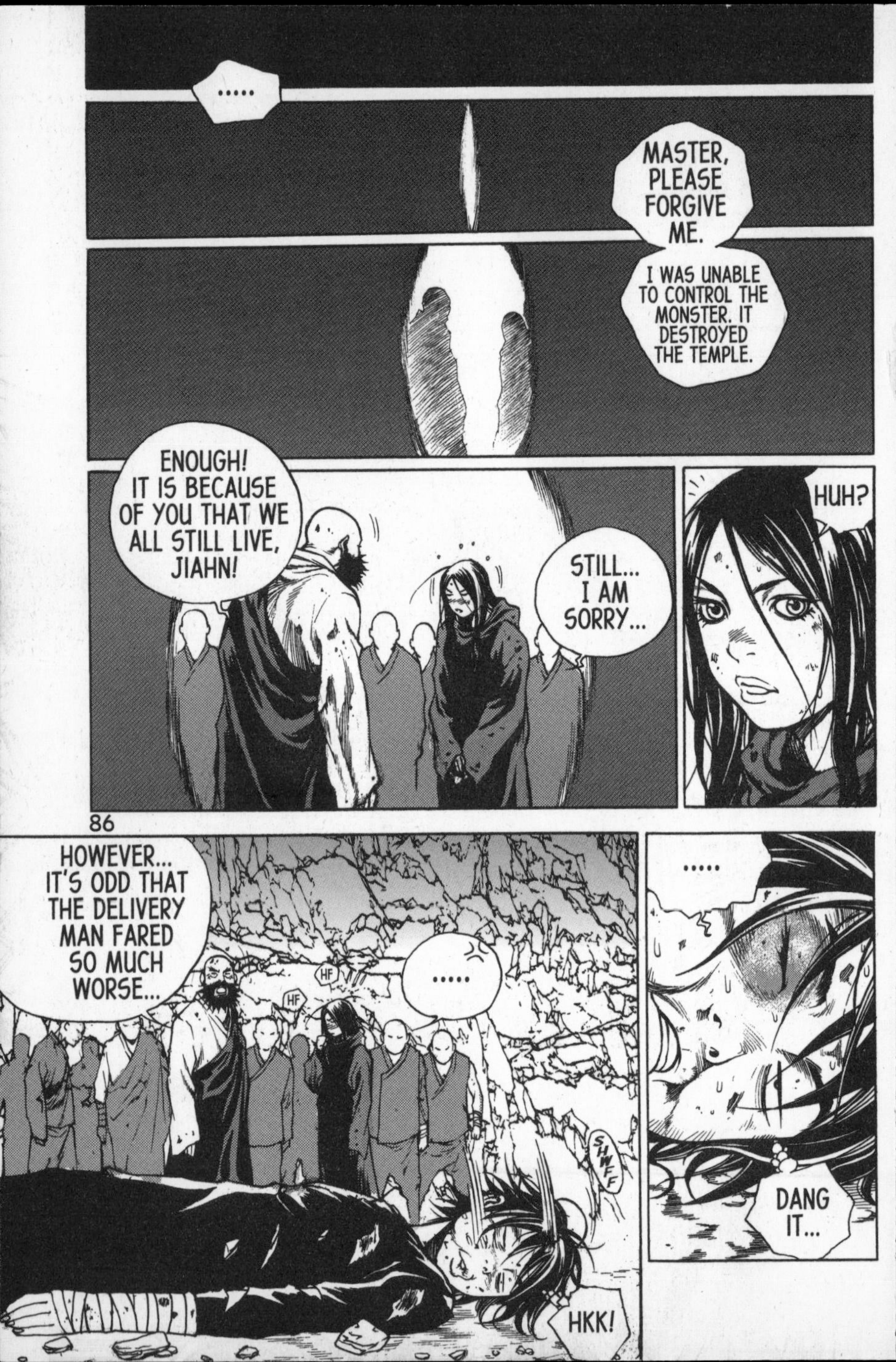
.....
MASTER, PLEASE FORGIVE ME.
I WAS UNABLE TO CONTROL THE MONSTER. IT DESTROYED THE TEMPLE.
ENOUGH! IT IS BECAUSE OF YOU THAT WE ALL STILL LIVE, JIAHN!
STILL... I AM SORRY...
HUH?
HOWEVER... IT'S ODD THAT THE DELIVERY MAN FARED SO MUCH WORSE...
HF
HF
.....
SHWFF
HKK!
.....
DANG IT...

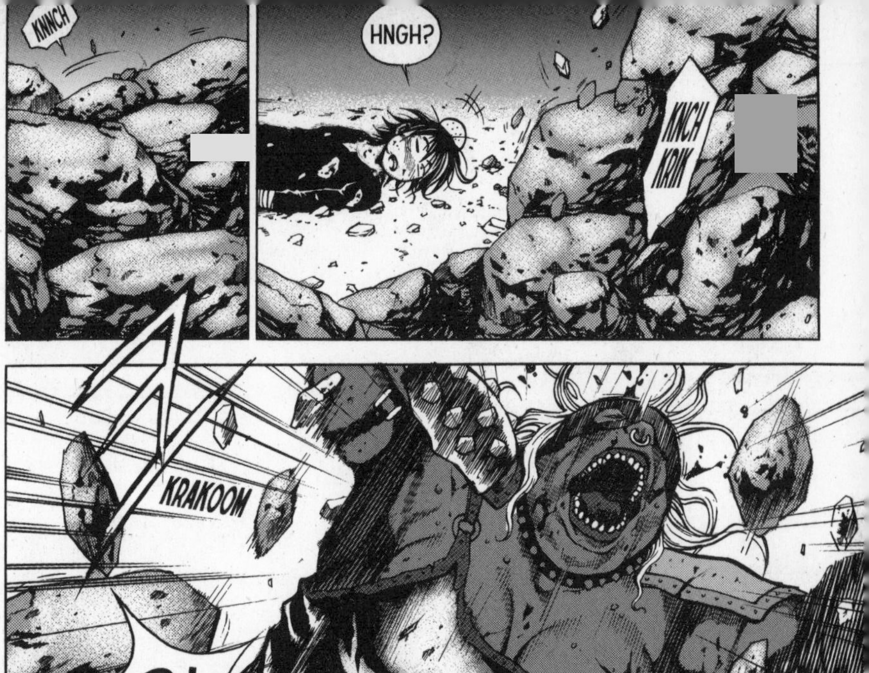
KNNCH
HNGH?
KNCH KRIK
KRAKOOM
?!

87

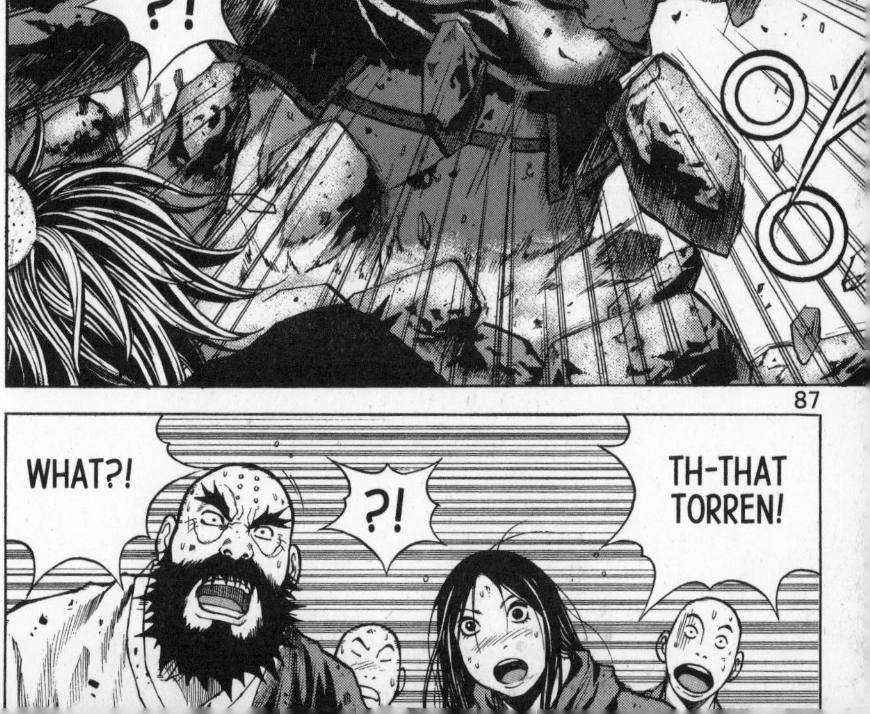
WHAT?!
?!
TH-THAT TORREN!

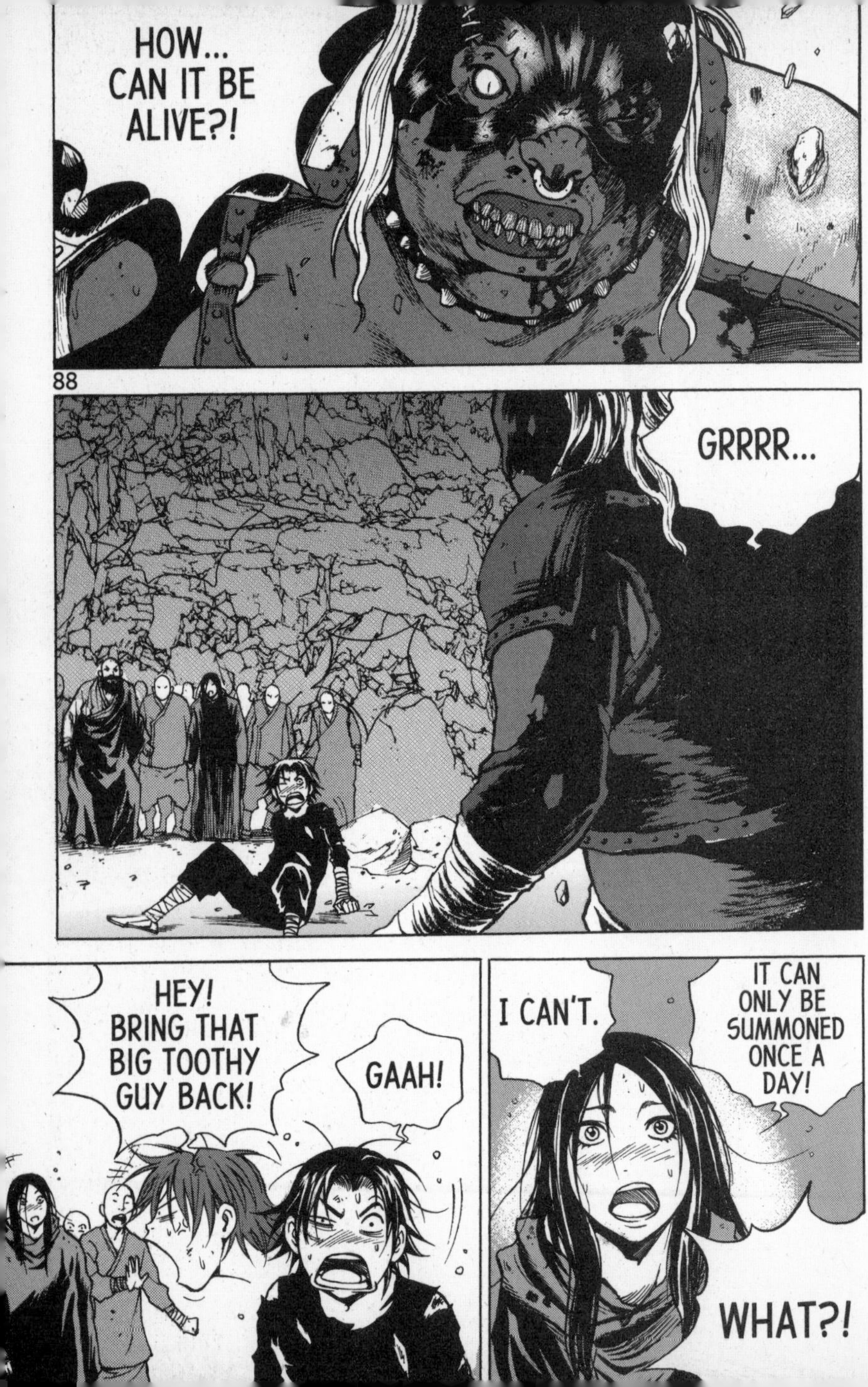
HOW... CAN IT BE ALIVE?!
GRRRR...
HEY! BRING THAT BIG TOOTHY GUY BACK!
GAAH!
I CAN'T.
IT CAN ONLY BE SUMMONED ONCE A DAY!
WHAT?!

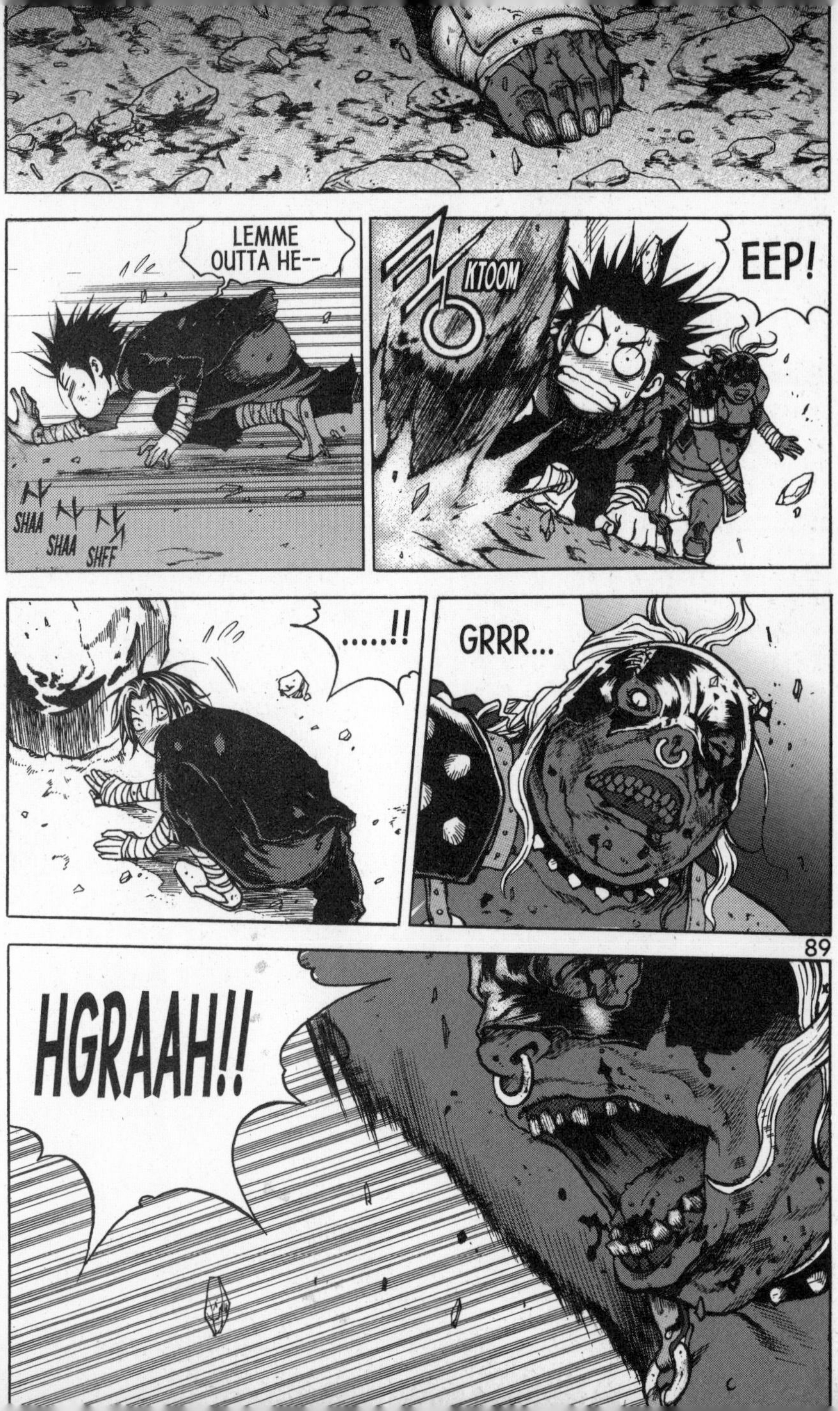
LEMME OUTTA HE--
SHAA
SHAA
SHFF
KTOOM
EEP!
.....!!
GRRR...
HGRAAH!!

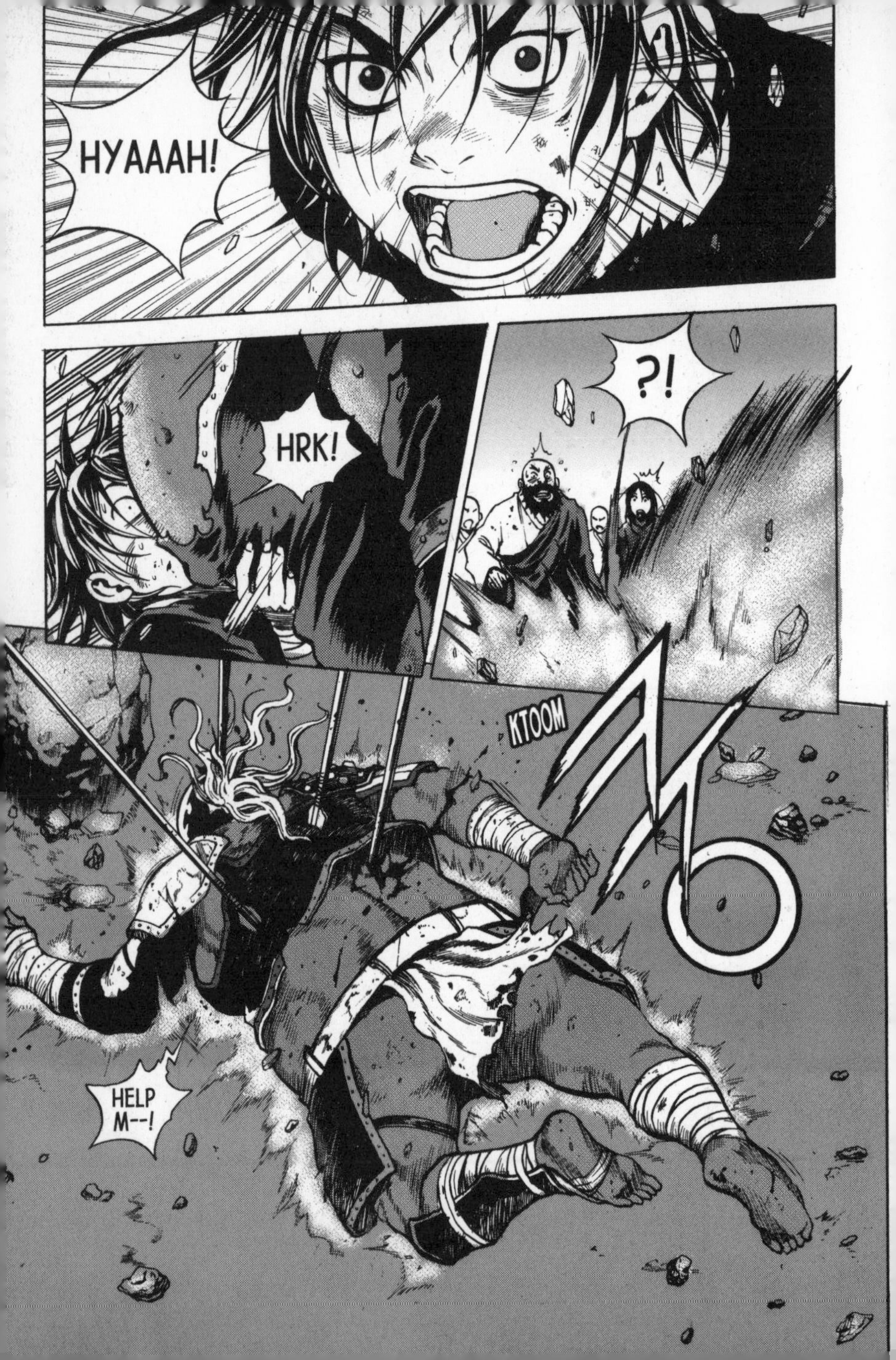
HYAAAH!
HRK!
?!
KTOOM
HELP M--!

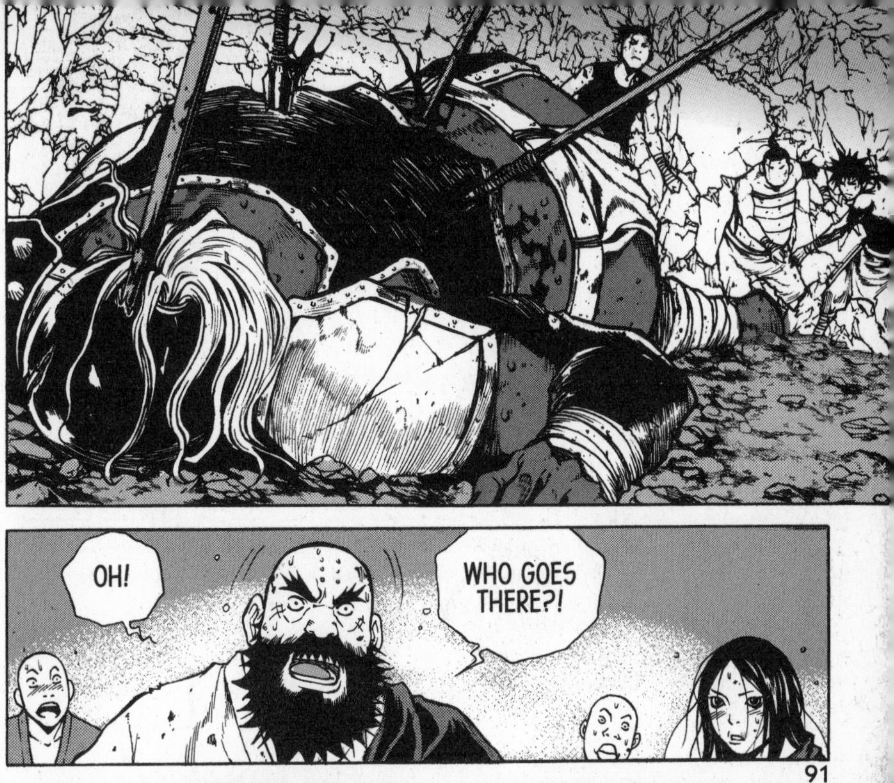

OH!
WHO GOES THERE?!

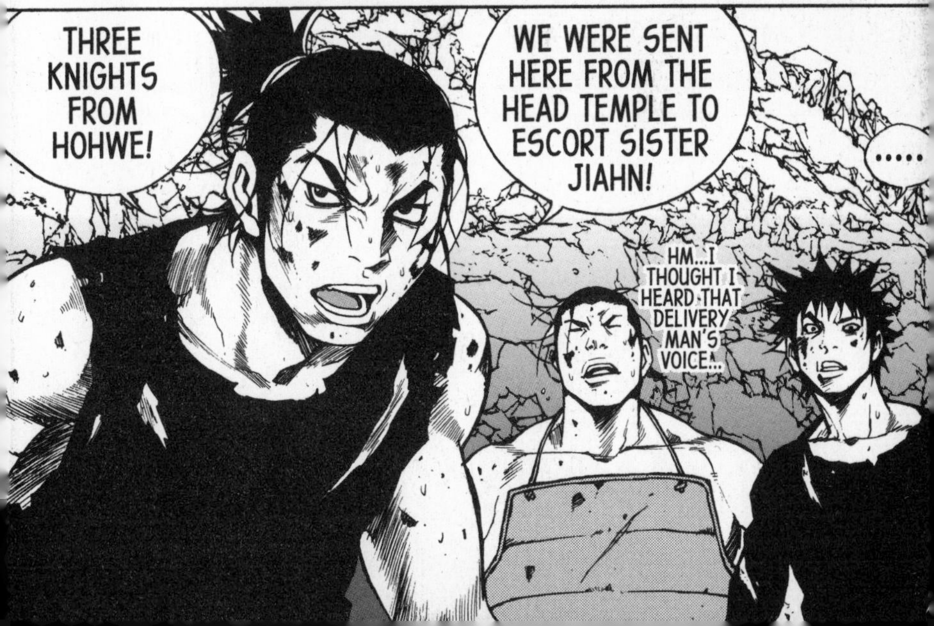

THREE KNIGHTS FROM HOHWE!
WE WERE SENT HERE FROM THE HEAD TEMPLE TO ESCORT SISTER JIAHN!
.....
HM...I THOUGHT I HEARD THAT DELIVERY MAN'S VOICE...

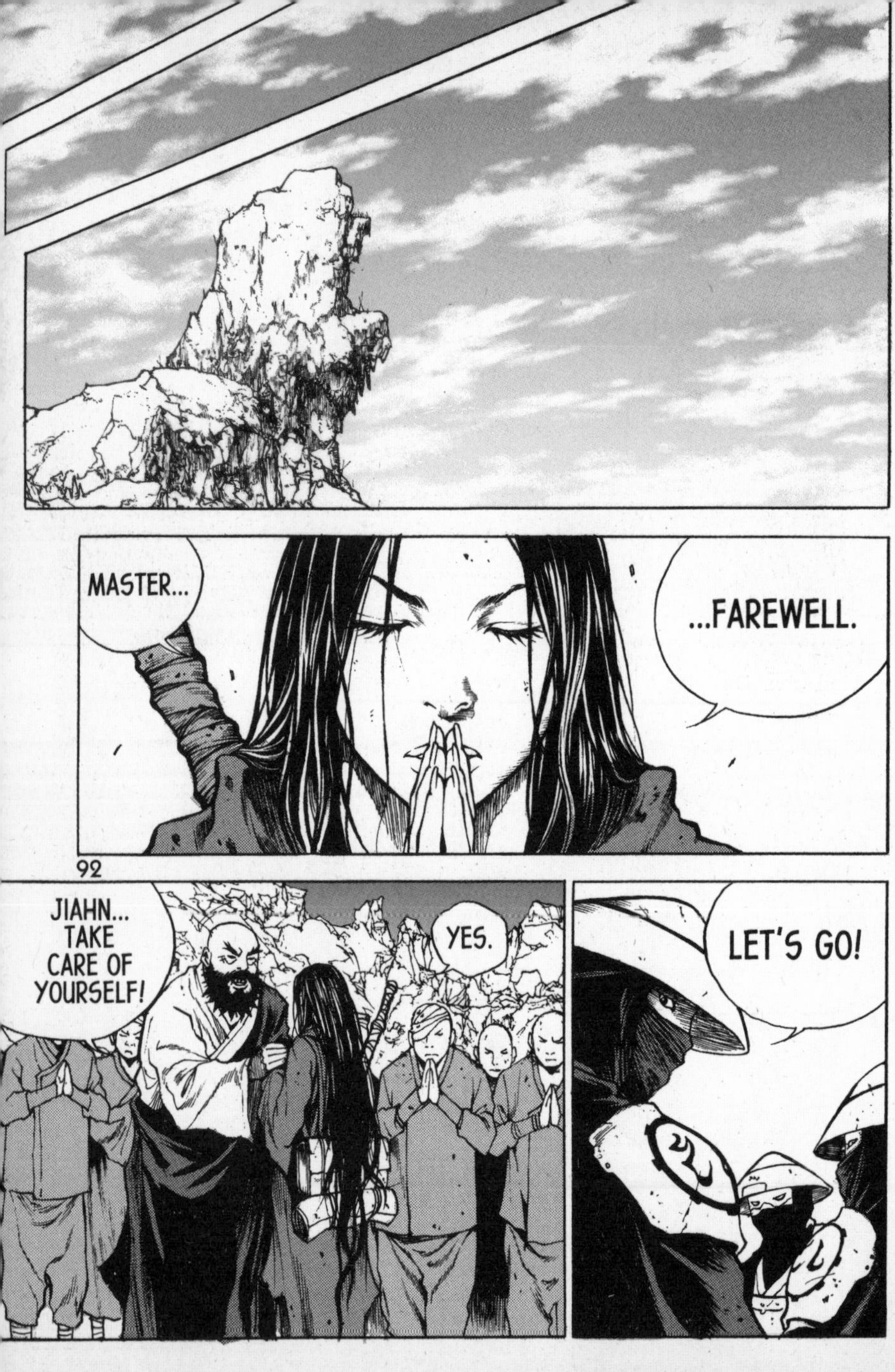
MASTER...
...FAREWELL.
JIAHN... TAKE CARE OF YOURSELF!
YES.
LET'S GO!

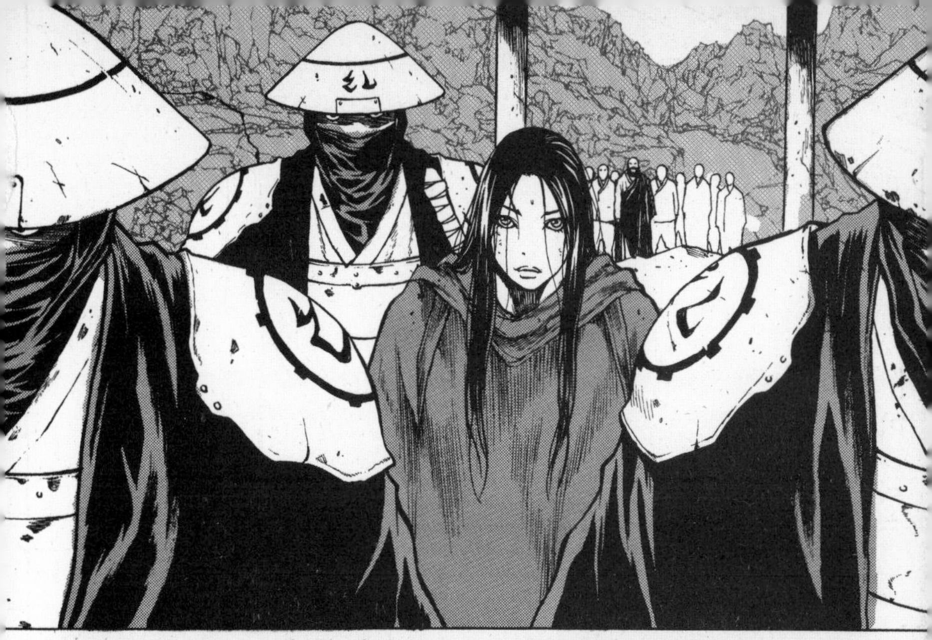

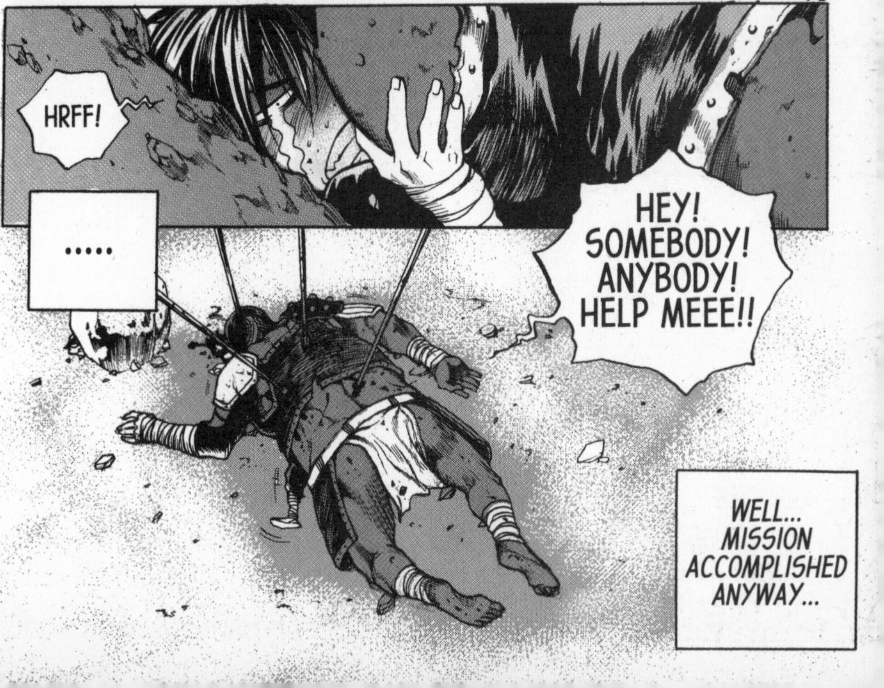
HRFF!
.....
HEY! SOMEBODY! ANYBODY! HELP MEEE!!
WELL... MISSION ACCOMPLISHED ANYWAY...

Ba-nya
the explosive delivery man

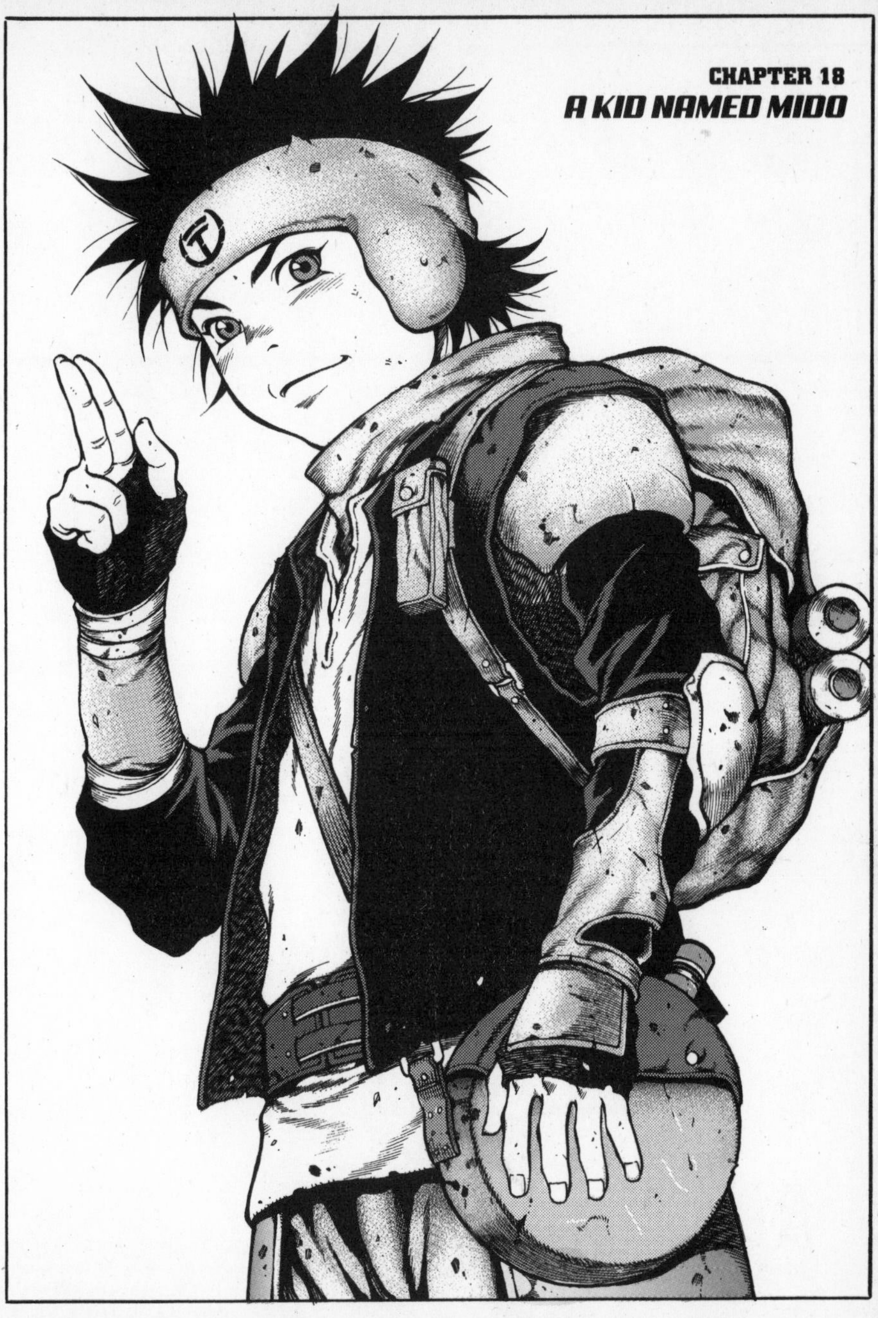

CHAPTER 18
A KID NAMED MIDO

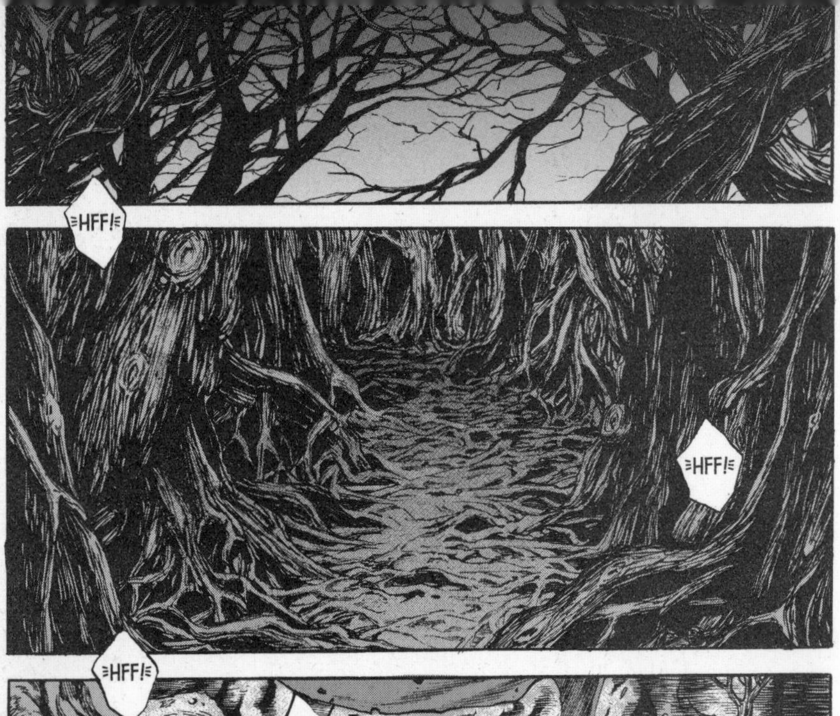
HFF!
HFF!
HFF!

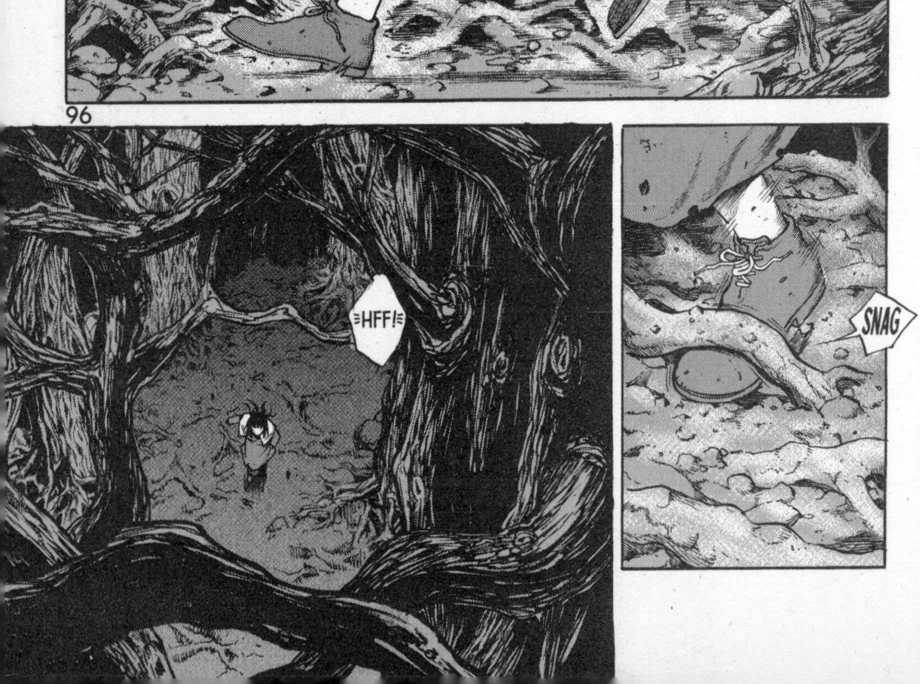
HFF!
SNAG

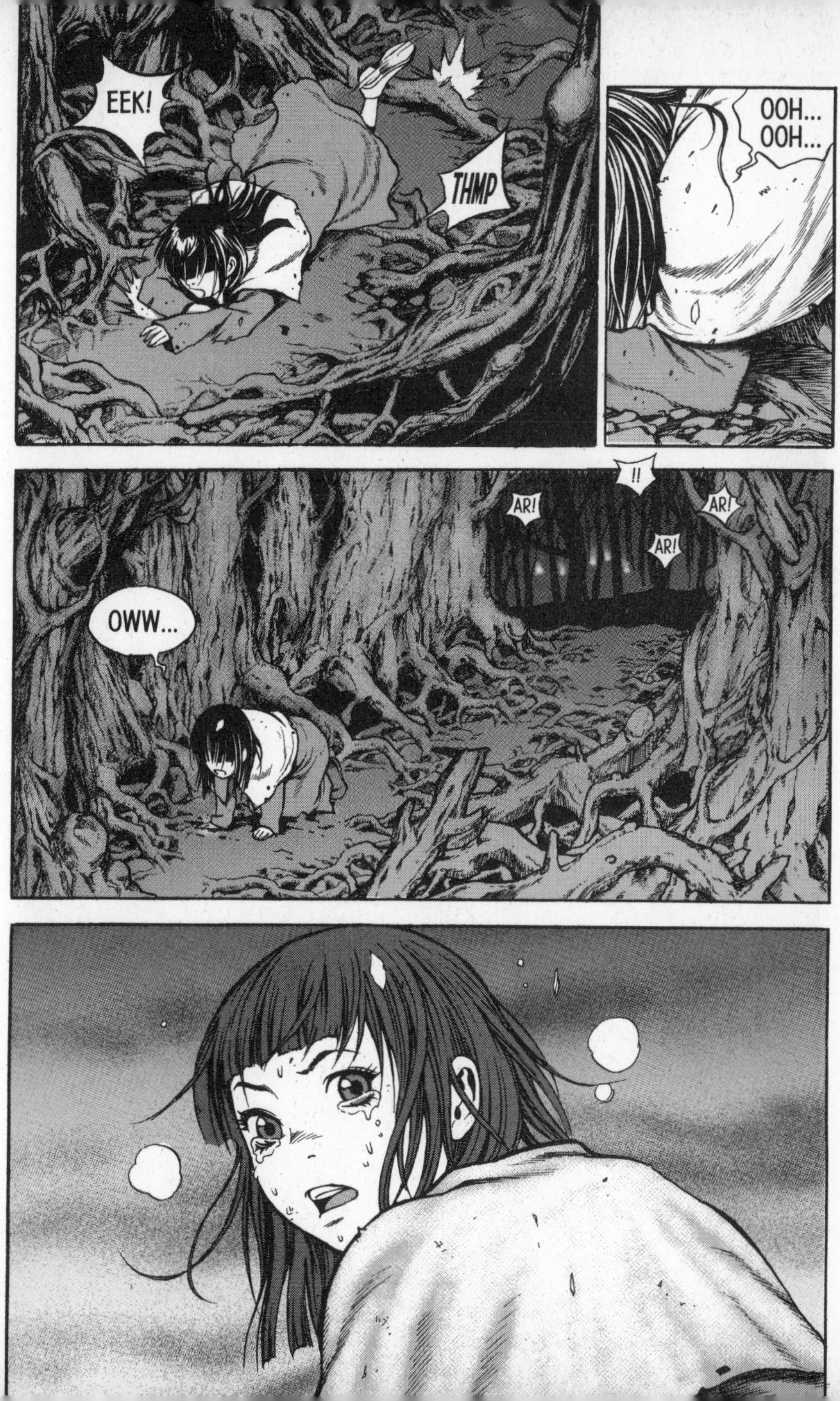
OOH...
OOH...
EEK!
THMP
!!
AR!
AR!
AR!
OWW...

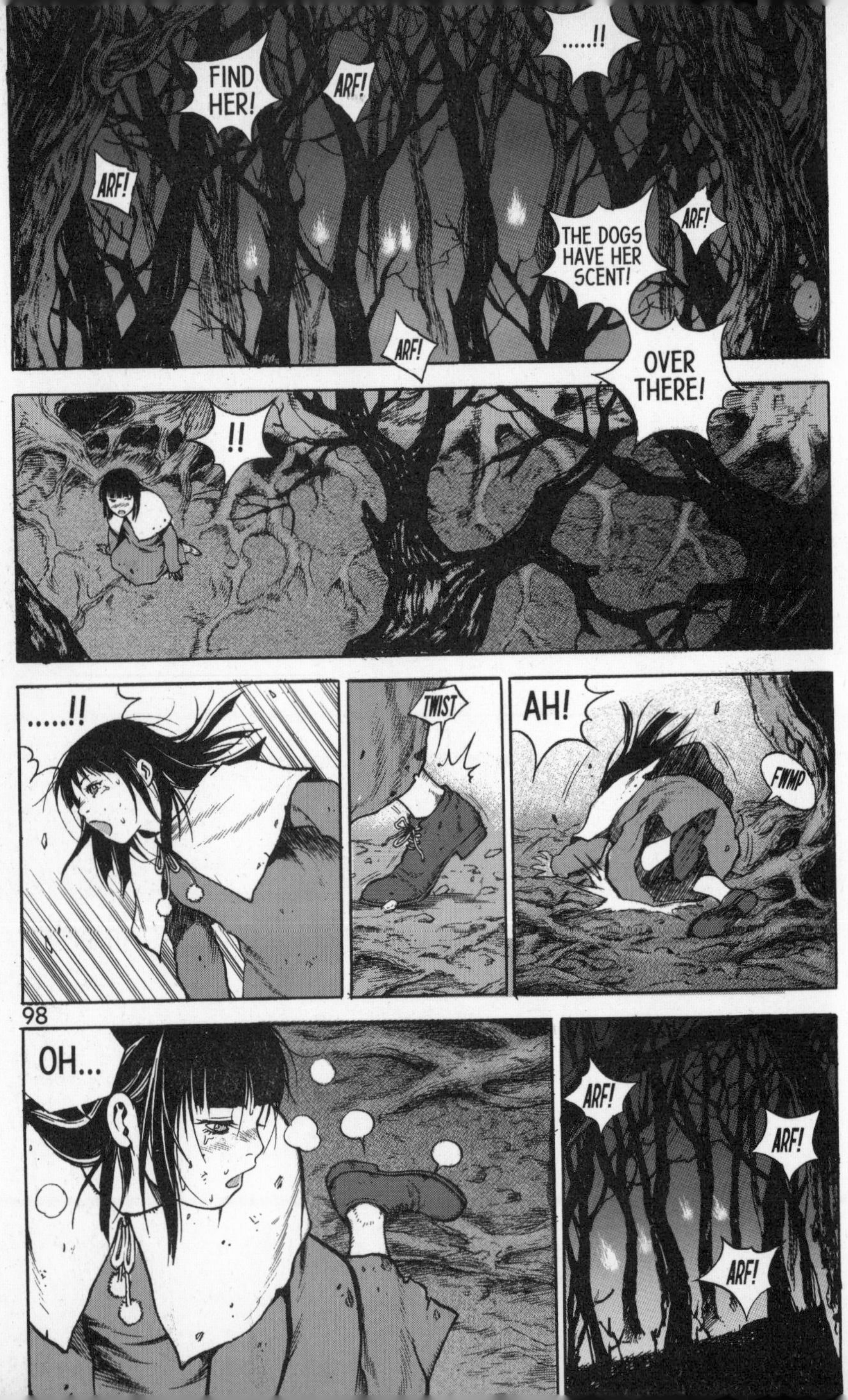
FIND HER!
ARF!
ARF!
.....!!
ARF!
THE DOGS HAVE HER SCENT!
ARF!
OVER THERE!
!!
.....!!
TWIST
AH!
FWMP
OH...
ARF!
ARF!
ARF!

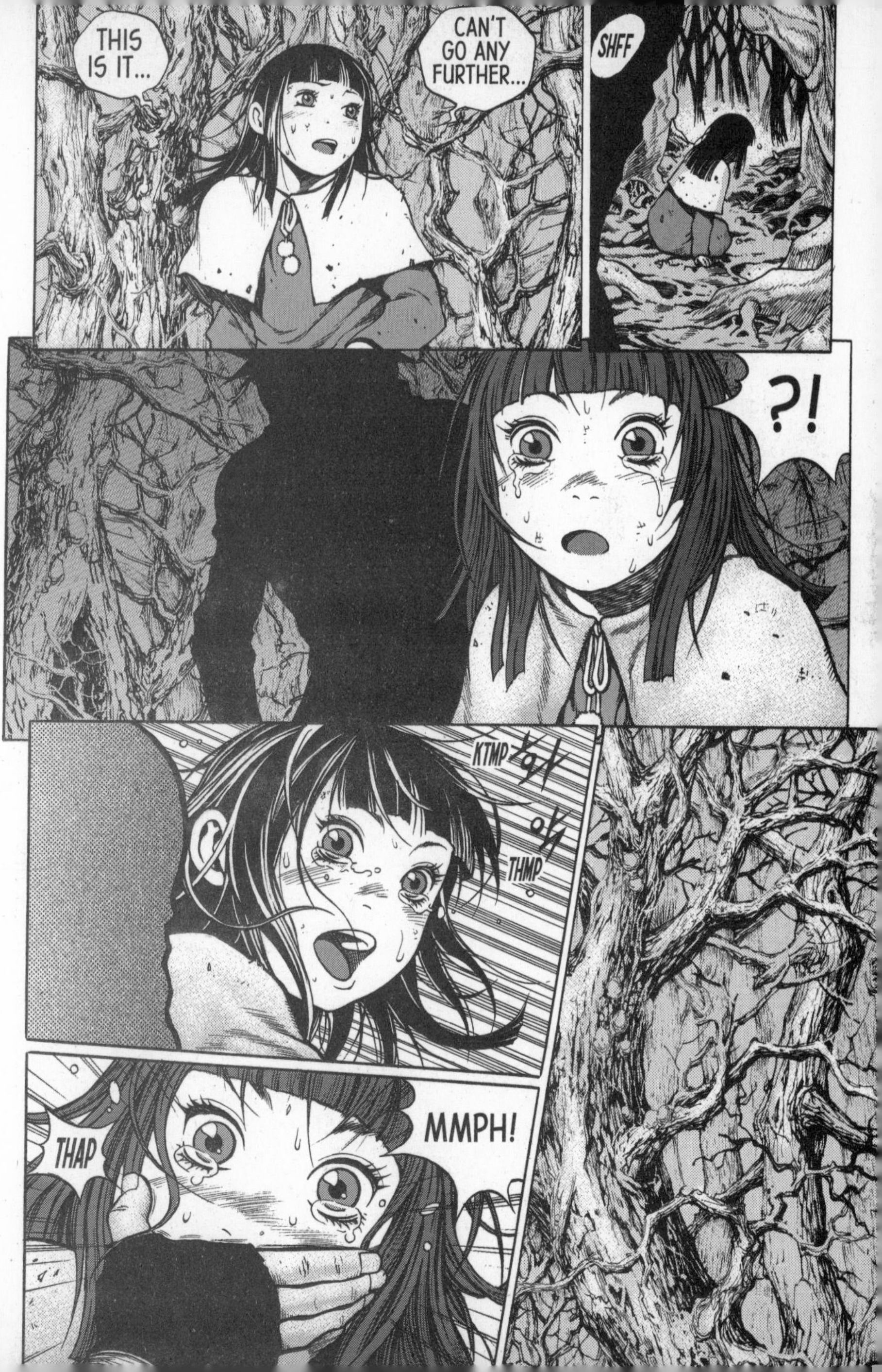
THIS IS IT...
CAN'T GO ANY FURTHER...
SHFF
?!
KTMP
THMP
MMPH!
THAP

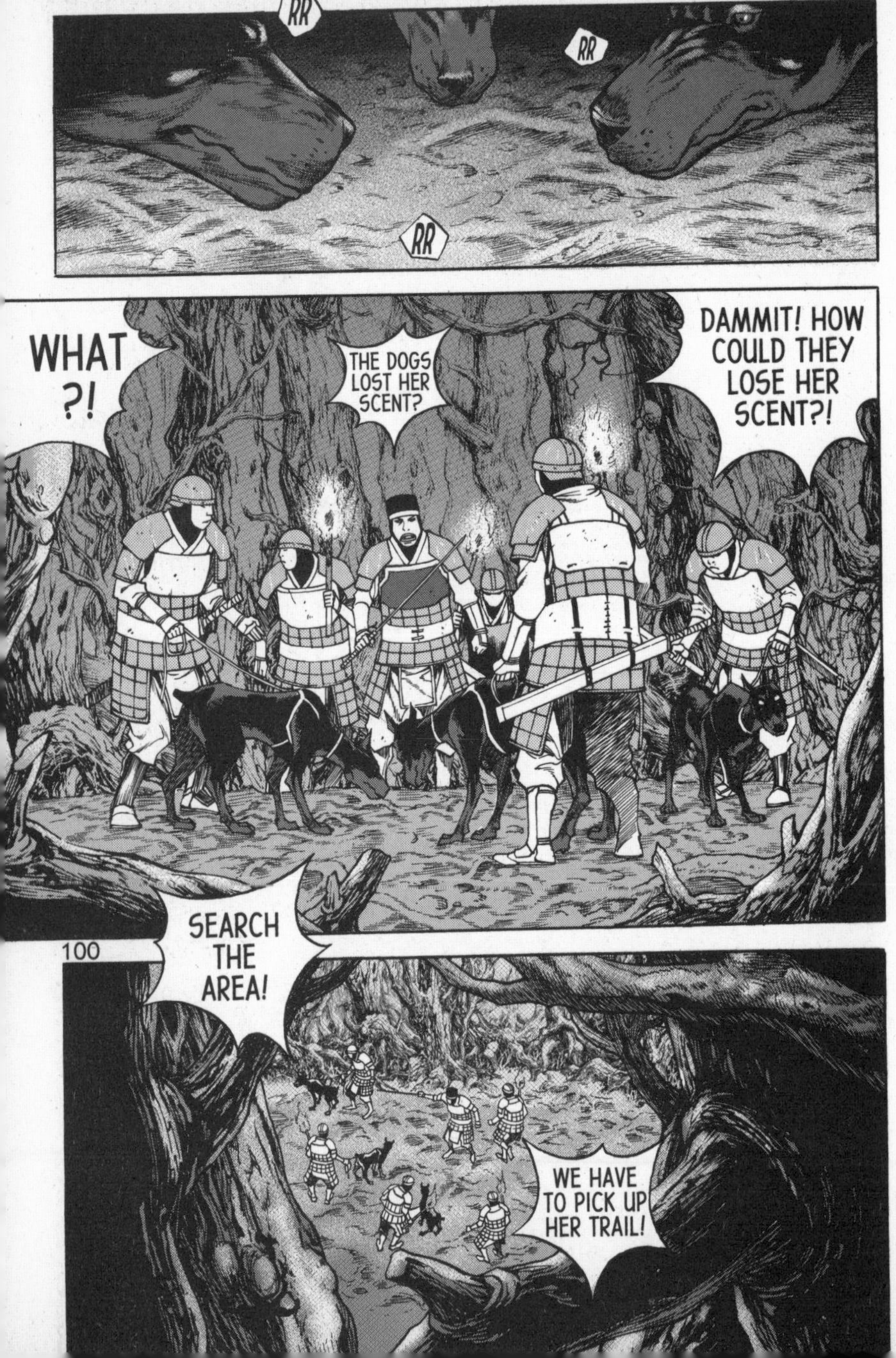
RR
RR
RR
WHAT ?!
THE DOGS LOST HER SCENT?
DAMMIT! HOW COULD THEY LOSE HER SCENT?!
SEARCH THE AREA!
WE HAVE TO PICK UP HER TRAIL!

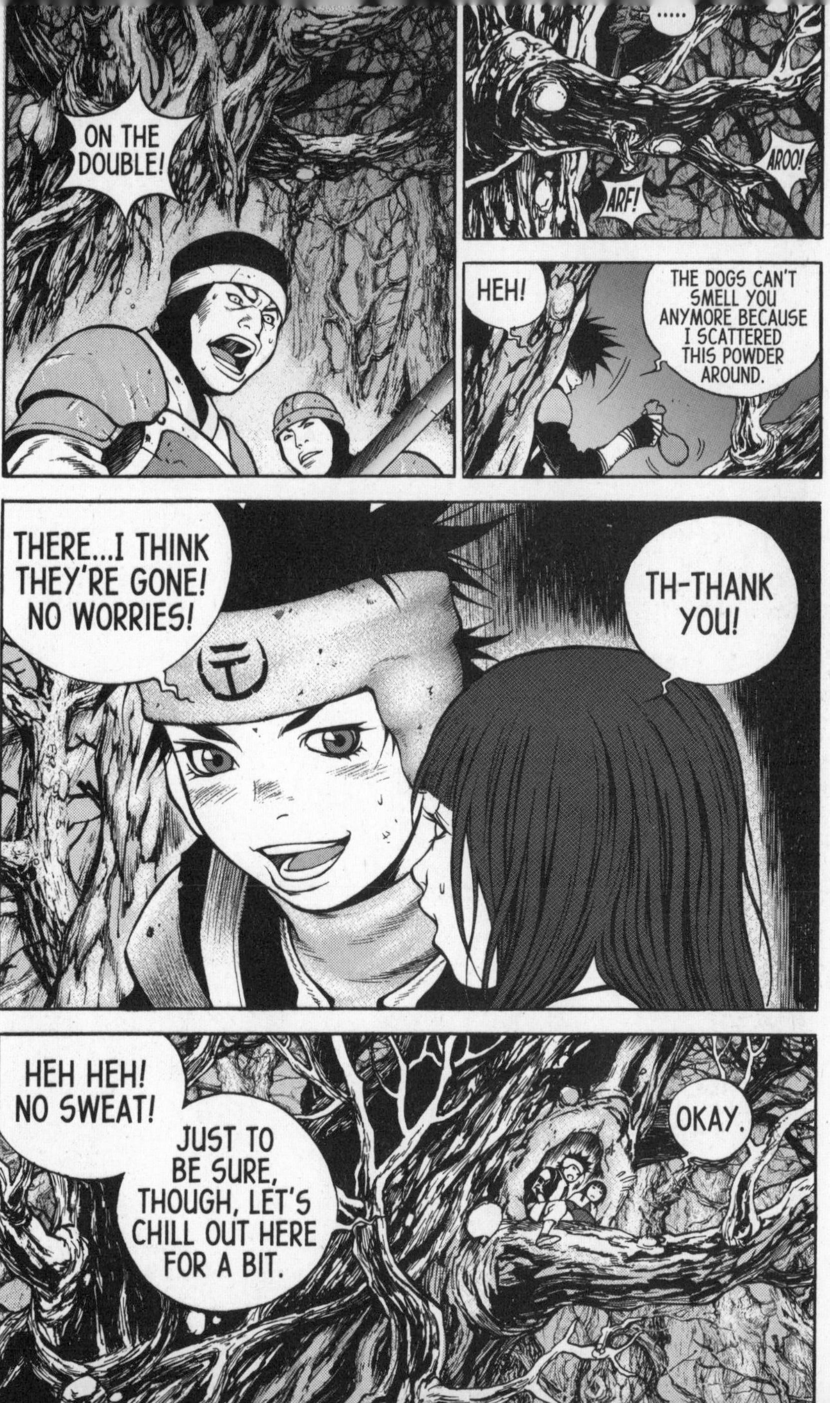

ON THE DOUBLE!
.....
ARF!
AROO!
HEH!
THE DOGS CAN'T SMELL YOU ANYMORE BECAUSE I SCATTERED THIS POWDER AROUND.
THERE...I THINK THEY'RE GONE! NO WORRIES!
TH-THANK YOU!
HEH HEH! NO SWEAT!
JUST TO BE SURE, THOUGH, LET'S CHILL OUT HERE FOR A BIT.
OKAY.

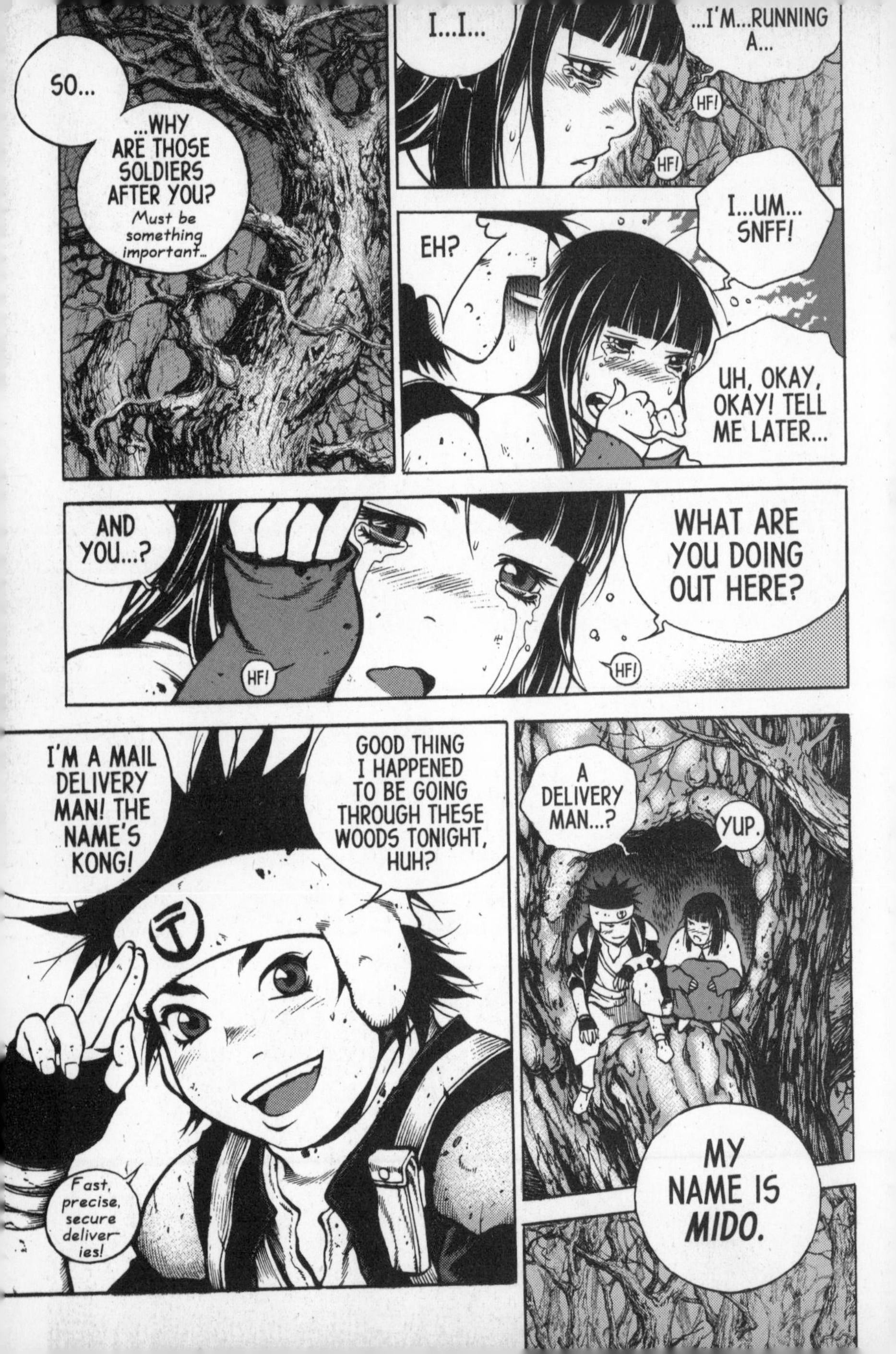
SO...
...WHY ARE THOSE SOLDIERS AFTER YOU?
Must be something important...
I...I...
...I'M...RUNNING A...
HF!
HF!
EH?
I...UM... SNFF!
UH, OKAY, OKAY! TELL ME LATER...
AND YOU...?
WHAT ARE YOU DOING OUT HERE?
HF!
HF!
I'M A MAIL DELIVERY MAN! THE NAME'S KONG!
GOOD THING I HAPPENED TO BE GOING THROUGH THESE WOODS TONIGHT, HUH?
Fast, precise, secure deliver-ies!
A DELIVERY MAN...?
YUP.
MY NAME IS MIDO.

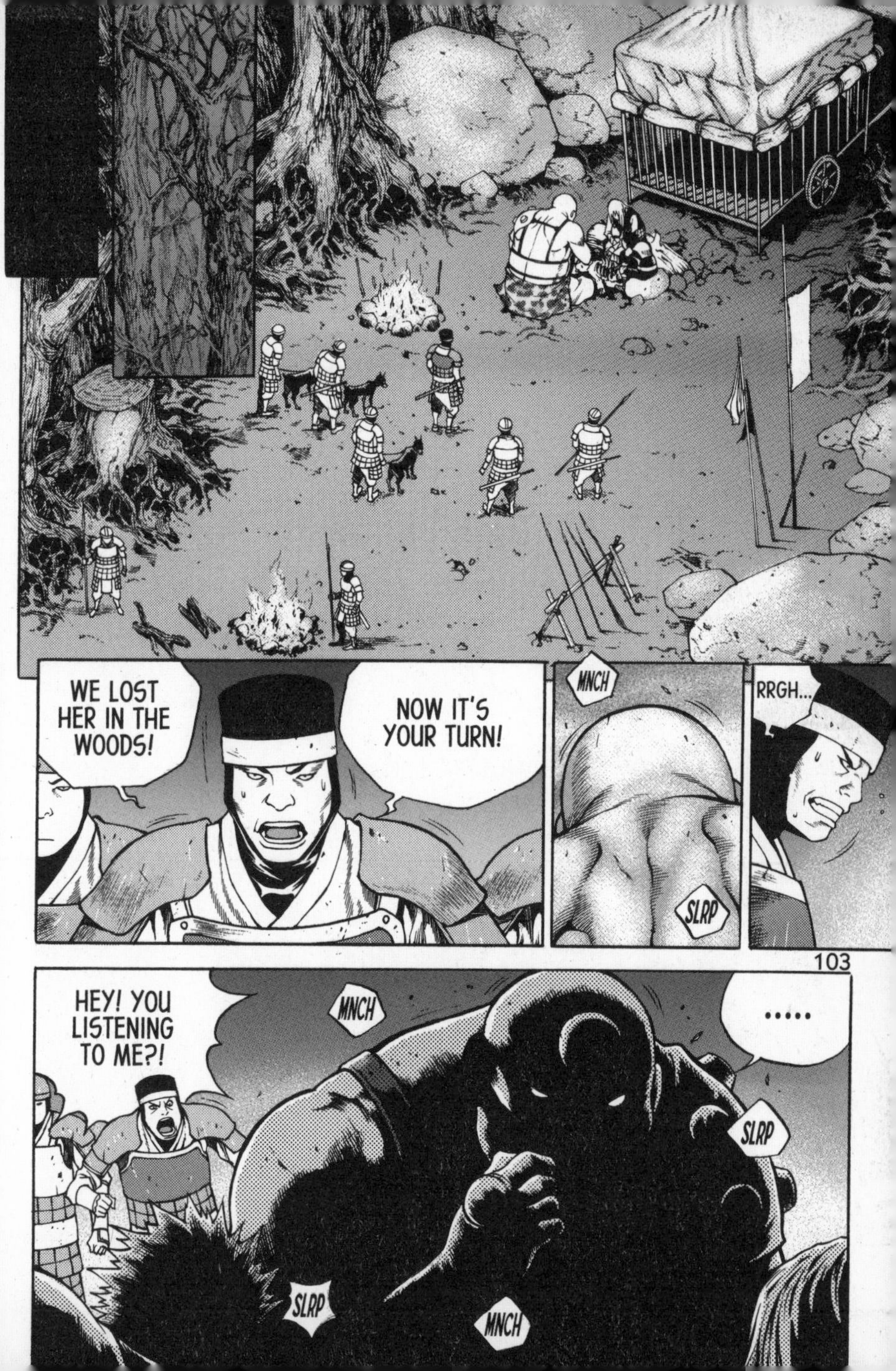
WE LOST HER IN THE WOODS!
NOW IT'S YOUR TURN!
MNCH
SLRP
RRGH...
HEY! YOU LISTENING TO ME?!
MNCH
.....
SLRP
SLRP
MNCH

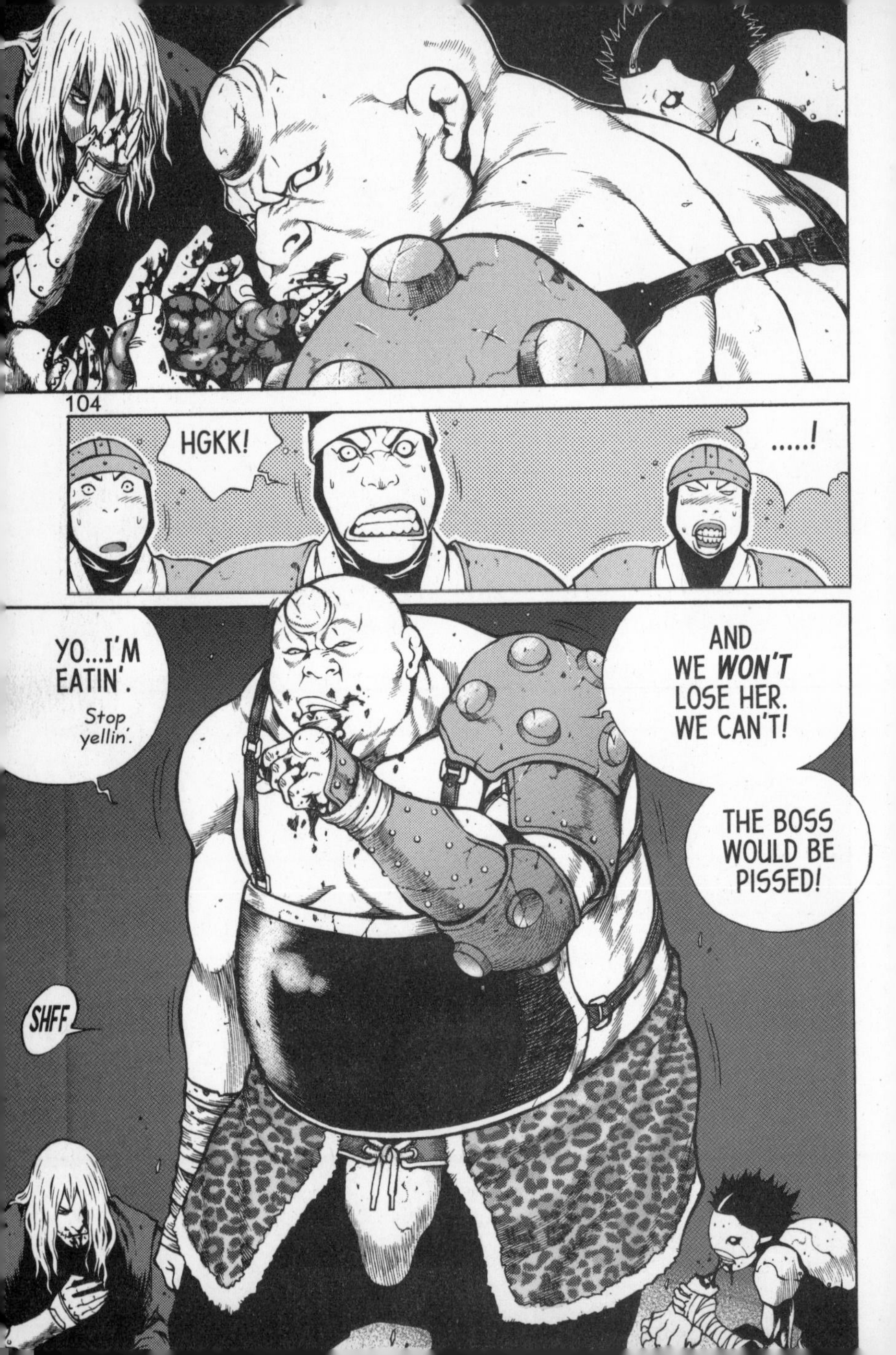
HGKK!
.....!
YO...I'M EATIN'.
Stop yellin'.
AND WE *WON'T* LOSE HER. WE CAN'T!
THE BOSS WOULD BE PISSED!
SHFF

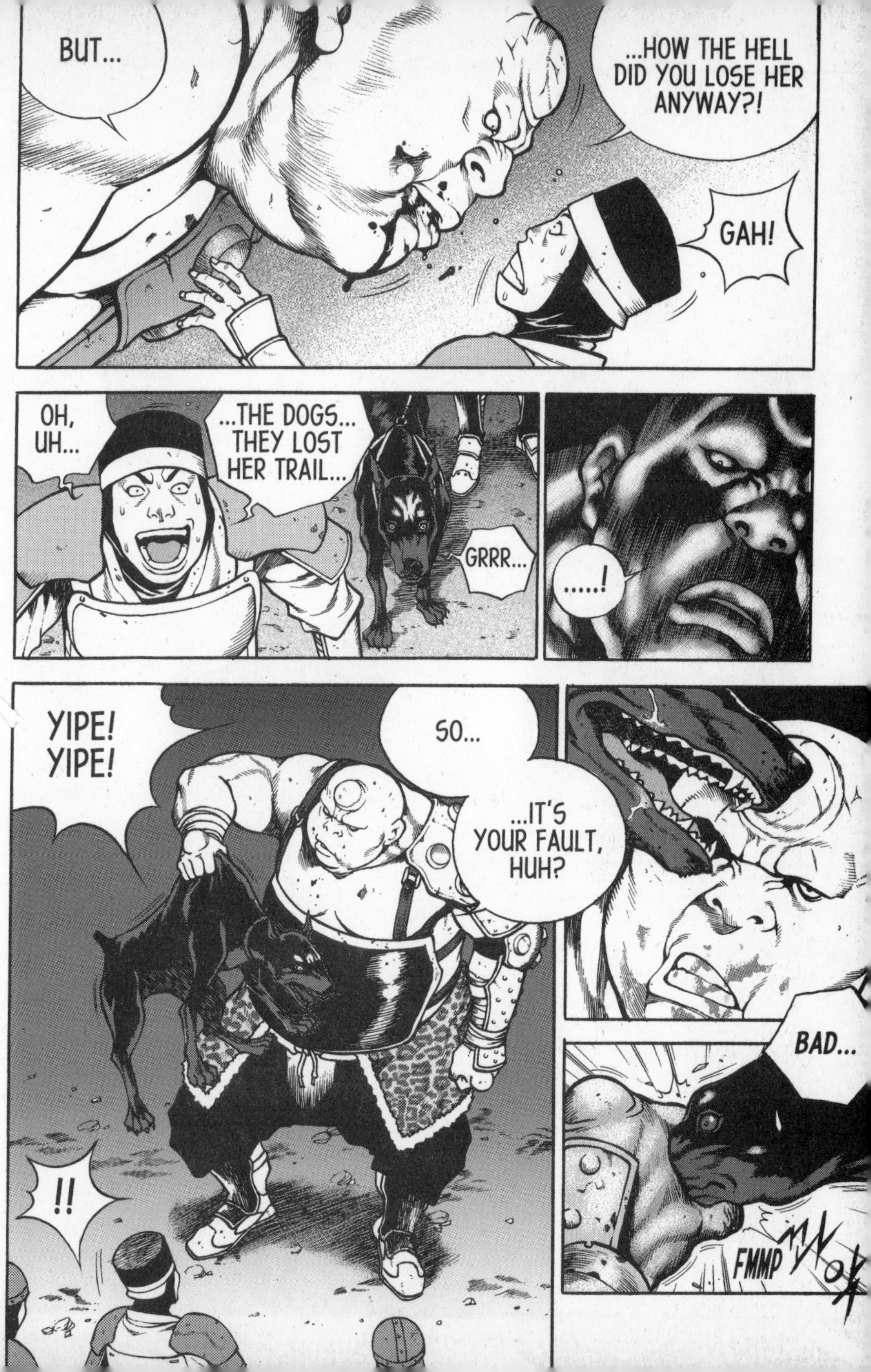
BUT...
...HOW THE HELL DID YOU LOSE HER ANYWAY?!
GAH!
OH, UH...
...THE DOGS... THEY LOST HER TRAIL...
GRRR...
.....!
YIPE! YIPE!
SO...
...IT'S YOUR FAULT, HUH?
!!
BAD...
FMMP

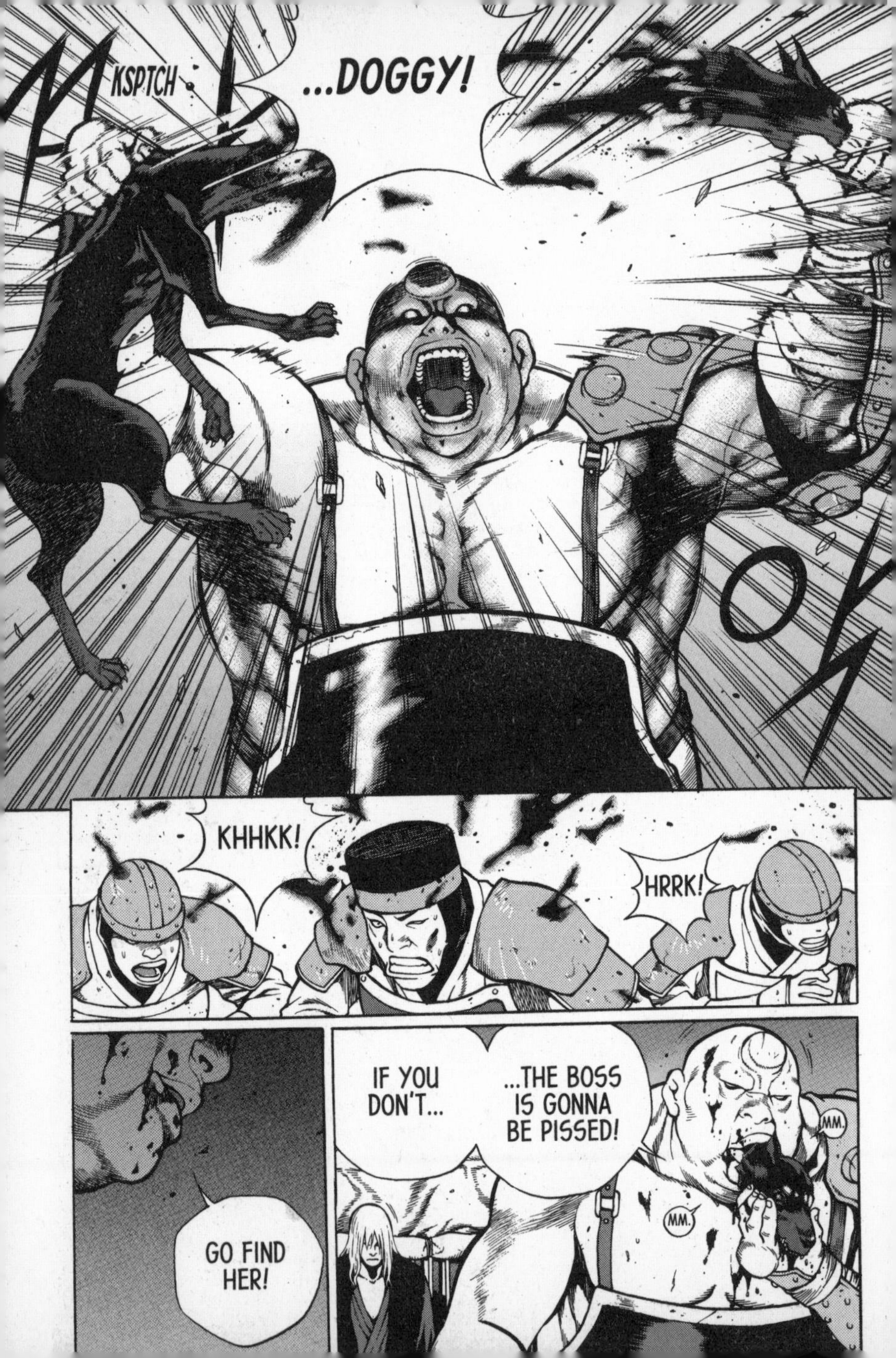
KSPTCH
...DOGGY!
KHHKK!
HRRK!
IF YOU DON'T...
...THE BOSS IS GONNA BE PISSED!
MM.
MM.
GO FIND HER!

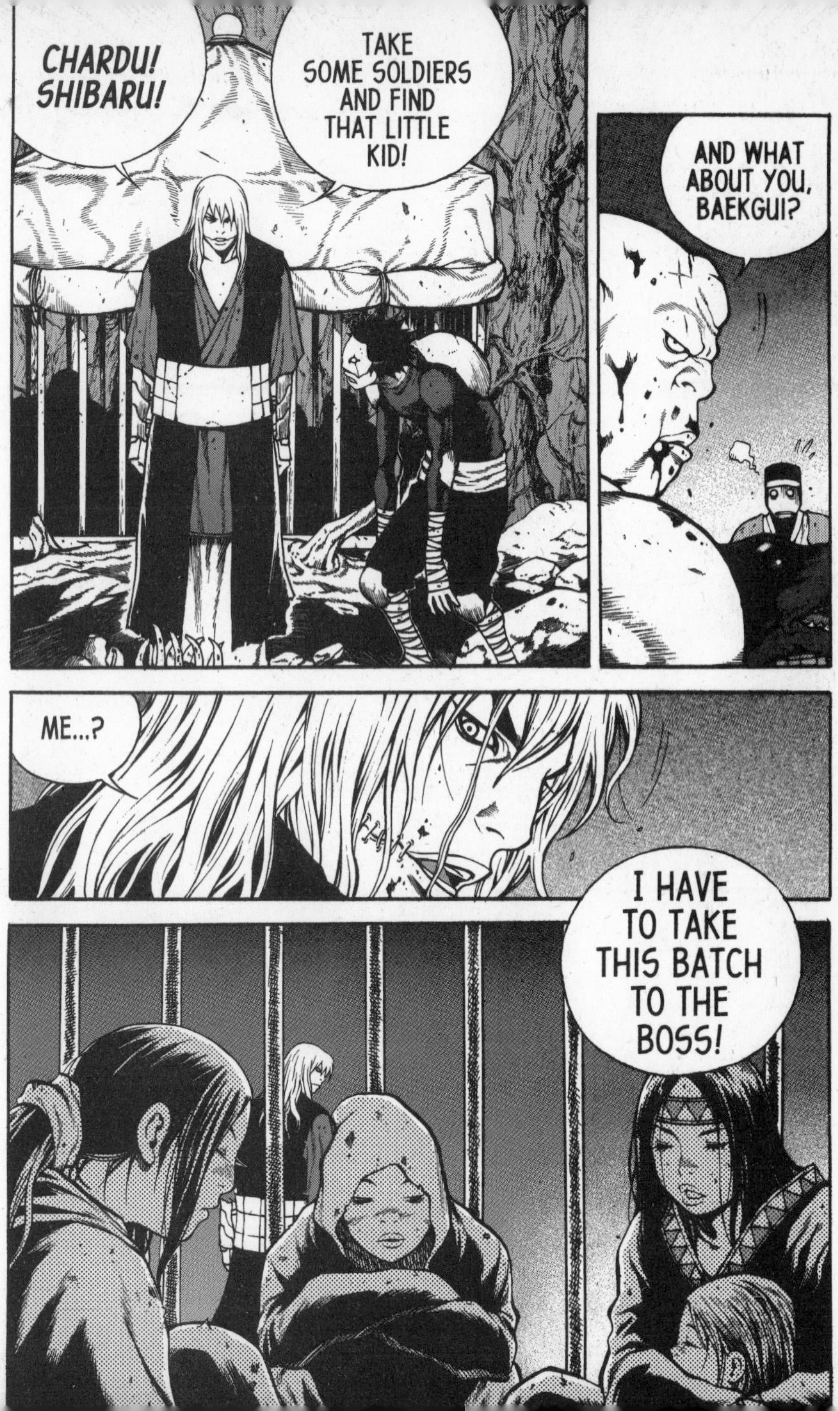
CHARDU! SHIBARU!
TAKE SOME SOLDIERS AND FIND THAT LITTLE KID!
AND WHAT ABOUT YOU, BAEKGUI?
ME...?
I HAVE TO TAKE THIS BATCH TO THE BOSS!

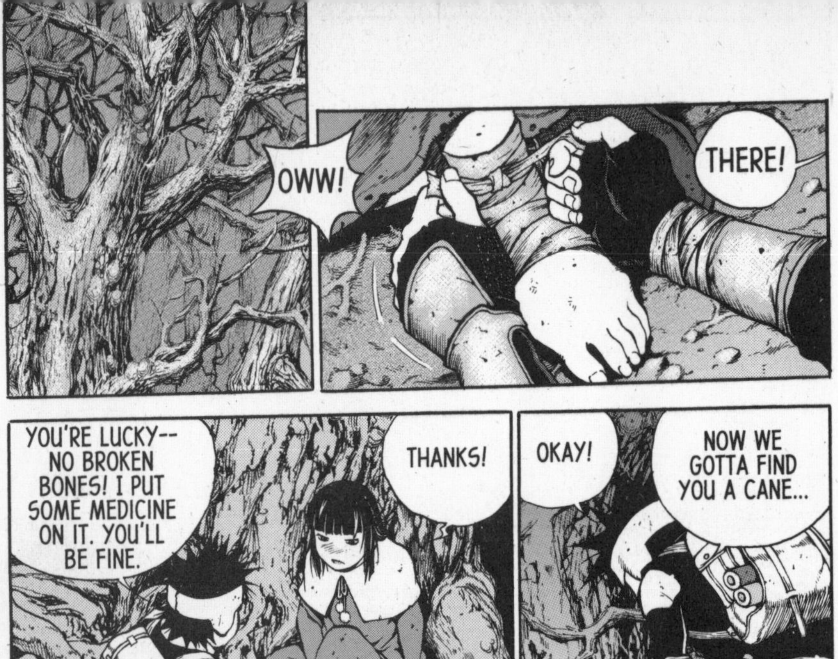
OWW!
THERE!
YOU'RE LUCKY-- NO BROKEN BONES! I PUT SOME MEDICINE ON IT. YOU'LL BE FINE.
THANKS!
OKAY!
NOW WE GOTTA FIND YOU A CANE...
NOPE, TOO THICK...
NOPE, TOO THIN...
.....

108

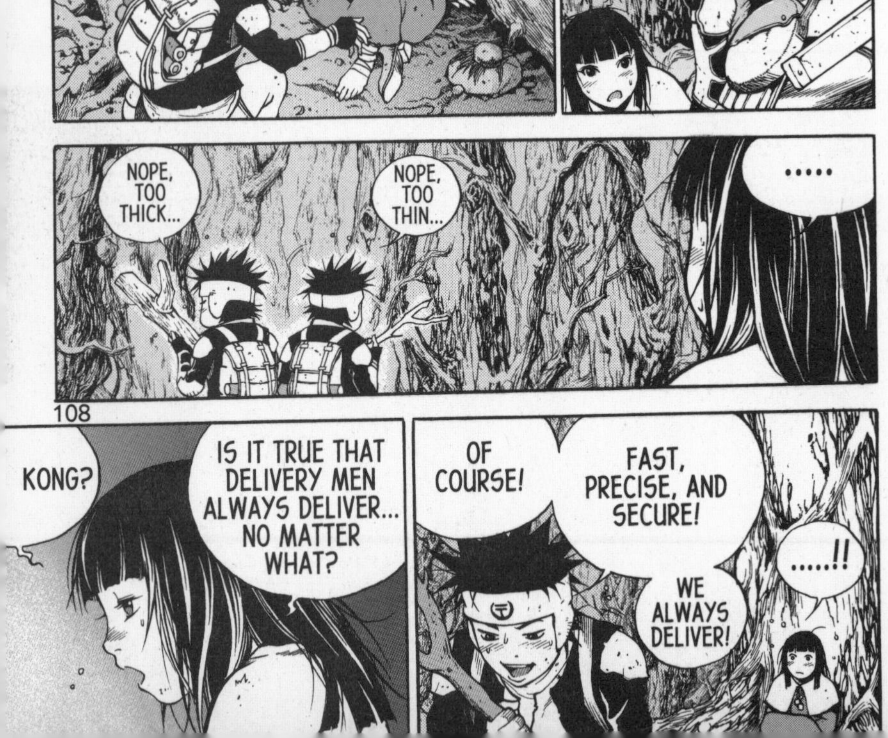
KONG?
IS IT TRUE THAT DELIVERY MEN ALWAYS DELIVER... NO MATTER WHAT?
OF COURSE!
FAST, PRECISE, AND SECURE!
WE ALWAYS DELIVER!
.....!!

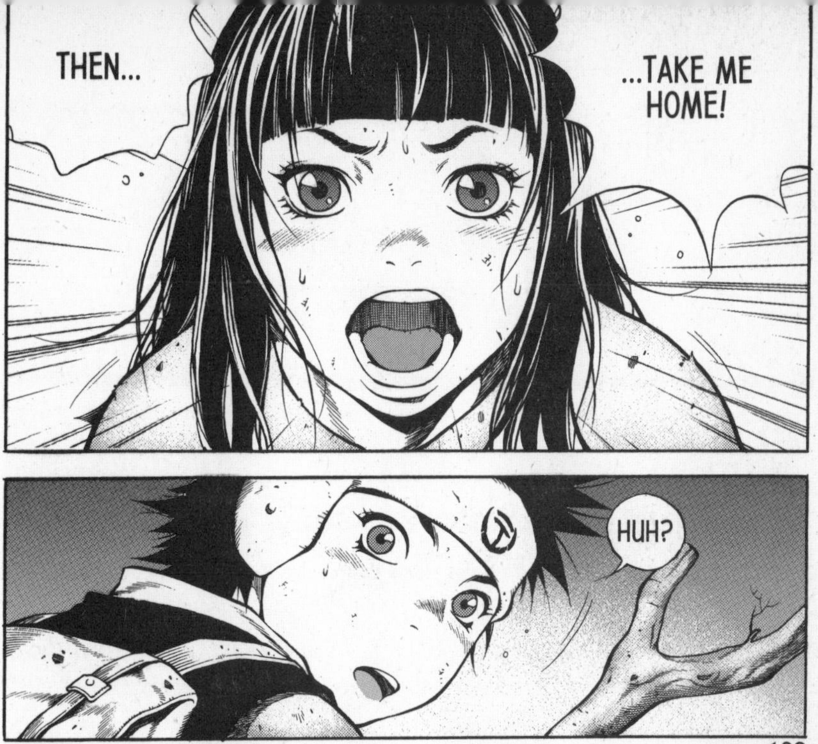
THEN...
...TAKE ME HOME!
HUH?

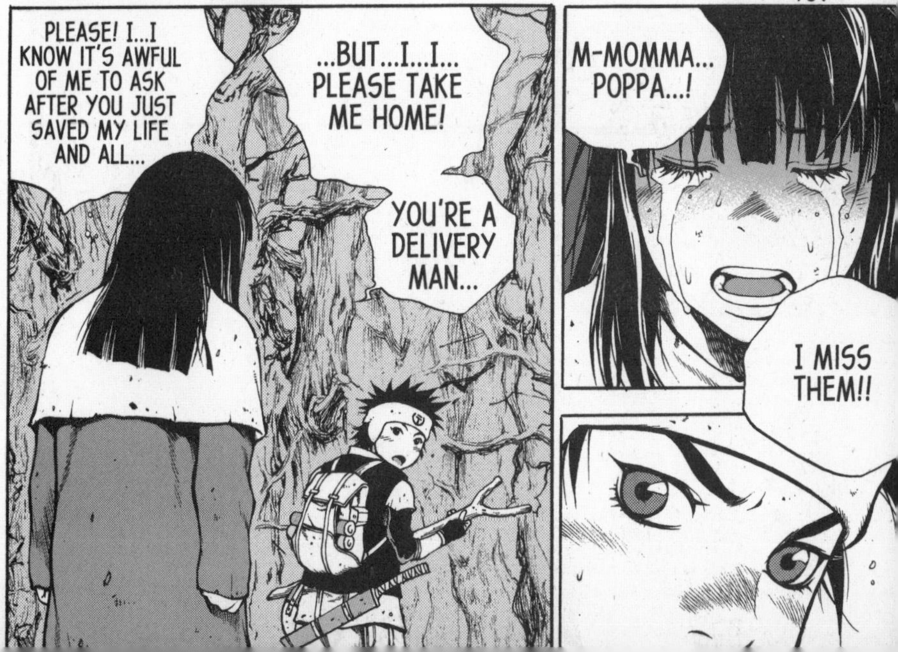
PLEASE! I...I KNOW IT'S AWFUL OF ME TO ASK AFTER YOU JUST SAVED MY LIFE AND ALL...
YOU'RE A DELIVERY MAN...
...BUT...I...I... PLEASE TAKE ME HOME!
M-MOMMA... POPPA...!
I MISS THEM!!

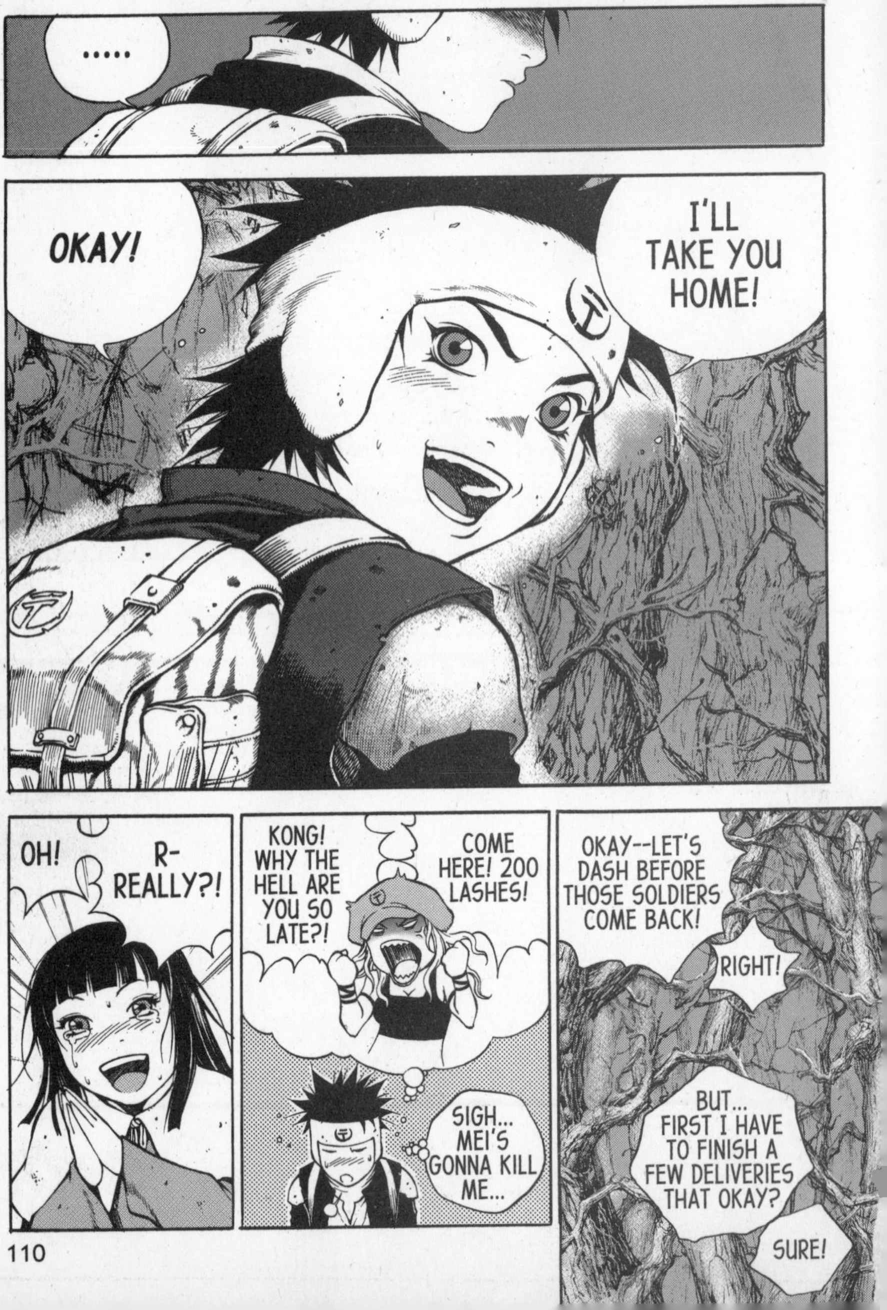
.....
OKAY!
I'LL TAKE YOU HOME!
OH!
R-REALLY?!
KONG! WHY THE HELL ARE YOU SO LATE?!
COME HERE! 200 LASHES!
SIGH... MEI'S GONNA KILL ME...
OKAY--LET'S DASH BEFORE THOSE SOLDIERS COME BACK!
RIGHT!
BUT... FIRST I HAVE TO FINISH A FEW DELIVERIES THAT OKAY?
SURE!

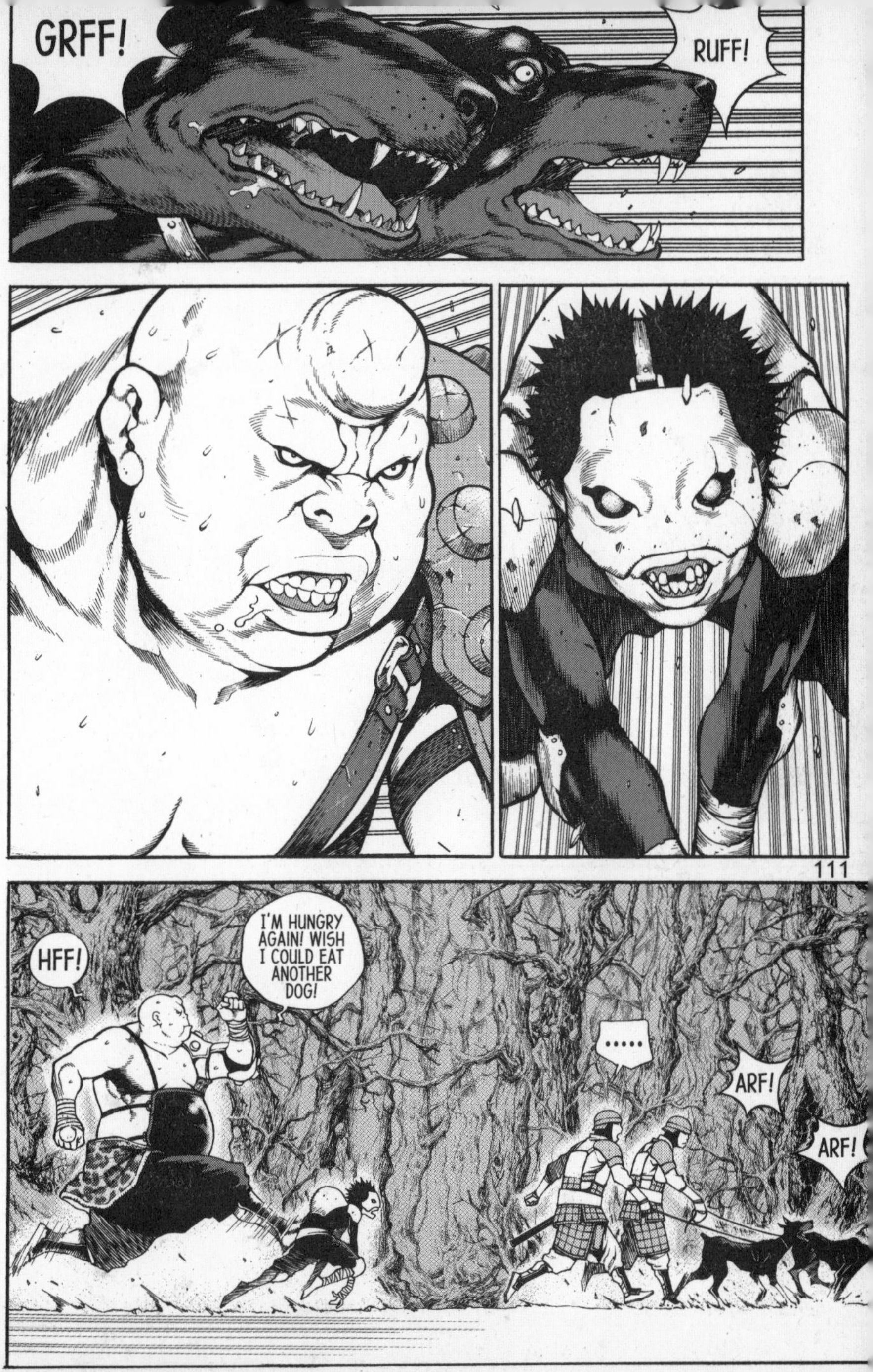
GRFF!
RUFF!
HFF!
I'M HUNGRY AGAIN! WISH I COULD EAT ANOTHER DOG!
......
ARF!
ARF!

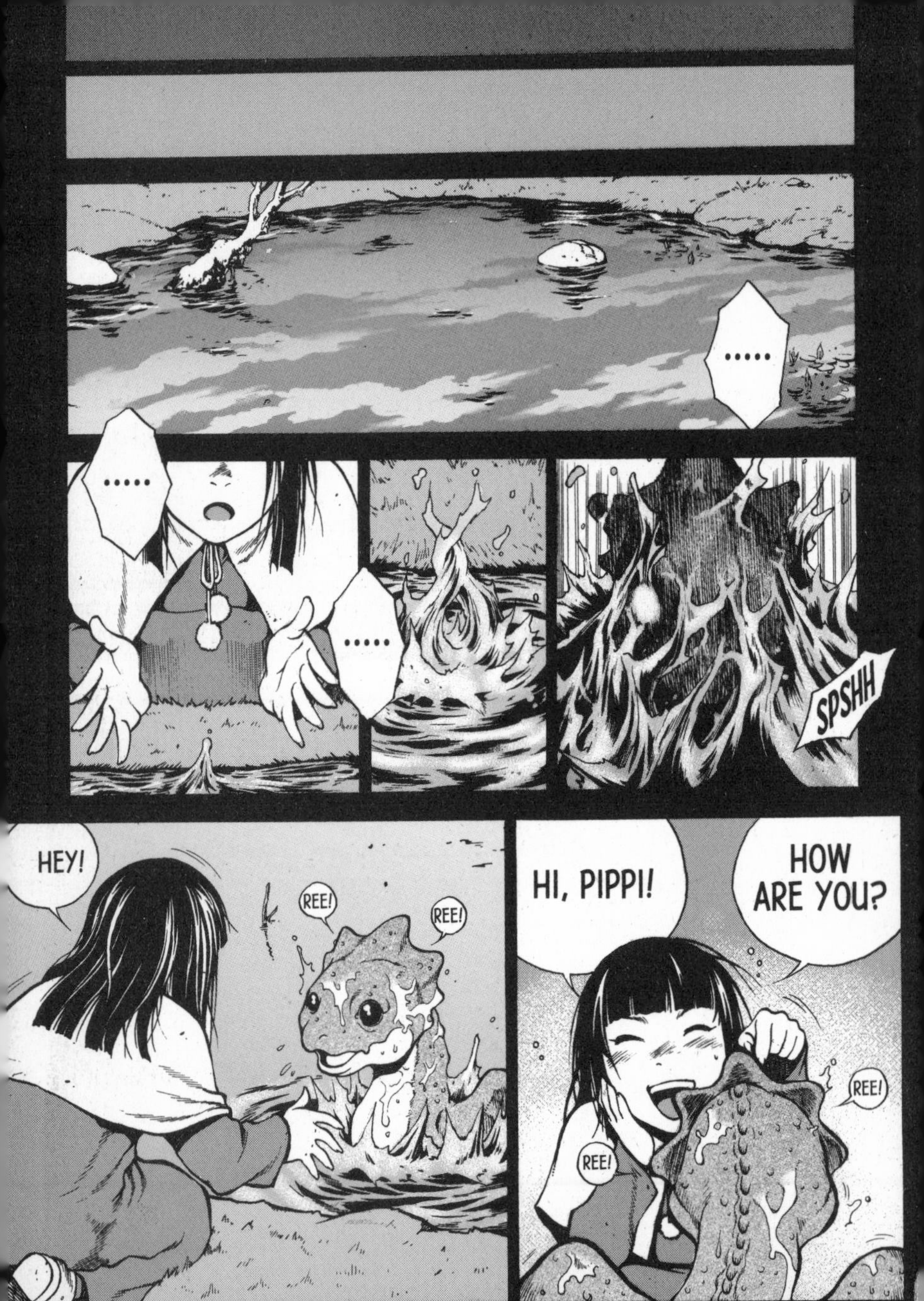
.....
.....
.....
SPSHH
HEY!
REE!
REE!
HI, PIPPI!
HOW ARE YOU?
REE!
REE!

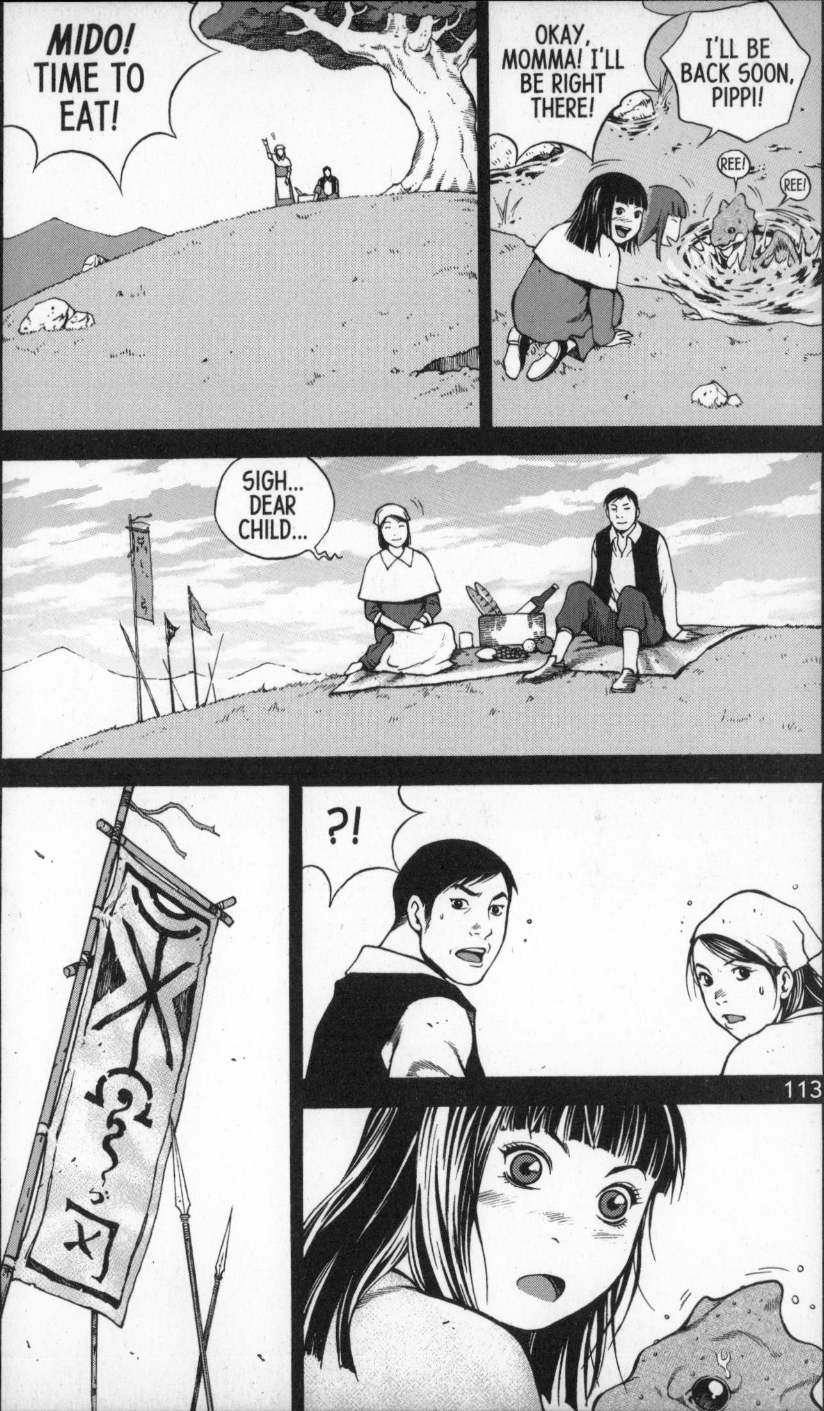
MIDO! TIME TO EAT!
OKAY, MOMMA! I'LL BE RIGHT THERE!
I'LL BE BACK SOON, PIPPI!
REE!
REE!
SIGH... DEAR CHILD...
?!

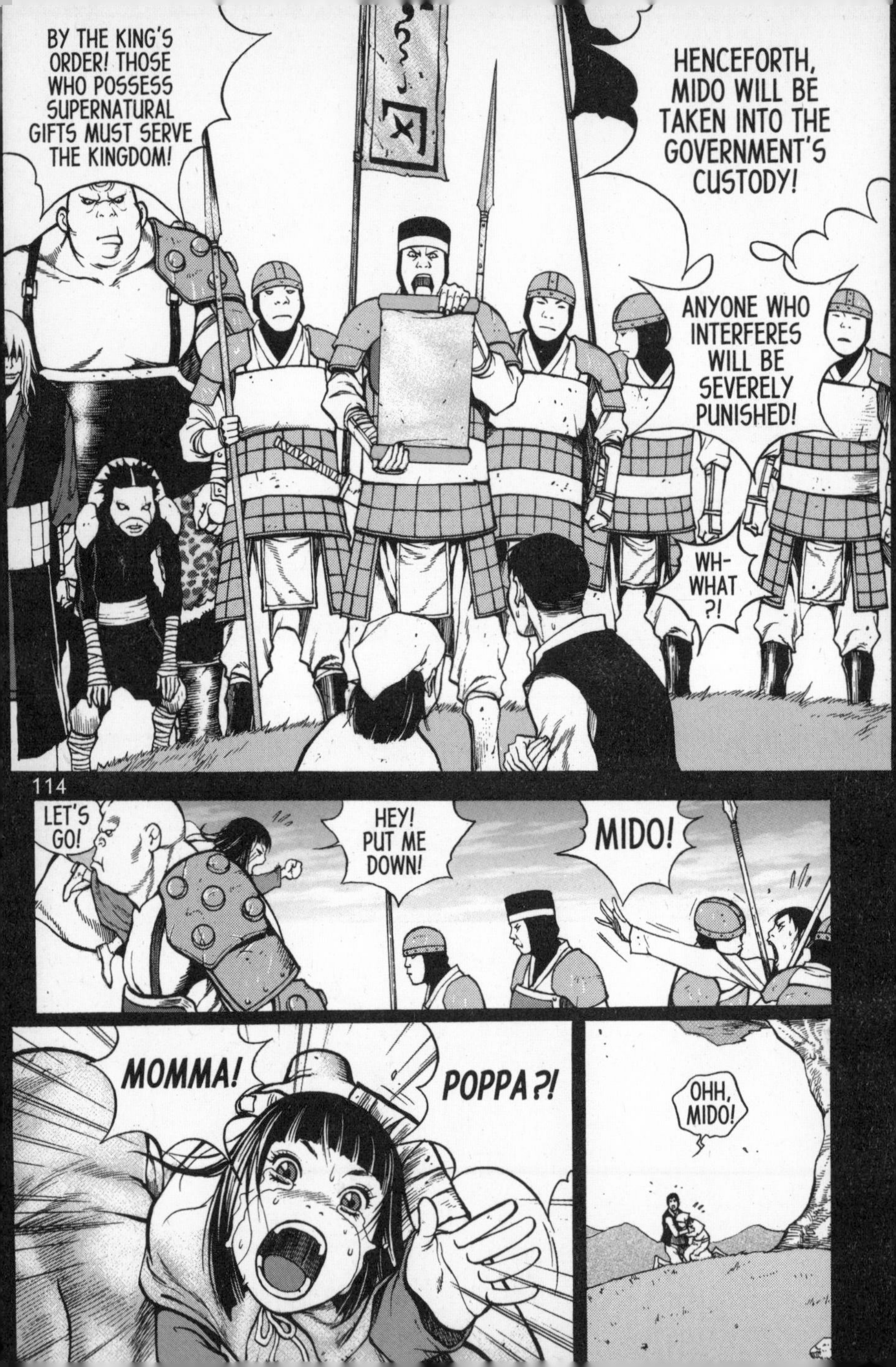
BY THE KING'S ORDER! THOSE WHO POSSESS SUPERNATURAL GIFTS MUST SERVE THE KINGDOM!
HENCEFORTH, MIDO WILL BE TAKEN INTO THE GOVERNMENT'S CUSTODY!
ANYONE WHO INTERFERES WILL BE SEVERELY PUNISHED!
WH-WHAT?!
LET'S GO!
HEY! PUT ME DOWN!
MIDO!
MOMMA!
POPPA?!
OHH, MIDO!

Ka-ga

the explosive delivery man

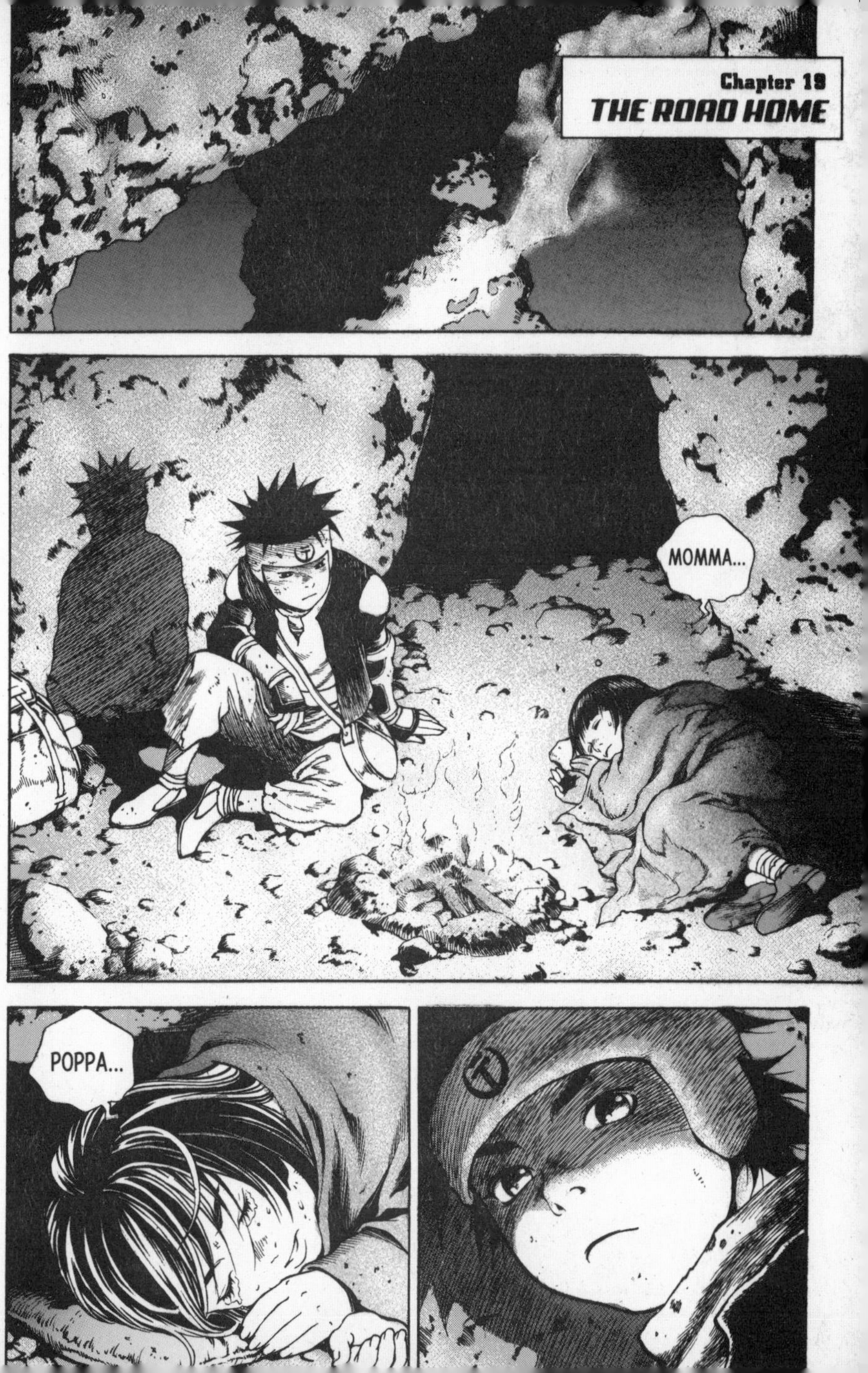
Chapter 19
THE ROAD HOME
MOMMA...
POPPA...

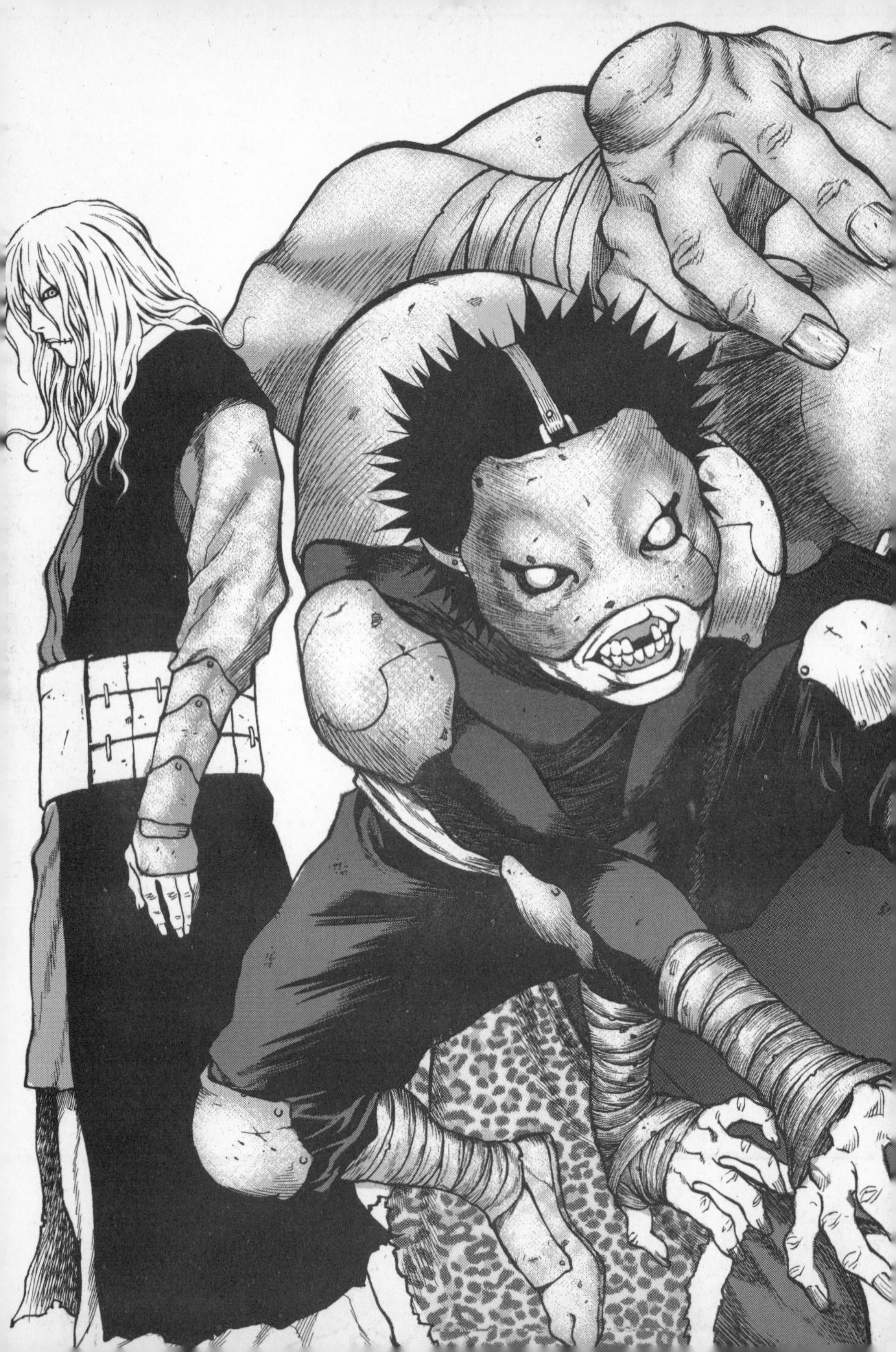

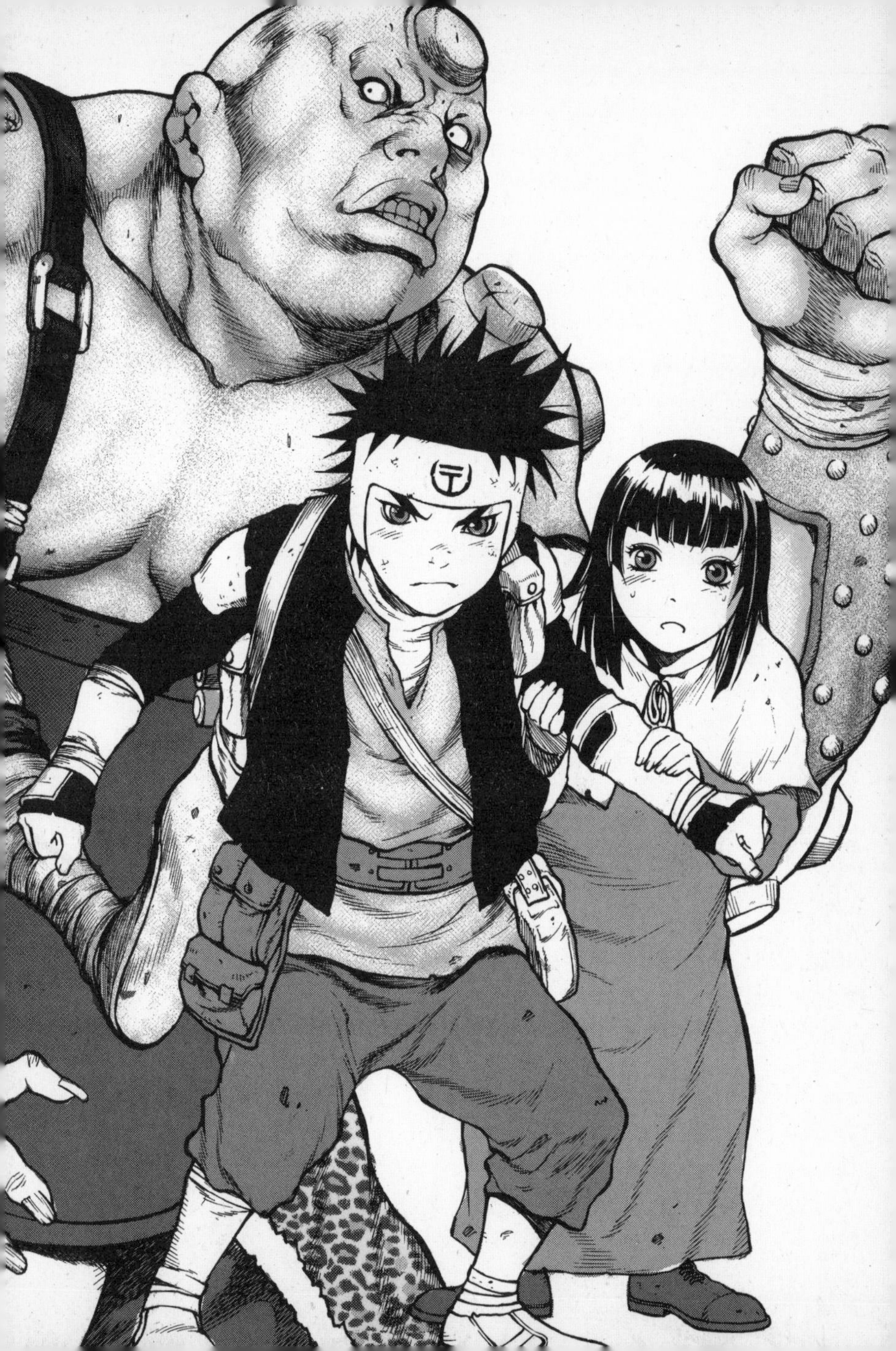

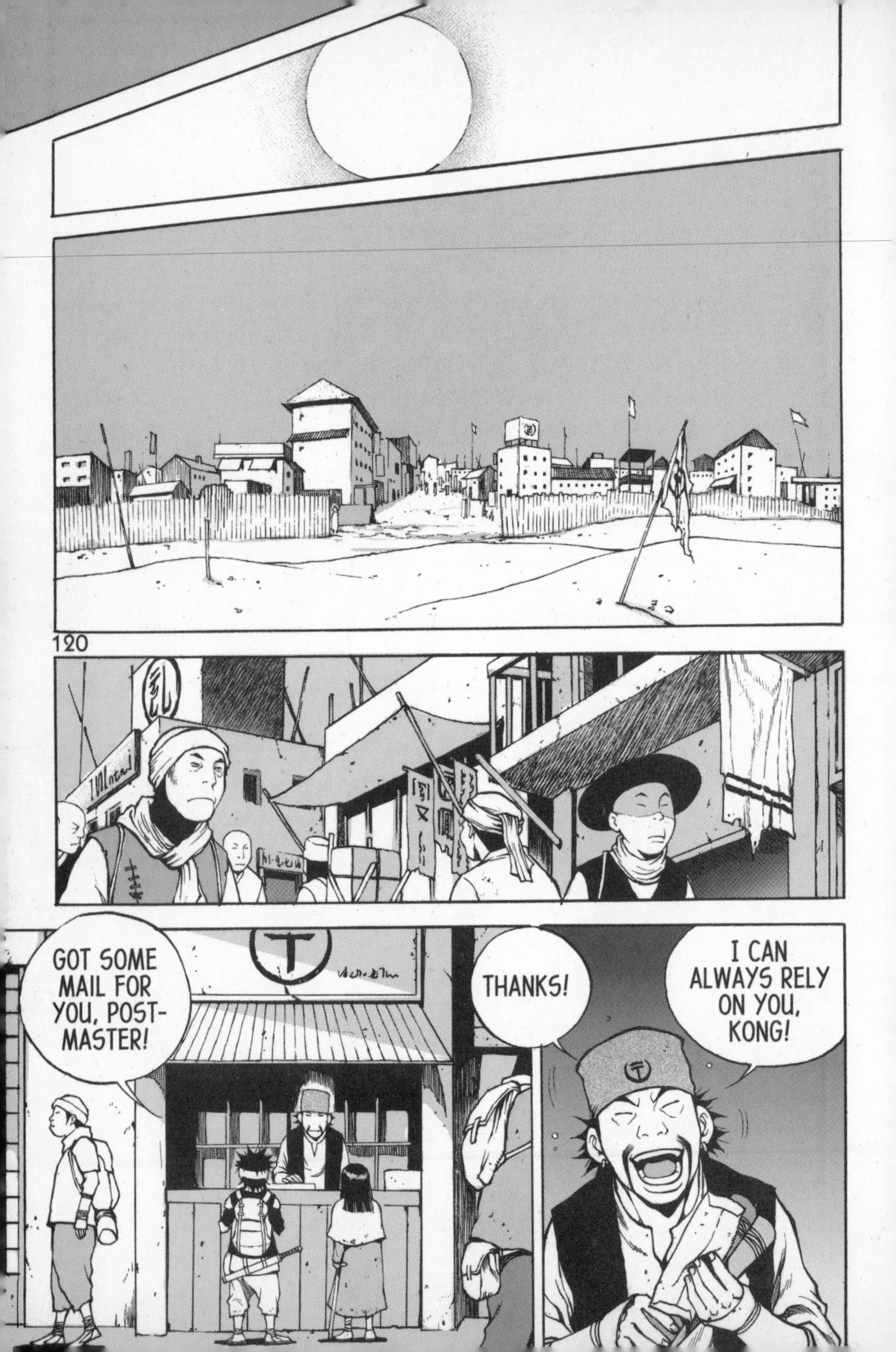
GOT SOME MAIL FOR YOU, POST-MASTER!
THANKS!
I CAN ALWAYS RELY ON YOU, KONG!

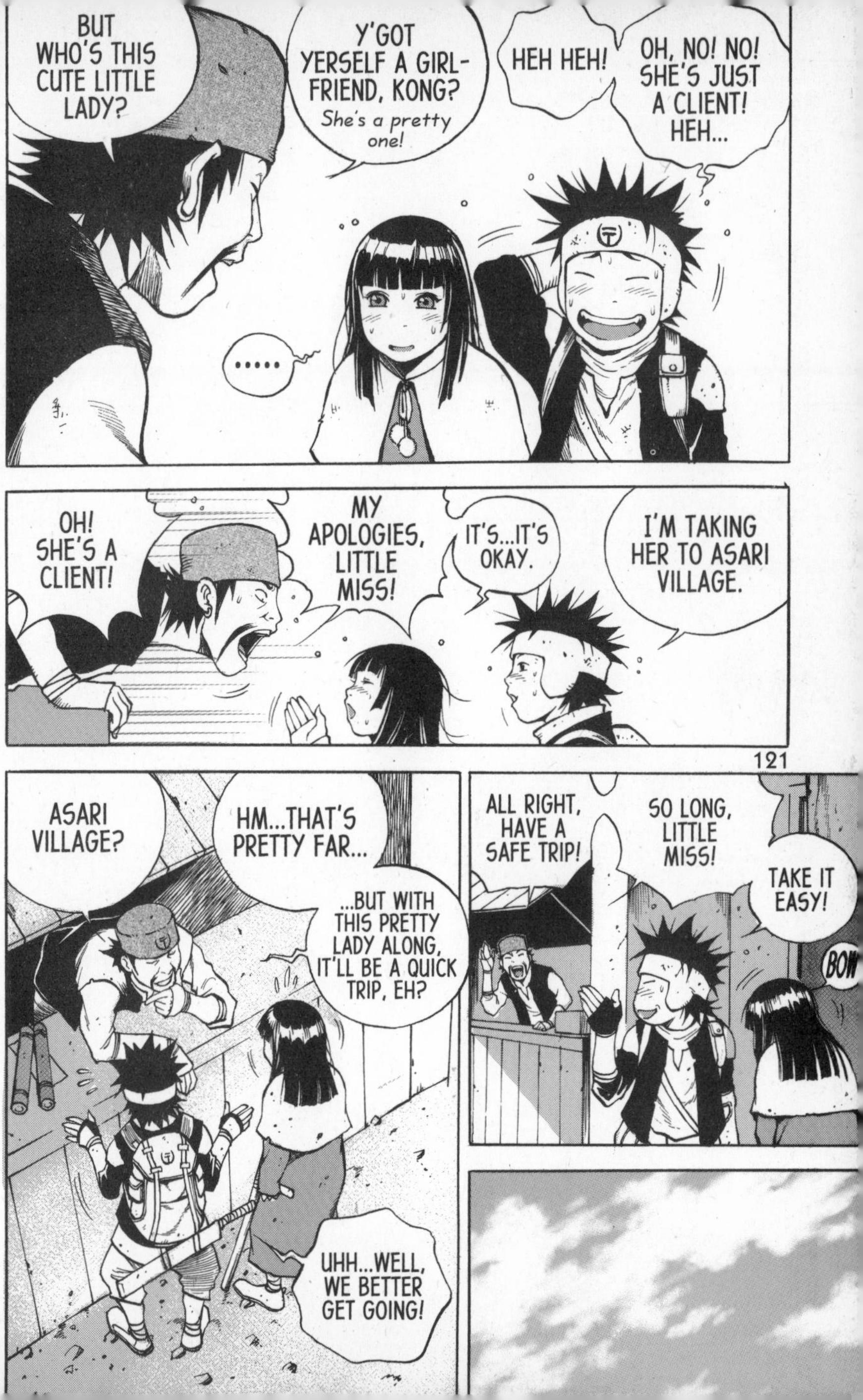
BUT WHO'S THIS CUTE LITTLE LADY?
Y'GOT YERSELF A GIRL-FRIEND, KONG? She's a pretty one!
HEH HEH!
OH, NO! NO! SHE'S JUST A CLIENT! HEH...
.....
OH! SHE'S A CLIENT!
MY APOLOGIES, LITTLE MISS!
IT'S...IT'S OKAY.
I'M TAKING HER TO ASARI VILLAGE.
ASARI VILLAGE?
HM...THAT'S PRETTY FAR...
...BUT WITH THIS PRETTY LADY ALONG, IT'LL BE A QUICK TRIP, EH?
UHH...WELL, WE BETTER GET GOING!
ALL RIGHT, HAVE A SAFE TRIP!
SO LONG, LITTLE MISS!
TAKE IT EASY!
BOW

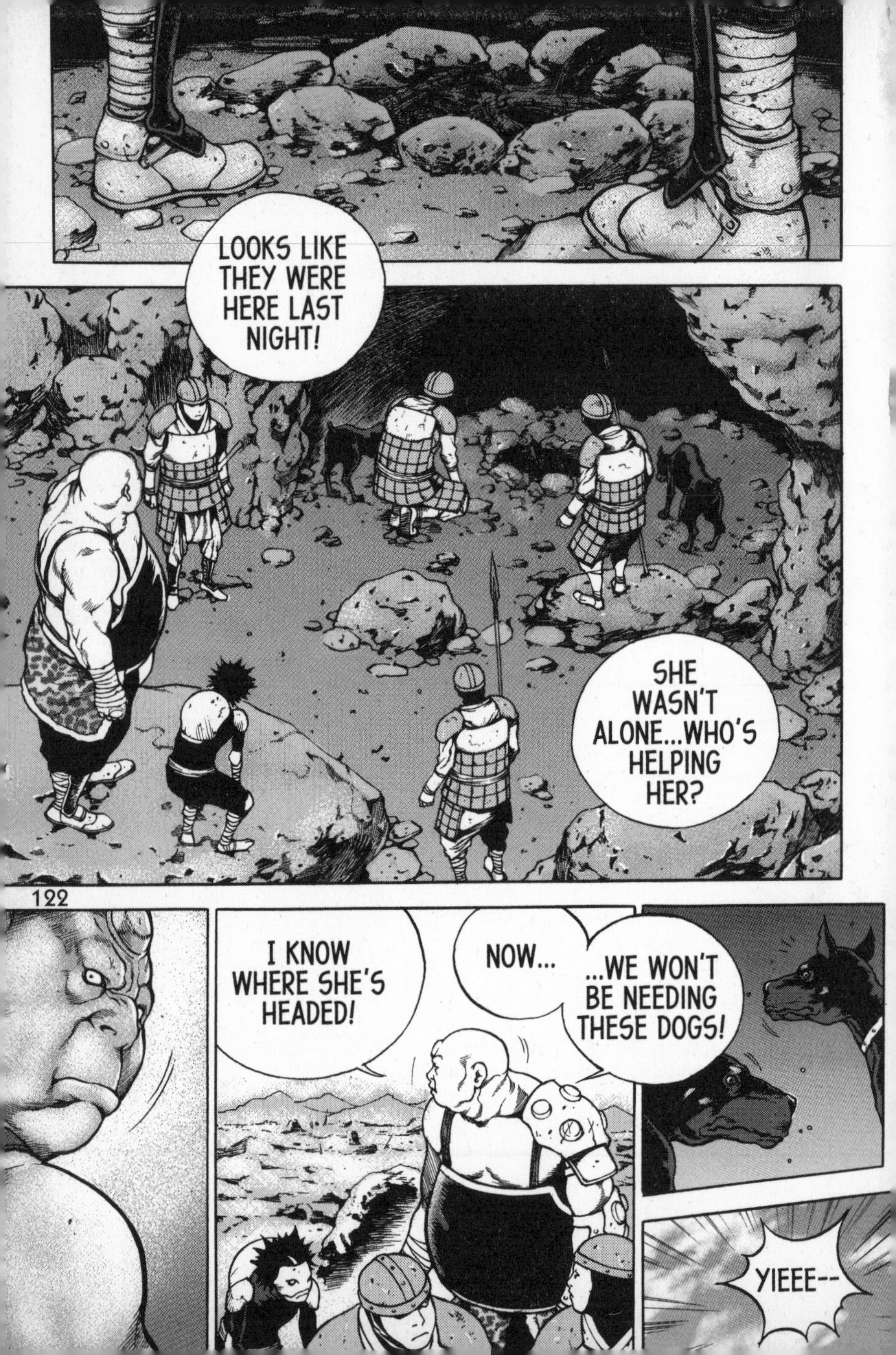
LOOKS LIKE THEY WERE HERE LAST NIGHT!
SHE WASN'T ALONE...WHO'S HELPING HER?
I KNOW WHERE SHE'S HEADED!
NOW...
...WE WON'T BE NEEDING THESE DOGS!
YIEEE--

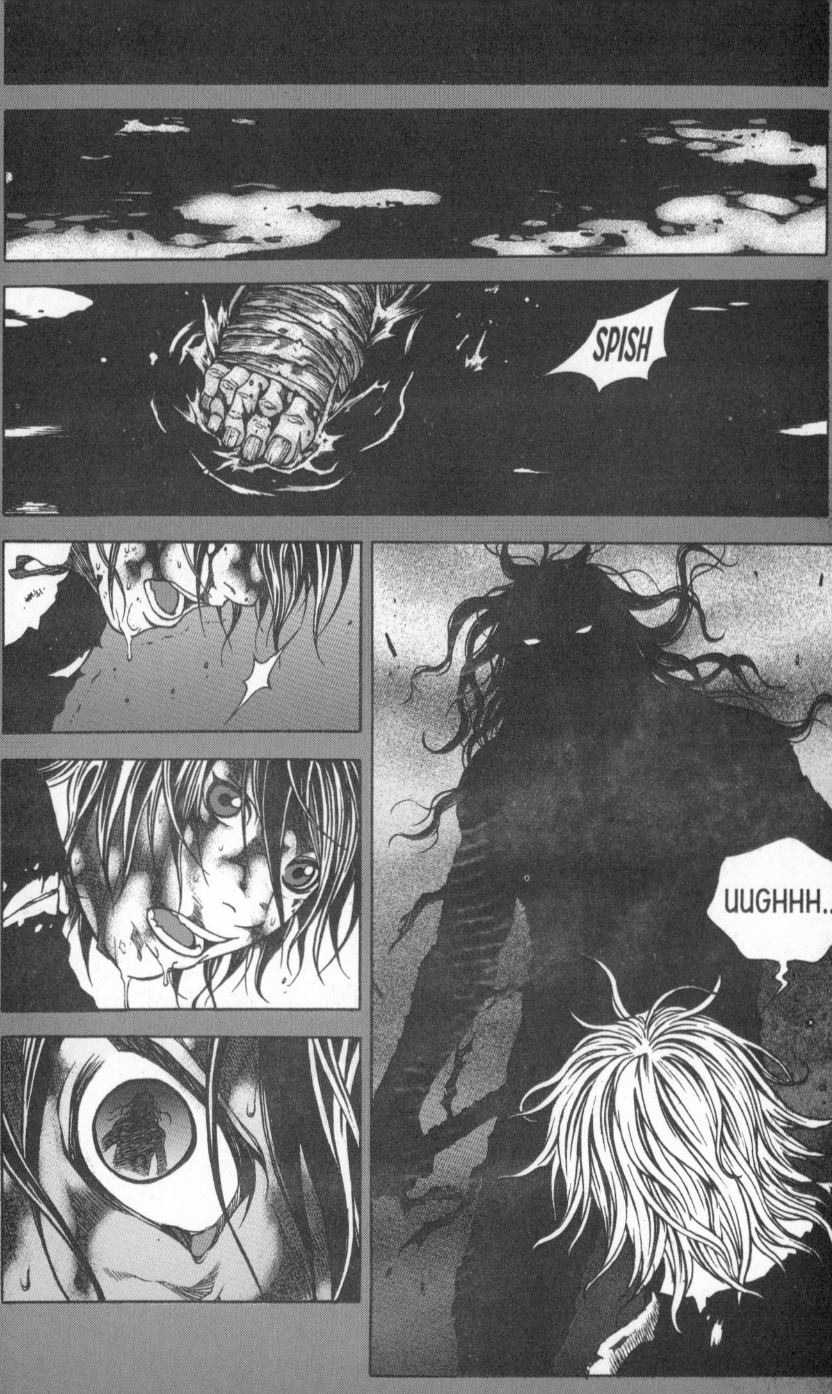
SPISH
UUGHHH...

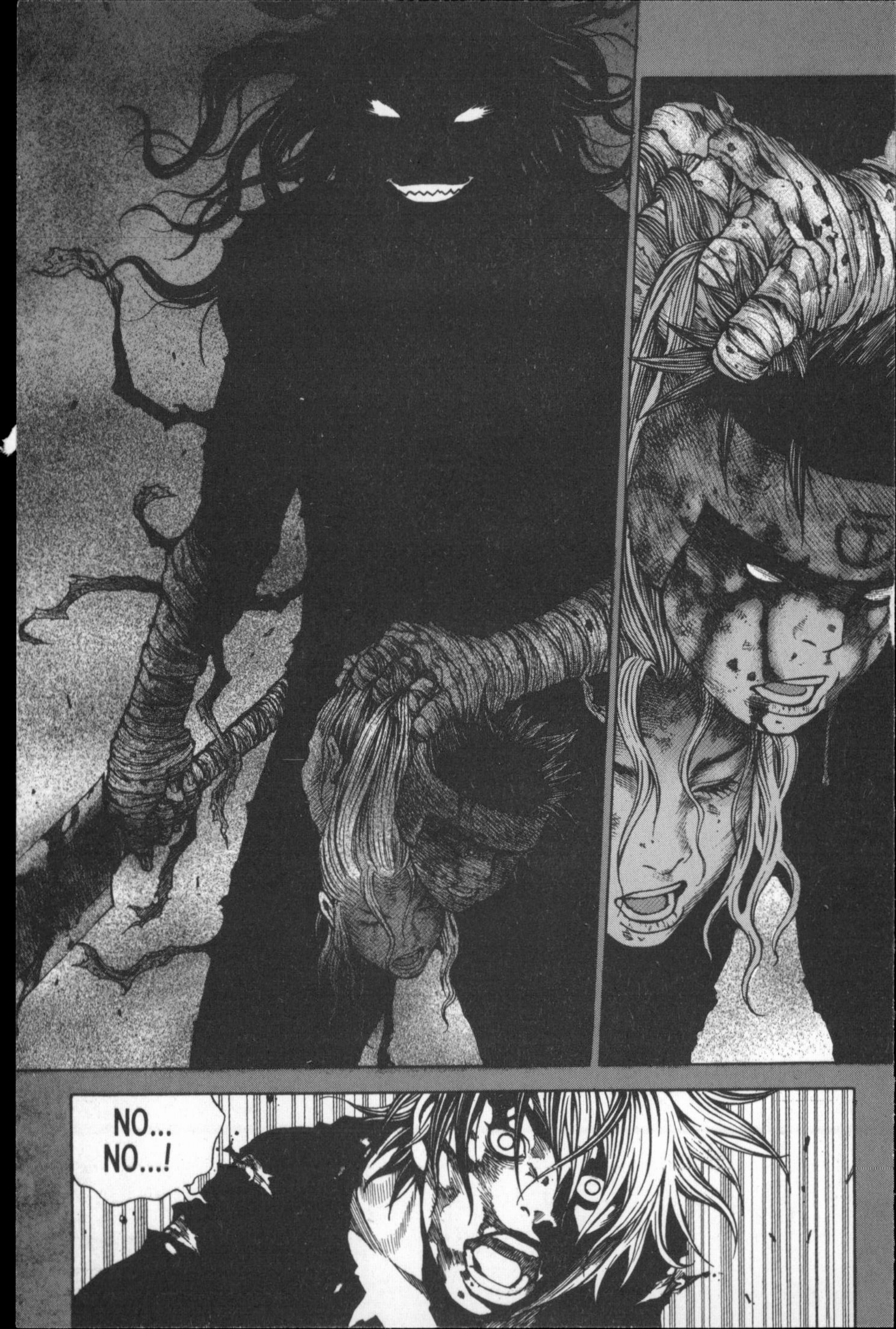
NO...
NO...!

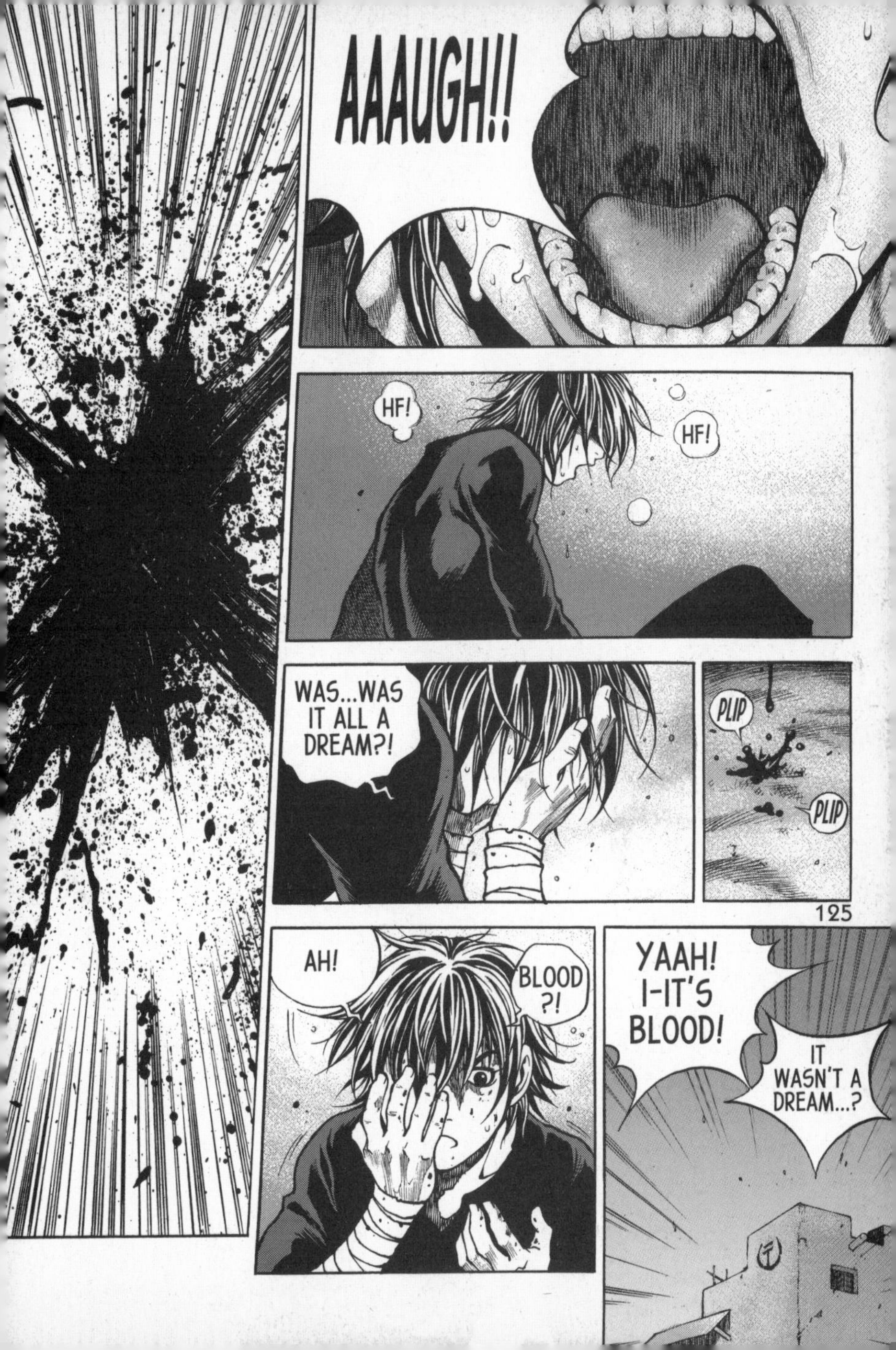
AAAUGH!!
HF!
HF!
WAS...WAS IT ALL A DREAM?!
PLIP
PLIP
BLOOD ?!
AH!
YAAH! I-IT'S BLOOD!
IT WASN'T A DREAM...?

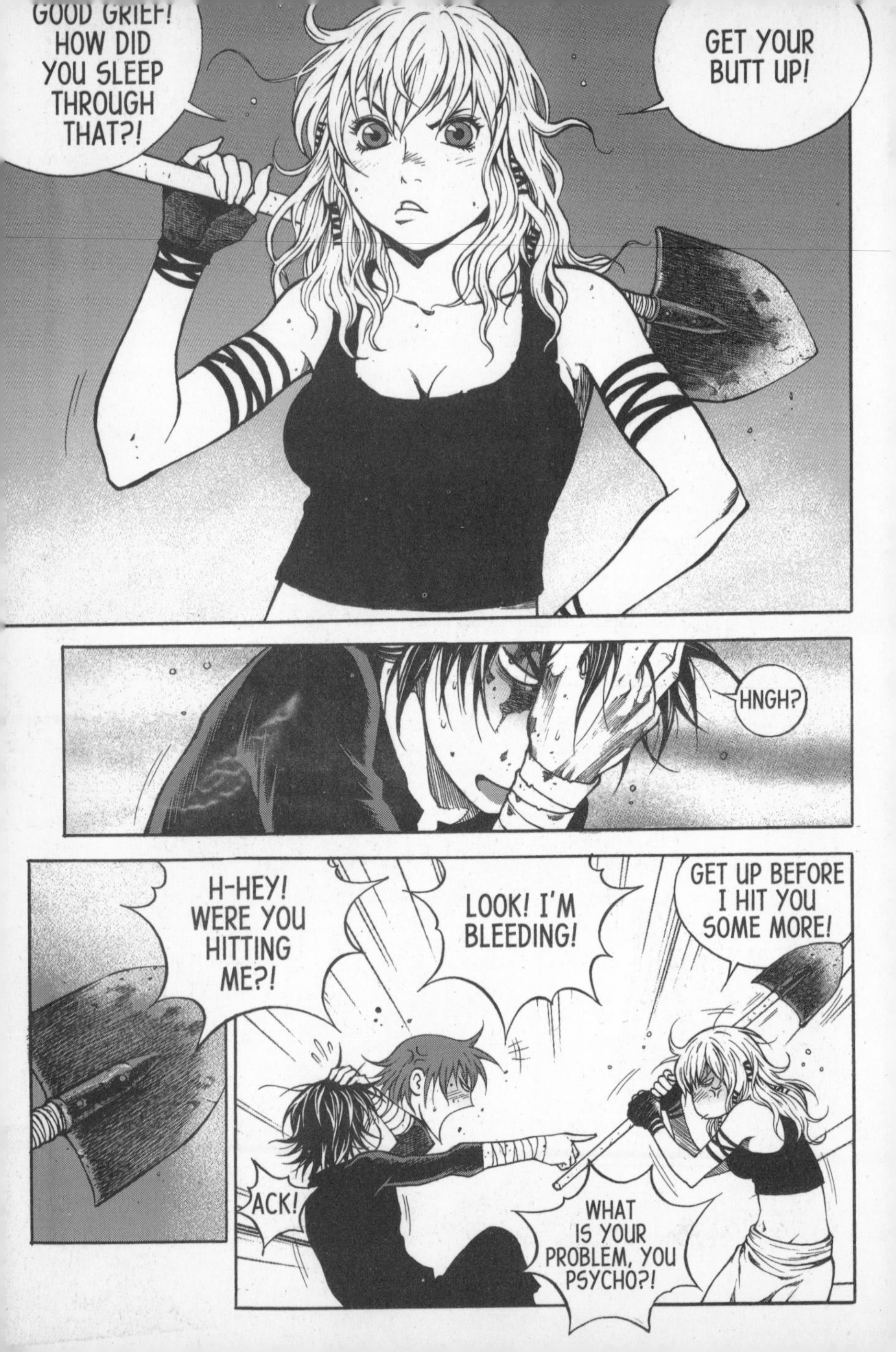
GOOD GRIEF! HOW DID YOU SLEEP THROUGH THAT?!
GET YOUR BUTT UP!
HNGH?
H-HEY! WERE YOU HITTING ME?!
LOOK! I'M BLEEDING!
GET UP BEFORE I HIT YOU SOME MORE!
ACK!
WHAT IS YOUR PROBLEM, YOU PSYCHO?!

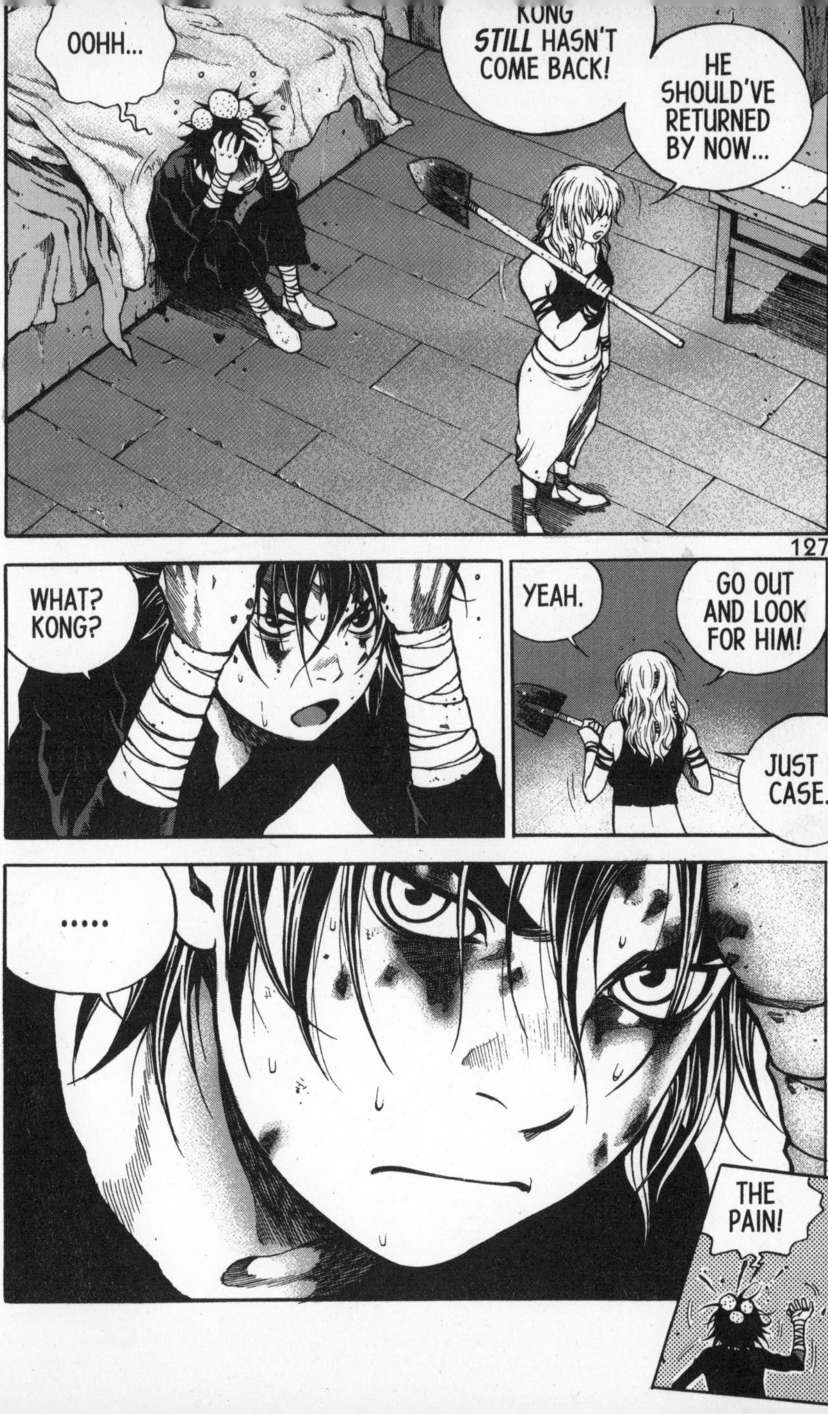
OOHH...
KONG STILL HASN'T COME BACK!
HE SHOULD'VE RETURNED BY NOW...
WHAT? KONG?
YEAH.
GO OUT AND LOOK FOR HIM!
JUST IN CASE...
.....
THE PAIN!

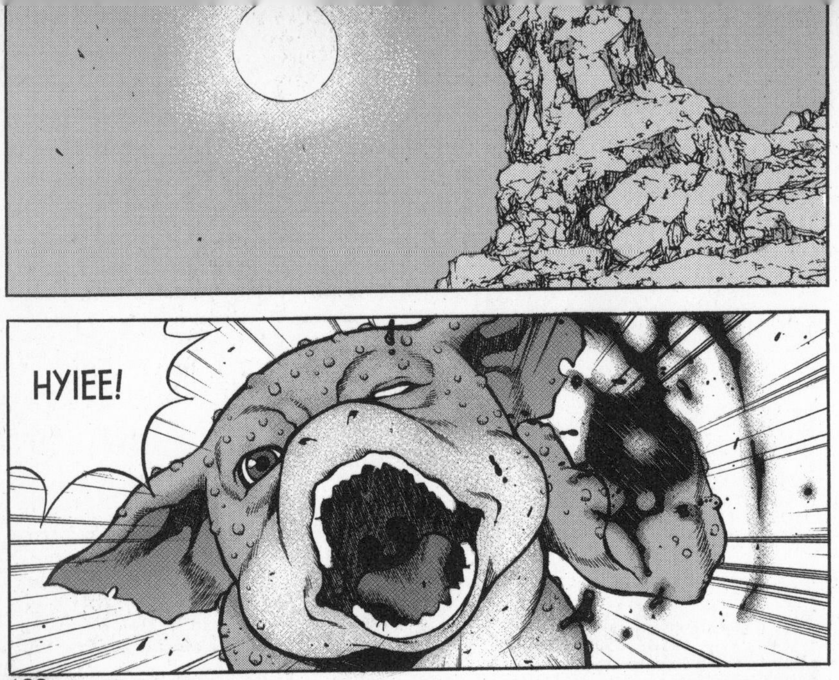
HYIEE!

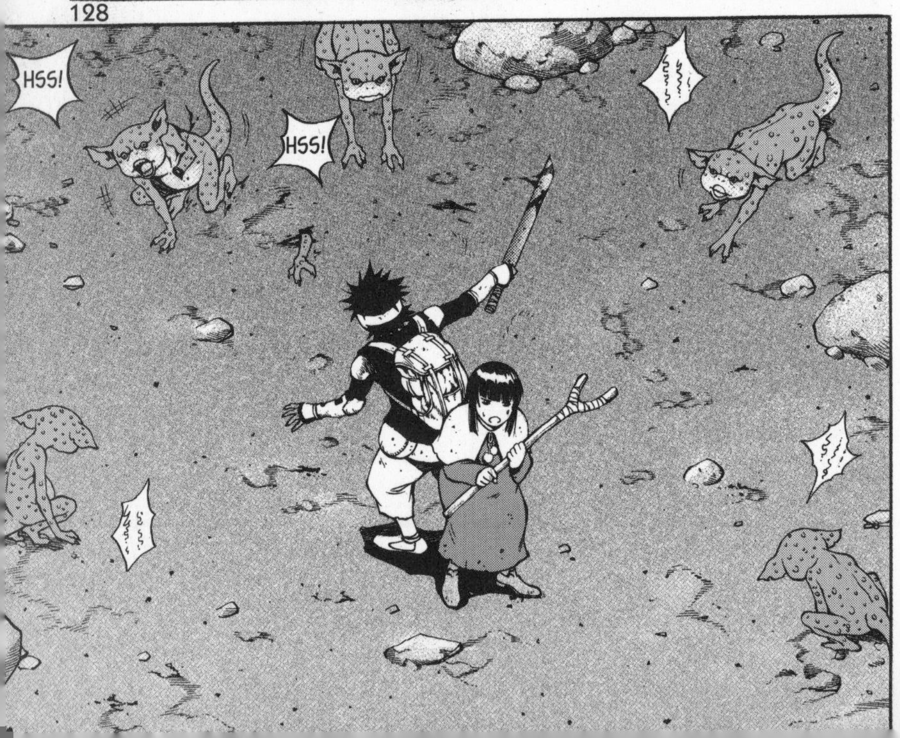
HSS!
HSS!

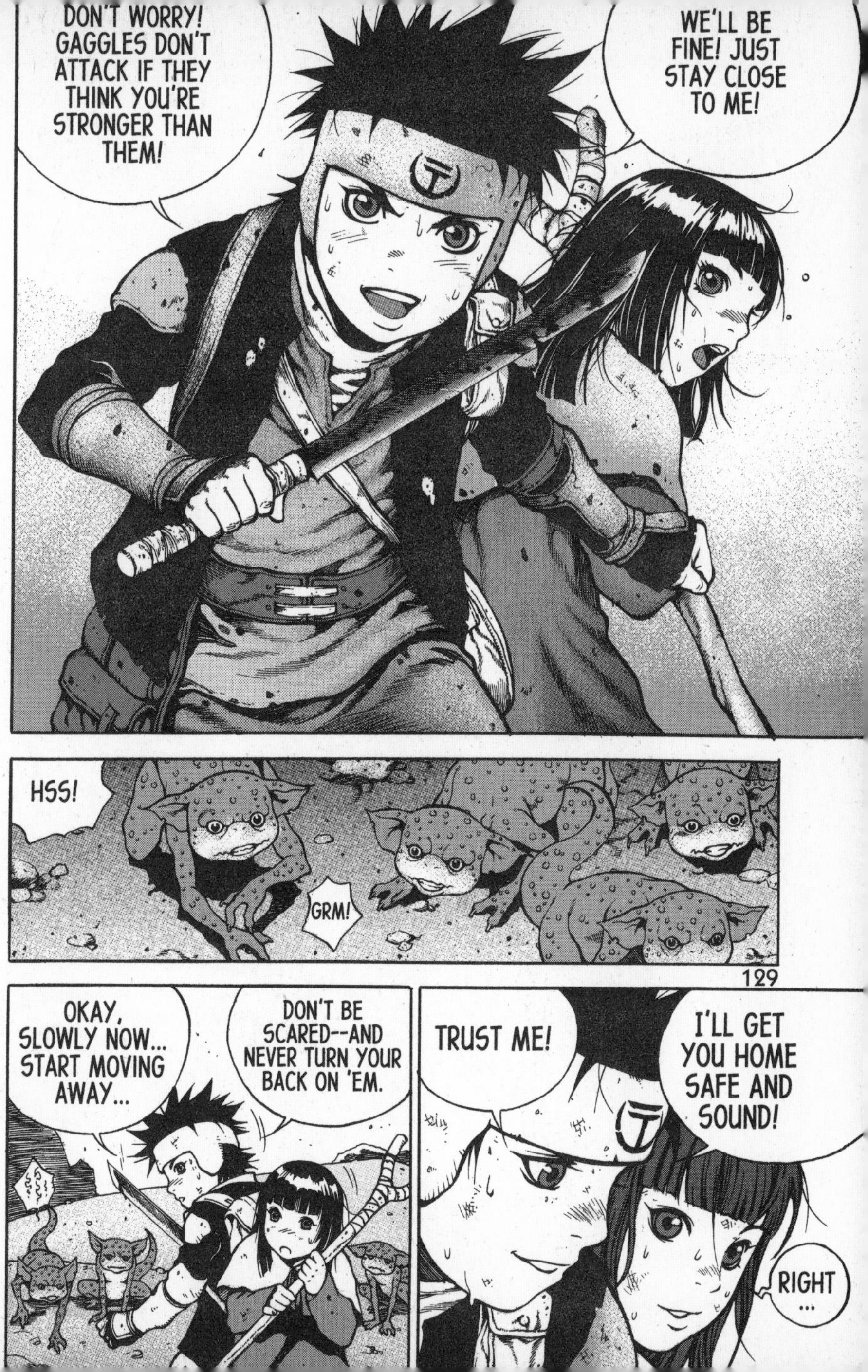
DON'T WORRY! GAGGLES DON'T ATTACK IF THEY THINK YOU'RE STRONGER THAN THEM!
WE'LL BE FINE! JUST STAY CLOSE TO ME!
HSS!
GRM!
OKAY, SLOWLY NOW... START MOVING AWAY...
DON'T BE SCARED--AND NEVER TURN YOUR BACK ON 'EM.
TRUST ME!
I'LL GET YOU HOME SAFE AND SOUND!
RIGHT ...

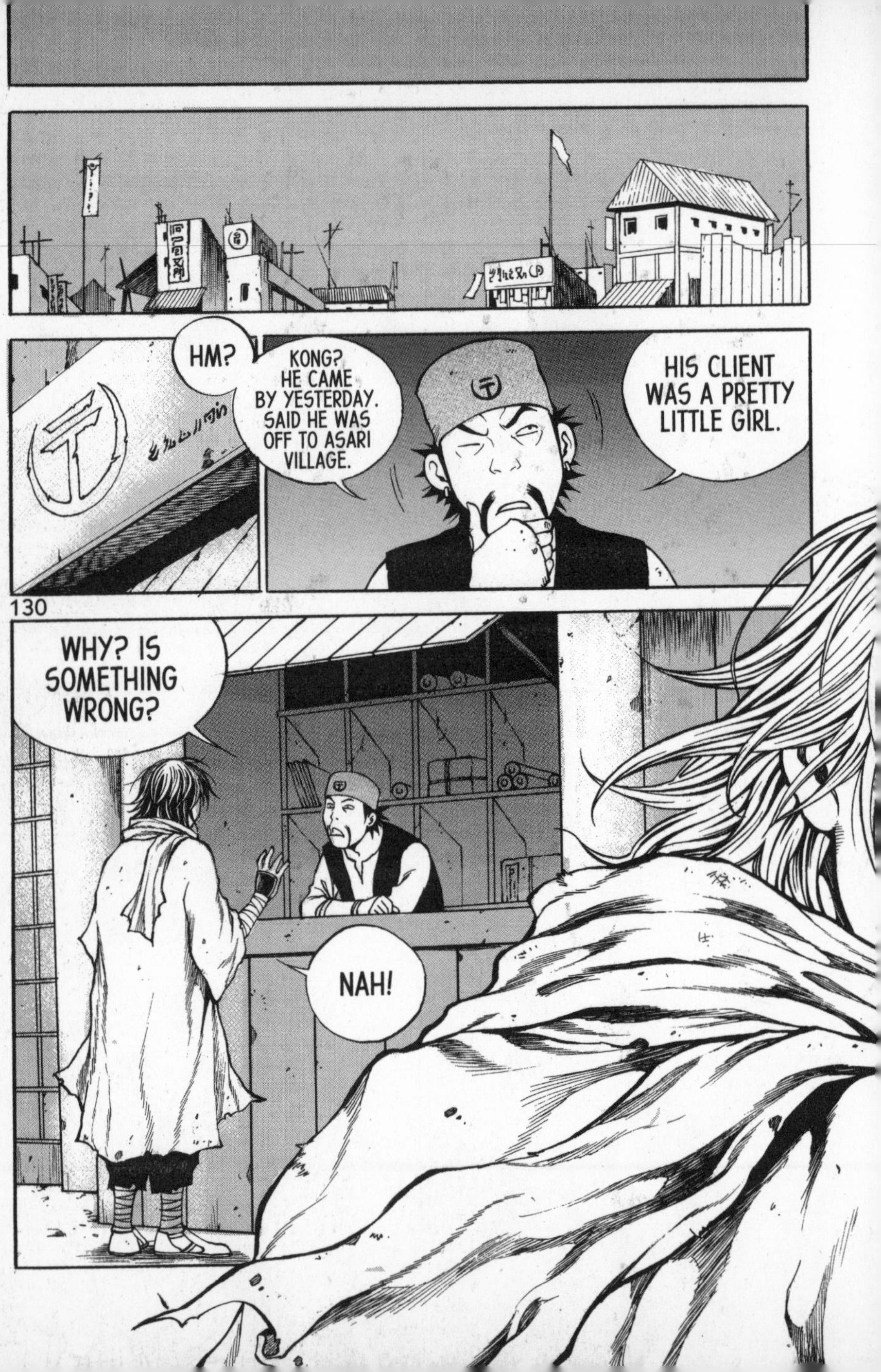
HM?
KONG? HE CAME BY YESTERDAY. SAID HE WAS OFF TO ASARI VILLAGE.
HIS CLIENT WAS A PRETTY LITTLE GIRL.
WHY? IS SOMETHING WRONG?
NAH!

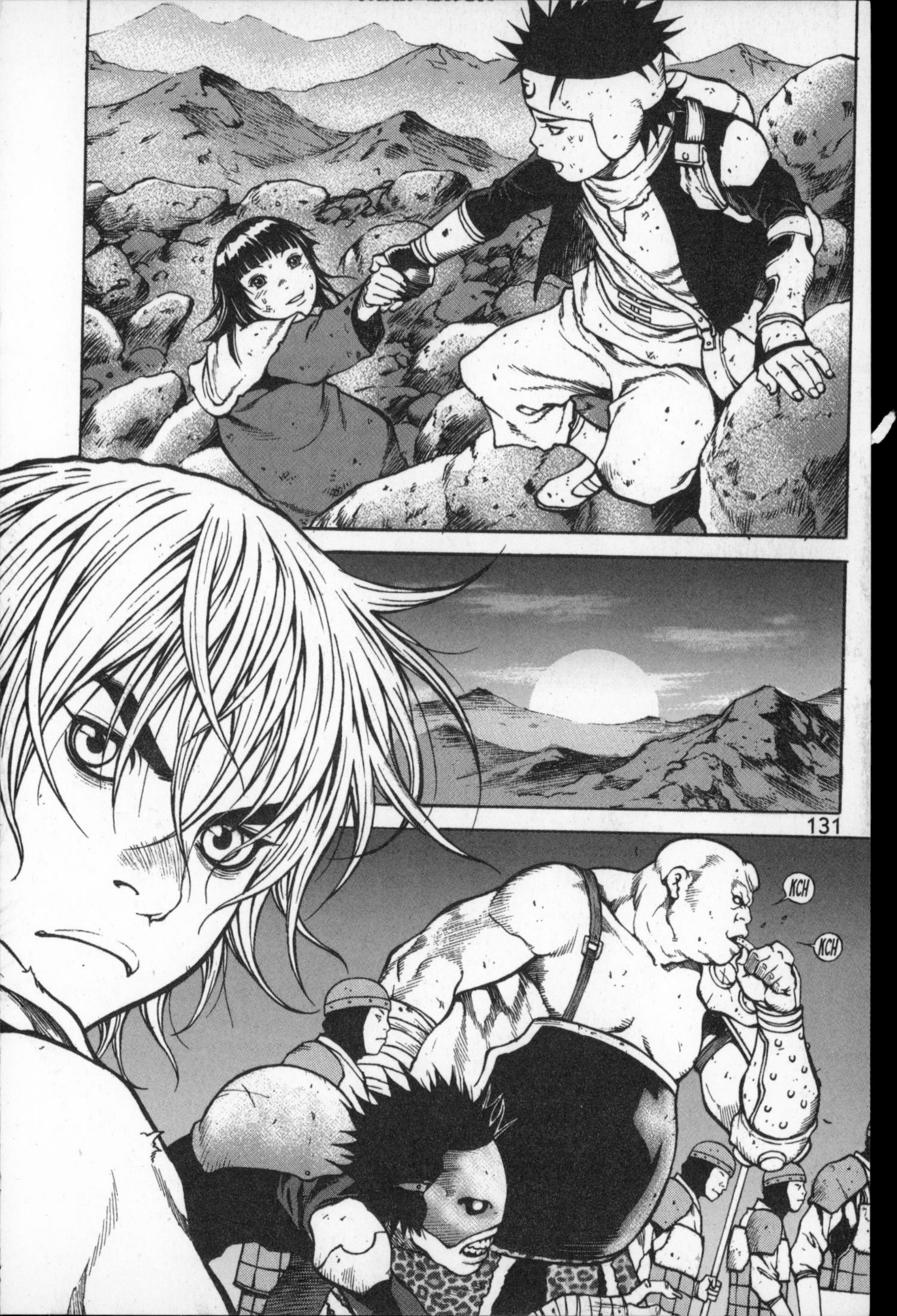
KCH
KCH

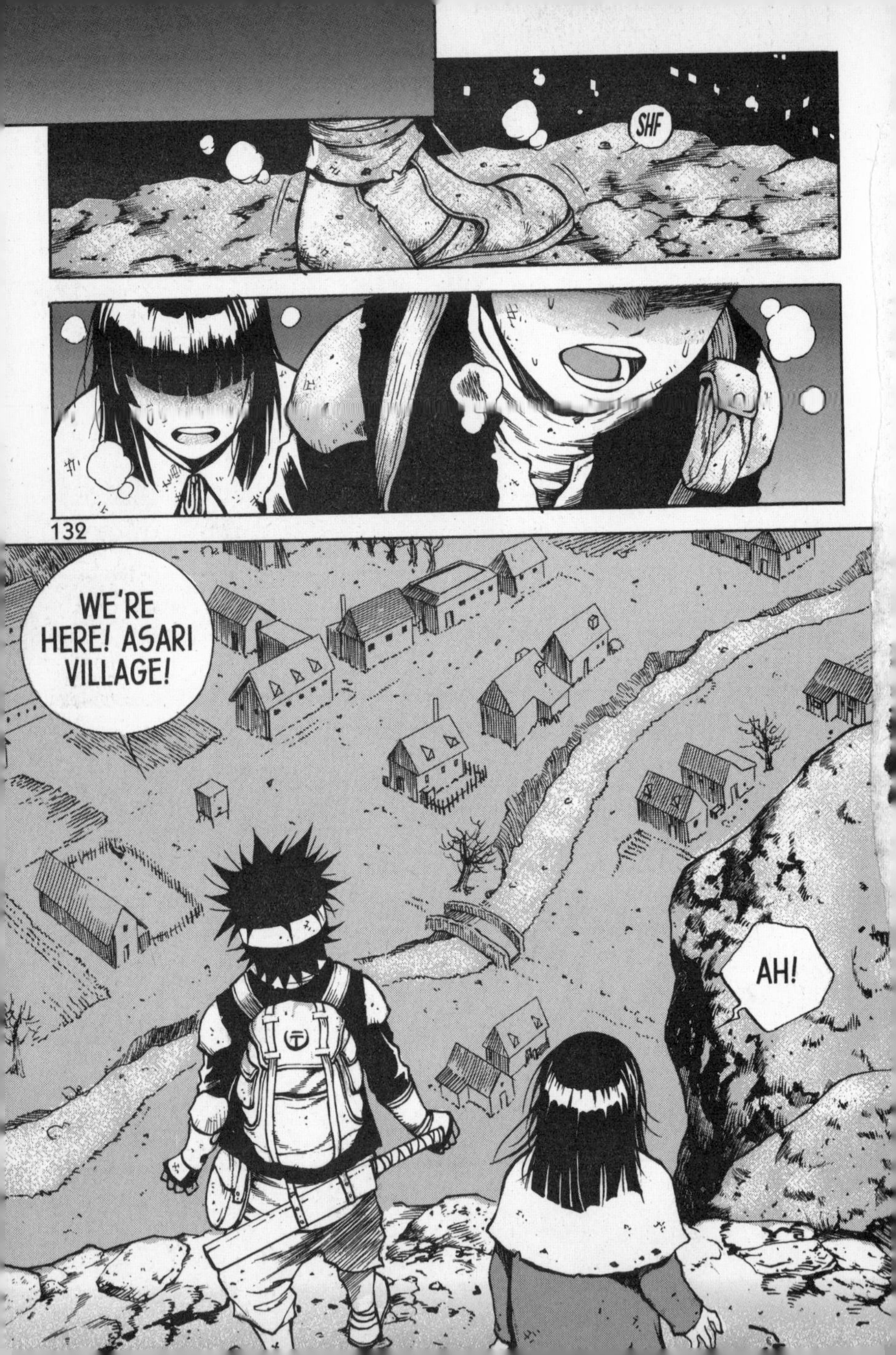
SHF
WE'RE HERE! ASARI VILLAGE!
AH!

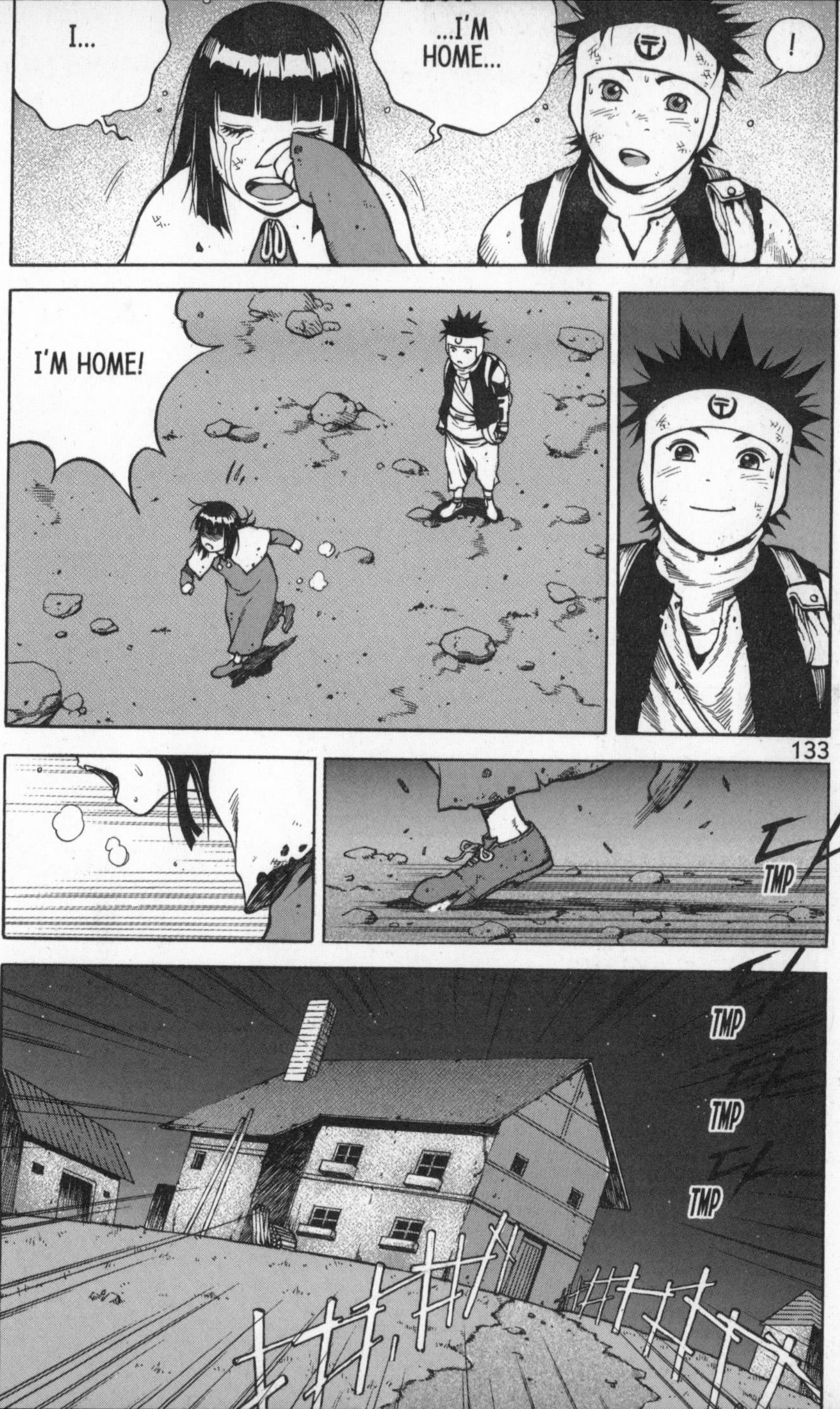
I...
...I'M HOME...
!
I'M HOME!
TMP
TMP
TMP
TMP

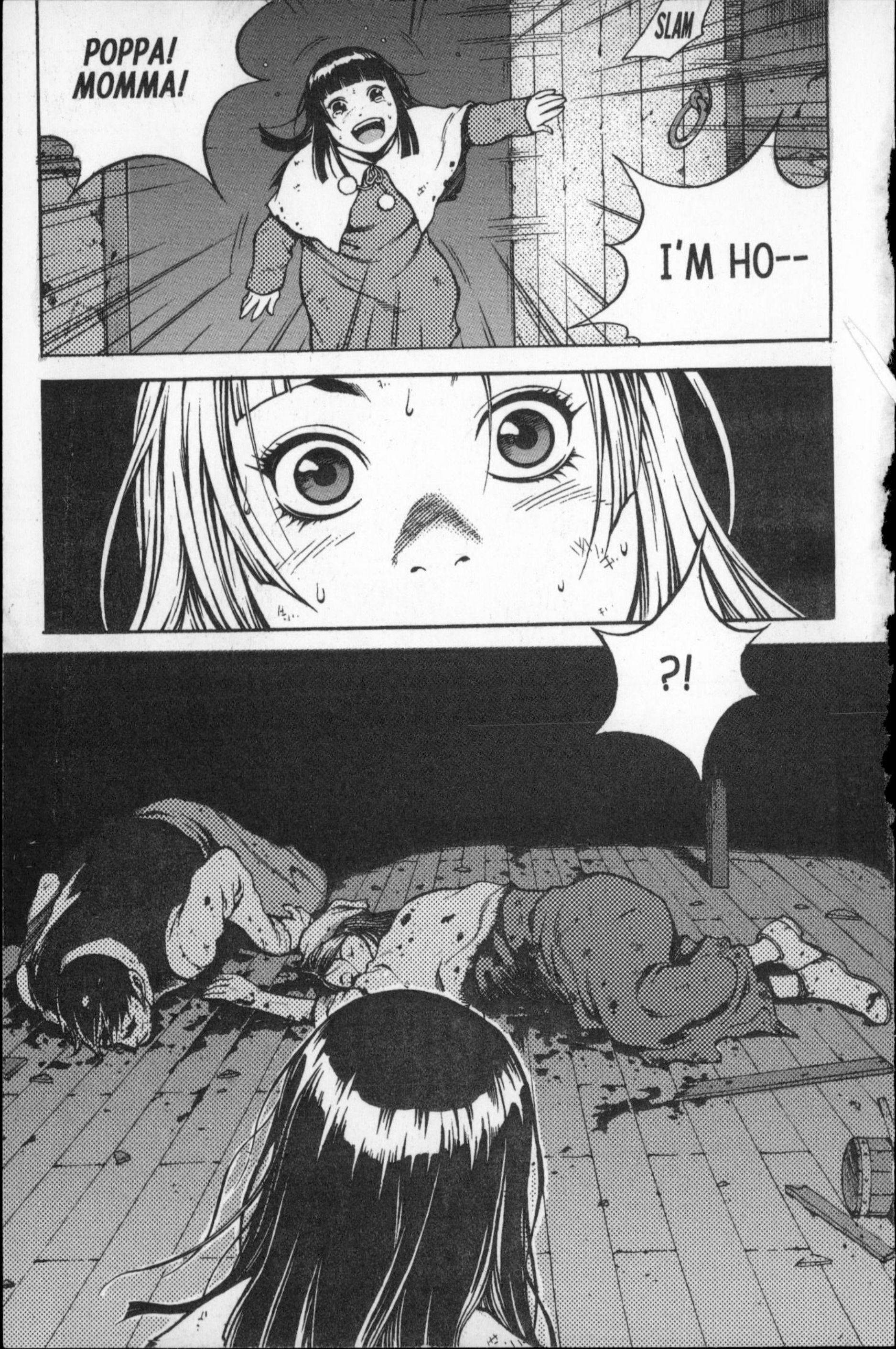
SLAM
POPPA! MOMMA!
I'M HO--
?!

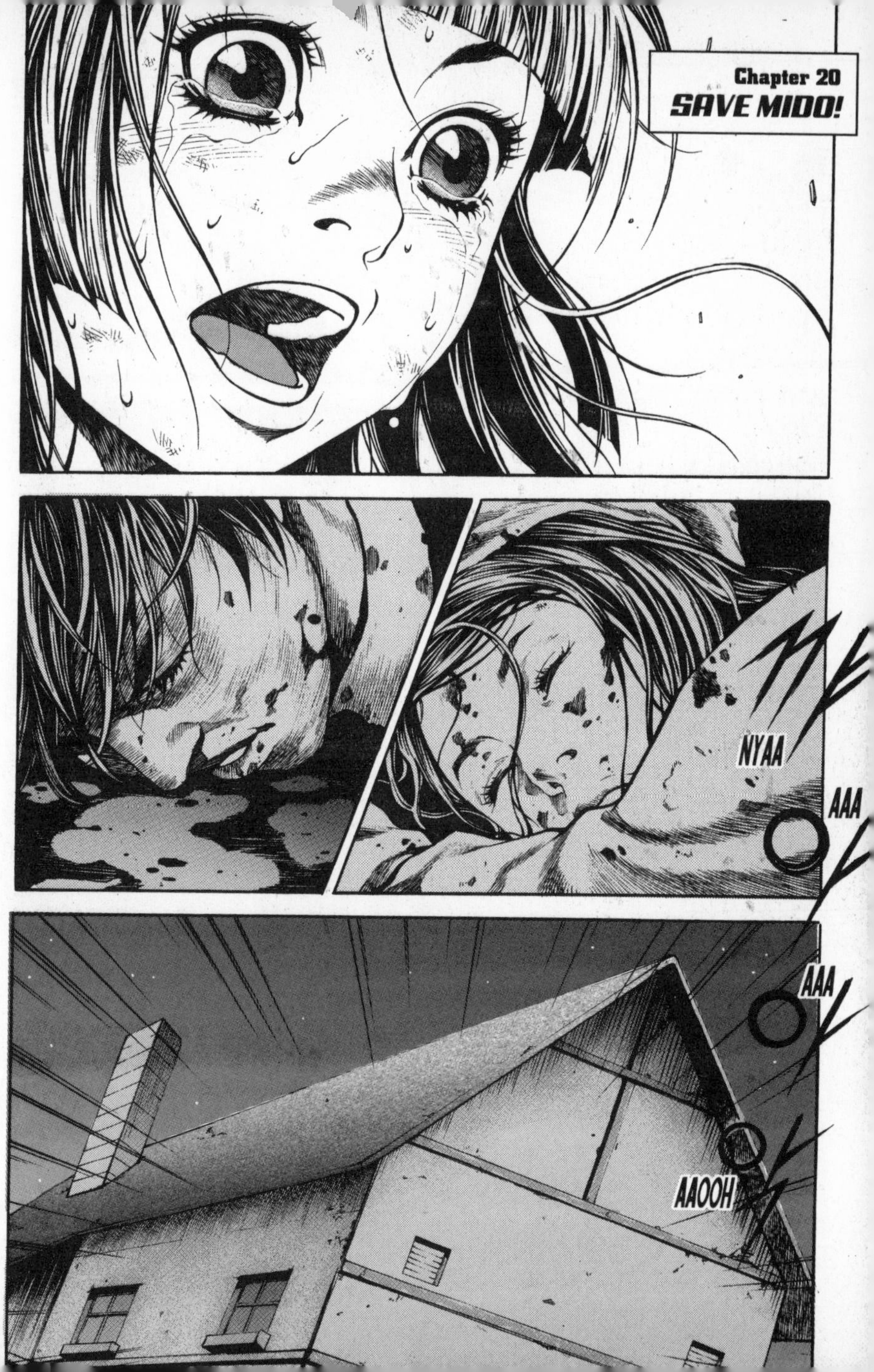
Chapter 20
SAVE MIDO!
NYAA
AAA
AAA
AAOOH

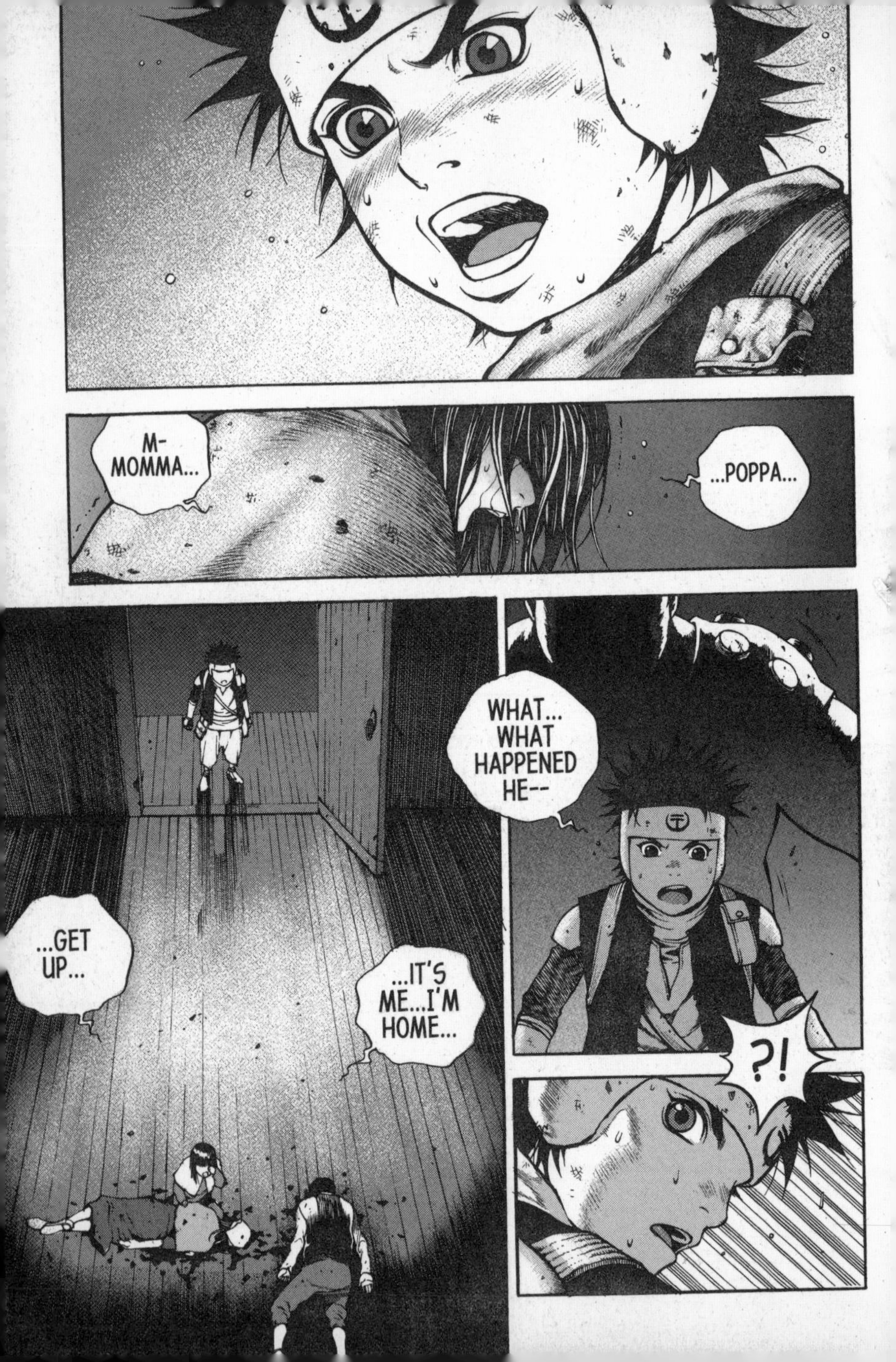
...POPPA...
M-MOMMA...
WHAT... WHAT HAPPENED HE--
?!
...IT'S ME...I'M HOME...
...GET UP...

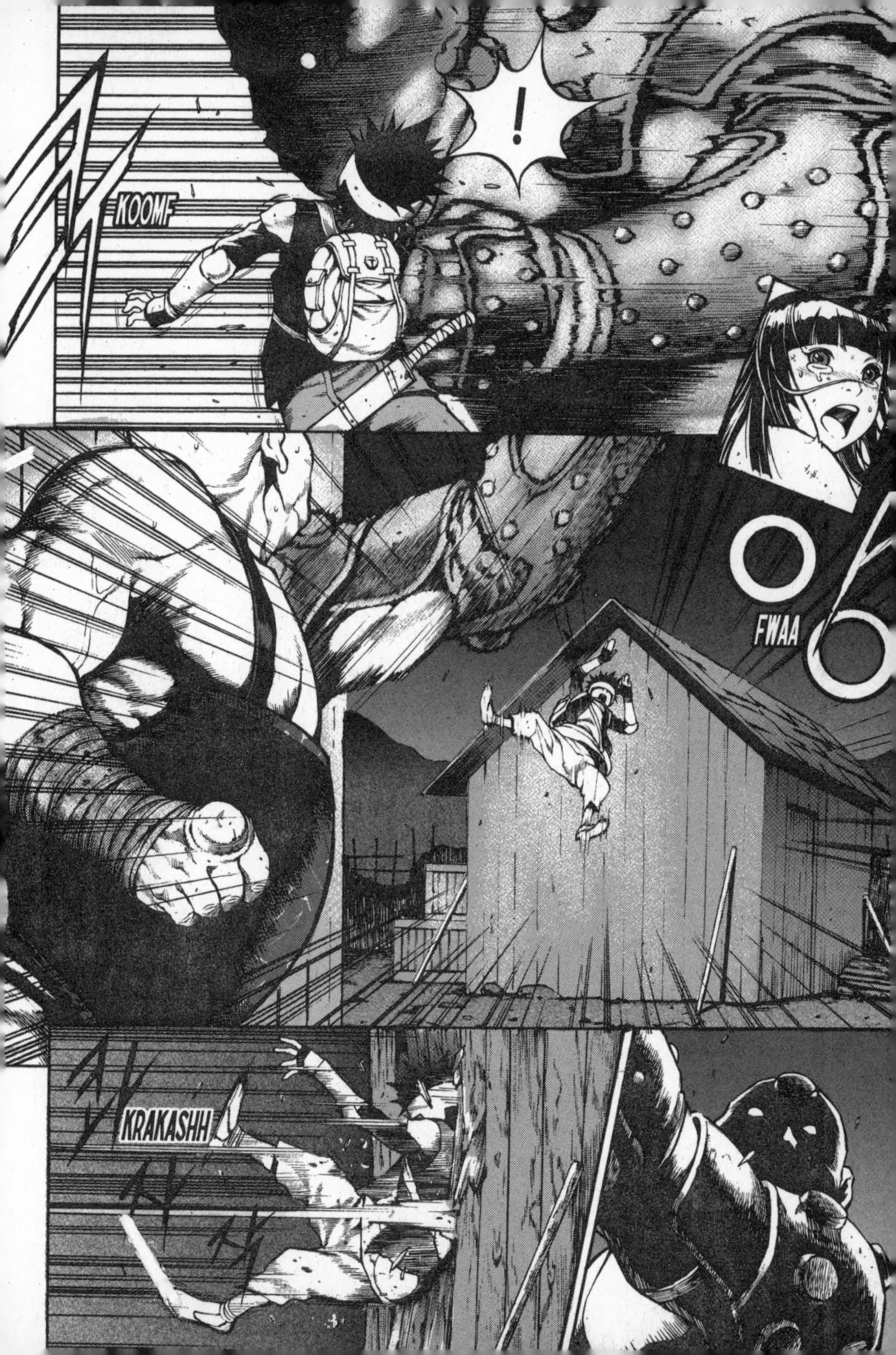
KOOMF
!
FWAA
KRAKASHH

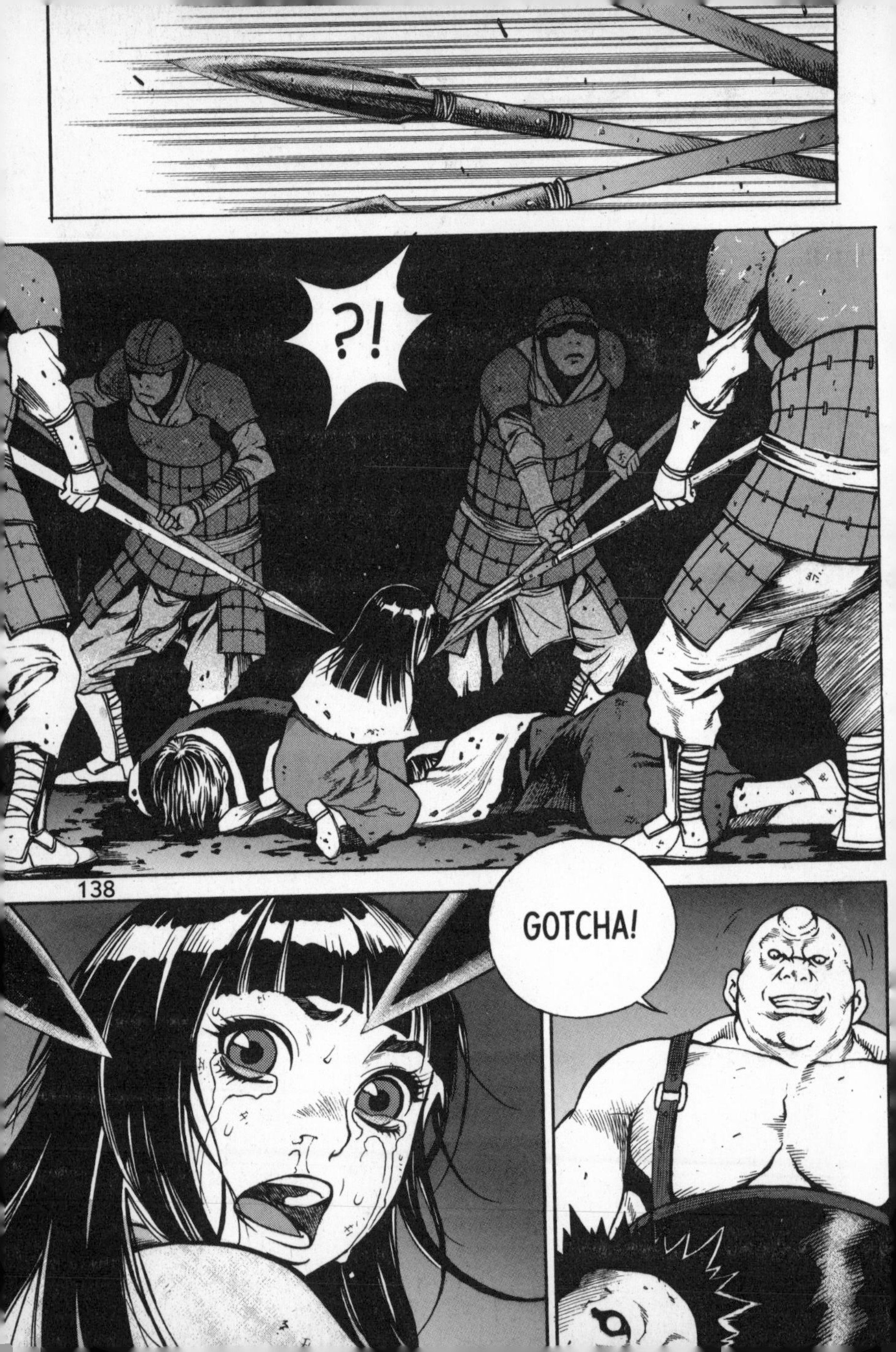
?!
GOTCHA!

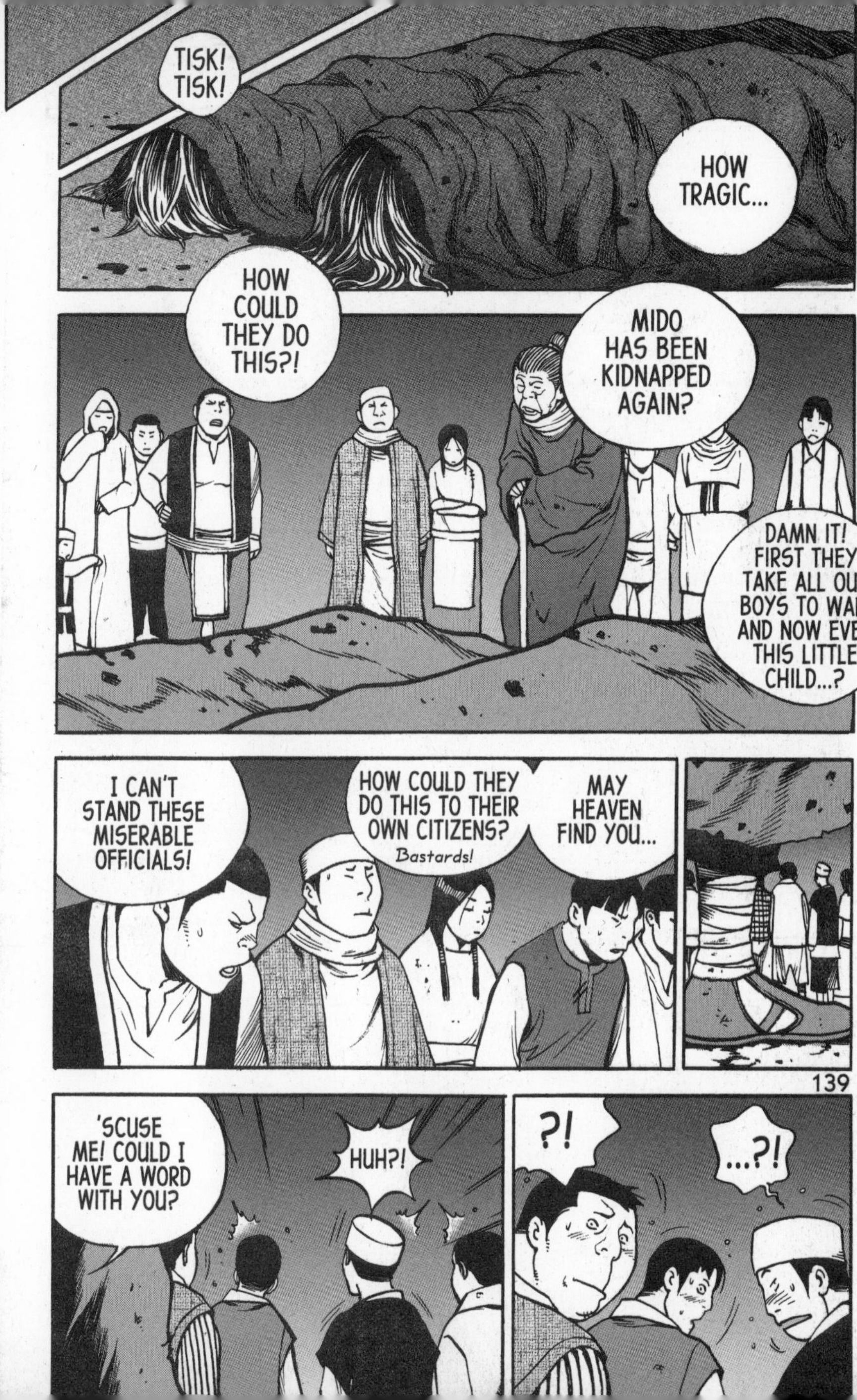
TISK! TISK!
HOW TRAGIC...
HOW COULD THEY DO THIS?!
MIDO HAS BEEN KIDNAPPED AGAIN?
DAMN IT! FIRST THEY TAKE ALL OUR BOYS TO WAR, AND NOW EVEN THIS LITTLE CHILD...?
I CAN'T STAND THESE MISERABLE OFFICIALS!
HOW COULD THEY DO THIS TO THEIR OWN CITIZENS?
Bastards!
MAY HEAVEN FIND YOU...
'SCUSE ME! COULD I HAVE A WORD WITH YOU?
HUH?!
?!
...?!

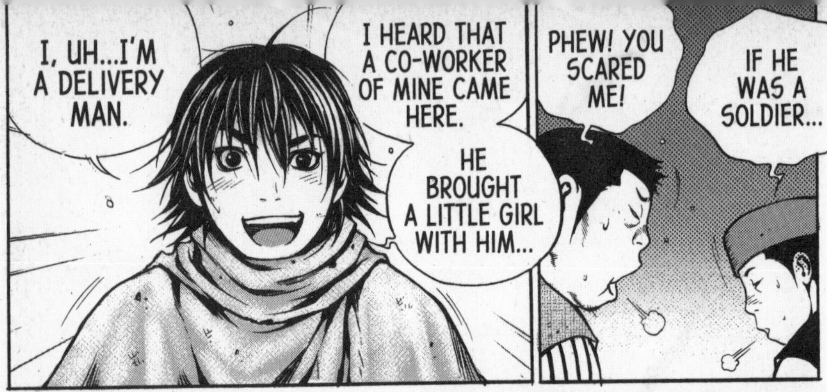
I, UH...I'M A DELIVERY MAN.
I HEARD THAT A CO-WORKER OF MINE CAME HERE.
HE BROUGHT A LITTLE GIRL WITH HIM...
PHEW! YOU SCARED ME!
IF HE WAS A SOLDIER...

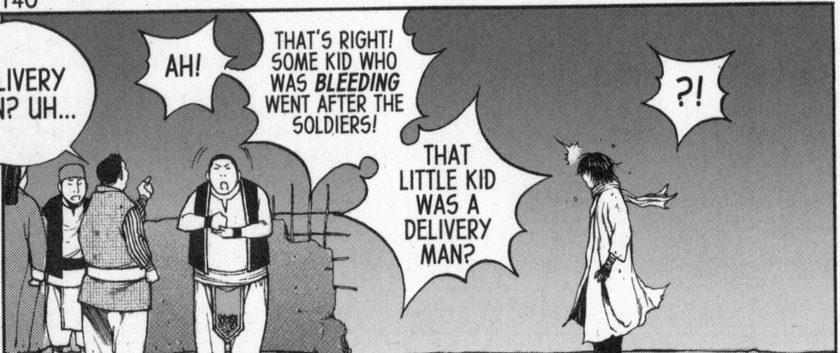
DELIVERY MAN? UH...
AH!
THAT'S RIGHT! SOME KID WHO WAS BLEEDING WENT AFTER THE SOLDIERS!
THAT LITTLE KID WAS A DELIVERY MAN?
?!

140

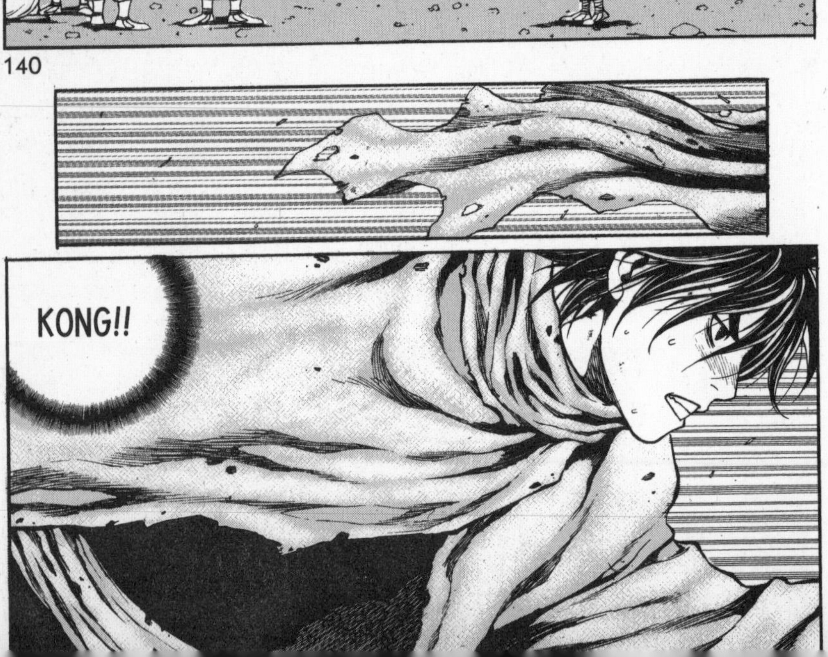
KONG!!

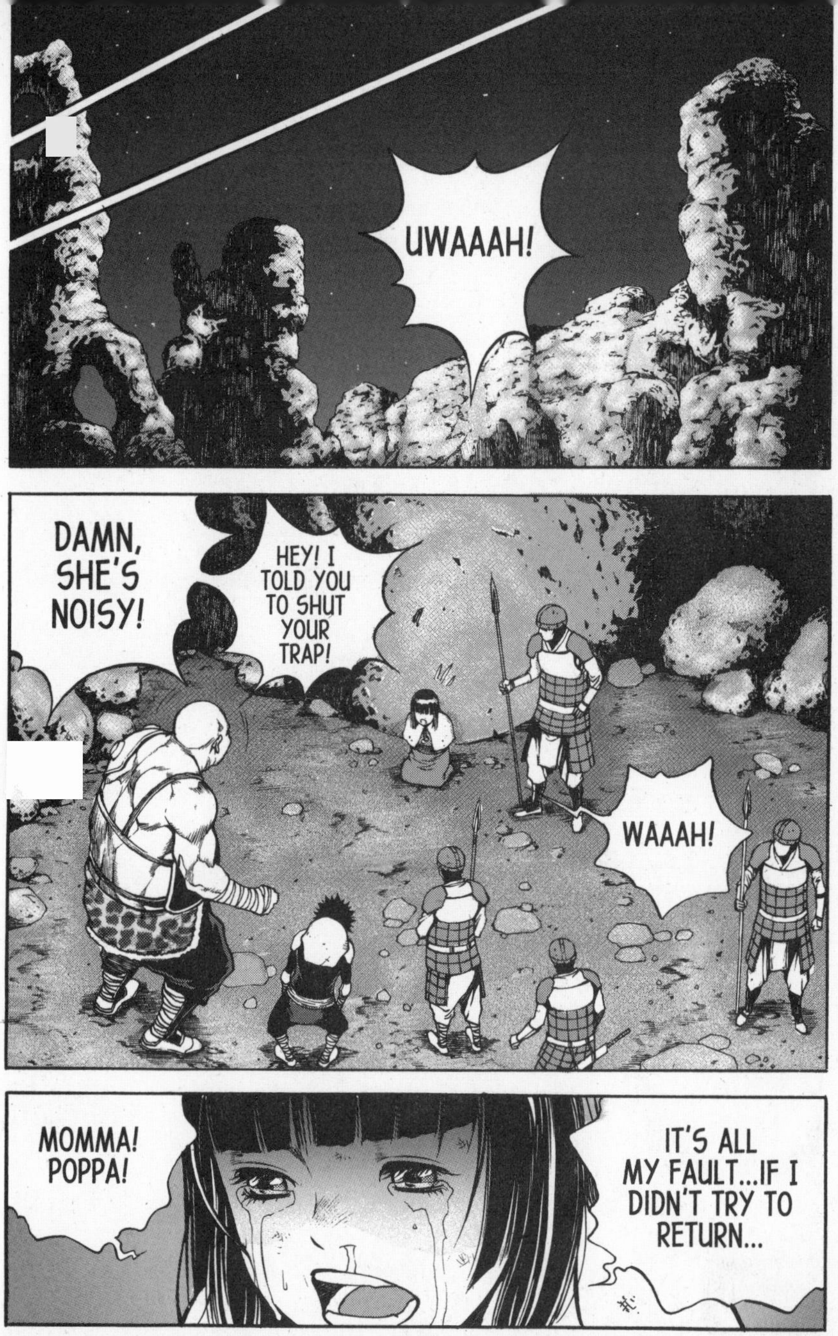
UWAAAH!
DAMN, SHE'S NOISY!
HEY! I TOLD YOU TO SHUT YOUR TRAP!
WAAAH!
MOMMA! POPPA!
IT'S ALL MY FAULT...IF I DIDN'T TRY TO RETURN...

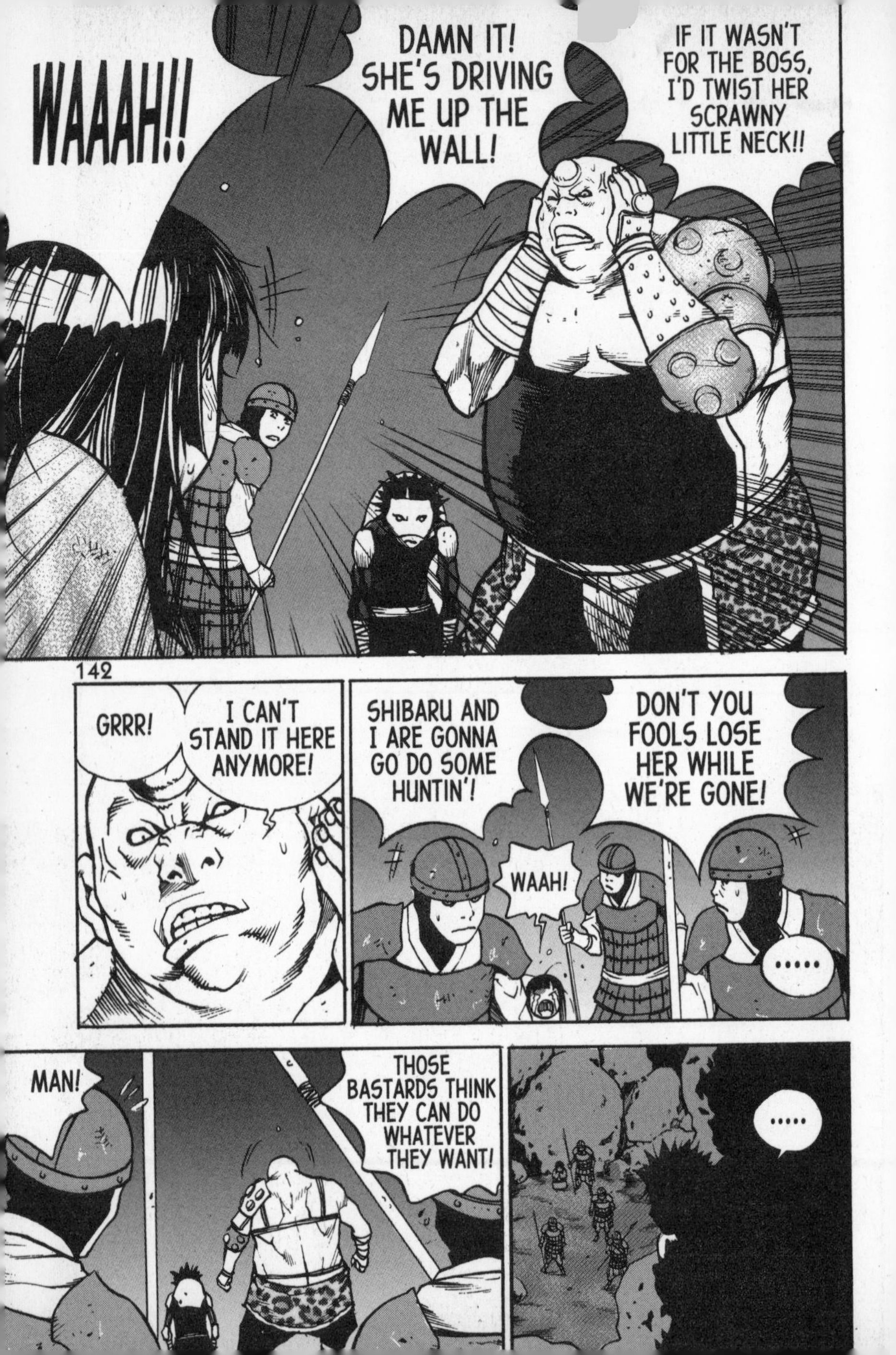
WAAAH!!
DAMN IT! SHE'S DRIVING ME UP THE WALL!
IF IT WASN'T FOR THE BOSS, I'D TWIST HER SCRAWNY LITTLE NECK!!
GRRR!
I CAN'T STAND IT HERE ANYMORE!
SHIBARU AND I ARE GONNA GO DO SOME HUNTIN'!
DON'T YOU FOOLS LOSE HER WHILE WE'RE GONE!
WAAH!
.....
MAN!
THOSE BASTARDS THINK THEY CAN DO WHATEVER THEY WANT!
.....

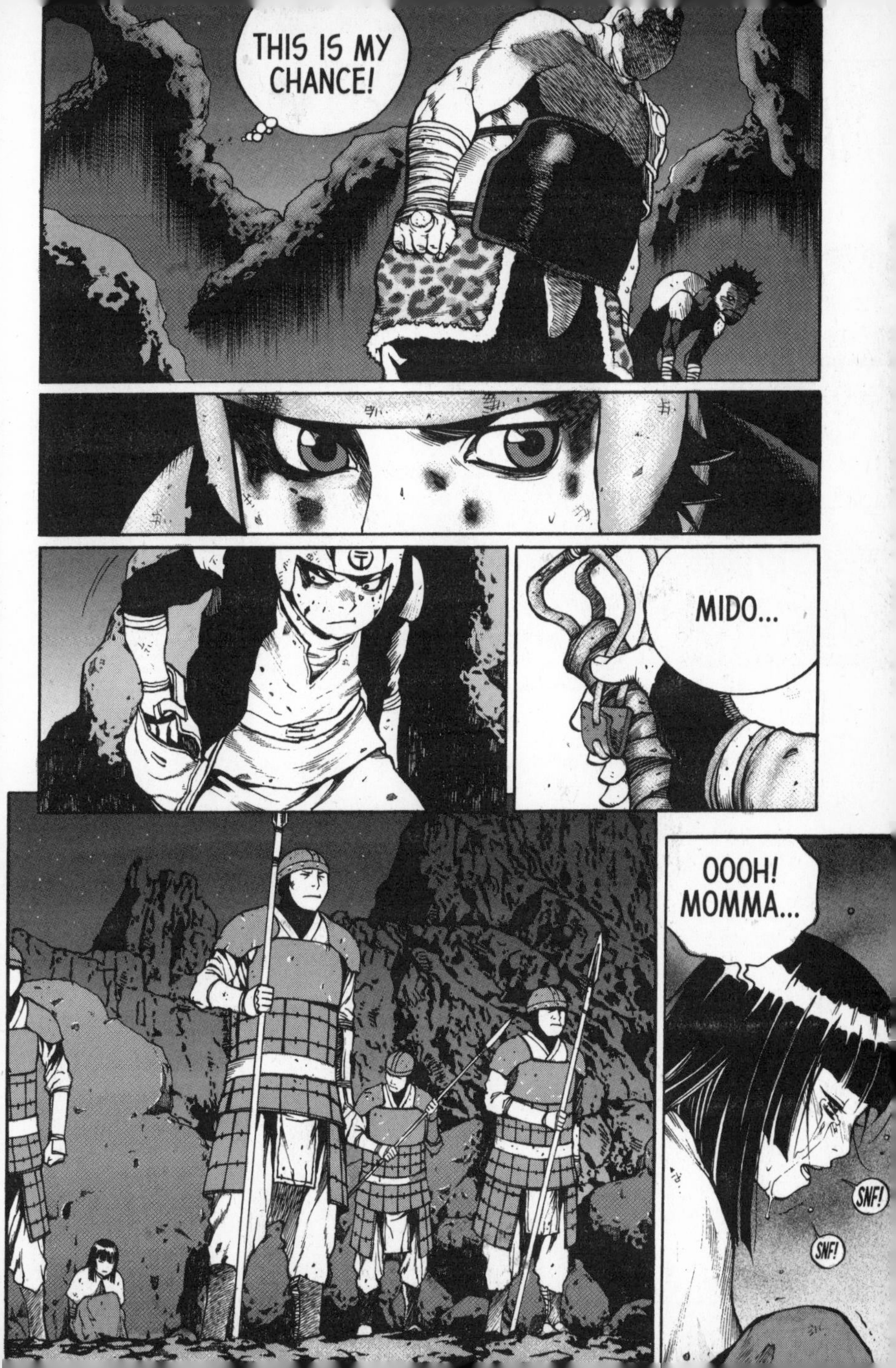
THIS IS MY CHANCE!
MIDO...
OOOH! MOMMA...
SNF!
SNF!

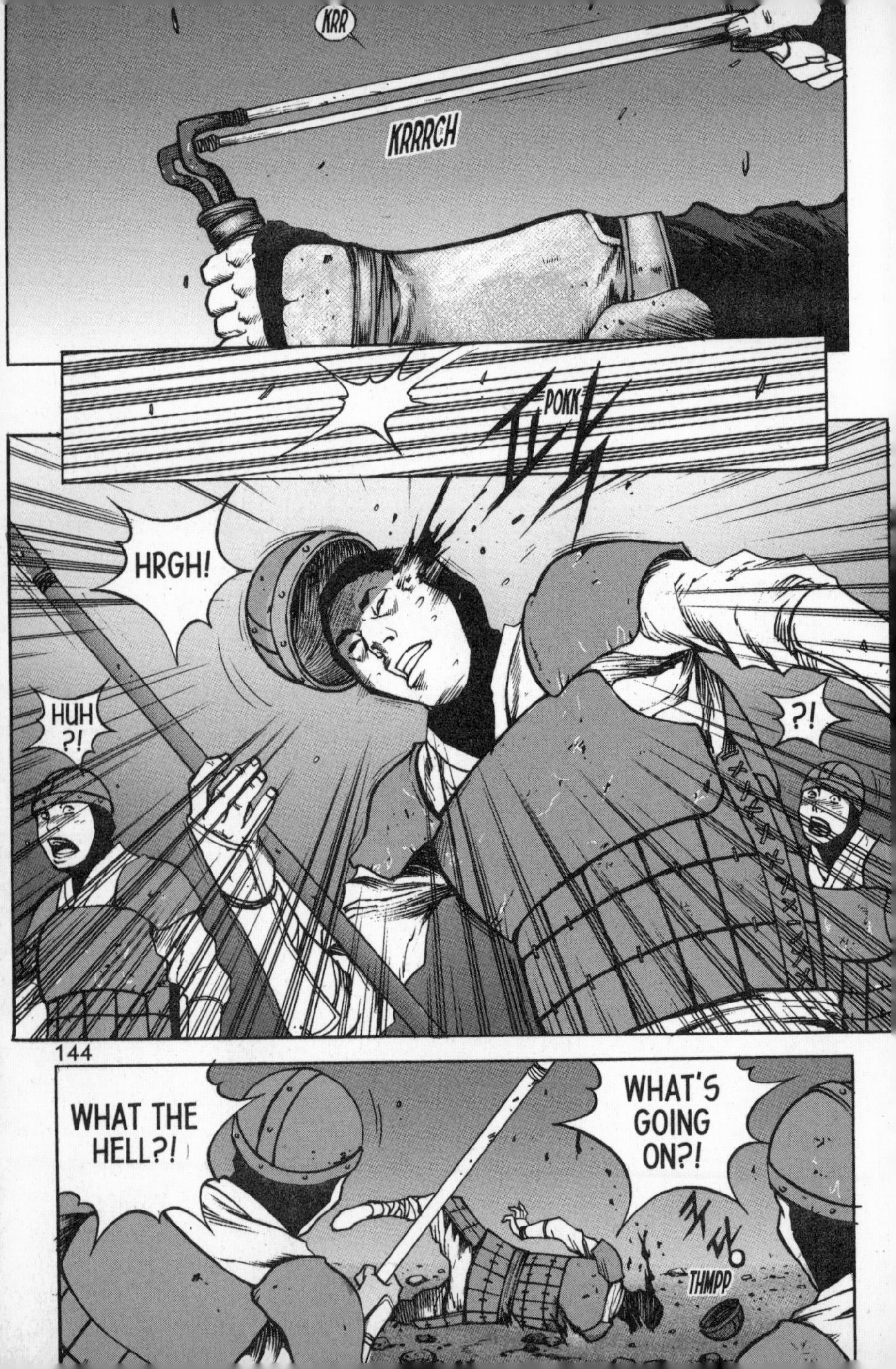
KRR
KRRRCH
POKK
HRGH!
HUH ?!
?!
WHAT THE HELL?!
WHAT'S GOING ON?!
THMPP

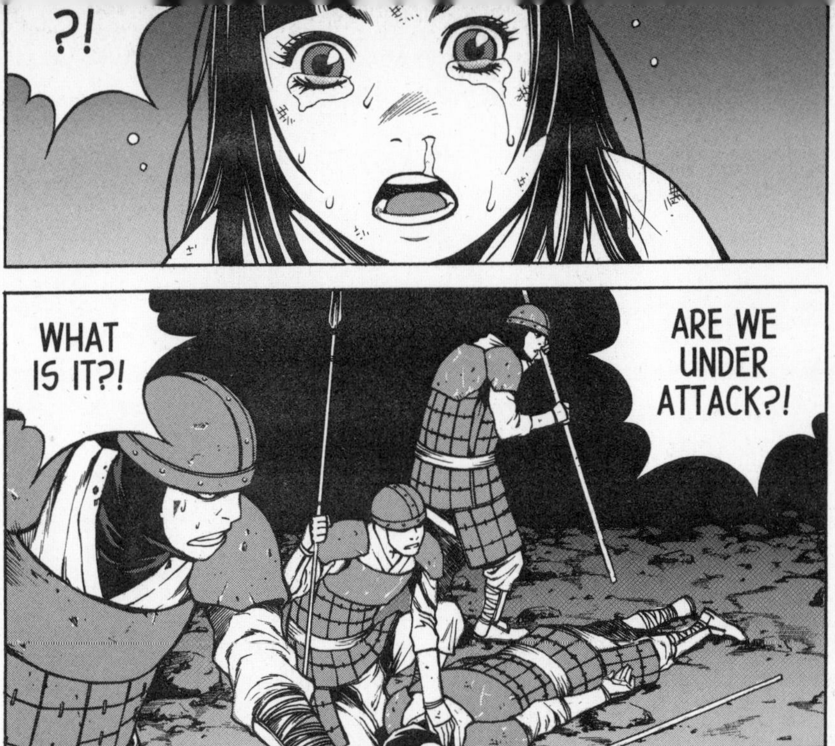
?!
ARE WE UNDER ATTACK?!
WHAT IS IT?!

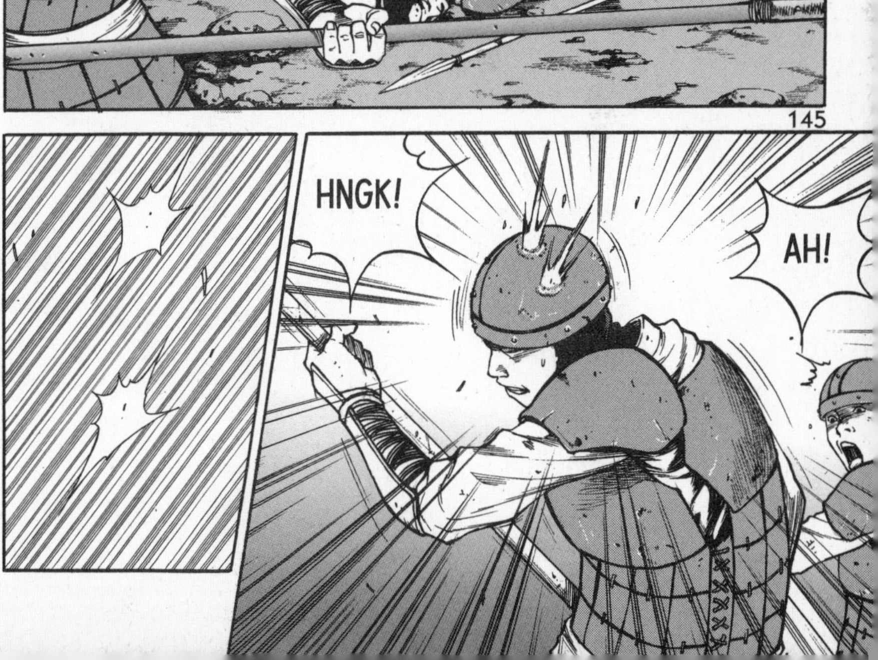
AH!
HNGK!

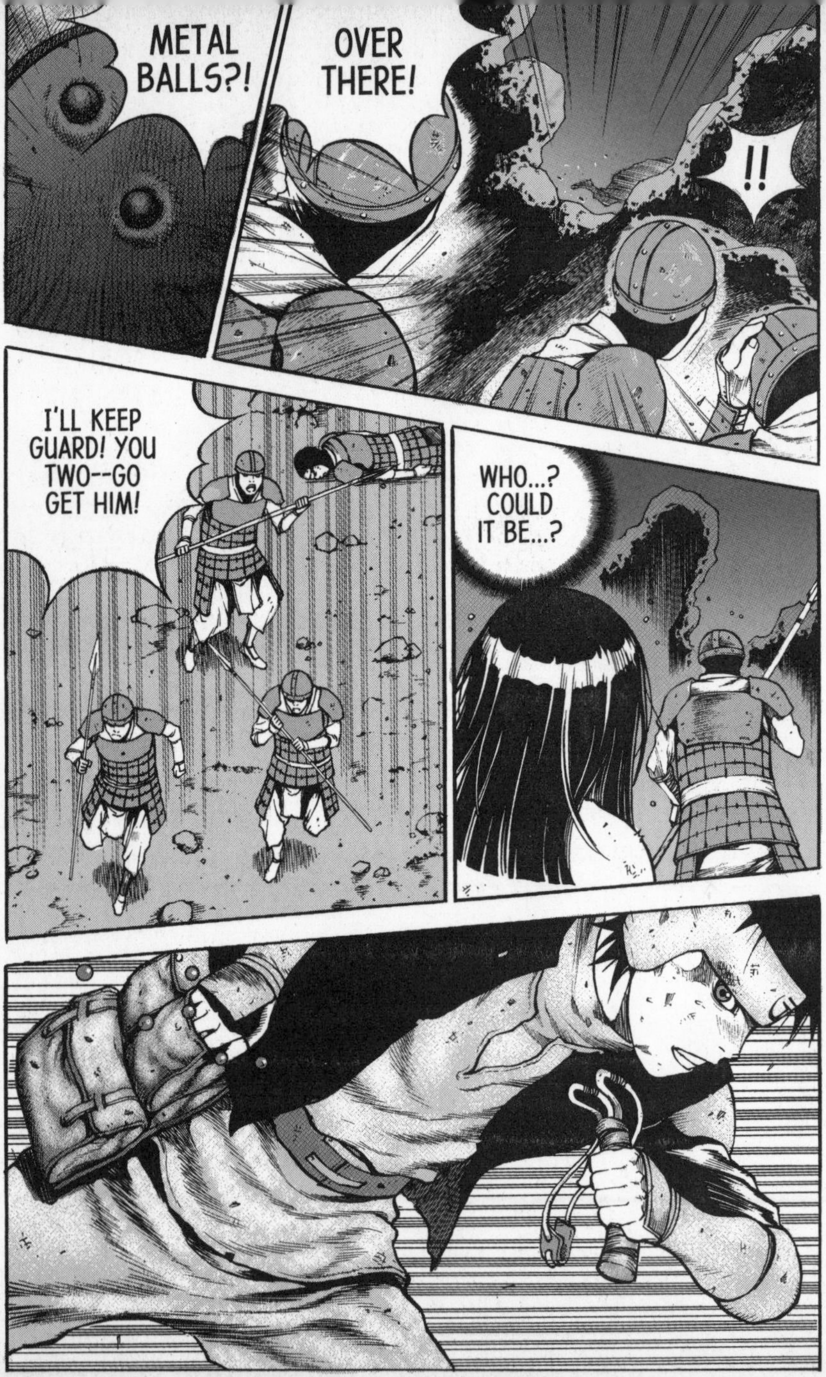
OVER THERE!
METAL BALLS?!
!!
WHO...? COULD IT BE...?
I'LL KEEP GUARD! YOU TWO--GO GET HIM!

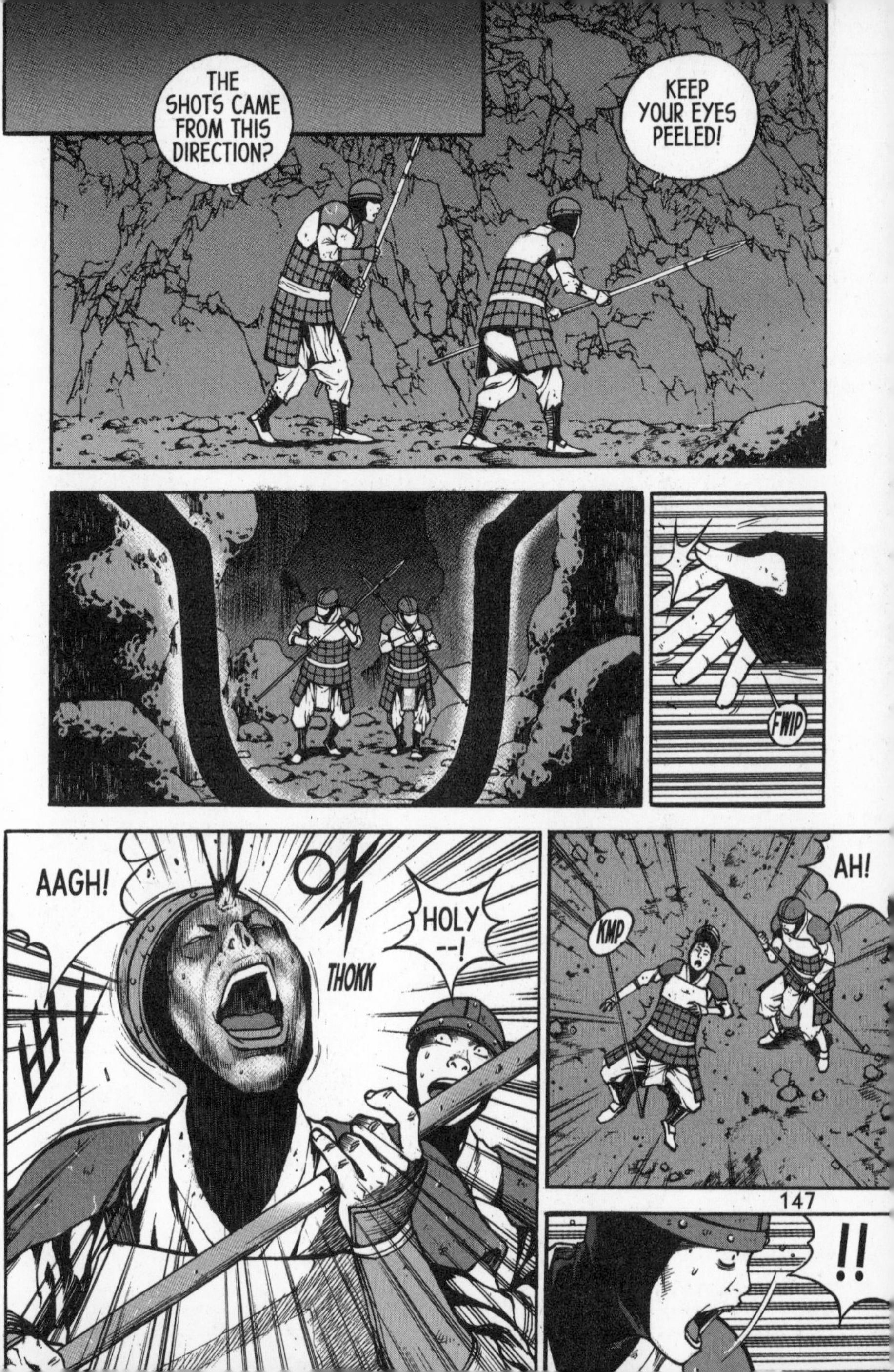
THE SHOTS CAME FROM THIS DIRECTION?
KEEP YOUR EYES PEELED!
FWIP
AAGH!
THOKK
HOLY --!
AH!
KMP
!!

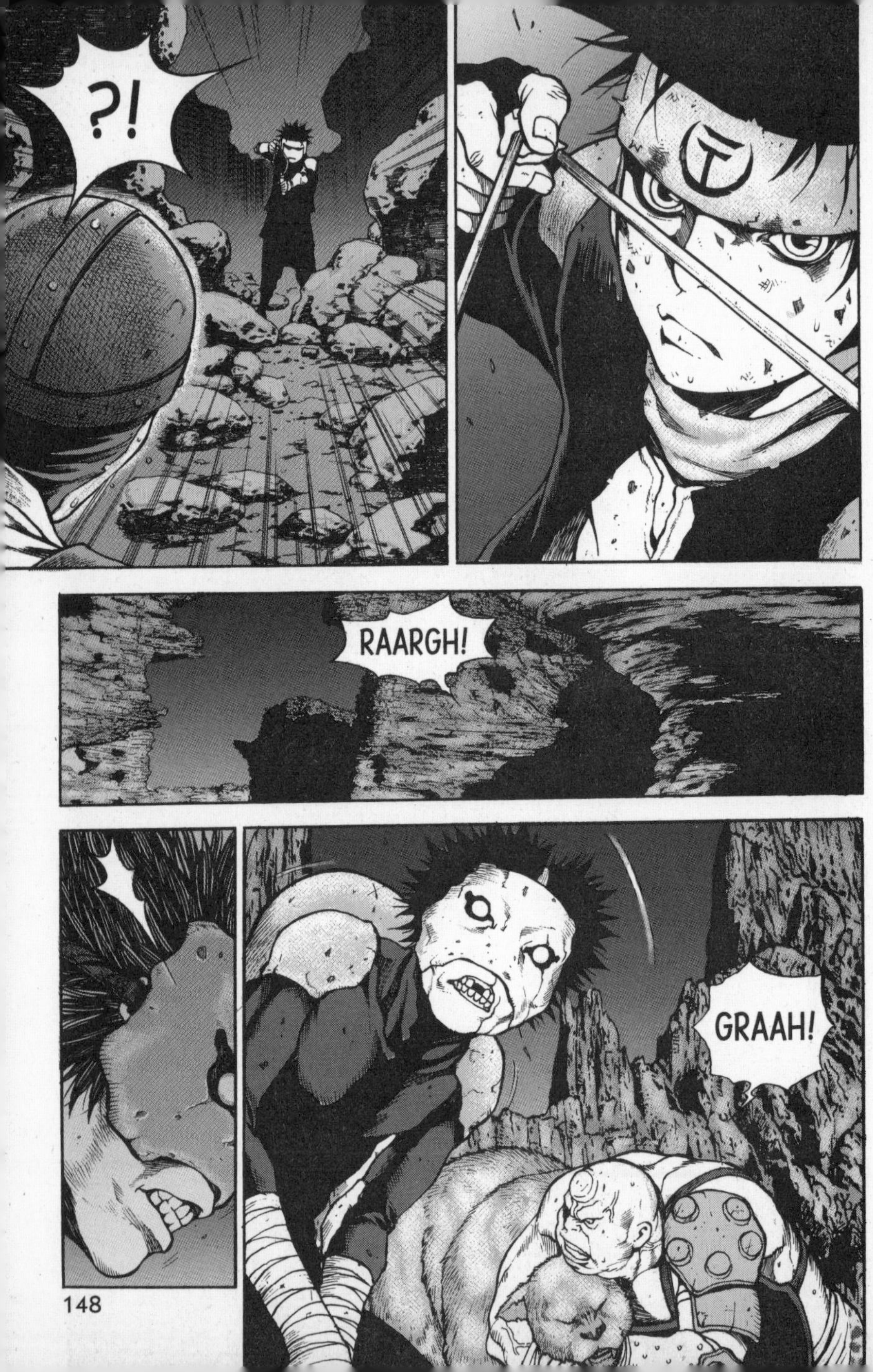
?!
RAARGH!
GRAAH!

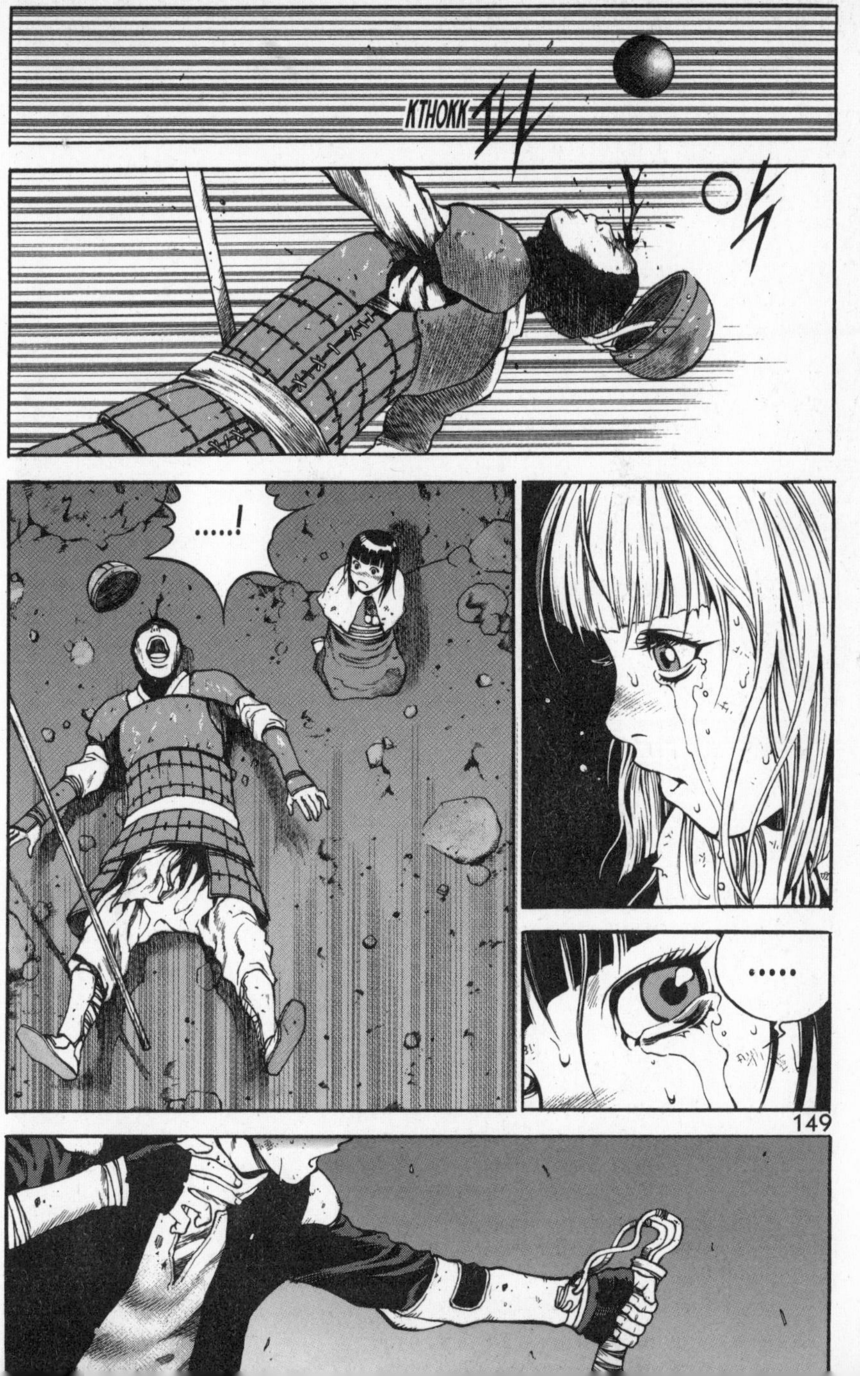
KTHOKK
.....!
.....

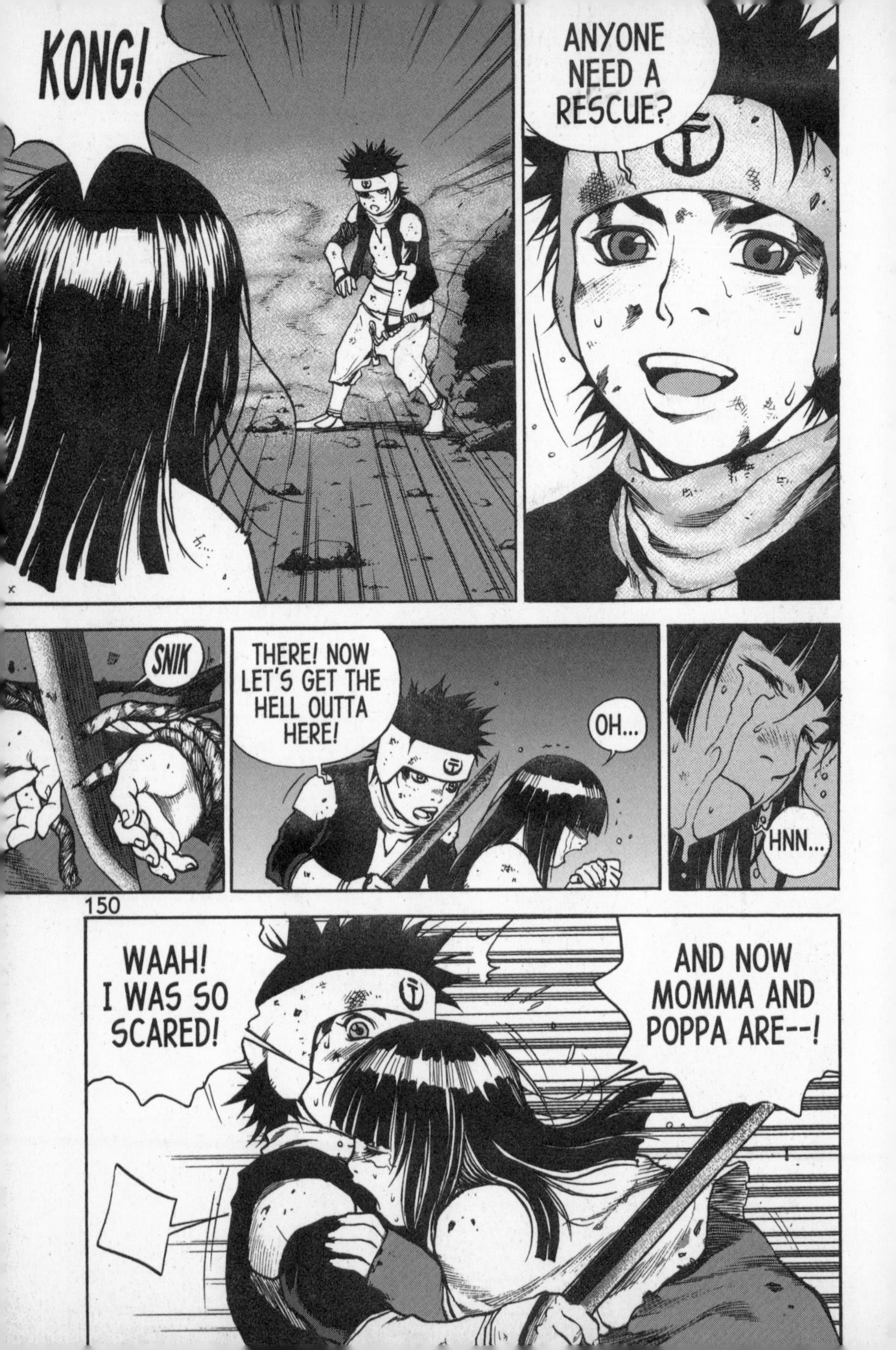
ANYONE NEED A RESCUE?
KONG!
SNIK
THERE! NOW LET'S GET THE HELL OUTTA HERE!
OH...
HNN...
AND NOW MOMMA AND POPPA ARE--!
WAAH! I WAS SO SCARED!

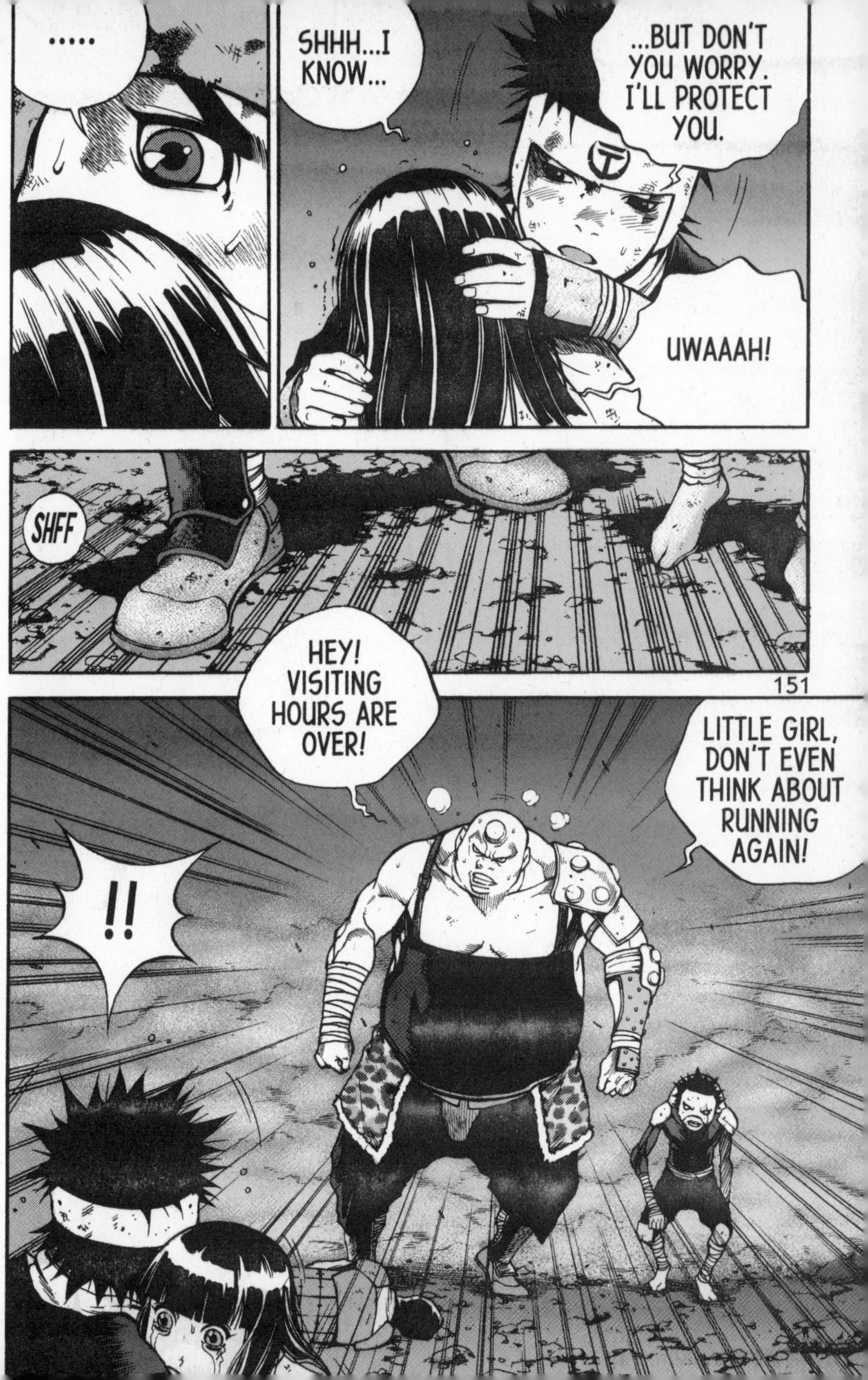

......
SHHH...I KNOW...
...BUT DON'T YOU WORRY. I'LL PROTECT YOU.
UWAAAH!
SHFF
HEY! VISITING HOURS ARE OVER!
LITTLE GIRL, DON'T EVEN THINK ABOUT RUNNING AGAIN!
!!

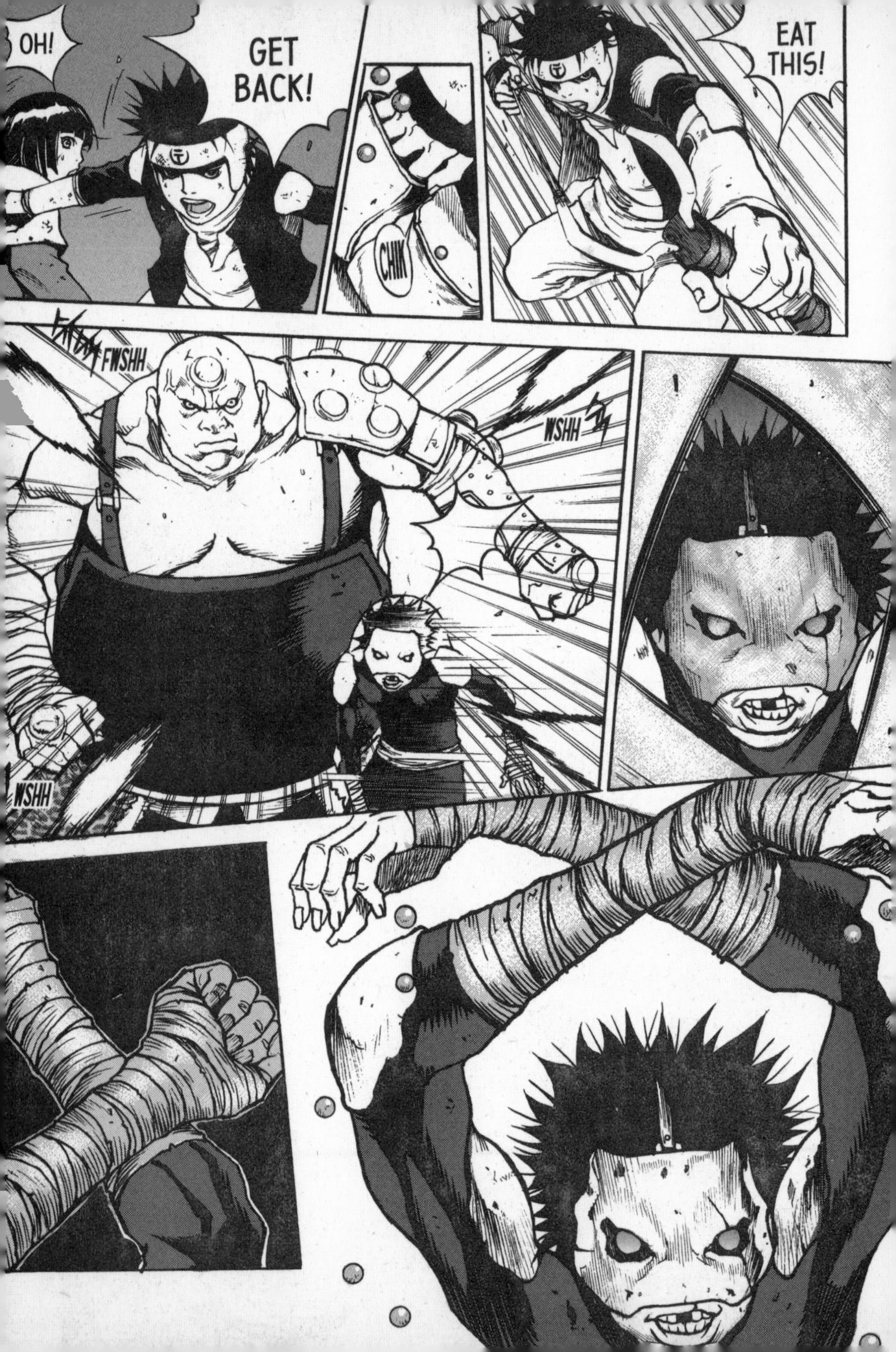

OH!
GET BACK!
CHIK
EAT THIS!
FWSHH
WSHH
WSHH

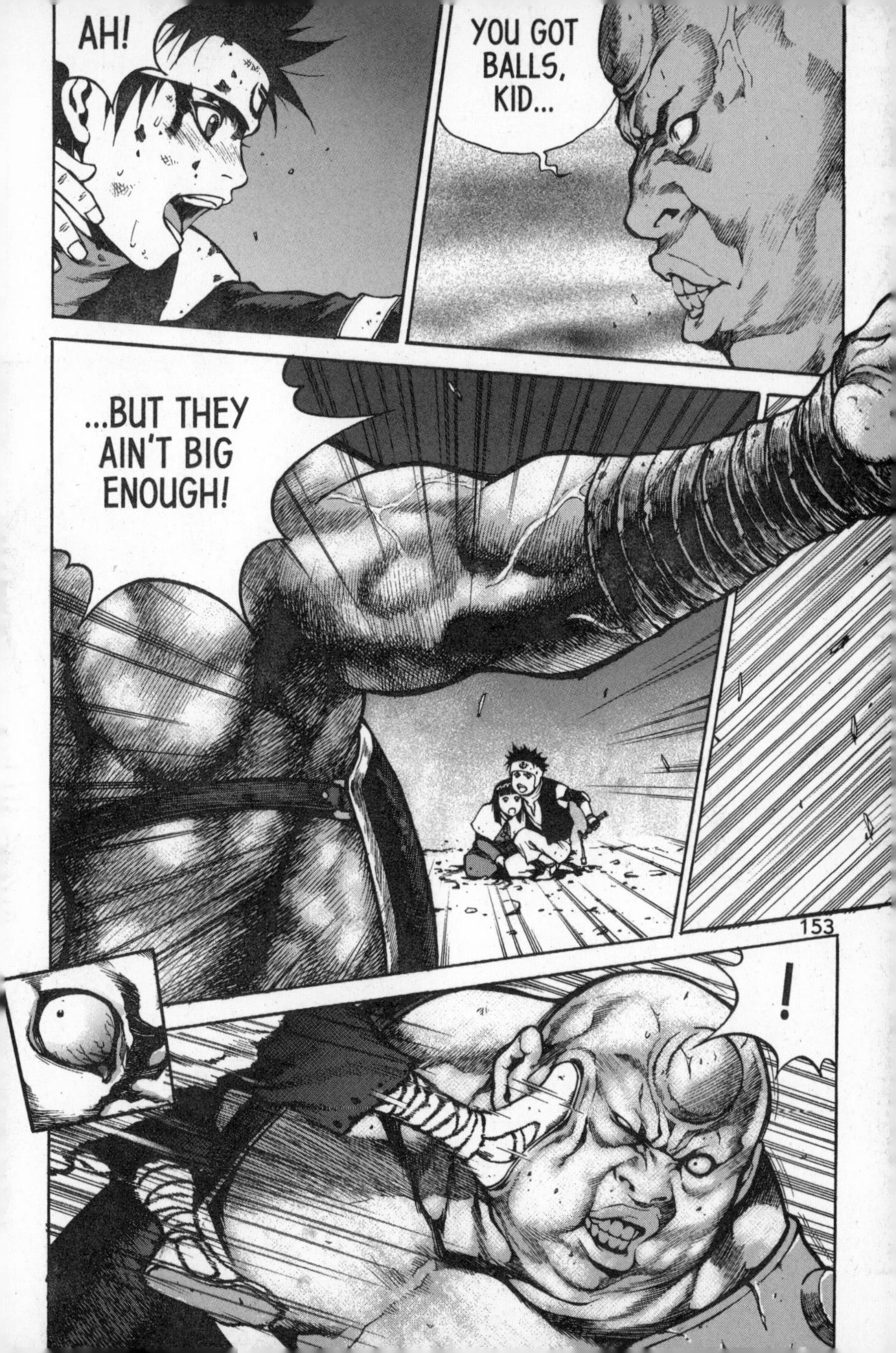
AH!
YOU GOT BALLS, KID...
...BUT THEY AIN'T BIG ENOUGH!
!

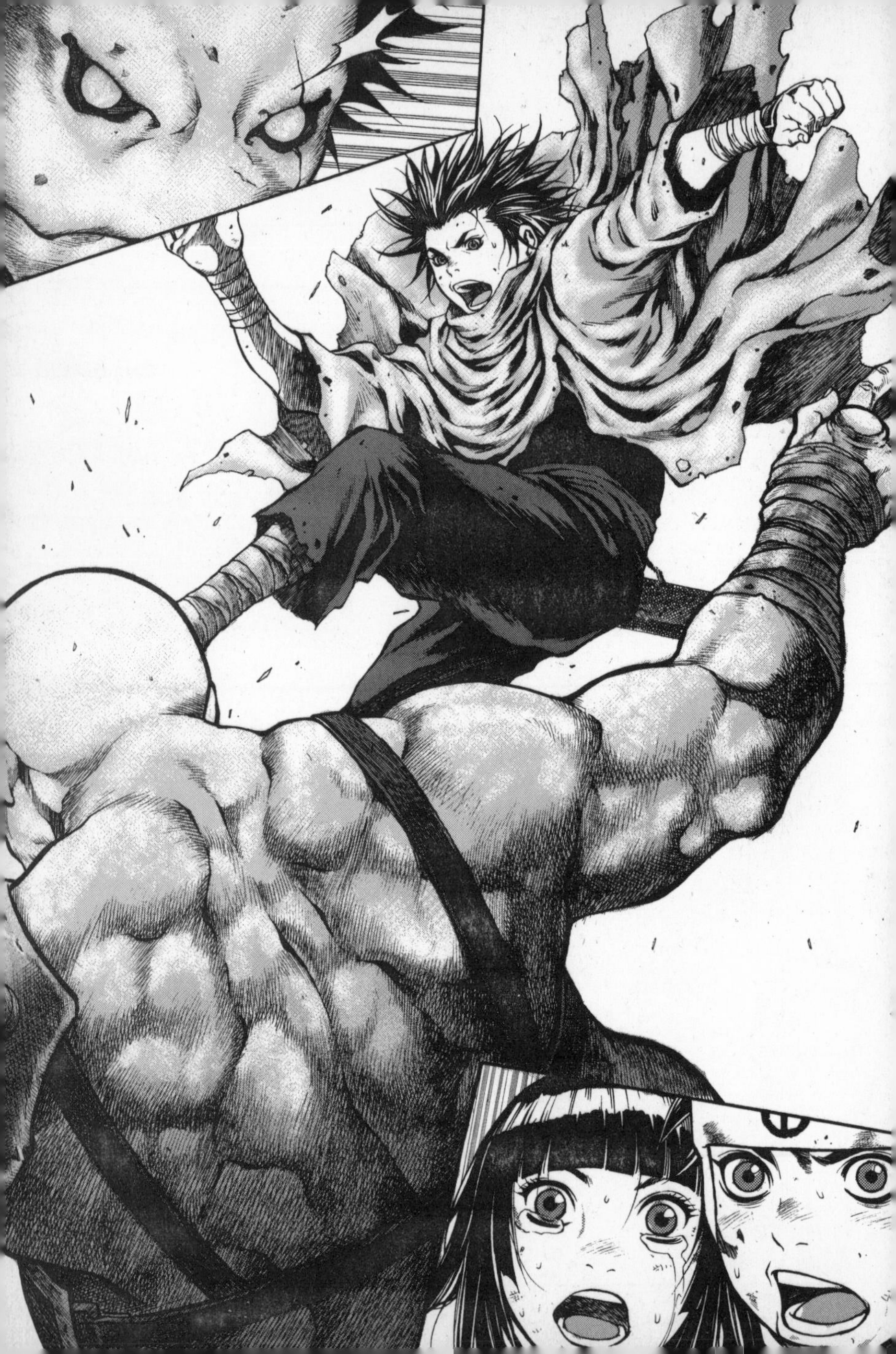

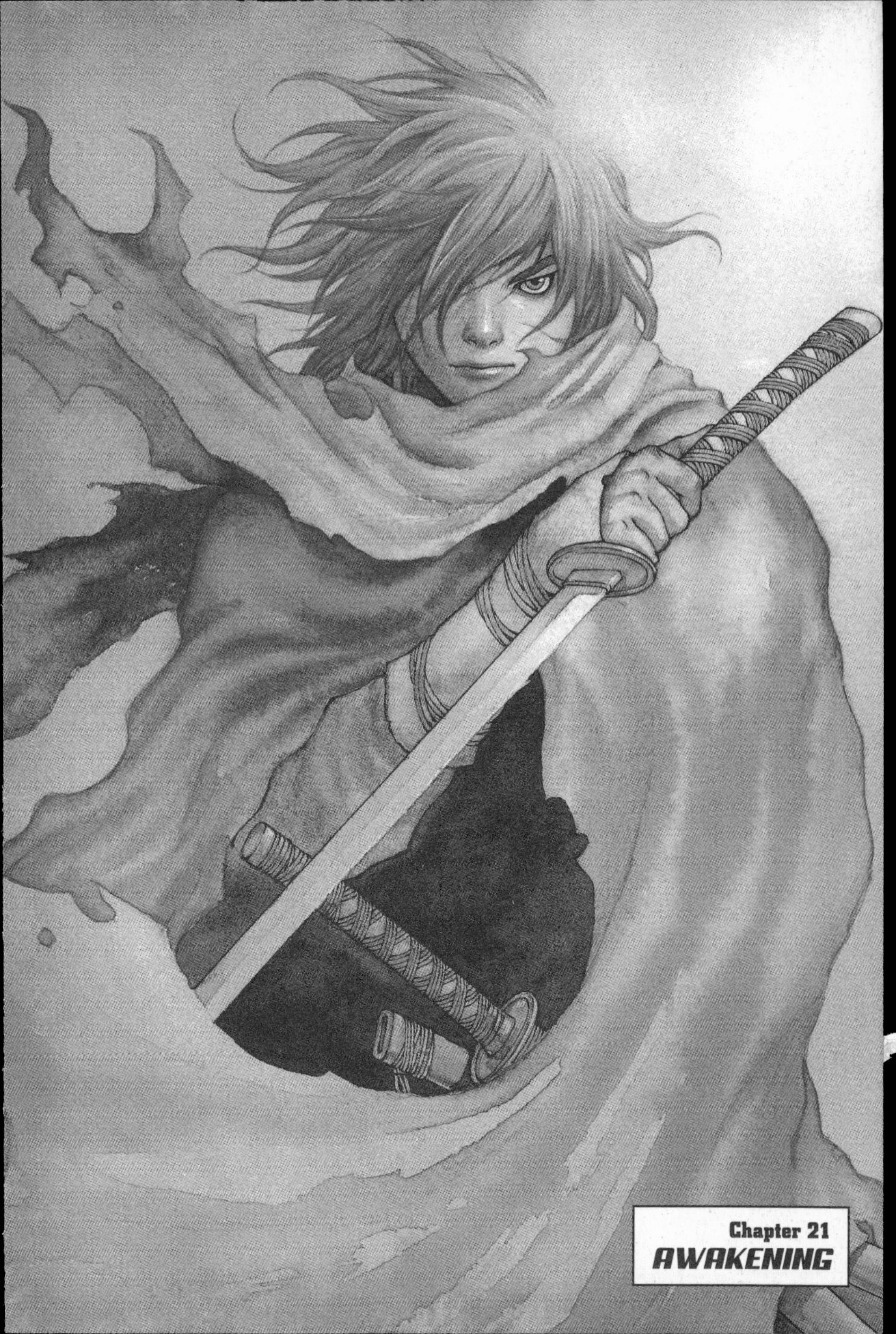
Chapter 21
AWAKENING

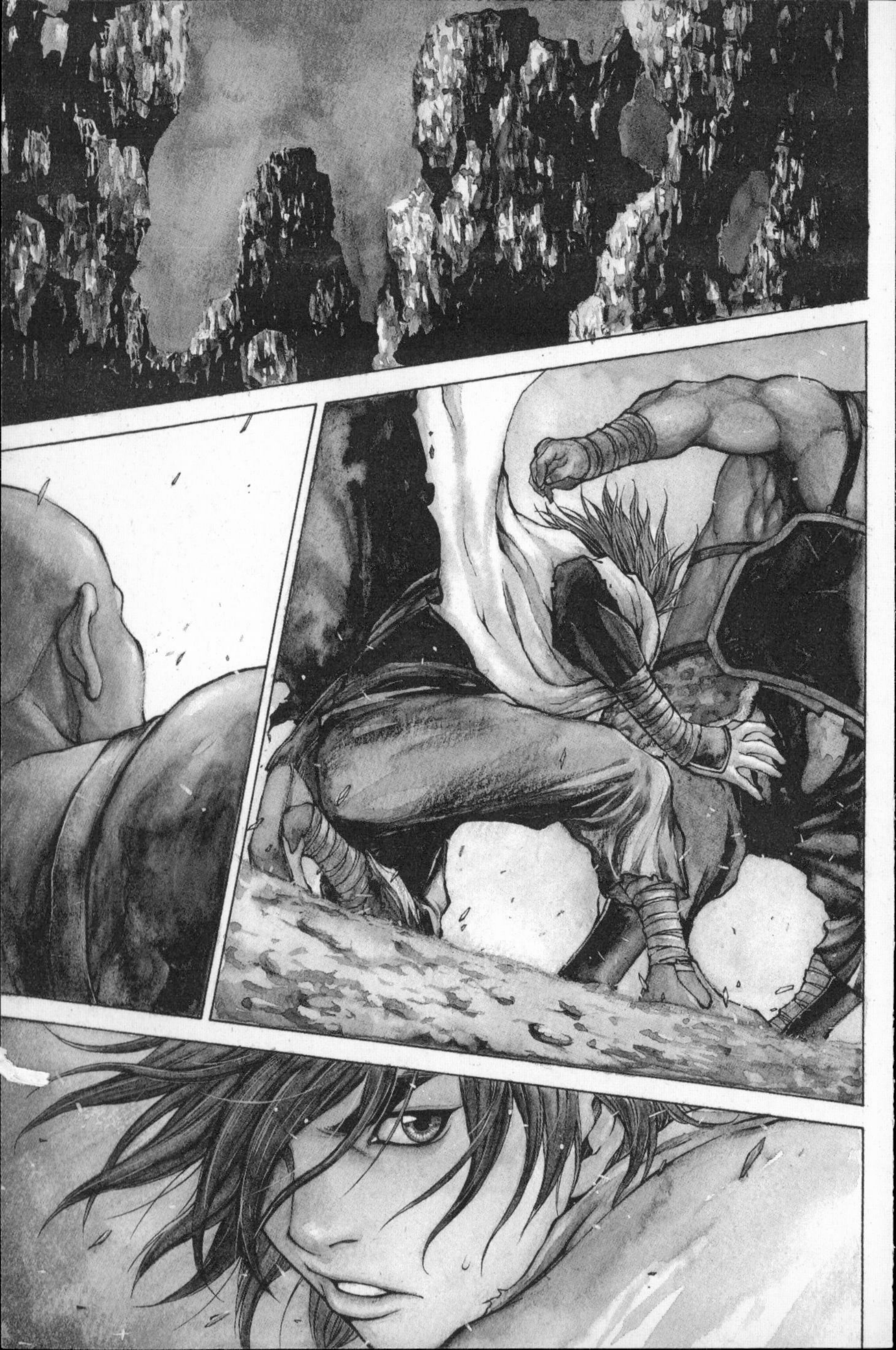

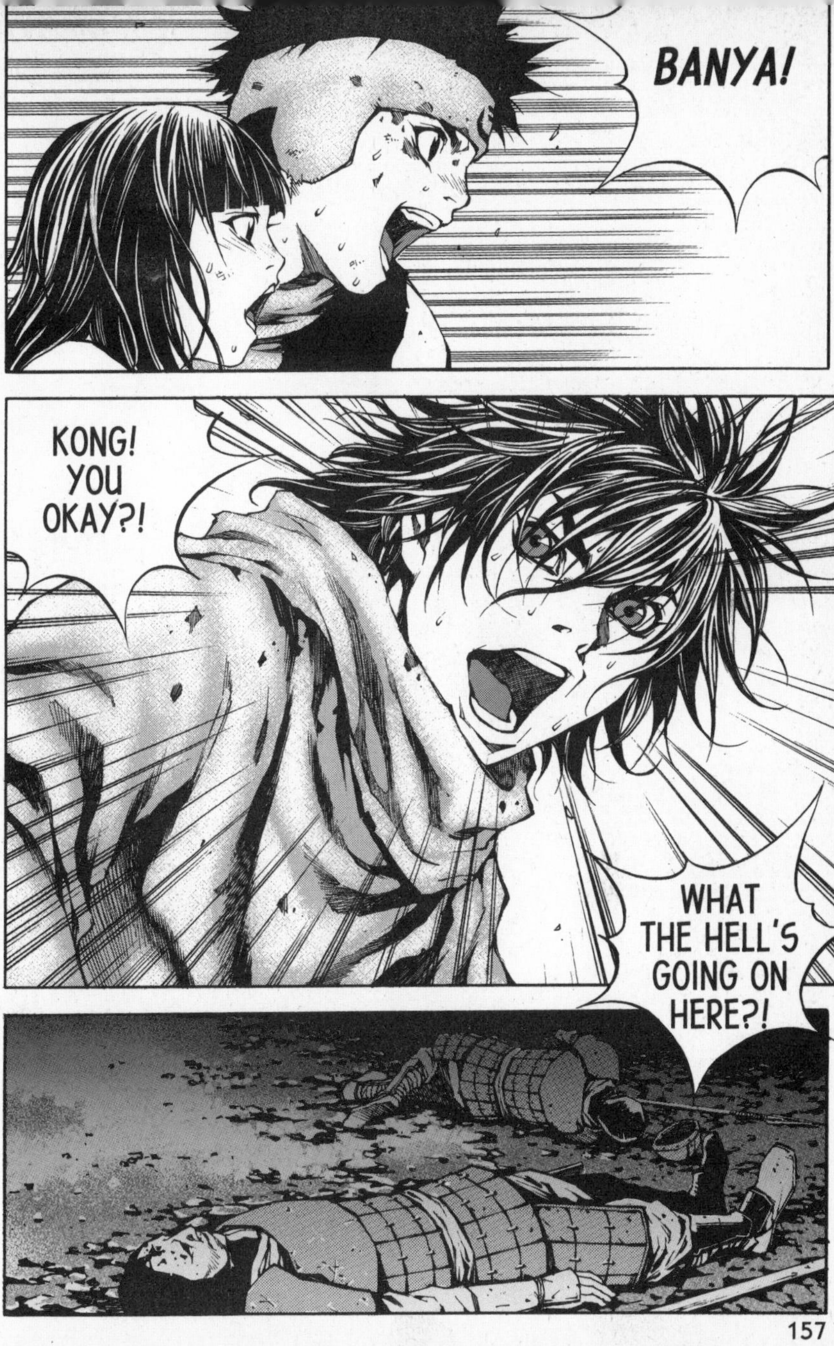
BANYA!
KONG! YOU OKAY?!
WHAT THE HELL'S GOING ON HERE?!

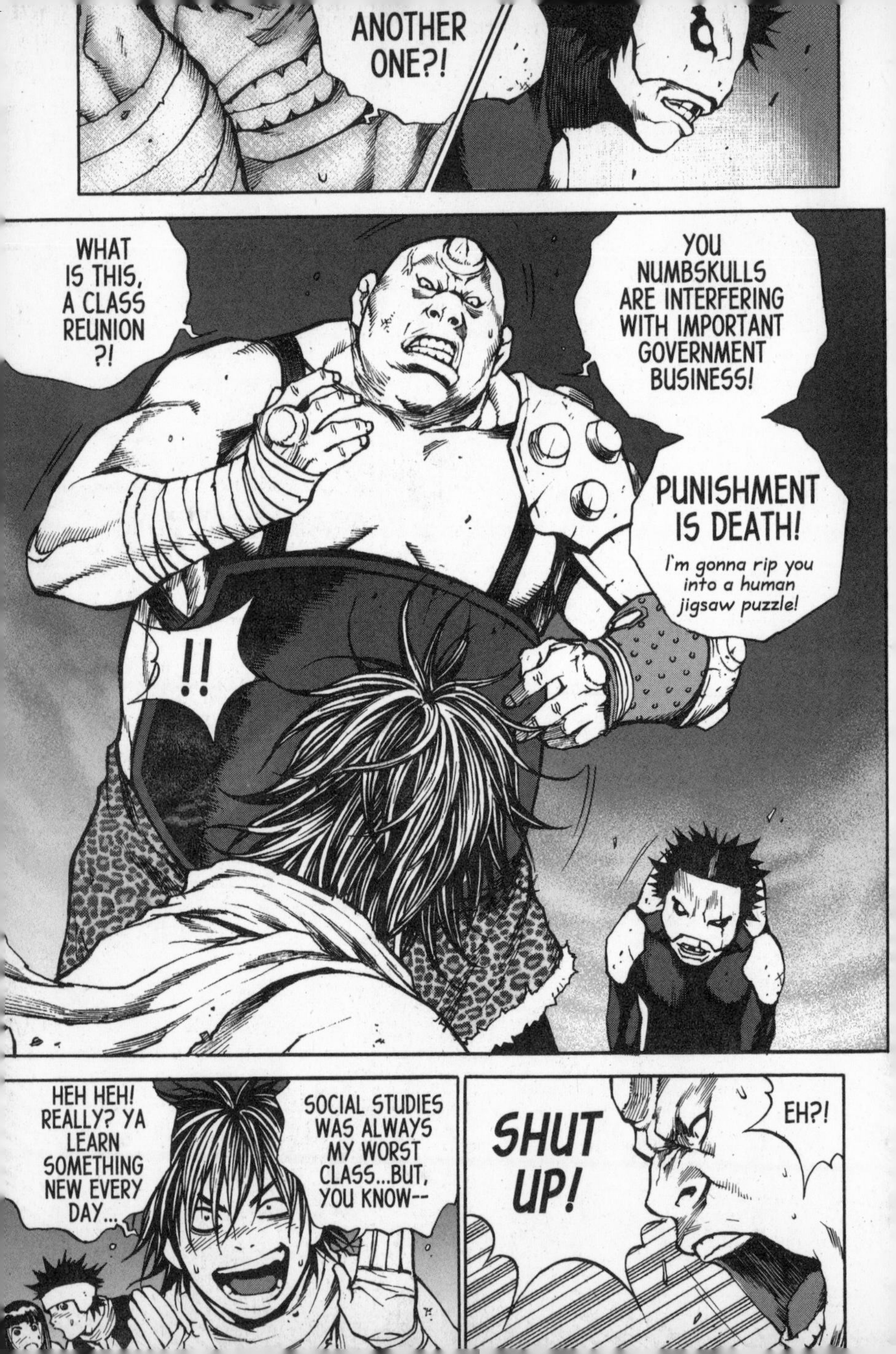
ANOTHER ONE?!
WHAT IS THIS, A CLASS REUNION ?!
YOU NUMBSKULLS ARE INTERFERING WITH IMPORTANT GOVERNMENT BUSINESS!
PUNISHMENT IS DEATH!
I'm gonna rip you into a human jigsaw puzzle!
!!
HEH HEH! REALLY? YA LEARN SOMETHING NEW EVERY DAY...
SOCIAL STUDIES WAS ALWAYS MY WORST CLASS...BUT, YOU KNOW--
SHUT UP!
EH?!

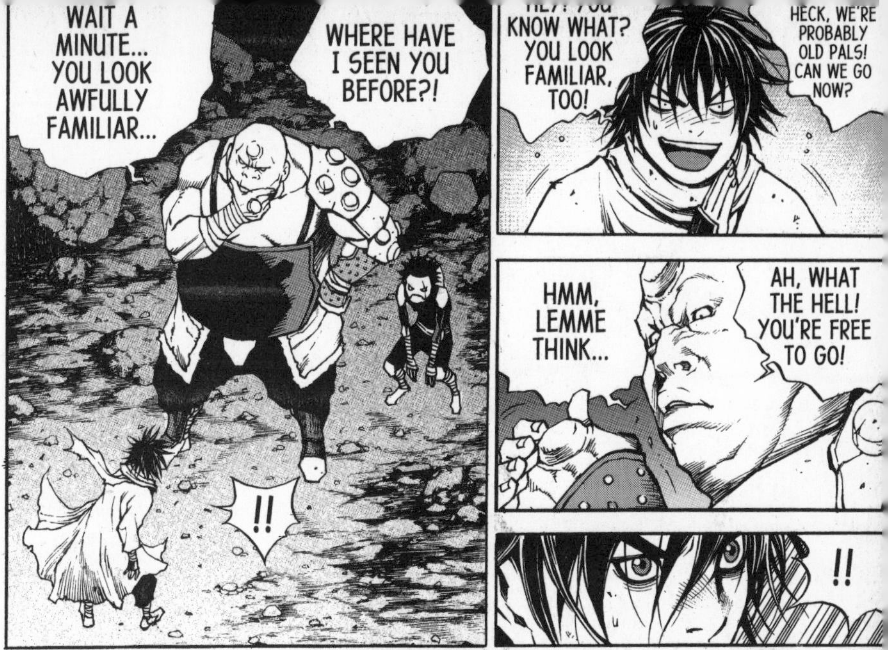
WAIT A MINUTE... YOU LOOK AWFULLY FAMILIAR...
WHERE HAVE I SEEN YOU BEFORE?!
!!
KNOW WHAT? YOU LOOK FAMILIAR, TOO!
HECK, WE'RE PROBABLY OLD PALS! CAN WE GO NOW?
HMM, LEMME THINK...
AH, WHAT THE HELL! YOU'RE FREE TO GO!
!!

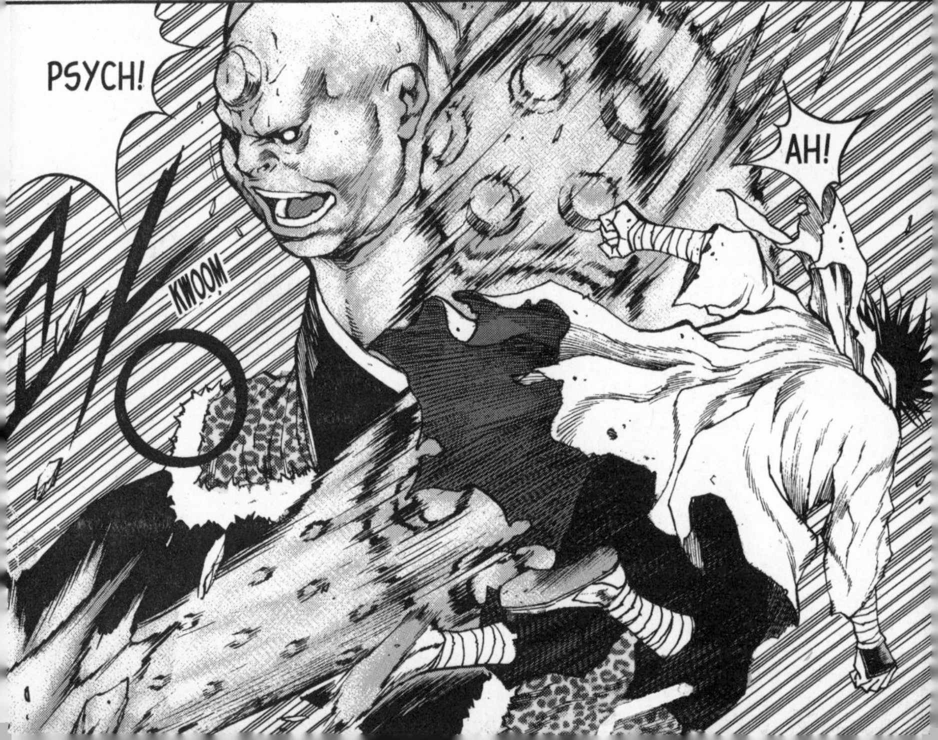
PSYCH!
KWOOM
AH!

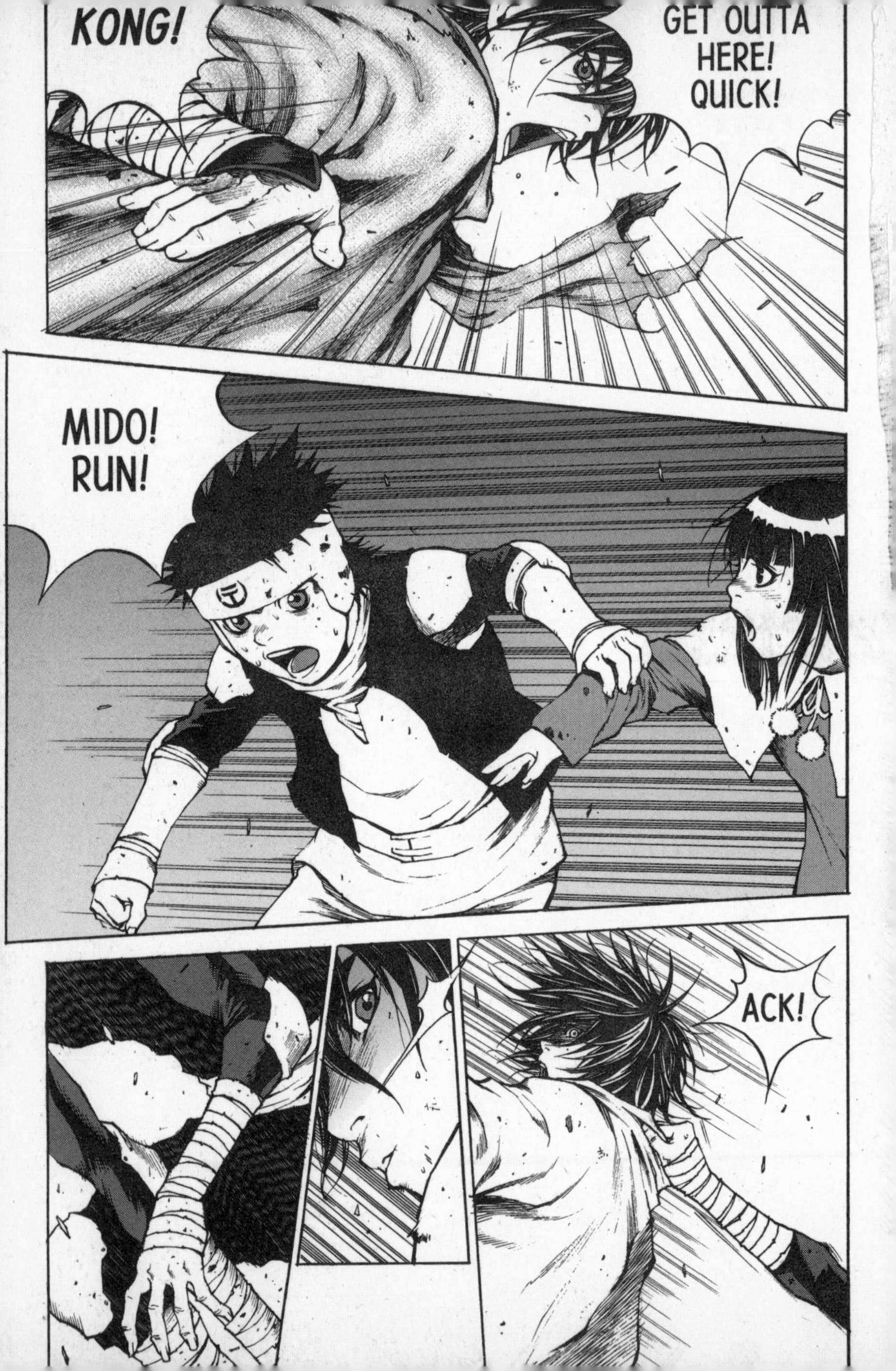
GET OUTTA HERE! QUICK!
KONG!
MIDO! RUN!
ACK!

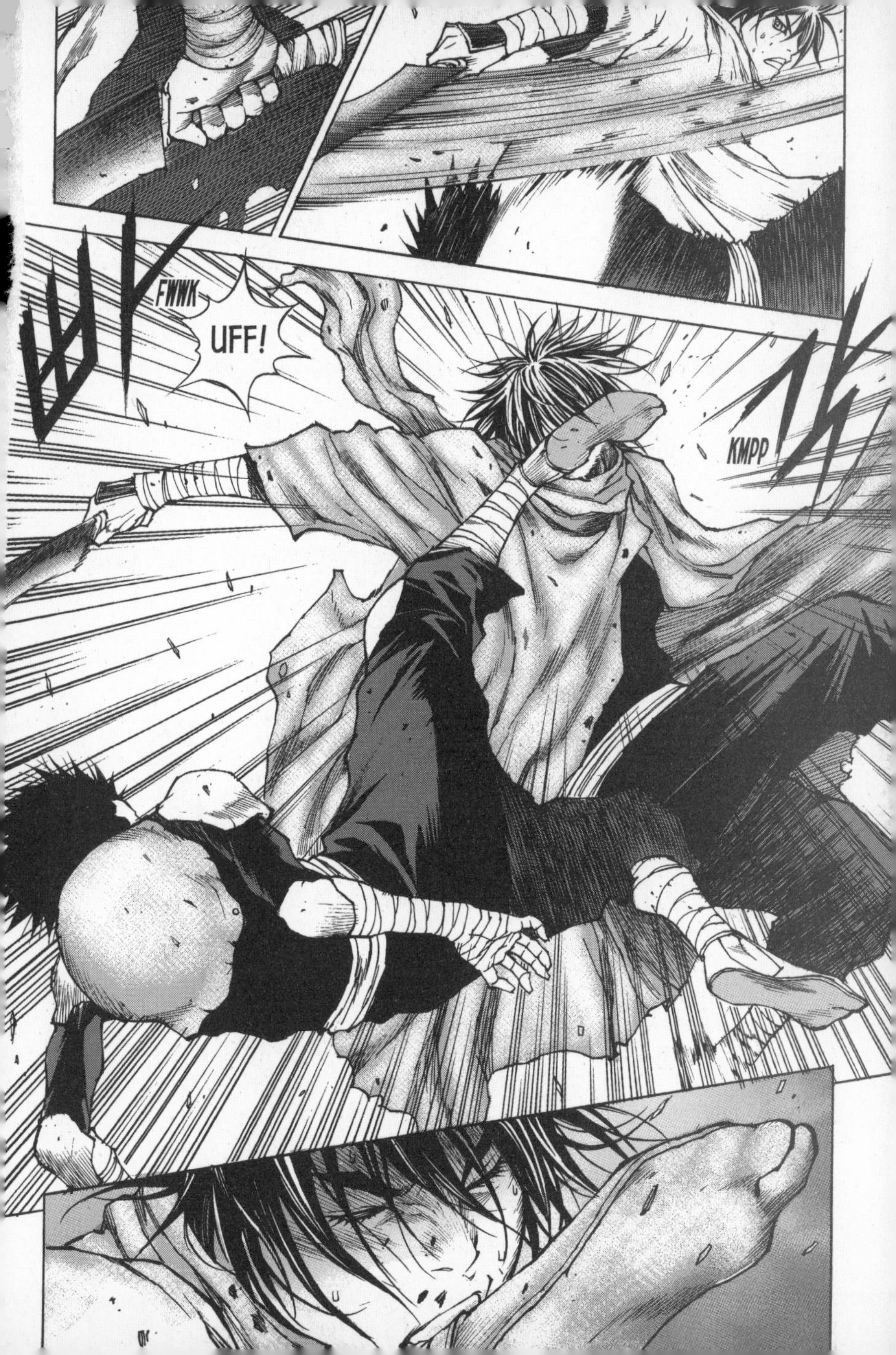
FWWK
UFF!
KMPP

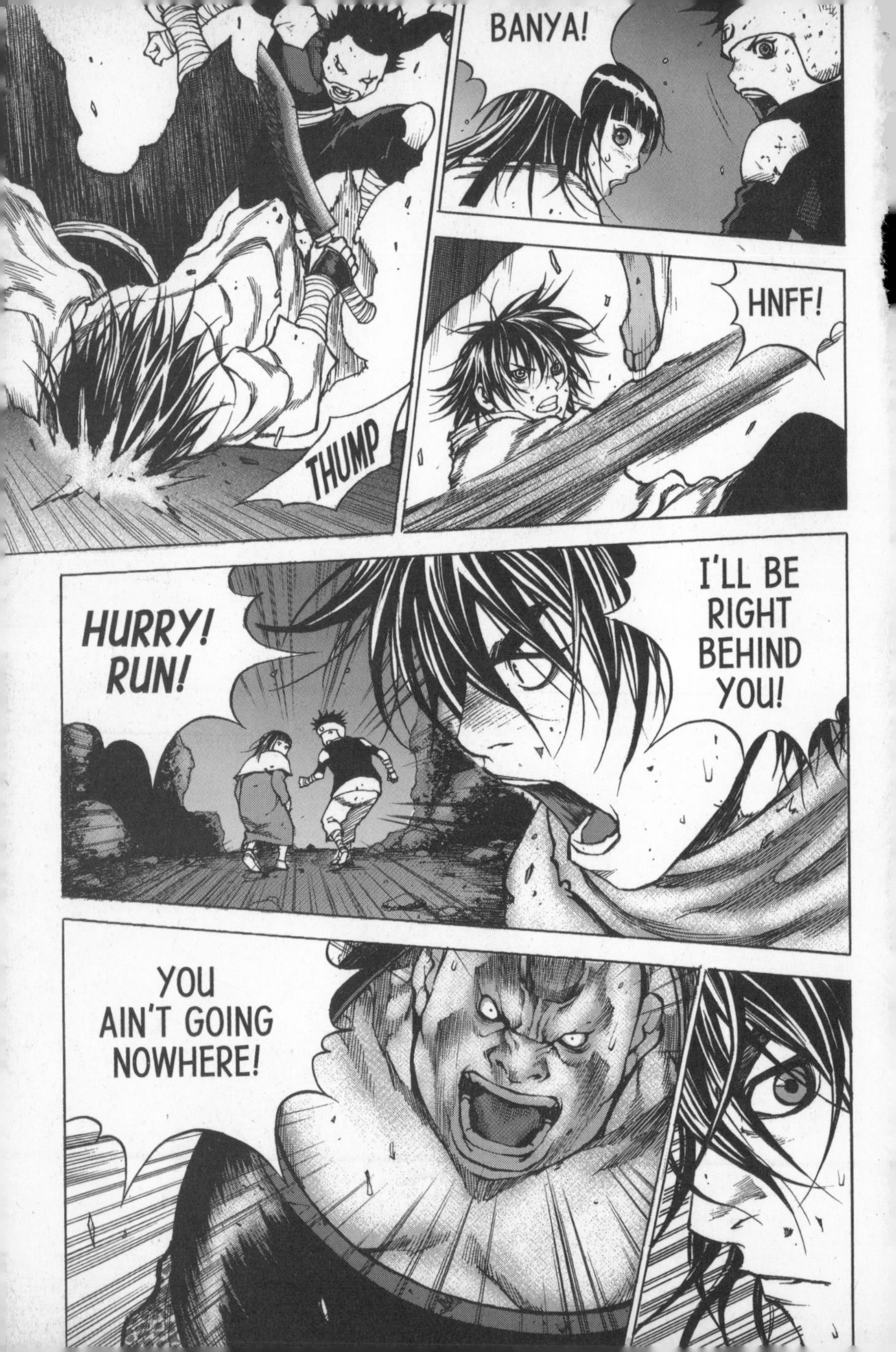
BANYA!
HNFF!
THUMP
I'LL BE RIGHT BEHIND YOU!
HURRY! RUN!
YOU AIN'T GOING NOWHERE!

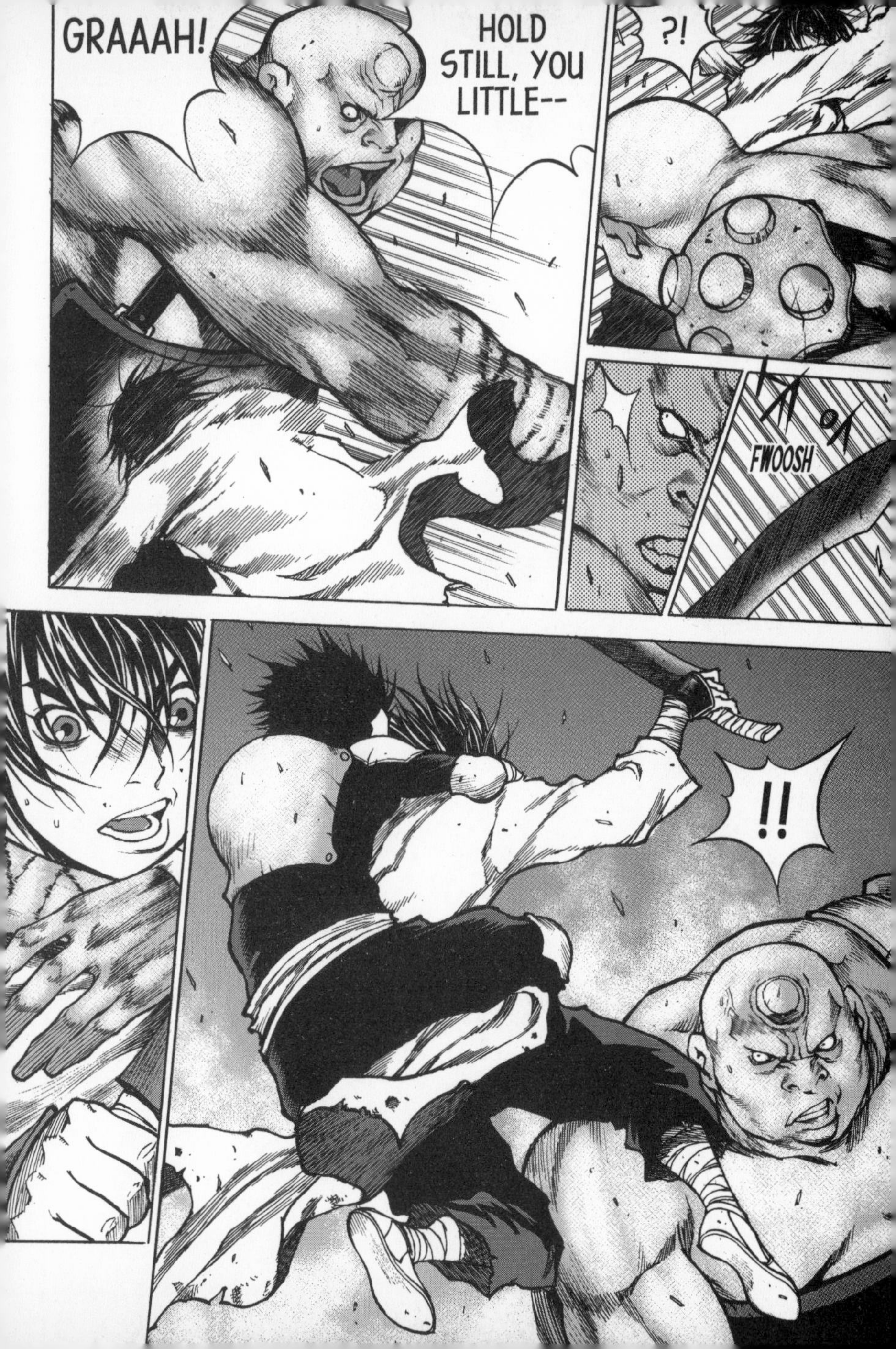
HOLD STILL, YOU LITTLE--
GRAAAH!
?!
FWOOSH
!!

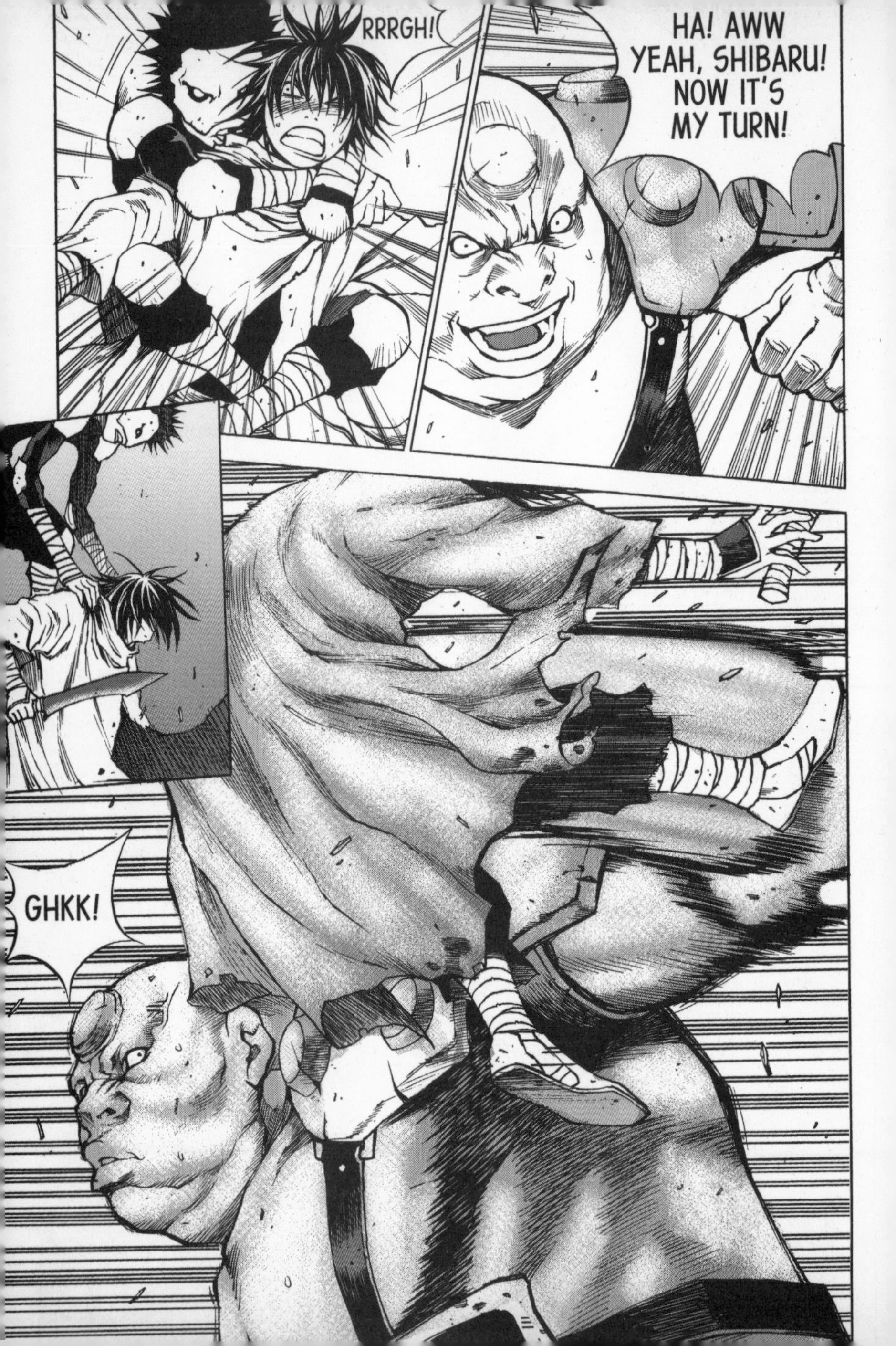
HA! AWW YEAH, SHIBARU! NOW IT'S MY TURN!
RRRGH!
GHKK!

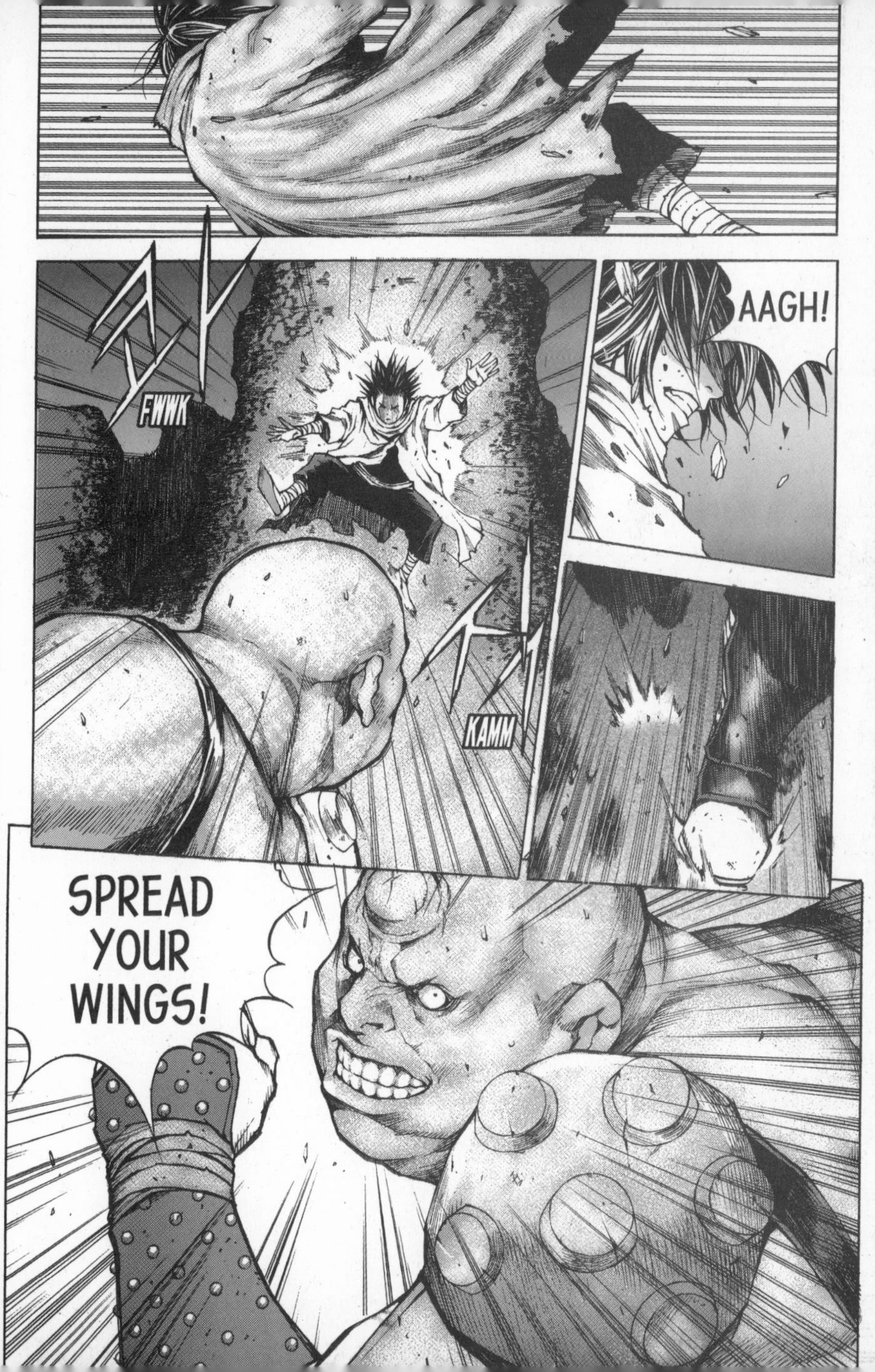
AAGH!
FWWK
KAMM
SPREAD YOUR WINGS!

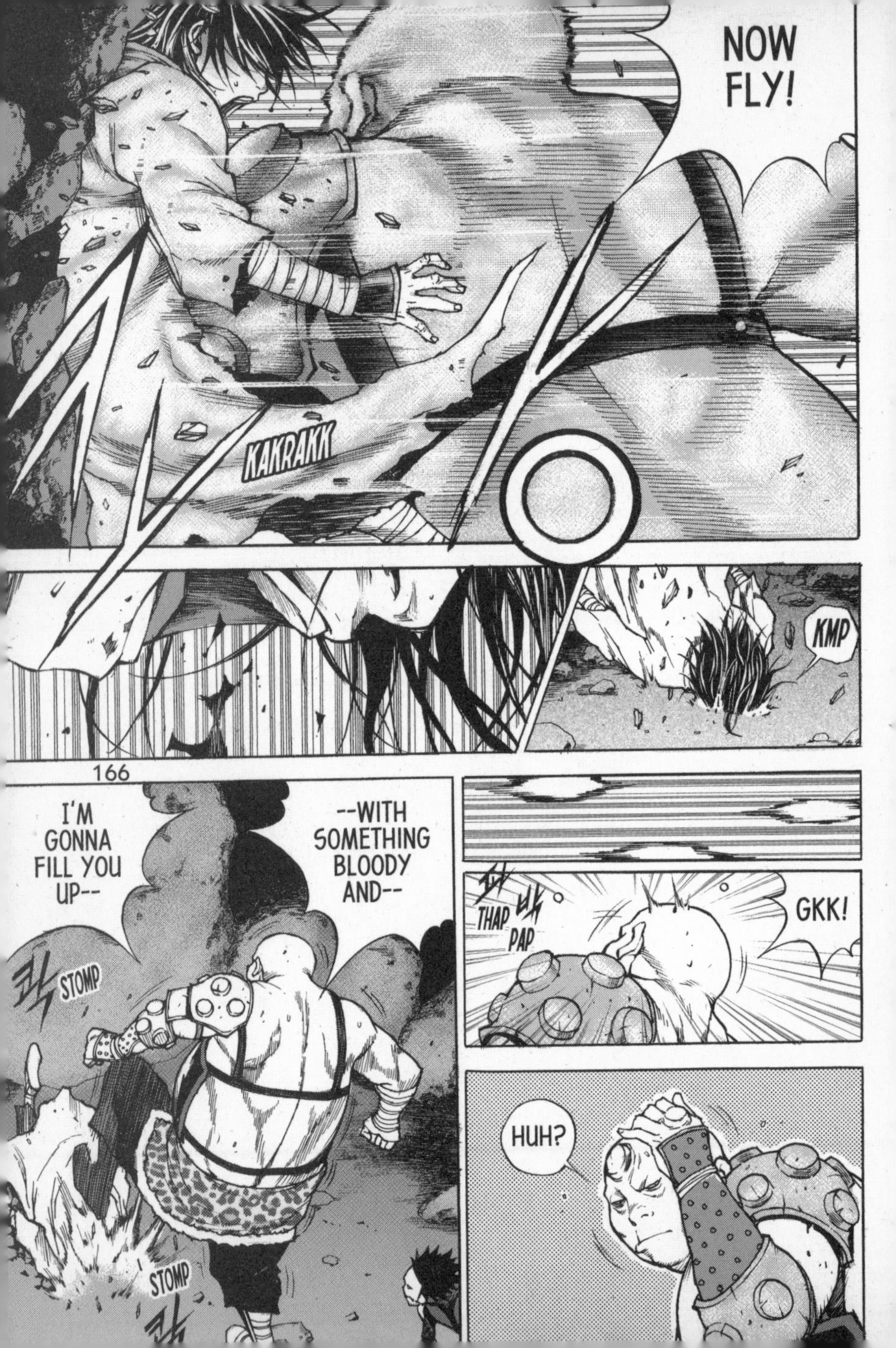
NOW FLY!
KAKRAKK
KMP
I'M GONNA FILL YOU UP--
--WITH SOMETHING BLOODY AND--
STOMP
STOMP
THAP
PAP
GKK!
HUH?

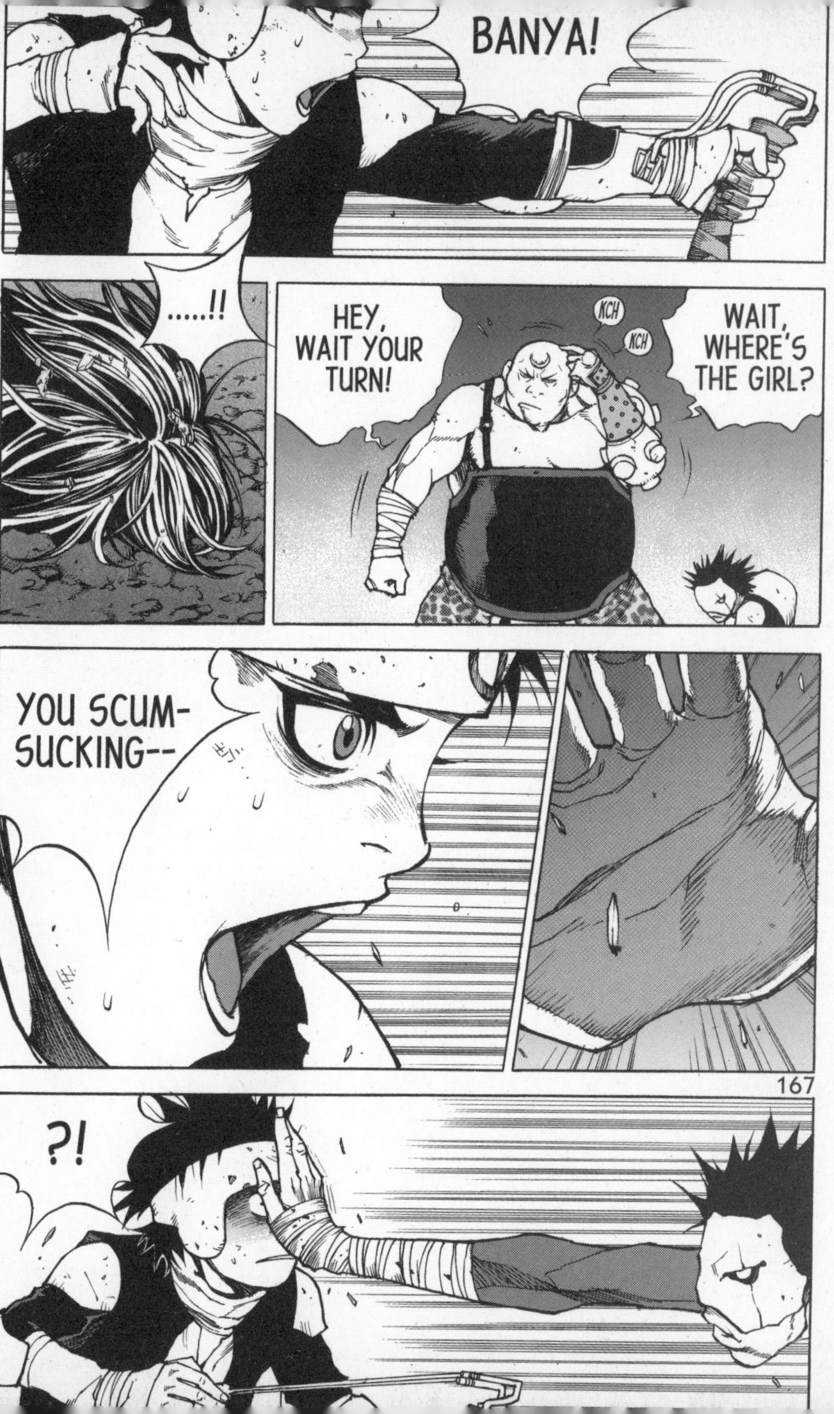
BANYA!
.....!!
HEY, WAIT YOUR TURN!
KCH
KCH
WAIT, WHERE'S THE GIRL?
YOU SCUM-SUCKING--
?!

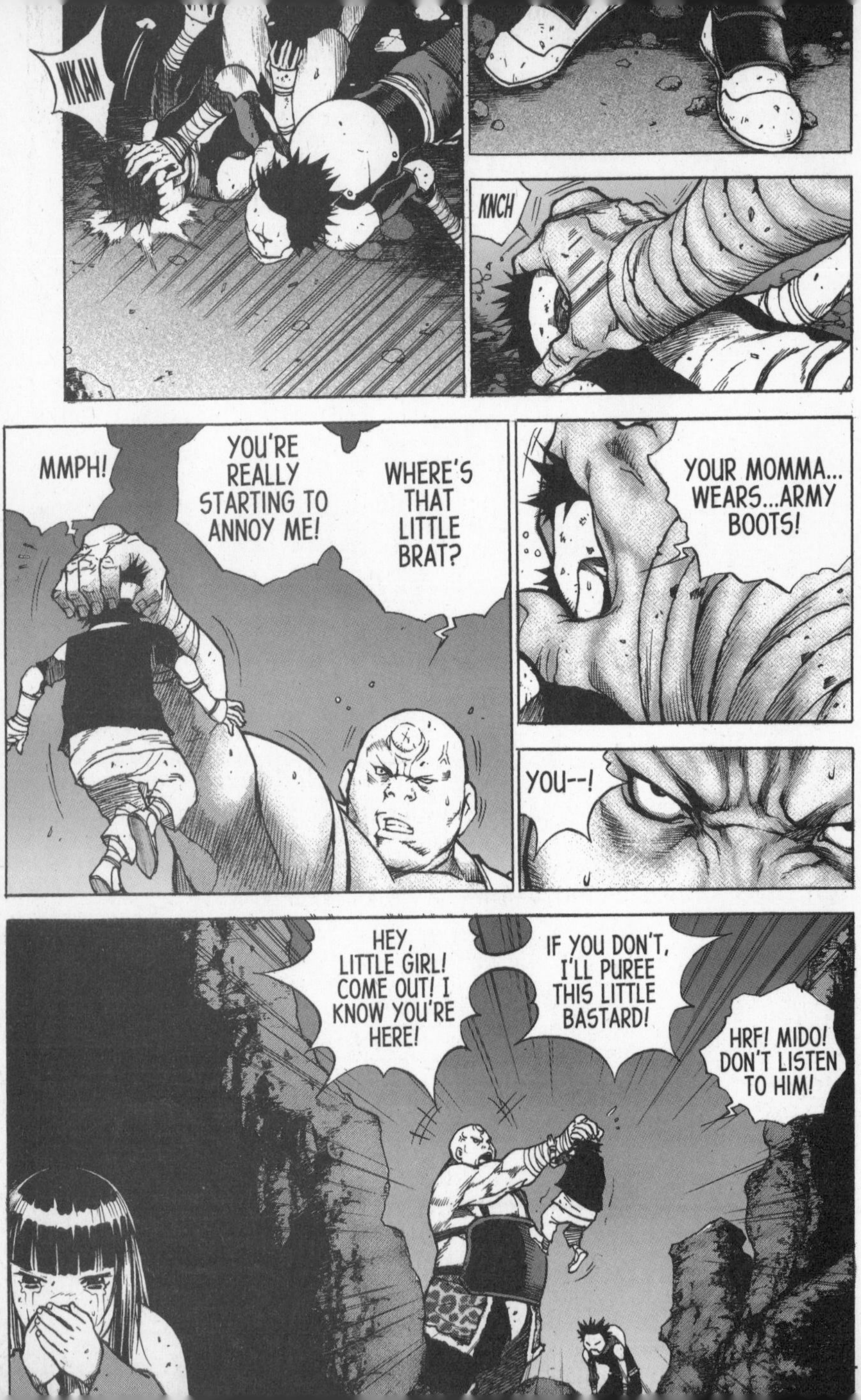
WKAM
KNCH
MMPH!
YOU'RE REALLY STARTING TO ANNOY ME!
WHERE'S THAT LITTLE BRAT?
YOUR MOMMA... WEARS...ARMY BOOTS!
YOU--!
HEY, LITTLE GIRL! COME OUT! I KNOW YOU'RE HERE!
IF YOU DON'T, I'LL PUREE THIS LITTLE BASTARD!
HRF! MIDO! DON'T LISTEN TO HIM!

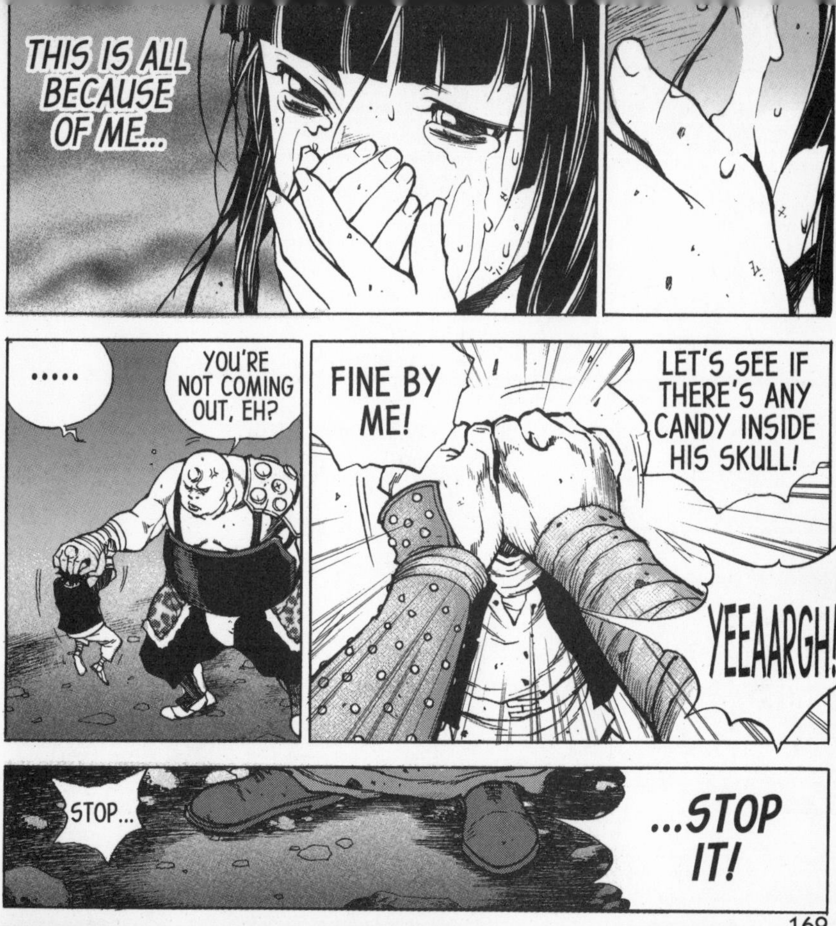
THIS IS ALL BECAUSE OF ME...
.....
YOU'RE NOT COMING OUT, EH?
FINE BY ME!
LET'S SEE IF THERE'S ANY CANDY INSIDE HIS SKULL!
YEEAARGH!
STOP...
...STOP IT!

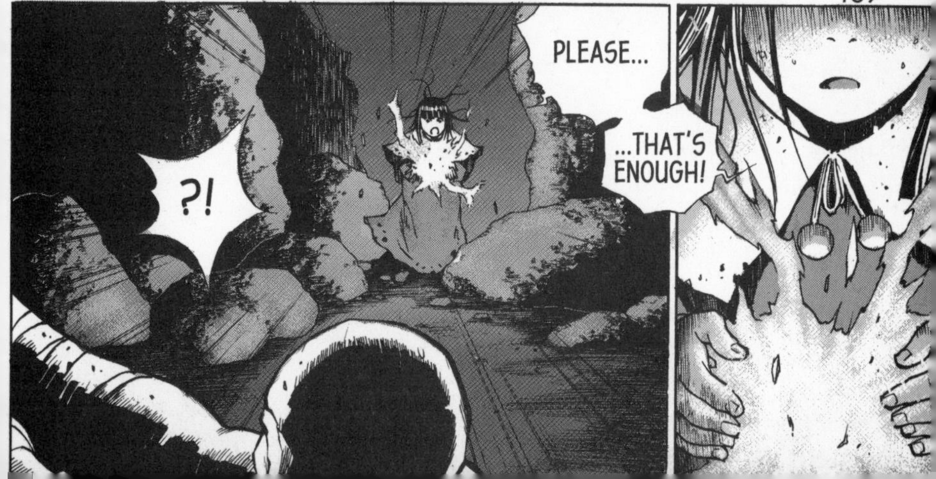
?!
PLEASE...
...THAT'S ENOUGH!

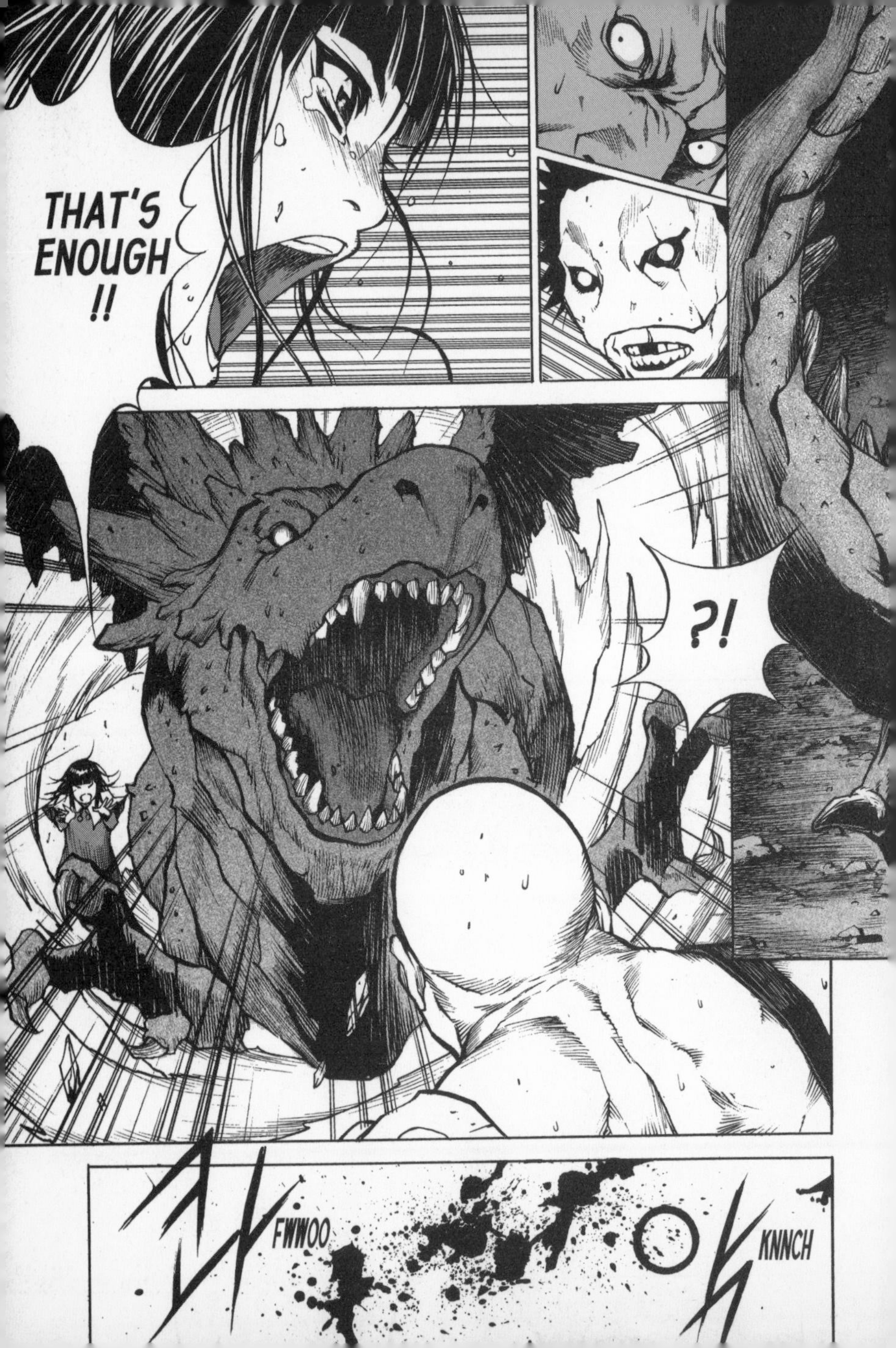
THAT'S ENOUGH !!
?!
FWWOO
KNNCH

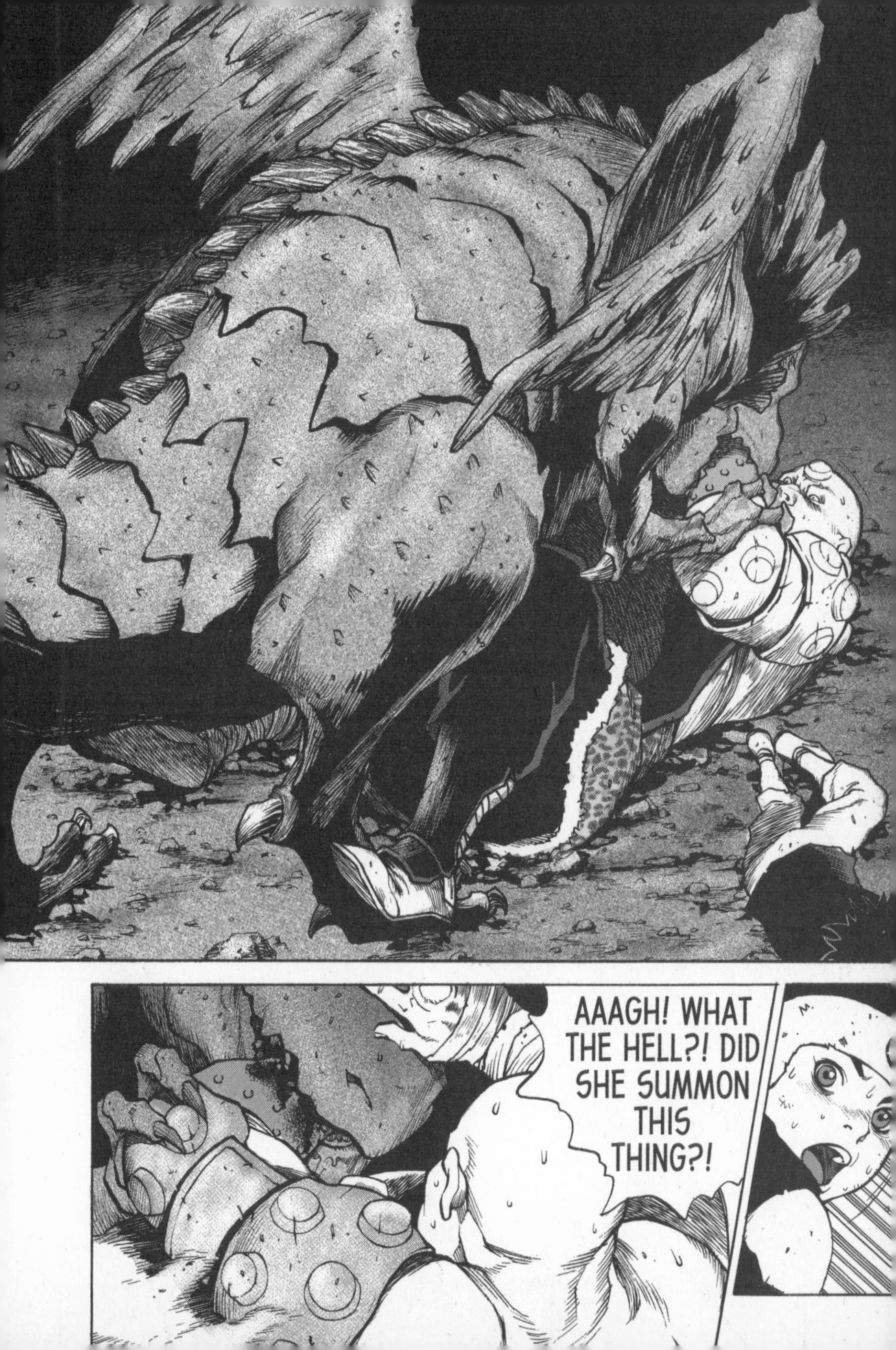
AAAGH! WHAT THE HELL?! DID SHE SUMMON THIS THING?!

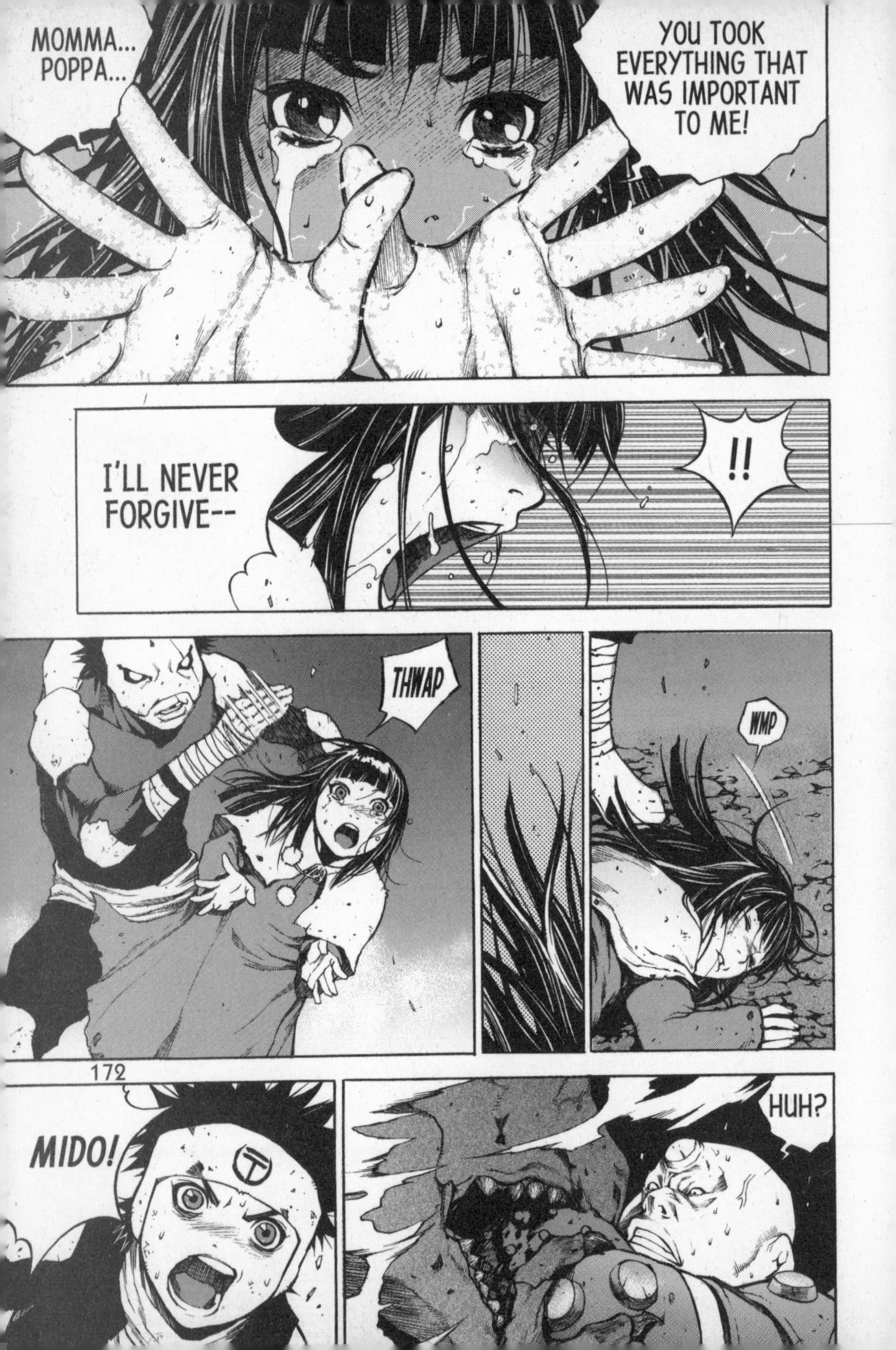
YOU TOOK EVERYTHING THAT WAS IMPORTANT TO ME!
MOMMA... POPPA...
!!
I'LL NEVER FORGIVE--
WMP
THWAP
HUH?
MIDO!

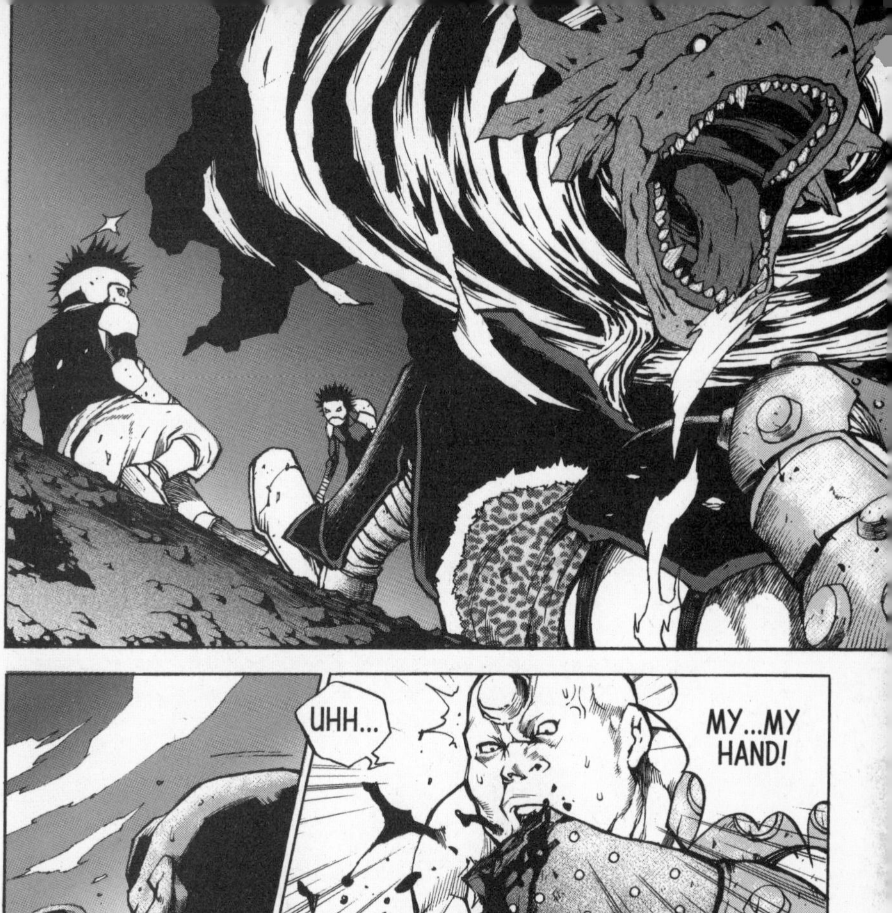
UHH...
MY...MY HAND!

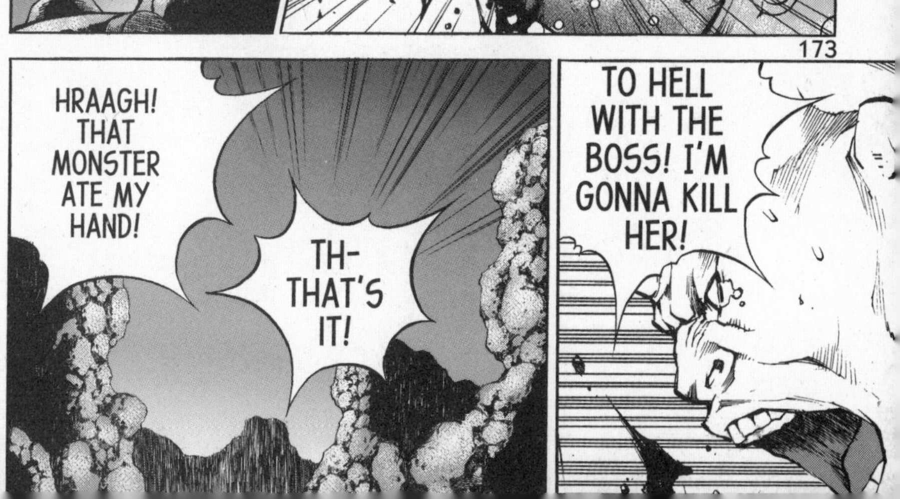
HRAAGH! THAT MONSTER ATE MY HAND!
TH-THAT'S IT!
TO HELL WITH THE BOSS! I'M GONNA KILL HER!

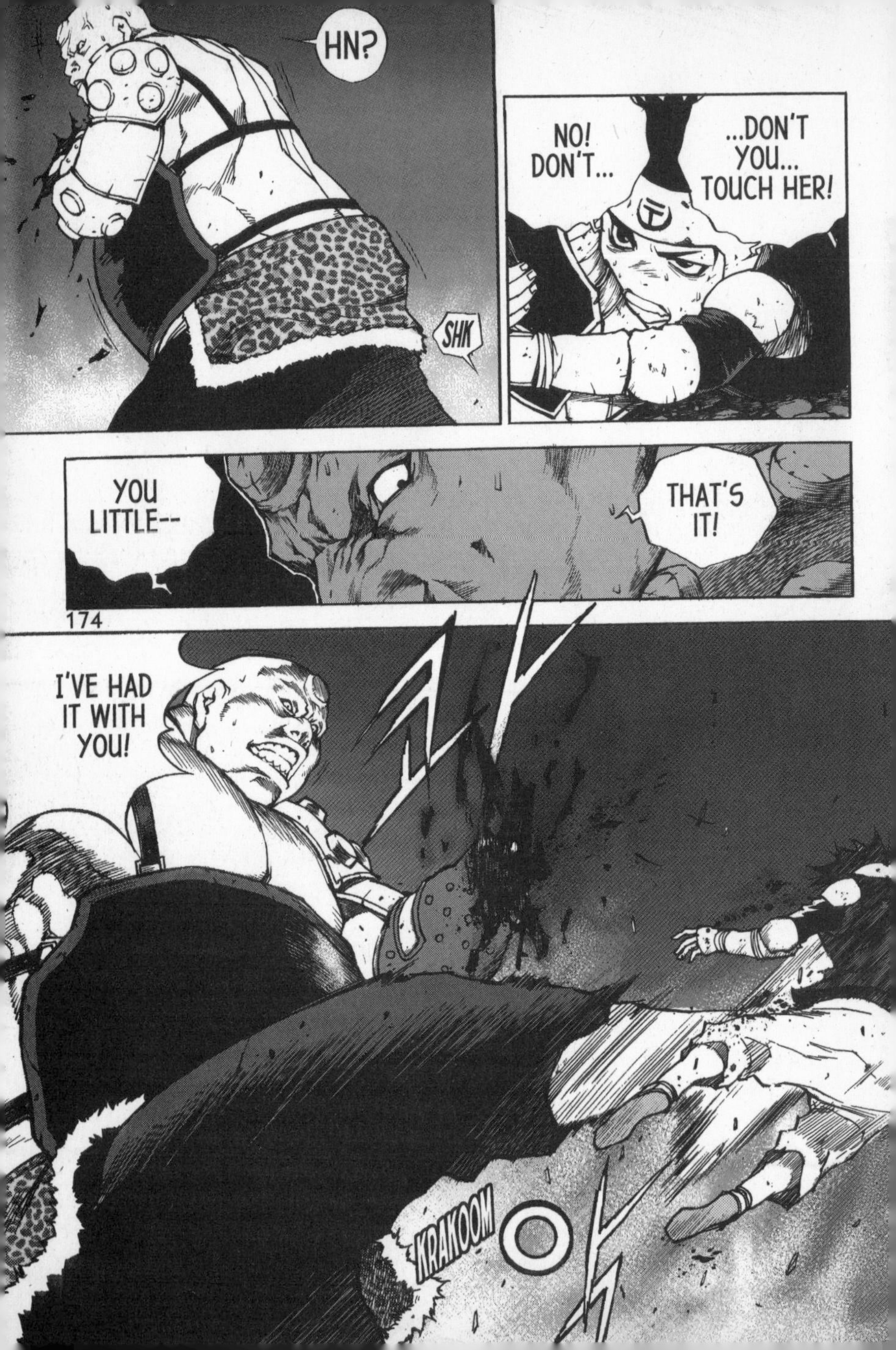

HN?
SHK
NO! DON'T...
...DON'T YOU... TOUCH HER!
YOU LITTLE--
THAT'S IT!
I'VE HAD IT WITH YOU!
KRAKOOM

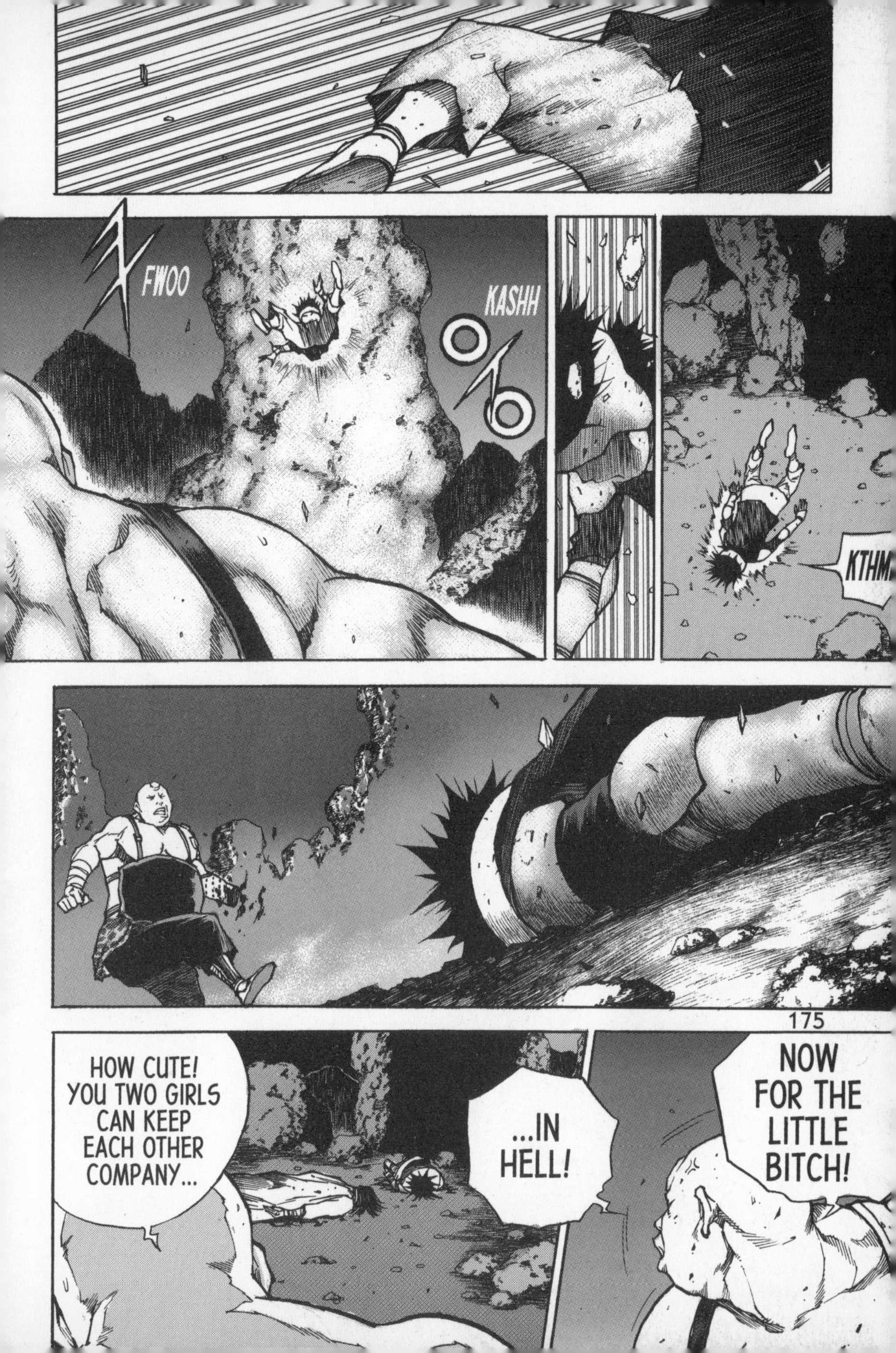

FWOO
KASHH
KTHM
HOW CUTE! YOU TWO GIRLS CAN KEEP EACH OTHER COMPANY...
...IN HELL!
NOW FOR THE LITTLE BITCH!

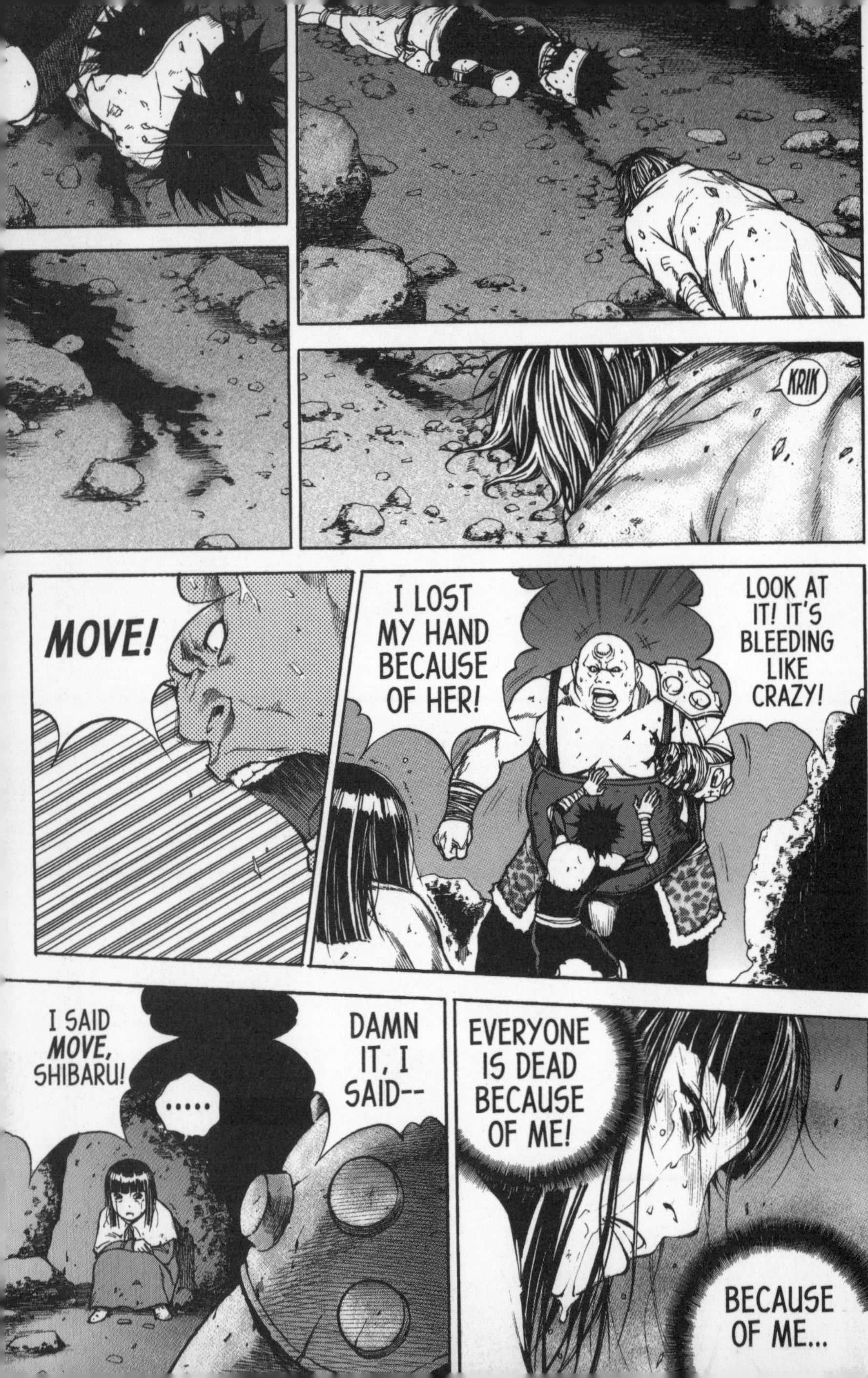
KRIK
LOOK AT IT! IT'S BLEEDING LIKE CRAZY!
I LOST MY HAND BECAUSE OF HER!
MOVE!
EVERYONE IS DEAD BECAUSE OF ME!
BECAUSE OF ME...
DAMN IT, I SAID--
I SAID MOVE, SHIBARU!
.....

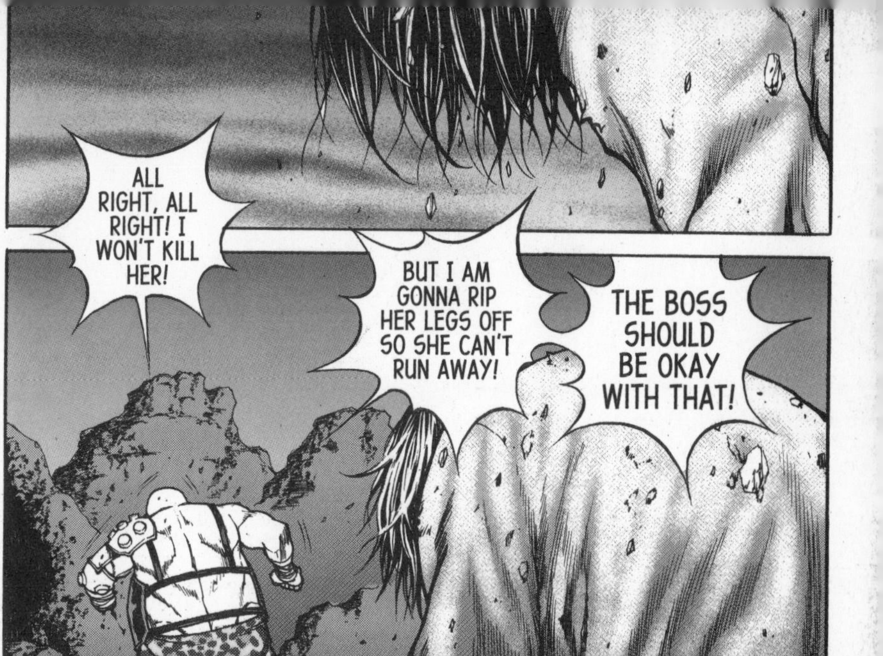
ALL RIGHT, ALL RIGHT! I WON'T KILL HER!
BUT I AM GONNA RIP HER LEGS OFF SO SHE CAN'T RUN AWAY!
THE BOSS SHOULD BE OKAY WITH THAT!

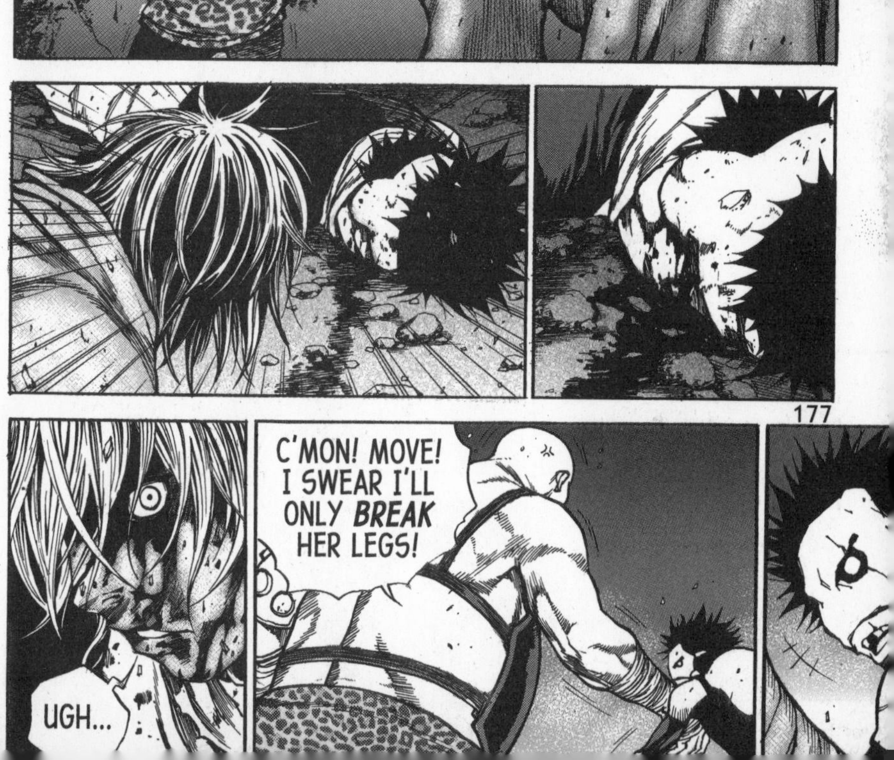
C'MON! MOVE! I SWEAR I'LL ONLY BREAK HER LEGS!
UGH...

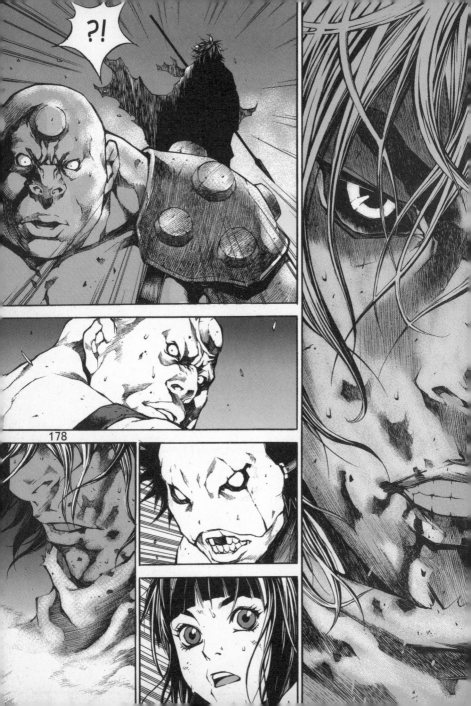

178

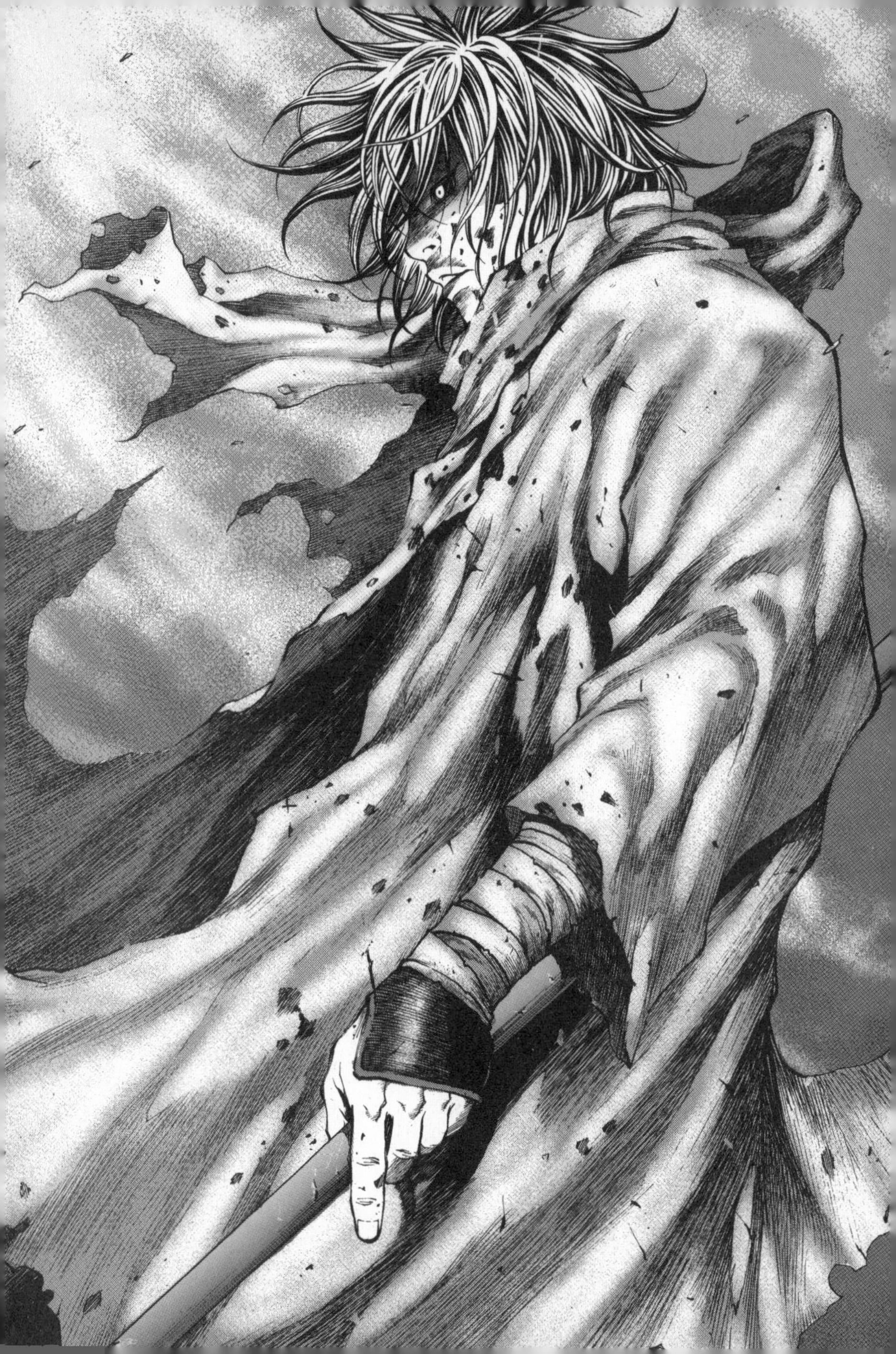

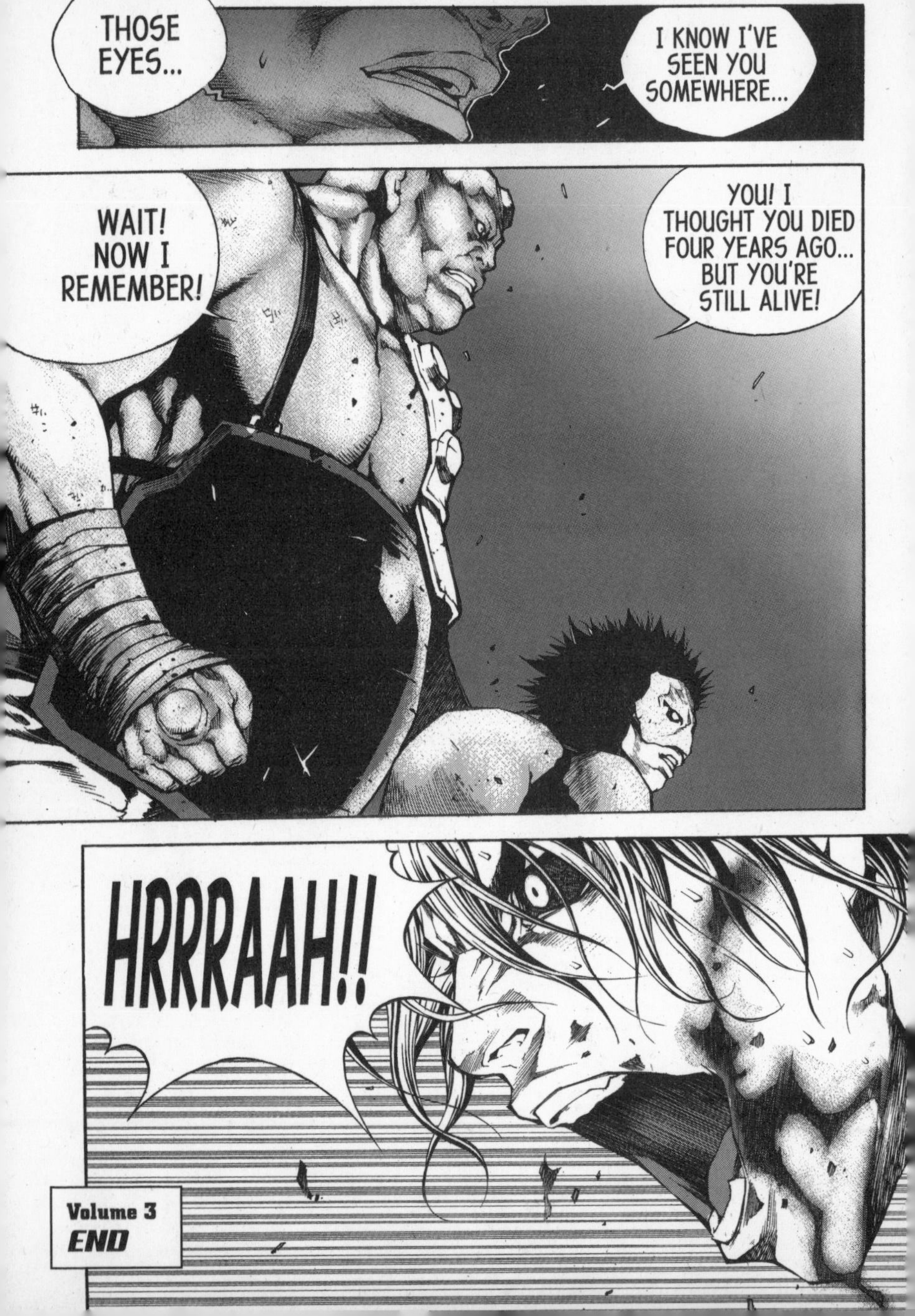
THOSE EYES...
I KNOW I'VE SEEN YOU SOMEWHERE...
WAIT! NOW I REMEMBER!
YOU! I THOUGHT YOU DIED FOUR YEARS AGO... BUT YOU'RE STILL ALIVE!
HRRRAAH!!
Volume 3 END

publisher
MIKE RICHARDSON

editor
PHILIP SIMON

editorial assistants
JEMIAH JEFFERSON and RYAN JORGENSEN

digital production
RYAN HILL

collection designer
M. JOSHUA ELLIOTT

art director
LIA RIBACCHI

Special thanks to Michael Gombos, Dr. Won Kyu Kim, J. Myung Kee Kim, and Julia Kwon.

English-language version produced by DARK HORSE COMICS.

BANYA: THE EXPLOSIVE DELIVERY MAN Volume 3

DARK HORSE MANHWA
A division of Dark Horse Comics, Inc.
10956 SE Main Street
Milwaukie OR 97222

darkhorse.com

To find a comics shop in your area, call the
Comic Shop Locator Service toll-free at 1-888-266-4226

First edition: March 2007
ISBN-10: 1-59307-705-X
ISBN-13: 978-1-59307-705-1

10 9 8 7 6 5 4 3 2 1
Printed in Canada

GRAPHIC
NOVEL
F
Ban
vol. 3

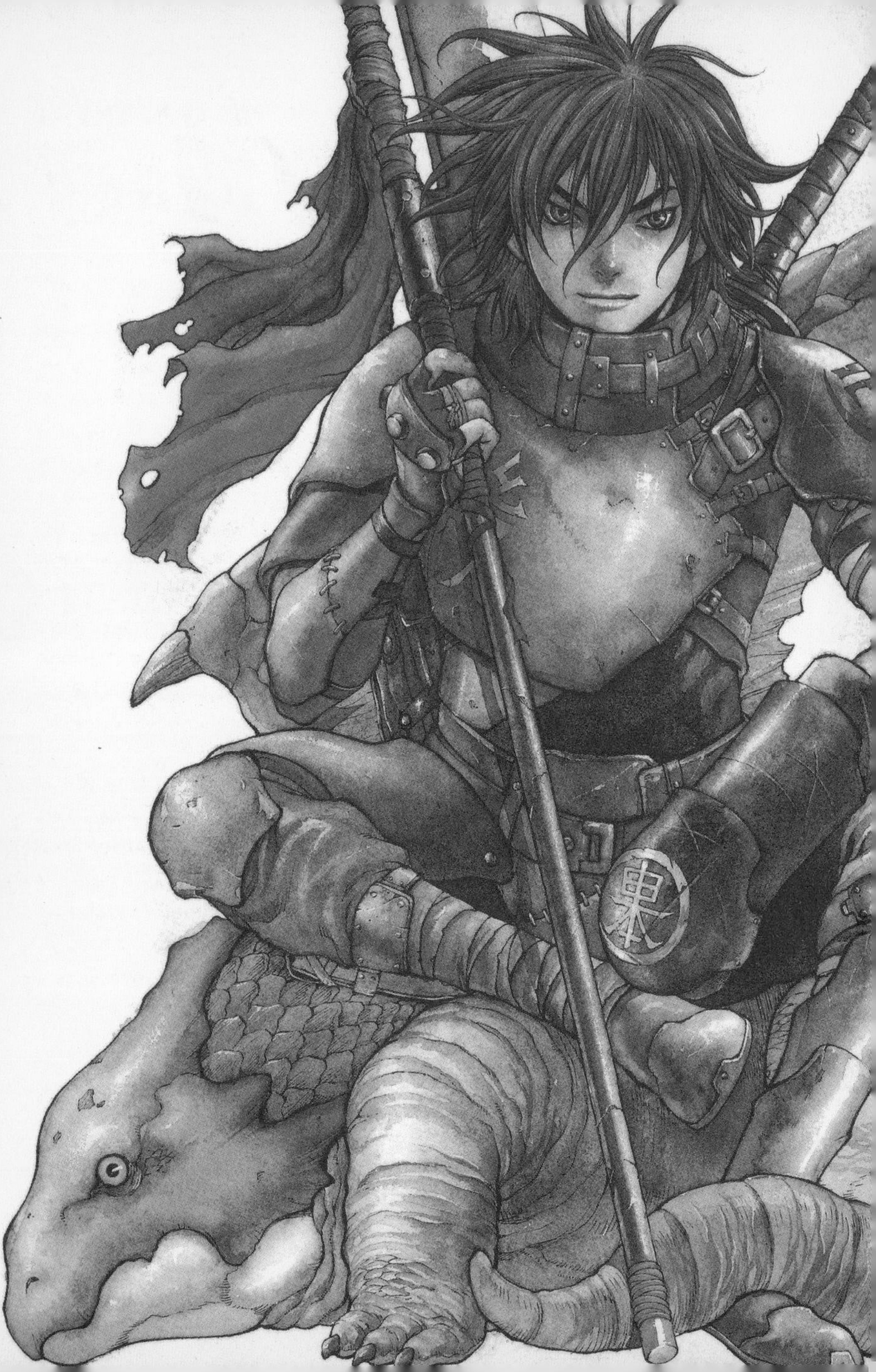

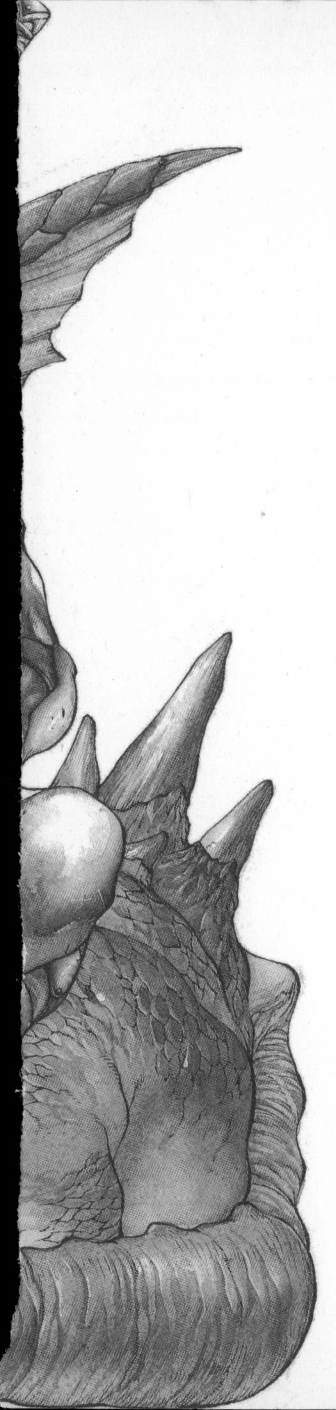

coming soon in

Banya

the explosive delivery man

volume 4!

Banya's kept his cool while mingling with the monstrous Torren, fighting off gargantuan pit bulls, and dodging giant Gwichi worms' sneak attacks—but now he's gone crazy with anguish and rage and is about to unleash a world of hurt on two mutated killers and the mastermind behind their cruel kidnapping sprees! *Banya*'s cast of heroes and villains grows and powerful armies gather, as Gaya's future falls in the hands of one determined man! Book 4, the penultimate volume of *Banya: The Explosive Delivery Man*, isn't all gloom and doom though, as Kim Young-Oh continues to mix incredible artwork and fast-paced storytelling with perfectly timed slapstick moments and surprising plot twists.

"This shamelessly entertaining story plays like a cross between *Dune, Mad Max,* and *Lord of the Rings,* blending fantasy and sci-fi elements with plenty of butt-kicking action sequences . . . The bottom line: *Banya* delivers. (Groan all you want, but it's true.)"

—Katherine Dacey-Tsuei, *PopCultureShock.com*

DARK HORSE MANHWA

AUTHOR'S NOTE

All of my time . . .
Where has it gone?
I once thought that I had a lot,
but I don't have enough now.

Is this any way to enjoy life?!

I have so many things to do,
but not enough time.
If I keep living like this,
I won't have any time left
when I really need it.

Somebody give me more time . . .

By Kim Young-Oh
Photograph by Noh Min-Yong

(Author's Note translated by Dr. Won Kyu Kim and J. Myung Kee Kim)